DOCUMENTATION		
Passenger Name _____		
Ship Name_____		
Date of Voyage _____		
Stateroom _____		

MEDITERRANEAN
By Cruise Ship

ANNE VIPOND

SEVENTH EDITION

YOUR PORTHOLE
COMPANION

OCEAN
CRUISE
GUIDES
Vancouver, Canada   Pt. Roberts, USA

Published by: Ocean Cruise
Guides Ltd.
Canada
325 English Bluff Road
Delta, BC V4M 2M9
Phone: (604) 948-0594
Email: info@oceancruiseguides.com

USA
PO Box 2041
Pt. Roberts, WA 98281-2041

Seventh Edition

Visit our web site: www.oceancruiseguides.com
Editors: Mel-Lynda Andersen, Debbie Parker (UK), Karen Stevens,
Stephen York (UK), Michael DeFreitas, William Kelly
Cover Artwork by Alan H. Nakano.
Cover Design by Ocean Cruise Guides.
Cartography: Reid Jopson, Doug Quiring, Cartesia – USA, OCG.
Design: Ocean Cruise Guides Ltd
Publisher: William Kelly

Printed in China.

Library and Archives Canada Cataloguing in Publication

Vipond, Anne, 1957
  Mediterranean by cruise ship : the complete guide to Mediterranean
cruising / Anne Vipond. -- 7th ed.

Includes index.
ISBN: 978-1-927747-13-1   ISSN 1921-8028

1. Cruise ships--Mediterranean Region--Guidebooks.   2. Mediterranean
Region--Guidebooks. I. Title

D973.V56 2016   910'.91822   C98910623-3

(Previous pages) Florence's Duomo; Bay of Kotor

(Opposite page) Villefranche

CONTENTS

PART ONE

GENERAL INFORMATION

Santorini

PART TWO

THE VOYAGE & THE PORTS

(with port walking maps on reverse side)

Villefranche

Back in the mists of antiquity, the lands bordering the Mediterranean Sea were the centre of the known world. Today, as the cradle of Western civilization, the Mediterranean offers cruise passengers a rich variety of destinations spanning 5,000 years of human history.

Nowhere else in the world is there such a concentration of architectural wonders and artistic masterpieces. Cities of past glory disarm visitors with their ancient ruins and Renaissance palaces, as well as their waterfront promenades, outdoor cafés and chic boutiques. Baroque churches face fountain-filled squares, medieval castles overlook golden beaches, and subtropical flowers flourish in a mild climate and sensuous setting that has long appealed to poets, painters and romantics.

The Mediterranean is a storied sea, and its layers of history and human drama inspire a passion for living. This intensity extends to affairs of the heart, with many a star-crossed romance unfolding beneath the Med's sunny skies.

Mark Twain described his Mediterranean cruise, which he took on board a steamer from New York in 1867, as "a picnic on a gigantic scale." By then the fashionable Grand Tour of Europe was so popular with British and American travellers that members of the wealthy class began seeking ever more exclusive modes of travel in the form of Pullman rail cars, stately hotels and lavish ocean liners.

Today we can all embark on a grand tour of the Mediterranean, where an expanding fleet of modern cruise ships now carries passengers from port to port in unsurpassed luxury and comfort. And when you step ashore at each port of call, the options range from exploring the nearby attractions on your own to booking an all-inclusive shore excursion that takes care of logistics while you enjoy the destination.

This guidebook is designed to help you make the most of your cruise. Each port of call is different, so a bit of beforehand reading will assist you in deciding what you would like to see and do without cramming too much into the time you have there.

At the end of the day, it matters not so much that you have seen everything there is to possibly see, but that you have enjoyed what you chose to focus on so you can return to your ship enriched by the experience and buoyed by the memories you've made.

– Anne Vipond

A cruise ship at anchor along the French Riviera.

PART I

GENERAL INFORMATION

Choosing Your Cruise

The Mediterranean Sea, bordered by three continents and over a dozen countries, offers an extraordinary diversity of cruise destinations, with ports of call ranging from grand cities to idyllic islands. Ships plying the Mediterranean are as diverse as their destinations, and some of the newest premium and contemporary ships offer Mediterranean cruises, along with a host of small luxury ships. (For more detail, please refer to The Cruise Lines glossary at the back of this book where the cruise lines servicing the English-speaking market are profiled.)

The length of a Mediterranean cruise can vary, usually ranging from one to two or more weeks, and both round-trip cruises and one-way cruises (which depart from one port and terminate at another) are available. The ships dock at the large ports, but often anchor and tender passengers ashore at smaller ports, such as some of those along the French Riviera or at the smaller Greek islands.

Each spring, following a winter in the Caribbean, ships begin arriving in the Mediterranean. Their transatlantic crossings often include stops at the Madeira and Canary Islands, as well as Morocco and Portugal, before entering the Mediterranean Sea. Some ships head to Southampton, England, which has become an important base port for cruises to the Med.

The Western Mediterranean encompasses Spain, France and Italy. Ports of call include Gibraltar, Cadiz, Valencia, Malaga and Mallorca, with Barcelona a major base port. The French ports of Marseille, Toulon, Nice, Monaco and others along the Côte d'Azur are also featured in western itineraries, as are Corsica and the Italian islands of Sardinia and Sicily.

The 'boot' of Italy lies in the middle of the Mediterranean and its famous ports and nearby cities are included in both western and eastern cruises. The Italian Riviera, Florence, Rome and Naples are all popular stops, as of course is Venice, where most ships dock overnight so their passengers can fully enjoy this enchanting city. Venice is also a major base port, as is Rome's seaport of Civitavecchia.

Greece's mainland ports and far-flung islands are highlighted

Santorini is one of many Greek islands visited by cruise ships.

in eastern cruises, as are the intriguing Turkish destinations of Istanbul and ancient Ephesus. An eastern cruise might also include the Black Sea, the Holy Land and Egypt's seaports of Alexandria and Port Said, both providing access to Cairo and the Great Pyramids. Athens and Istanbul are base ports for eastern cruises.

When choosing a cruise, you're well advised to visit a travel agent who specializes in cruises. Look for an agency displaying the CLIA logo, indicating its agents have received training from Cruise Lines International Association. These cruise specialists are a good source of information, with personal knowledge of many ships. They are able to provide pertinent detail regarding on-board atmosphere, itineraries, pricing and potential upgrades if you book early. They can also help you select a cabin suited to your specific needs, e.g. one that's close to the facilities you plan to frequent, or connecting staterooms for families. Booking early, especially during the 'wave season' (January through March), offers the best discounts, selection, choice of dinner sittings and potential upgrades. Waiting for last-minute deals is tempting, but it's not always possible to get a good deal on last-minute flights.

Booking your flights with the cruise line will save you the time-consuming process of monitoring airfares. These air/sea packages vary with each cruise line and don't necessarily save you any money, but unexpected expenses due to flight delays and missed travel connections are covered by the cruise line. Pre- and post-cruise hotel packages are also available through the cruise lines, and these packages include transfers between airport, hotel and pier.

Spring and fall are the best months for cruising the Med, although ships remain throughout the summer. Mid-summer temperatures in southern Italy and parts of Greece can climb into the 90s F, while the weather in fall is pleasantly warm and sunny. August is the month in which many Europeans take their vacations, temporarily closing their businesses in the city and heading to the coastal resorts. The first Saturday in August is one of the busiest travel days in southern Europe.

Shore Excursions

The cruise lines offer **organized shore excursions** for the convenience of their passengers, and these are described in detail on their websites, with the option of pre-booking your shore excursions online. Shore excursions can also be booked once you've boarded the ship and can be cancelled up to 24 hours before arriving in the applicable port of call.

The cost of a shore excursion varies, depending on its length (half day / full day) and the activities involved. Most shore excursions are fairly priced and the local tour operators used are reliable and monitored by the cruise companies, with the added advantage that the ship will wait for any of its overdue excursions.

Full-day shore excursions organized by the cruise lines are usually a combination of driving tour, guided walking tour and lunch at a local restaurant, with an interlude for shopping. The tour guides are local people providing narration of the sights and answering any questions you might have. When joining a ship-organized excursion, the decision to tip your guide or driver is personal. If you like the service, a small tip is appreciated.

Independent-minded passengers need not feel that pre-booked shore excursions are their only option when exploring various ports of call. If the ship docks right beside a town or city centre, a person can simply set off on foot to do some sightseeing and shopping. If the town centre is a few miles from the port, the cruise lines often offer a **shuttle**

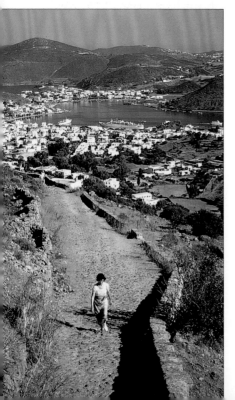

service. In some instances, such as Rome and Florence, where the city is an hour or more away from its seaport, your options include taking a train or hiring a taxi. Passengers who like the idea of exploring these cities on their own but wish to avoid any anxiety about getting back to the ship on time, may want to consider a ship-organized excursion that provides motorcoach transportation to the city centre but leaves you to see the sights on your own before reboarding the motorcoach at a pre-appointed time for the ride back to the ship.

To avoid lineups at major museums, buy your ticket in advance online or buy a city card that includes free or discounted entry to most major attractions.

Train travel in Europe is very efficient and a convenient way to see a port's nearby attractions. The ship's shore excursion manager will likely have a current schedule, which is also posted at the local train station. Double-check the schedule at the other end before leaving the station. Although the trains generally run on schedule, it's best not to plan your return train ride too close to the ship's time of departure, just in case there's an unforeseen delay. Local currency is needed to purchase a ticket. There are two classes of tickets, with first class being more expensive but allowing you to ride in slightly better cars. A rail pass is another option

Local attractions can often be reached on foot, such as those on the Greek island of Patmos.

if you're planning an extended stay in Europe before or after your cruise.

Hop-on/hop-off sightseeing buses are a good way to tour a city, such as Barcelona, and they usually have a stop near the cruise port. Regular transit buses can be a good way to cover short distances, but are not recommended for longer trips, as they make frequent stops and are not always as reliable as trains for keeping to their schedules. Bus tickets are usually sold at newsstands in the local currency.

Taxis may seem expensive, but if you're splitting the fare with a few other people it can often be more economical than a ship's

Missing Your Ship

One of the most discussed issues for cruise passengers is whether to take a ship-organized shore excursion at the ports of call or strike out on your own. This is not a simple issue, because each port is different and everyone has their own idea what they want to see and do while in port. My usual choice for visiting a city located some distance from the cruise port is to take a ship's shuttle if available. This way I can explore the sights on my own without any worry about getting back to the ship. Cruise ships are very punctual about departing on time and will delay their departure only if one of their excursions hasn't returned. Everyone else is responsible for returning to the ship on time.

I learned this lesson the hard way in Egypt, where my husband Bill and I spent the day touring Cairo independently, then nearly missed our ship docked in Alexandria. We arrived back at the port as the ship, having pulled away from the dock, was steaming out of the harbour. Amid frantic shouting and arm waving, we paid the crew of the pilot boat to take us out to our ship. As we pulled alongside the moving ship,

a maintenance door several decks above us opened and a jacob's ladder came tumbling down. I grabbed the ladder first and climbed up the side of the hull. Two crewmen at the top of the ladder eagerly helped me aboard where a waiting ship's officer greeted me with the words, "I'll need to see your cruise card."

I was still a bit shaken by this near-miss when we decided to take the train from the port of Civitavecchia into Rome. We spent a full morning and early afternoon visiting famous sites and walking the streets of Rome before returning to Termini station to catch the train back to port. All seemed well until the train ground to a halt just outside the Vatican. As the minutes ticked by we waited nervously for the train to start moving again. Finally, after a 30-minute delay, Bill and I figured we had to do something. Some fellow cruise passengers were on the train and it was decided that we would all wait another ten minutes before getting off the train and hiring enough taxis to get us all back to the ship. Fortunately the train started moving a few minutes later and we arrived at the port with just minutes to spare.

Sightseeing in car-free Venice is done by boat and on foot. Rented scooters are one way to get around small ports of call.

hail a taxi in a large city, the driver will simply charge you the metered fare.

Renting a car or motor scooter can be a good way to explore an island destination, but is not recommended when visiting large cities where traffic can be extremely congested and fast-paced. Boat travel is another option in some ports such as Venice, where large boats serve as local buses and taxis come in the form of motor boats. At Naples, ferries and hydrofoils transport visitors to nearby Sorrento and to the isle of Capri, and at some small ports, such as Cinque Terre, boat transport is the best way to tour the area.

The local sights to be seen on Mediterranean shore excursions include ancient ruins, medieval fortresses and Renaissance palaces. There is often a fair amount of

excursion. Keep in mind that some taxi drivers make better 'guides' than others, and be sure to agree on the fare before getting into the taxi. To avoid possible miscommunication due to a language barrier, it's a good idea to write on a piece of paper the exact amount both parties have agreed upon and show it to the driver to be certain he understands what you are willing to pay at the end of the trip. Don't hesitate to bargain with a few drivers before making your decision, and a tip is warranted if the driver proves to be pleasant and helpful. If you

walking involved, especially at the ruins where stone steps and uneven grades are common. In medieval towns and city quarters, where the roads are too narrow for vehicles, on foot is often the only way to explore the winding cobblestone streets.

Pre- and Post-Cruise Stays

If time allows, fly to your port of embarkation at least a day before the cruise begins, thus avoiding the stress of making same-day travel connections. Better yet, stay two or three nights at your embarkation port to recover from jet lag, relax and have time to enjoy the local sights. Southampton, Barcelona, Nice, Genoa, Rome (Civitavecchia), Venice, Athens (Piraeus) and Istanbul are all used as base ports for Mediterranean cruises. If your cruise ends at a different port than where it started, consider staying a few nights before flying home.

A water taxi pulls up to the Baglioni Hotel Luna in Venice.

Be sure to book your accommodations ahead of time, either through your travel agent or as part of a pre- or post-cruise package offered by the cruise line. The hotel packages offered by the cruise lines usually utilize four- and five-star hotels, thus ensuring their clients a consistent level of comfort and service, and transfers between hotel and pier are included. If you're booking a hotel independently, reservations are advisable in the major cities.

Once you have checked into your hotel, remember that the concierge and front desk staff offer a wealth of information for foreign visitors. They can direct you to the best shops and restaurants, and will usually provide miscellaneous services upon request, such as obtaining information on local tours or calling a taxi and confirming the destination and fare with your driver. If you're part of an organized cruisetour, an experienced guide employed by the cruise line will be available to answer questions.

Land Tours

A cruise is a perfect opportunity to combine a vacation at sea with a land-based holiday, whether you do so independently or by booking a cruisetour package with the cruise line.

A fully escorted cruisetour is an ideal way to see more of a European country. The tours offered by the cruise lines are a seamless form of travel, for the cruise companies maintain the same level of service on land as at sea, with well-planned itineraries, deluxe hotel accommodations and professional tour direction. Hotels are centrally located, within walking distance of major attractions and shopping streets, and several hosted meals are often part of the package, while plenty of free time allows clients to do a bit of independent sightseeing, leisurely shopping or lingering in a sidewalk café.

Some cruise lines offer tours to the Moorish stronghold of Toledo.

The group travels by comfortable motorcoach or high-speed train, and the tour guides employed by the cruise companies are well-educated and highly qualified to introduce visitors to the history, culture and cuisine of the country they are visiting. All tours must be booked at the same time as the cruise, as part of a cruisetour package. Land tours vary with each cruise line.

Italy is well covered by land tours, including a variety of three- and five-day itineraries that feature Venice, Rome and Florence. Milan and Lake Como are also featured in some land tours, as are the hilltop towns of Tuscany. Spain's interior is covered by land tours combined with cruises out of Barcelona, with Seville and Madrid included in five-night itineraries.

Touring On Your Own

If you plan to embark on an independent tour outside the major cities, your options include

renting a car or purchasing a rail pass. If you cherish total independence and the freedom to hop from village to village, stopping on a whim to admire a valley view or coastal lookout, then **renting a car** is probably for you. Obtain an International Driver's Permit before leaving home, especially if you'll be travelling in areas where you are not fluent in the language.

When reserving a car, confirm a number of details, such as whether the 'all-inclusive' rate includes GPS, taxes, unlimited kilometres and drop-off charges. Be aware that not all rental depots are open on Sundays, and filling stations may be closed on Sundays in parts of Italy and Spain. European cars are generally smaller than North American models, with a 'compact' comfortably holding two people and two pieces of luggage; the next size up is usually worth the extra cost. Standard-shift transmissions are popular in Europe, but auto-matics are available in larger cars at higher rates and are usually in high demand during the summer tourist season. If you plan to use a credit card for insurance, ask for a copy of the policy's coverage; theft protection insurance is also required in some countries. Never leave valuables in a rental car.

Rail travel is another option for independent travel in Europe, where high-speed trains have become a more efficient way to get around than taking short-haul flights. These newer trains provide direct links between major cities in Europe, while traditional rail travel on the slower-moving trains remains a comfortable and relaxing way to see the countryside as you settle into your window seat and watch the scenery slide by.

An extensive rail system connects countries, cities, towns and villages, and most train stations

High-speed trains pull into the Atocha Station in Madrid.

Train travel is an efficient and pleasant way to get around Europe. (Above and left) Nice's train station.

are centrally located – whether in a resort town or a large city – so your hotel will likely be just a short taxi ride away.

In 1958, Western Europe's railroads developed the idea of an easy-to-use, multi-country, prepaid ticket for unlimited mileage use, and that concept evolved into the popular Eurailpass, which now comes in a variety of forms.

The range of passes offered by Rail Europe is exhaustive, including the EurailDrive Pass with which a person can combine four days of unlimited train travel with two days of car rental through Avis or Hertz. The flexible Eurorail Select pass has replaced the Europass and provides unlimited first-class train travel within a two-month period for lengths of five, six, eight or 10 days, and is valid in four bordering countries.

To obtain more information about Rail Europe's selection of passes, visit the company's website at *www.raileurope.com*. All passes must be purchased before you leave for Europe, and reservations are required for some trains.

Porters and luggage carts are not always available, so you must be prepared to handle your own baggage if travelling by train.

Accommodations should be reserved in advance when travelling independently. Each country offers unique and varied accommodations, and it's best to do some research ahead of time.

Places to stay in Portugal include *pousadas* (stately castles), which are palaces and private manor houses that have been converted into hotels. In Spain, many of the *paradores* (state-operated tourist hotels) are housed in castles, palaces, monasteries and convents that have been refurbished into three- and four-star hotels.

France offers everything from grand hotels to family-run country inns serving regional cuisine. And in Italy, an umbrella organization called *Agriturismo* ('farm stays') provides information on an extensive network of rural bed-and-breakfast inns. Located on quiet country roads, with views of valley fields and vineyards, these Italian B&B's are housed in country estates and quaint farmhouses.

There are hundreds of monasteries and convents throughout Europe, many of which welcome overnight visitors who enjoy the spartan but clean and quiet accommodations and the warm hospitality. Be prepared to climb stairs to the upper-floor rooms and expect certain restrictions, such as a midnight curfew.

Villa rentals are also popular with people travelling as a small group, and properties are available in Greece, France, Spain and Portugal, as well as Italy. For instance, it's possible to rent a *palazzetto* in Venice that accommodates four to eight people and is within walking distance of St. Mark's Square for US$2,000 to $3,000 per week.

There are numerous websites providing information on villa rentals. Those that include details and photos of each property, and allow you to book directly with the villa owner, are your best bet.

Hotel Loggiato dei Serviti in Florence is a former monastery.

Documentation

Several weeks prior to your cruise departure date you will receive (or be able to print out) all pertinent documentation for your trip, including your cruise ticket, airline ticket and a mandatory pre-registration form that can be completed on-line, or faxed or mailed to the cruise line. Before your departure, leave a detailed travel itinerary with a family member or friend, in case someone needs to contact you while you're away. Include the name of your ship, its phone number and the applicable ocean code, as well as your stateroom number – all of which will be included in your cruise documentation. With this information, a person can call the international telephone operator and place a satellite call to your ship in an emergency.

A valid passport is required for travel to all countries bordering the Mediterranean. A few countries in the Mediterranean region also require an entry visa, and your travel agent or the cruise line can advise you beforehand of any visa requirements your cruise might entail.

As a precaution, you should photocopy the identification page of your passport, along with your driver's licence and any credit cards you will be taking on your trip. Keep one copy of this photocopied information (including the emergency telephone number listed on the back of each credit card) with you, separate from your passport and wallet, and leave another copy at home.

Travel insurance is recommended. A comprehensive policy will cover trip cancellation, delayed departure, medical expenses, personal accident and liability, lost baggage and money, and legal expenses. You may already have supplementary health insurance through a credit card, automobile club policy or employment health plan, but you should check these carefully. Carry details of your policy with you and documentation showing that you are covered by a plan.

Currency

When travelling abroad, it's best to take various forms of currency – cash, credit cards and bank cards. If you're staying in a foreign city for a few days before or after your cruise, obtain some petty cash in that country's currency to cover taxi fares and other incidentals. Major credit cards are accepted by most hotels and restaurants, and ATM machines are widespread in larger cities.

Once you're aboard your ship, travellers checks can be cashed at the Front Desk and many of the ships have an ATM on board, usually located near the Front Desk. Most ships also have a currency exchange facility on board, offering a competitive rate on foreign

currencies, so that passengers needn't spend time at each port of call exchanging funds into local currency. The rates offered by local currency exchange offices can vary and some will charge a higher commission on Sundays.

The euro is the official currency in the majority of member nations of the European Union, making money transactions much simpler for cruise passengers visiting countries such as Greece, Italy, France, Spain, Portugal, Malta and Cyprus.

One euro is divided into 100 centimes and there are eight coins, worth 1, 2, 5, 10, 20 and 50 centimes, and 1 and 2 euros. There are seven bank-notes in denominations of 5, 10, 20, 50, 100, 200 and 500 euros. Approximate rates of exchange at press time: 1 EUR = 1USD and .75 GBP.

For major purchases or expenses, a credit card is recommended (rather than carrying large amounts of cash) and although a currency conversion fee is charged (usually 2 or 3%), the difference in service charges between using a credit card or withdrawing cash in the local currency from an ATM is not substantial. It's best to carry several credit cards, and married couples should arrange for at least one set of separate cards (without joint signing privileges) in case one spouse loses his or her wallet and all of the couple's joint cards have to be cancelled. It's also wise to take along a handful of small US bills and euros to cover possible tips for guides and other sundries when ashore.

What to Pack

Pack casual attire for daytime wear – both aboard the ship and in port. The weather will be generally dry and sunny, but spring and fall temperatures in the Mediterranean can vary from cool to hot, so pack clothes that can be layered. Cool, loose cotton clothes are recommended for the summertime heat, as are sunglasses and a wide-brimmed hat. A comfortable pair of rubber-soled shoes is essential for walking along cobblestone streets, and a light sweater or jacket will fend off the air-conditioning in restaurants, museums and aboard motorcoaches. Some European ports, such as Venice, can be chilly in late October, so pack one warm sweater or jacket if you're travelling at this time of year.

The dress code for churches and monasteries dictates that legs and shoulders be covered, so keep this in mind when heading ashore – either wear slacks or carry a wrap that can be tied around your waist as an ankle-length cover-up before entering religious sites. In Muslim countries, conservative attire is recommended, and removal of shoes is mandatory before entering mosques.

Your evening wear should include something suitable for the formal nights held on board most large ships. Women wear gowns or cocktail dresses, and men favor suits. For informal evenings, the women wear dresses, skirts or slacks, and the men

Visitors to monasteries must cover their shoulders and legs.

wear jackets with either a shirt and tie or an open-necked sports shirt.

Check with your travel agent regarding on-board facilities; for instance, most cabins will have a built-in hair dryer. Many ships have coin-operated launderettes with ironing boards; those that don't usually provide laundry service at an extra charge. Steam pressing and dry cleaning are standard services on most ships, and it's easy to do hand washing in your cabin. Poolside towels are provided by the ship, as are beach towels for taking ashore.

To save room in your suitcase, pack sample sizes of toothpaste and other toiletries, which can also be purchased on board the ship. Rolling instead of folding your clothes saves room and reduces wrinkles, especially if tissue paper is used.

If you wear prescription eyeglasses, consider packing a spare pair. Keep prescribed medication in original, labelled containers and carry a doctor's prescription for any controlled drug. Other items you may want to bring along are a small pair of binoculars and a pocket calculator for tabulating exchange rates. And be sure to keep all valuables, including your camera and expensive jewellery, in your carry-on luggage, as well as all prescription medicine and documentation, such as your passport, tickets and a copy of your insurance policy. Last but not least, be sure to leave room in one of your suitcases for souvenirs.

Health Precautions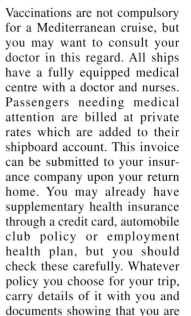

Vaccinations are not compulsory for a Mediterranean cruise, but you may want to consult your doctor in this regard. All ships have a fully equipped medical centre with a doctor and nurses. Passengers needing medical attention are billed at private rates which are added to their shipboard account. This invoice can be submitted to your insurance company upon your return home. You may already have supplementary health insurance through a credit card, automobile club policy or employment health plan, but you should check these carefully. Whatever policy you choose for your trip, carry details of it with you and documents showing that you are covered by a plan.

The overall standards of cleanliness on board cruise ships are extremely high, yet contagious viruses that are spread by person-to-person contact (such as the **Norovirus**, which is a brief but severe gastrointestinal illness) do occasionally plague a small percentage of passengers. To avoid contracting such a virus, practice frequent, thorough handwashing with warm, soapy water.

Motion sickness is not a widespread or prolonged problem for most passengers, but for those who are susceptible, a number of remedies are available. One is a special wrist band, the balls of which rest on an acupressure point. These 'sea bands' are available at most drug stores. Another option is to chew meclizine tablets (usually available at the ship's infirmary) or take Dramamine, an over-the-counter antihistamine. It's best to take these pills ahead of time, before you feel too nauseous, and they may make you drowsy. Fresh air is one of the best antidotes, so stepping out on deck is often all that's needed to counter any queasiness. Other simple remedies include sipping ginger ale, nibbling dry crackers and an apple, or lying down.

To avoid traveller's diarrhea, it's best to drink bottled water when ashore, but don't worry about drinking wine. Studies have shown that a glass of wine – either red or white – is a good way to fend off traveller's diarrhea. Wine contains a mild disinfectant that quickly destroys a variety of bacteria that can cause stomach problems.

Connecting with Home

Text messaging and e-mail are replacing phone calls as the most convenient and inexpensive way to reach someone while you're away. Most cruise ships provide satellite-based broadband service that allows you to use your wireless devices while at sea. Bulk rates are usually offered and, with recent increases to bandwidth capacity and onboard Wi-Fi capability, some ships are now offering a flat daily rate for unlimited connectivity.

Large ships provide Internet cafes where passengers can access on-line computers and are charged for their use on a

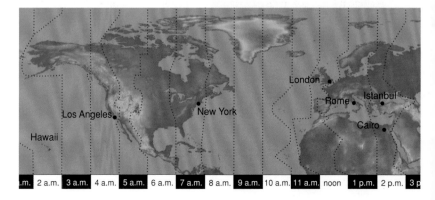

per-minute basis (either pay-as-you-go or package plans starting at about US$20 for 30 minutes). Transmission at sea is slower than on land and load-intensive pages will sometimes time-out.

Mobile phones are the easiest way to call home, but check with your service provider for detail on your phone's roaming capability and the attendant charges. A roaming package bought before-hand is one option. Another option if you're carrying a smart phone is to purchase a local pre-paid SIM card. Calls can also be placed through the ship's radio office or by placing a direct satel-lite telephone call. This is expen-sive, however, and unless the call is urgent you may want to wait and place your call from a land-based phone. Refer to the map (previous page) for time differ-ences before placing a call.

Vacation Photos

Digital images have largely replaced photographs, but the goal of capturing your holiday's highlights remains the same. If you're using a digital camera, be sure to have plenty of flash card memory storage and pack an extra battery pack, which can be recharged in your stateroom. Shoot at a fine setting for print-quality reproduction.

The ship's photo gallery is a good place to purchase shots taken by the ship's photographers of you and your travel compan-ions. These make good memen-tos of your cruise, capturing your embarkation and arrivals at the ports of call. On formal nights, when everyone is looking their best and feeling relaxed, the ship's photographers are set up at locations around the ship to take studio-quality portraits that are displayed the next day in the photo gallery. There is no sitting fee and no obligation to purchase these framable prints but people often do because it's a convenient way to obtain a professional por-trait.

Security

While security is not a major con-cern when on board the ship, you should take some precautions when venturing ashore. Property crime can occur anywhere, but tourists are especially vulnerable

because they carry large amounts of money, as well as cameras and other valuables. Keep all credit cards and most of your cash securely stowed in an inside pocket of your clothes or shoulder bag, and keep a few small bills in a readily accessible pocket so you're not pulling out your wallet to pay for small impromptu purchases from street vendors.

Be aware of potential thieves. Many operate in pairs, with one creating a distraction, such as dropping a handful of coins, while the other lifts their victim's wallet. Don't wear expensive jewellery and don't wear a fanny pack because a professional pickpocket with surgical scissors can quickly snip the strap and lift your pack without you even noticing. An inside jacket pocket with a zipper or a money belt concealed beneath your clothes are more secure ways to carry money and credit cards.

Situations requiring caution include any place where there are crowds of people, and at airports and train stations, where you should never turn your back on your luggage. When hiring a taxi, watch to make sure every piece of luggage is loaded into the trunk, and never leave valuables in a rented car.

Shopping

Most stores and upscale shops accept all major credit cards, but it's best to have local currency (in most cases the euro) for small and impromptu purchases. Value Added Tax is attached to most purchases in Europe, and North American visitors can obtain a refund by first requesting a refund form in the store where they make their purchase, then having it stamped by customs staff in the airport prior to departure. Refunds can be obtained on the spot or after you are home, by sending the form to the appropriate office. Check with your travel agent or local customs office before leaving home to determine your duty-free allowances.

The Mediterranean is rich in centuries-old craftsmanship, and memorable souvenirs include hand-painted ceramics, lustreware, terracotta pottery and decorative tiles. Hand-woven carpets, embroidered linens and delicate laceware are other traditional crafts, as is gold filigree jewelry. In the major cities and tourist resorts you will find boutiques selling high-fashion clothing, leather goods and jewellery.

Italian craftsmanship on display in a Sicilian shop window.

Western civilization began along the shores of the Mediterranean, and its well-travelled waters have transported heroes and emperors, poets and prophets, to their appointments with destiny. Over the centuries Homer's wine-dark sea has lived up to his description of it being capricious and powerful, peaceful and calming. For the officers of modern cruise ships, the Mediterranean no longer presents the same challenges it did to such legendary seafarers as Odysseus, and passengers cruising the Med can simply sit back and ponder the complex workings of a modern cruise ship.

Navigational Challenges of the Mediterranean

Ship captains generally regard the Mediterranean, the world's largest inland sea, as one of the safest and easiest cruise areas to navigate. Thoroughly charted, the Mediterranean is surprisingly deep in places. Thirty miles west of Greece's Peloponnese Peninsula, along a major subduction zone, the depths plunge to over 15,000 feet. Conversely, sea depths become shallow at river mouths, where silt carried downstream and deposited on a river's delta can alter the course of tributaries and reduce water depths at harbour entrances.

Although strong currents are not a prevalent hazard in the Mediterranean, two passes of concern are the Strait of Messina (lying between Sicily and the 'toe' of Italy) and the Dardanelles (leading to the Sea of Marmara and Istanbul). In both cases, however, currents rarely exceed five knots, which modern ships can handle without difficulty. (For a map of the prevailing currents in the Mediterranean, see page 41, Natural Phenomena.)

The enclosed Mediterranean produces smaller waves than an open ocean, but there can be steep seas if the winds are strong. Strong winds and choppy waves can occur in the Sea of Crete, the Tyrrhenian Sea (between the Straits of Messina and Naples), and the area between Barcelona

The upper decks of modern cruise ships provide excellent viewing for passengers. Shown here, a ship off the Sicily coast.

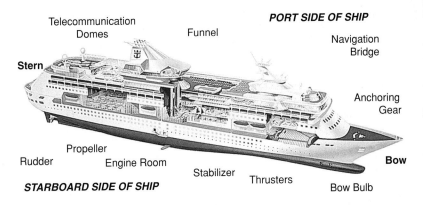

and Marseille where ships cross the Gulf of Lions. Extremely windy conditions in Marseille and Villefranche sometimes prompt ships to re-route to Toulon.

Numerous harbours in the Mediterranean are man-made, and some are centuries old with narrow entrances. For example, the entrances to Marseille, Livorno and Civitavecchia are very tight and require close attention from the crew. The entrance to the ship dock at Venice is also very narrow, and the west side of the docking area is shallow.

How Ships Move

Ships are pushed through the water by the turning of propellers, two of which are mounted at the stern. A propeller is like a screw threading its way through the sea, pushing water away from its pitched blades. Props are 15 to 20 feet in diameter on large cruise ships and normally turn at 100 to 150 revolutions per minute. It takes a lot of horsepower – about 60,000 on a large ship – to make these propellers push a ship along. The bridge crew can tap

into any amount of engine power by moving small levers that adjust the propeller blades to determine the speed of the ship. Most modern ships use diesel engines to deliver large amounts of electricity to motors that smoothly turn the propeller shafts. The use of electric motors to turn prop shafts greatly reduces ship vibration and passengers rarely detect the workings of the ship. Some ships use electric motors mounted on pods hung from the stern of the ship, like huge outboard engines. These pods can swivel 360 degrees.

The cruising speed of most ships in the Med is normally between 15 and 20 knots, depending on the distance to the next port. Distances at sea are measured in nautical miles (1 nautical mile = 1.15 statute miles = 1.85 kilometres).

Modern cruise ships are vastly different from those of the Golden Age of ocean liners, which were designed for the rigours of winter storms in the North Atlantic. Ships built today are generally taller, shallower, lighter and powered by smaller, more compact engines. Although their steel hulls are thinner and welded together in numerous sections, modern ships are as strong as the older ocean liners because of advances in construction technology and metallurgy.

A ship's size is determined by measurements that result in a figure called tonnage. There are approximately 100 cubic feet to a measured ton. Cruise ships used to be considered large if they exceeded 30,000 tons. Today, many of the ships being built are over 100,00 tons, with some exceeding 200,000 tons.

At the stern of every ship, below its name, is the ship's country of registry, which is not necessarily where the cruise company's head office is located. Certain countries grant registry to ships for a flat fee, with few restrictions or onerous charges, and ships often fly these 'flags of convenience' for tax reasons.

A ship's bow bulb reduces the vessel's fuel consumption.

The Engine Room

Located many decks below the passenger cabins is the engine room, a labyrinth of tunnels, catwalks and bulkheads connecting and supporting the machinery that generates the vast amount of power needed to operate a ship. A large, proficient crew keeps everything running smoothly, but this is a far cry from the hundreds of workers once needed to operate coal-burning steam engines before the advent of diesel fuel.

Technical advancements have helped to reduce fuel consumption and improve ship handling. These advancements include the bow bulb, stabilizers and thrusters. The bow bulb, positioned just below the waterline, displaces the same amount of water that would be pushed out of the way by the ship's bow. This virtually eliminates a bow wave, resulting in fuel savings as less energy is needed to push the ship forward. Stabilizers are small, wing-like appendages that protrude amidships below the waterline and act

to dampen the ship's roll in beam seas. Thrusters are port-like openings with small propellers that are located at the bow (and sometimes at the stern) which push the bow (or stern) of the ship as it approaches or leaves a dock. Thrusters have greatly reduced the need for tugs when docking.

The amount of soot smoke from today's ships is a fraction of that produced by earlier ships, but stricter emission regulations have prompted the retrofitting of ships with exhaust-cleaning systems (called scrubbers). A growing number of ships have also been configured to plug into shoreside electrical power (cold ironing) when docked.

The Bridge

The bridge (located at the bow of the ship) is an elevated, enclosed platform that bridges (or crosses) the width of the ship, providing an unobstructed view ahead and to either side from the bridge wings. It is from the ship's bridge that the highest-ranking officer – the captain – oversees the operation of the ship. The bridge is manned 24 hours a day by two

(Top) Banks of navigational aids are located on the ship's bridge. (Above) A captain uses the bridge wing controls while docking.

officers working four hours on, eight hours off, in a three-watch system. They all report to the captain, and their various duties include recording all course changes, keeping lookout and making sure the junior officer keeps a fresh pot of coffee going. The captain does not usually have a set watch but will be on the bridge when the ship is entering or leaving port, and transiting a

Pilot boats can face tough seas delivering personnel to a ship.

channel. Other conditions that would bring the captain to the bridge would be poor weather or when there are numerous vessels in the area, such as commercial fishboats.

An array of instrumentation provides the ship's officers with pertinent information. Radar is used most intensely in foggy conditions or at night. Radar's electronic signals can survey the ocean for many miles, and anything solid – such as land or other boats – appears on its screen. Radar is also used for plotting the course of other ships and for alerting the crew of a potential collision situation. Depth sounders track the bottom of the seabed to ensure the ship's course agrees with the depth of water shown on the official chart.

The helm on modern ships is a surprisingly small wheel. An automatic telemotor transmission connects the wheel to the steering mechanism at the stern of the ship. Ships also use an 'autopilot' which works through an electronic compass to steer a course. The autopilot is used when the ship is in open water. When docking the ship, the captain controls the ship from one of the two bridge wings.

Other instruments monitor engine speed, power, angle of list, speed through water, speed over ground and time arrival estimations. When entering a harbour, large ships must have a pilot on board to provide navigational advice to the ship's officers. When a ship is in open waters, a pilot is not required.

Tendering

At some ports, the ship will anchor off a distance from the town and passengers are tendered ashore in the ship's launches. Passengers on organized shore excursions will be taken ashore first, so if you have booked an excursion you will assemble with your group in one of the ship's public areas. Otherwise, wait an hour or so to board a tender, when the line-ups will be shorter.

Ship Safety

Cruise ships are one of the safest modes of travel. The International Maritime Organization maintains high standards for safety at sea, including regular fire drills for the crew as well as frequent ship inspections for cleanliness and seaworthiness. A mandatory life-boat drill takes place within 24 hours of embarkation, usually just before leaving port. All passengers must comply and are directed to either an assigned lifeboat station or to a designated lounge for briefing. Directions are displayed on the back of each cabin door and staff are on hand to guide passengers through the safety drill.

Hotel Staff

The Front Desk (or Purser's Office) is the pleasure centre of the ship and the Hotel Manager's rank is second only to that of the Captain. In terms of staff, the Hotel Manager (or Passenger Services Director) oversees the largest. It is his or her responsibility to make sure beds are made, meals are served, wines are poured, entertainment is provided and tour buses arrive on time. Hotel managers typically have many years of experience on ships, working in various departments before rising to this position. Most have graduated from a

(Top) Tendering passengers ashore is usually done efficiently but requires a bit of patience to safely get off and on the tender. (Above) A ship's hotel manager oversees all of the service staff.

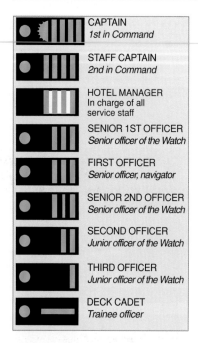

CAPTAIN	1st in Command
STAFF CAPTAIN	2nd in Command
HOTEL MANAGER	In charge of all service staff
SENIOR 1ST OFFICER	Senior officer of the Watch
FIRST OFFICER	Senior officer, navigator
SENIOR 2ND OFFICER	Senior officer of the Watch
SECOND OFFICER	Junior officer of the Watch
THIRD OFFICER	Junior officer of the Watch
DECK CADET	Trainee officer

(Above) An officer's rank is easily discerned by the stripes on the sleeves. (Below) The front desk (purser's office) handles all passenger queries and accounts.

university or college program in management, and have trained in the hotel or food services industries, where they learn the logistics of feeding hundreds of people throughout a cruise.

A Hotel Manager's management staff includes a Purser, Food Services Manager, Beverage Manager, Chief Housekeeper, Cruise Director and Shore Excursion Manager. All ship's staff wear a uniform and even if a hotel officer doesn't recognize a staff member, he will know at a glance that person's duties by their uniform's colour and the distinguishing bars on its sleeves. The hotel staff on cruise ships come from countries around the world.

Checking In

Upon arrival at the cruise terminal, you will be directed to a check-in counter and asked to offer up a credit card to be swiped for any onboard expenses. In exchange, you will receive a personalized plastic card which acts both as your onboard credit card and the door key to your stateroom. It is also your security pass for getting off and on the ship at each port of call. Carry this card with you at all times.

Life Aboard

Cruise ship cabins – also called staterooms – vary in size, from standard inside cabins to outside suites complete with a verandah. Whatever the size of your stateroom, it will be clean and comfortable. A telephone and television are standard features, and storage space includes closets and

A standard outside stateroom with balcony is usually about 250 square feet.

drawers ample enough to hold clothes and miscellaneous items. Valuables can be left in your stateroom safe or in a safety deposit box at the front office, also called the purser's office.

If your budget permits, an outside cabin – especially one with a verandah – is preferable for enjoying the scenery and orienting yourself at a new port. When selecting a cabin, keep in mind its location in relation to the decks above and below. Being below the disco is fine if that's where you plan to be in the wee hours, but not if you like to retire early. If you're prone to seasickness, cabins located on lower decks near the middle of the ship will have less motion than a top outside cabin near the bow or stern. Some people like being near a set of elevators for the convenience while others are bothered by the sounds associated with people getting on and off the lifts. Discuss your preferences with

your cruise agent when booking. For families, most large ships have a number of standard cabins that can accommodate a third and fourth passenger. Another option is to book interconnecting cabins or a family suite.

Both casual and formal dining are offered on the large ships, with breakfast and lunch served in the buffet-style lido restaurant or at an open seating in the main dining room. Dinner traditionally was served at two sittings in the main dining room, with passengers asked to indicate their preference for first or second sitting. While this traditional two-sitting format is still offered on the large ships, flexible dining times are also offered for passengers who prefer to dine at a time of their choosing. Luxury cruise lines usually offer a choice of open-seating restaurants.

Large ships also offer alternative dining – small specialty restaurants that require a reservation and for which there is usually a surcharge (about US$25 per person). Room service is also available, free of charge, for light meals and snacks.

Specialty restaurants (above) are an alternative to the ship's main dining rooms (left).

Things to Do

There are so many things to do on a modern cruise ship, you would have to spend a few months onboard to participate in every activity and enjoy all of the ship's facilities. A daily newsletter, delivered to your stateroom, will keep you informed of all the ship's happenings. If exercise is a priority, you can swim in the pool, work out in the gym, jog around the promenade deck, join the aerobics and dance classes or join in the table tennis and volley-ball tournaments. Perhaps you just want to soak in the jacuzzi, relax in the sauna or treat yourself to a massage and facial at the spa.

Stop by the library if you're looking for a good book, a board game or an informal hand of bridge with your fellow passengers. Check your newsletter to see which films are scheduled for the movie theatre or just settle into a deck chair, breathing the fresh sea air. Your days on the ship can be as busy or as relaxed as you want. You can stay up late every night, enjoying the varied entertainment in the ship's lounges, or you can retire early and rise at dawn to watch the ship pull into port. When the ship is in port, you can remain onboard if you wish or you can head ashore, returning to the ship as many times as you like before it leaves for the next port. Ships are punctual about departing, so be sure to get back to the ship at least a half hour before it is scheduled to leave.

Although bridge tours (of the navigation area of the ship) are not always available due to security concerns, tours of the kitchen and of backstage entertainment areas are offered on most ships. If you have an interest in these areas, check with the front desk for tour opportunities.

Children and teenagers are welcome on the majority of cruise ships (with the exception of small luxury ships) and these offer an ideal environment for family vacations. Most large ships provide a playroom for children and a disco-type club for teenagers. Supervised activities are offered on a daily basis, and security measures include parents checking their small children in and out of the playroom. Kids have a great time participating in activities ranging from ball games to arts and crafts, all overseen by staff with experience in education, recreation or a related field. Each cruise line has a minimum

(Top) The central atrium on a large ship. (Above and below) Games room and Internet cafe.

(Top to bottom) Pool decks on modern ships are expansive and often include dedicated areas for children. Outside teak decks are excellent venues for exercising.

age for participation (usually three years unless accompanied by a parent) and some also offer private babysitting. Childrens facilities and programs vary from line to line, and from ship to ship. For details, contact your cruise agent or visit the cruise lines' websites.

Extra Expenses

There are few additional expenses once you board a cruise ship. Your stateroom and meals are paid for, as are any stage shows, lectures, movies, lounge acts and other activities held in the ship's public areas. However, shore excursions, which are optional, are an extra expense. Also, if you make use of the personal services offered on board – such as dry cleaning or a spa treatment – these are not covered in the basic price of a cruise. There is usually an extra charge to dine at one of the ship's specialty restaurants, and any drinks you order in a lounge will be an additional expense. You will also be charged for wine or other alcoholic beverages you order with your meals. Wine packages are usually available and can be good value.

Gratuities for staff are another extra expense, with each cruise line providing their own guidelines on how much each crew-member should be tipped – provided you are happy with the service. On luxury ships, gratuities are covered by the all-inclusive fare; on premium and contemporary ships tipping is expected.

Tips were traditionally handed out the last night at sea, in cash, but most cruise lines now offer a service that automatically bills an aggregate amount for gratuities (about $13 per passenger per day) to your shipboard account – which can be adjusted at your discretion. These gratuities do not cover bar bills, to which a 15% tip is automatically added.

Most ships are cashless societies in which passengers sign for incidental expenses. These are itemized on a final statement that is slipped under your cabin door during the last night of your cruise and settled at the front office by pre-approved credit card. You can, if you like, occasionally check your account on your stateroom TV or at the Front Desk and clear up any discrepancies before receiving a final printout of your bill. It's best to do this before the final night of your cruise to avoid long line-ups.

(Above) A poolside bar is an ideal spot for relaxing. (Below) A couple enjoys a romantic moment at the ship's rail.

C ataclysmic events, once thought to be caused by the actions of angry gods, have since been explained by scientific data and an understanding of seismic activity. Yet, rather than discredit ancient myths, the scientific evidence offered by modern geologists and oceanographers may prove that certain legendary events did occur. Indeed, the earth did shake from time to time with deafening force, huge waves did wash ashore, and islands did rise from the sea.

Such phenomena is currently happening between the coasts of Sicily and Tunisia where a submerged volcanic island called Graham Island (known in Italian as Isola Ferdinandea) is rising to the sea's surface due to seismic activity in the area. It last emerged in 1831 when its six-month appearance sparked a diplomatic debate among Britain, Spain and the Bourbon court of Sicily, all claiming ownership of the tiny island.

This time around, in hopes of claiming this new territory for Italy the moment it reappears, Sicilian divers have planted a flag on the submerged rock, which lies about 20 feet below the surface.

Through radiocarbon dating of sediment cores, scientists can now explain phenomena from the distant past, such as the formation of the Black Sea. According to the evidence, in about 5500 BC a worldwide rise in sea levels caused waters of the Mediterranean Sea to spill into the Bosporus strait and transform an existing freshwater lake into the Black Sea. This has prompted speculation that the subsequent flooding of shorelines and displacement of people may have been the basis for Noah's ark in the Book of Genesis.

Tectonic Beginnings

The Mediterranean, the world's largest inland sea, was originally a vast ocean stretching across half the globe. Its surrounding land masses emerged some 30 million years ago when collisions of the earth's crustal plates created mountain ranges and deep sea rifts, such as the Red Sea, which formed when Africa and Arabia split.

The Mediterranean Sea marks the boundary of two major plates – the Eurasian and African. Much of this boundary – from the toe of Italy's 'boot' to the coast of

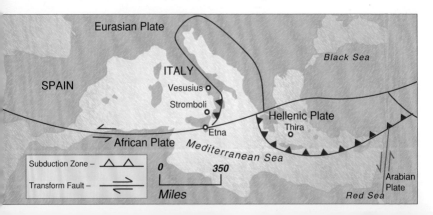

Eurasian Plate

Black Sea

ITALY

SPAIN

Vesusius ○

Stromboli ○

Hellenic Plate

Thira ○

○ Etna

African Plate   Mediterranean Sea

Subduction Zone – △ △

Transform Fault –

0   350

Miles

Arabian Plate

Red Sea

Turkey – is a subduction zone. The world's most destructive earthquakes occur along such zones, where the leading edge of one plate is pushing beneath the edge of another. Transform faults – where the edges of two plates are sliding past one another – run along the Mediterranean's North African coastline and extend from Turkey to the Red Sea.

The biblical cities of Sodom and Gomorrah were quite likely destroyed not by 'fire and brimstone' but by earthquakes. In more recent times, earthquakes have shaken western Turkey, northern Morocco, Greece and Italy, where a series of quakes have battered parts of central Italy, including one registering 6.3 on the Richter scale that struck the mountain city of L'Aquila and nearby medieval towns, reducing historic bell towers to rubble and killing more than 300 people. Aftershocks were felt as far away as Rome, 60 miles to the west.

Seismic activity on Sicily in 2002 resulted in 200 small quakes, which rattled the island's east side in the vicinity of **Mount Etna**, Europe's largest and most active volcano.

Volcanic Eruptions

The ancient Romans named their god of fire Vulcan, and volcanoes continue to threaten parts of modern Italy. Sicily's **Mount Etna** erupted more than 60 times in the first six months of 2000. Huge 'bombs' of lava, 4.5 feet in diameter, shot from Etna's main summit cone, followed by explosions of ash from the northern vent area and slow lava flows that poured from the volcano's youngest crater on its southeastern flank. Ash fell on nearby villages, and trenches were dug to divert the flow of magma away from the town of Linguaglossa. In October 2002 a stream of lava destroyed some ski lift pylons as it flowed toward Piano Provenzana, a plateau used by visitors as a starting point for mountain hikes. Scientists surmise that Etna is evolving from a predictable 'hotspot-type' of volcano to a more violent 'island-arc' variety.

Mount Vesuvius, standing on the eastern shore of the Bay of Naples, is the only active volcano on the European mainland. Its cataclysmic eruption of 79 AD buried Pompeii, Herculaneum and Stabiae under cinders, ashes and mud. Vesuvius has frequently erupted since then, including three times in the 20th century, and scientists predict another catastrophic eruption.

The height of the main cone is about 4,000 feet (1,200 m) and is half encircled by the ridge of a second summit Monte Somma.

Stromboli, one of Italy's Lipari Islands, is an active volcano.

The lower slopes of Vesuvius are quite fertile, where vineyards produce the famous Lachryma Christi wine.

To the west of Naples lies a hidden 'super volcano' similar to the Yellowstone caldera in the U.S. state of Wyoming but more menacing due to its densely populated location. Called **Campi Flegrei** (from the Greek word for burning), this eight-mile wide crater of boiling mud and sulphurous steam holes has become a tourist attraction, but one that is being closely monitored by the Vesuvius Observatory in Naples. Scientists there have devised a plan for drilling two miles below the surface to reach the caldera's massive chamber of molten rock. This will allow them to detect any signs of a pending eruption, which could be catastrophic.

Stromboli is an active volcano with several craters for which the 'Strombolian' form of volcanic eruption is named. This fairly mild type of eruption consists of a continuous discharge of viscous lava which produces luminous clouds. In December 2002, after 20 years of relative quiet, Stromboli began erupting with unusual force, suggesting a new interaction between its magma and seawater. Residents of the tiny volcanic island had to evacuate when part of Stromboli's lava field slid down a steep slope into the Tyrrhenian Sea, triggering a huge harbour wave.

The Mediterranean's legendary volcanoes include the Greek island of **Santorini** (Thira), which is the site of an exploded volcano, its harbour a flooded crater.

A Storied Sea

The strong local winds that blow across the Mediterranean Sea – such as the hot, dry sirocco from the south, and the cold mistral from the north – were believed by ancient mariners to be controlled by gods. Inspiring several myths were the currents and whirlpools that plague the **Strait of Messina**, which lies between mainland Italy and the island of Sicily. The whirlpools in particular were attributed to the sea monster Scylla, who lived on the rocks on the mainland side of the strait, where she would seize and devour sailors. Odysseus passed through this strait in his wanderings, as did Jason and the Argonauts.

The enclosed Mediterranean is an almost tideless sea, and its currents are generally estuarine in nature. This two-way circulation is created by extensive evaporation of the surface waters, which become saltier and heavier than waters at lower levels, causing the surface waters to sink to the bottom of the seabed and eventually flow out through the **Strait of Gibraltar** where less salty (and lighter) Atlantic water flows into the Mediterranean. During World War II, German submarines that were trapped by the Allied blockade of the Strait of Gibraltar would sneak out of the Mediterranean by silently drifting seaward on these bottom currents.

The Mediterranean once supported a brilliant array of sponges, corals and fish species, and tales of dolphins rescuing people from drowning date back to Greek mythology. In recent times, the sea has suffered from over-fishing and pollution.

When Jacques-Yves Cousteau, in the summer of 1943, slipped into the warm waters of a cove on the French Riviera to test the Aqualung he had developed with a French engineer, the Mediterranean teemed with life. By the early 1970s, Cousteau was so concerned with the drastic decrease in marine life he founded the Cousteau Society to spread his ardent advocacy of the seas.

Military exercises in the Mediterranean also pose a threat to the sea's marine life. When a dozen Cuvier's beaked whales beached themselves on the coast of the Kyparissiakos Gulf in May 1997, a Greek researcher suggested that a NATO test using very loud, low-frequency sounds designed to detect quiet diesel and nuclear submarines may have disoriented the whales. And when the corpses of 22 dolphins washed up on the south coast of France in March 1998, naval operations were again suspect.

Another troubling trend is the rise in water temperature, with a growing number of tropical fish species making the Mediterranean Sea their permanent home. They are arriving from the Red Sea and the Atlantic Ocean off Africa, and are thriving in part because the Mediterranean's indigenous species have been weakened by environmental stress and overfishing.

When the ancient Greeks, using ropes and stone weights, began diving beneath the sea's surface in search of sponges and sunken treasure, they feared the mysterious creatures of the deep. Today the fear is the serious threat of their extinction.

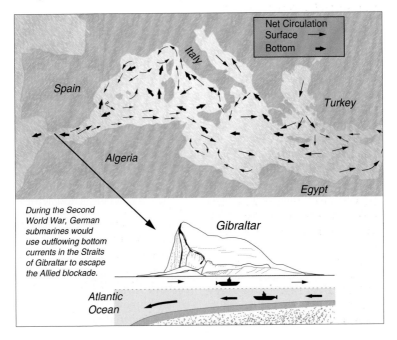

Net Circulation
Surface ⟶
Bottom ⟶

Italy

Spain

Turkey

Algeria

Egypt

During the Second World War, German submarines would use outflowing bottom currents in the Straits of Gibraltar to escape the Allied blockade.

Gibraltar

Atlantic Ocean

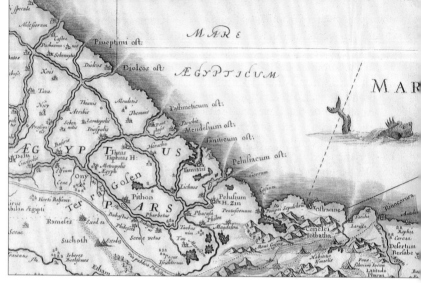

ANCIENT MARINERS

Since the beginning of time, shipping has determined human history. Early civilizations formed along the banks of navigable rivers or the coastlines of warm seas, and the ideally situated Mediterranean became the cradle of maritime endeavour.

As early as 3500 BC the **Egyptians** were sailing boats on the Nile, and by 2500 BC they were making tentative voyages into the Mediterranean Sea, tracing the coast by day and anchoring at night. Egypt was also the first Mediterranean nation to engage in shipbuilding. Early boats were made from bundles of papyrus reeds lashed together, their ends raised and bound, while those made of wood consisted of planks 'sewn' together with ropes. The larger boats were multi-oared and rigged with a steering oar. Over time, the Egyptians became skilled shipwrights, adept at dovetailing and scarfing hundreds of small timbers together to make watertight hulls for there were no tall trees in Egypt from which to cut long planks used later when Europeans developed seagoing water craft.

When Egyptian power waned in the 12th century BC, Phoenician mariners began dominating the Mediterranean. They sailed to the edges of the known world, and eventually ventured beyond the Pillars of Hercules (Strait of Gibraltar) at the Mediterranean's western entrance, travelling north to England in search of tin, and south along the coast of Africa.

The Phoenicians, whose territory corresponded roughly with modern-day Lebanon, established numerous colonies along the shores of the Mediterranean, including **Carthage** on the north coast of Africa, which eventually became a powerful city-state and rival of imperial Rome.

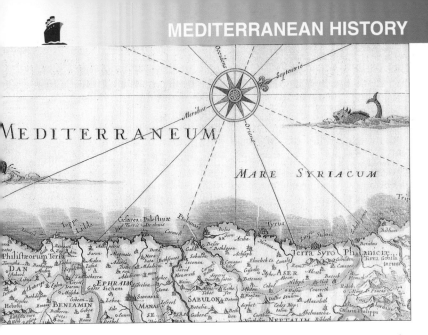

Navigation & Chartmaking

Mediterranean is a Latin word meaning 'sea in the midst of lands.' Strong local winds blow across this inland sea, and the early sailors used these winds as a means of navigation when sailing from one port to another. Greek mariners, when out of sight of land, used four winds to determine their position. The Boreas blew from the north, the Euros from the east, the Notos from the south and the Zephuros from the west. Each wind was identified in relation to the sun's bearing or, at night, by the star Polaris.

As longer voyages were taken, four more winds, from the of northeast, southeast, southwest and northwest, were added to the wind-rose – the compass of ancient mariners. Over time the system was expanded until there were 32 winds, representing the 32 points of the wind-rose.

The first pilot books were written around 500 BC. The mouth of the Nile was a starting point from which the pilot would guide mariners, in a clockwise direction, from port to port. Tides, which are minimal in the Mediterranean, were believed to be controlled by sea monsters until a Greek navigator and astronomer named Pytheas, who lived in Massilia (modern Marseille) in the 4th century BC, discovered that tides were connected with the moon.

As early as the 6th century BC, the Greek philosopher Pythagoras realized that the earth was spherical. Eratosthenes, keeper of Alexandria's great library in the 3rd century BC, expanded on Pythagoras's theory and devised a method for measuring the earth's circumference, which incorporated existing surveys of the Nile river. He constructed a map of the known world using parallels and meridians that passed through important places, such as Rhodes (the maritime centre of the known world) and the Pillars of Hercules, which marked the Mediterranean's western entrance.

In the 1st century AD, Marinus of Tyre created the first marine charts, with Rhodes remaining the primary meridian and parallel. But it was Ptolemy (85-160 AD), perhaps the greatest cartographer of all, who first projected part of the spherical earth's surface onto a plane surface. A Greek born in Egypt, Ptolemy spent most of his life in Alexandria, where he studied mathematics and astronomy. He wrote many works, the most famous being *Geographica*, compiled into eight books and containing an atlas of the known world. This great work was lost with the fall of the Roman Empire, but it resurfaced in 1400

An important port as early as 400 BC, Rhodes was used by ancient cartographers as the central reference point on maps.

AD in Constantinople and was eventually translated into Latin. The development of printing allowing for its wide distribution and it became the basis for mapping new world discoveries throughout the 15th and 16th centuries.

Ship Design

In the beginning, small merchant ships plied the waters between Phoenicia, Egypt and Greece, carrying such luxury items as spices, perfumes and fine pottery for trade. Baskets filled with stones were used as anchors, but as ships grew larger, iron hooks were designed to dig into the sea bed. When the Phoenician sailors began making longer voyages, they built larger ships which carried, in addition to oars, a square sail for running before the wind.

The **Romans**, skilled engineers, began to build larger and stronger ships for transporting military supplies and troops to outlying outposts of Rome's expanding empire. These broad,

full-bodied ships could carry up to 400 tons of cargo, and were used for shipping grain and other foodstuffs from their colonies. They were propelled by sails and steered by two deep oars, one on each quarter.

An innovative application of nautical know-how was used by the Romans during construction of the **Colosseum** in the 1st century AD, when a retractable sail-cloth was rigged as a sun shade for spectators. The sailors living in a camp nearby were adept at handling the wooden pulleys and ropes used to furl this cloth roof in heavy rains and winds, then unfurl it in fair weather.

Merchant ships, designed to carry cargo, were often accompanied by galleys for protection. War galleys were long, narrow vessels designed for speed and rowed by slaves and prisoners of war who were chained to benches. A beak or metal point was fixed on the bow and was used for ramming enemy vessels with the intent of piercing their hulls and sinking them. The crew of ancient warships used catapults for firing missiles and incendiaries such as Greek Fire, which was a flammable substance of sulphur, naphtha and quicklime.

Attached to the ship's beak was a figurehead. Associated with a sea deity for protection, this figure had eyes enabling the ship to 'see' its way swiftly across the water. The Egyptians mounted figures of various holy birds on the prows of their ships and the Romans often used a centurion.

A number of superstitions and rituals still practiced by modern mariners originated in ancient times. The tradition of breaking a bottle of champagne across a new ship's bow began as a cruel ritual during antiquity when a new galley had to 'taste blood' to be successful in battle. To this end, galleys were launched by rolling them across slaves tied to the keel blocks. Their bodies, when

Ptolemy's famous map of North Africa, drafted in the 2nd century, was remarkably accurate.

A felucca on the Nile (above).
Traditional beaks are still seen
on Venetian gondolas (below).

crushed, would splash blood against the ship's hull.

Galleys were eventually rigged as sailing vessels, and by the 15th century, the caravel – a three-masted sailing vessel with a roundish hull – was being used by the Portuguese and Spanish for ocean-going exploration. The galley continued to be used in the eastern Mediterranean until the 18th century.

Traditional boats that are still in use include the felucca, a lateen-rigged sailing vessel once used in the Mediterranean and still seen on the Nile, as is the *dahabeeyah*, a large river vessel with high lateen sails. The word *dahabeeyah* is Arabic for 'golden' and was originally applied in reference to the gilded barges Egyptian rulers used for river processions and ceremonies of state. Cleopatra's barge was described by Shakespeare in *Antony and Cleopatra* as "a burnished throne" with a golden poop, silver oars and purple sails "so perfumed the winds were love-sick with them".

The Venetian *bucentaur*, from the Italian *buzino d'oro* (meaning 'golden bark'), was another sumptuously decorated vessel. The state galley of the doges (rulers of Venice), it was used in an annual symbolic ceremony called 'the wedding of the sea' which commemorated Venice's victory over the Dalmatian pirates in 1000 AD. Venice's most famous vessel is the **gondola**, which dates to at least the 11th century and is still used today as a popular mode of transport for tourists transiting the city's canals. Long, sleek and efficient, its hull shape embodies the principles of the wave line theory of modern shipbuilding. With a flat bottom and a high prow and stern, it is propelled by a single oarsman – called a gondolier – positioned near the stern. The bright metal beak at the bow, called a ferro, is shaped like the ancient *rostrum tridens*.

Naval Battles

The Mediterranean's early naval fleets set off on raiding or trading expeditions, and were eventually organized for conquest and defense as naval supremacy became critical to an empire's survival.

When the Athenian navy destroyed a Persian fleet off the Aegean island of Salamis in 480 BC, this great naval victory established the maritime supremacy of **Athens** and ushered in the city-state's golden age under the leadership of Pericles. The port of Piraeus, linked to Athens by a fortified corridor called the Long Walls, became an important naval centre holding nearly 300 war galleys. Fifty years later, the rival city-state of Sparta, aided by the Persians, defeated the Athenian navy and tore down the Long Walls.

In the 3rd century BC, following its conquest of central and southern Italy, **Rome** began to look seaward. The North African city of Carthage ruled the western Mediterranean, and Rome's designs on Sicily drew these two city-states into a protracted conflict. Rome eventually emerged as victor, with the Romans now referring to the Mediterranean as Mare Nostrum ('Our Sea').

Rome's first naval hero was Gaius Duillius, who led a fleet to victory against the Carthaginians off the coast of Sicily during the First Punic War in 260 BC. Duillius carried boarding bridges and designed grappling irons which he used to bind his ships to those of the enemy. Thus aided, he captured fifty ships at the Battle of Mylae and was the first Roman to achieve victory over the naval power of Carthage. His great triumph was honoured in Rome with the raising of a column in the Roman Forum adorned with the beakheads of the captured vessels. Hailed as a hero, he was attended by a torch-bearer and flute player whenever he walked the streets of Rome in the evening.

Ancient galleys of the Mediterranean were rigged with a square sail for running before the wind.

Piracy & Plunder

The fall of the Roman Empire was followed by the rise of piracy, and throughout the Middle Ages pirates plagued the Mediterranean. Coastal trading ports were fortified with walls and bastions, and chains were drawn across harbour entrances during times of attack. Sacking and plundering coastal settlements was highly lucrative, and became even more so when oared galleys were replaced with sailing ships, which expanded a pirate's range of operation.

The most famous pirates of the Mediterranean operated from the coast of north Africa. Many were displaced Moors of Spain who had been driven into exile in the 15th century by the Catholic forces of Ferdinand and Isabella. Bent on revenge against Christians in general and the Spanish in particular, they were called **Barbary pirates** for the Berber settlements from which they embarked on their raids. These notorious corsairs, who lived by plunder, operated out of Tripoli, Tunis and Algiers, all of which were military republics that broke free of Turkish rule in the mid-1600s.

The Barbary pirates specialized in the capture and sale of slaves, with some venturing as far away as Iceland. The most feared were the Barbarossa brothers, whose names struck terror in the hearts of Christians. From 1510 to 1545, they burned, pillaged and murdered in raids along the Spanish and Italian coasts. One brother was eventually killed by Spanish troops but the other retired with vast riches to a palace he had built at Constantinople.

Despite numerous attempts to stamp out piracy in the Mediterranean, it wasn't completely eliminated until 1830 when a French fleet bombarded and captured the port of Algiers, the last stronghold of organized piracy.

ANCIENT EGYPT

The mysterious monuments, rituals and relics of ancient Egypt may seem strange and unconnected to modern life, but they have in fact influenced the art, culture and conceptions of subsequent civilizations, including our own. More than four thousand years ago, during the time of the Old Kingdom (2686-2181 BC), the Egyptians devised a solar calendar based on a year of 365 days. They also invented the sun dial, the water clock and various mathematical formulas, including one for calculating the area of a circle. Their knowledge of medicine was remarkably advanced, having developed an understanding of the circulatory system.

The chair, one of the oldest forms of furniture, dates from the Old Kingdom, as does taxation, which was based on a biennial census of farmers' produce. The world's first recorded labour strike occurred during the reign of Rameses III, in the 12th century BC, when royal tomb-workers from the village of Deir

El-Medina on the Theban west bank staged protests in front of several mortuary temples.

Wages back then were paid in the form of food rations. Emmer-wheat, used for making stone-ground flour, and barley, used for brewing a thick, soup-like beer, were highly valued as staples of the Egyptian diet. The wealthier classes dined on meat, salted fish, lettuce and cucumbers, and such fruits as dates, figs and pome-granates. The nobility also drank wine, which was stored in stone vessels. Noblemen and their families lived in villas with gardens, and kept house pets, including cats, monkeys and dogs.

We know all of this and more because the Egyptians invented one of the earliest forms of writing. Hieroglyphs, meaning 'priestly carvings' in Greek, were pictorial symbols for words, sounds or syllables, and were carved and painted on the walls of temples and tombs to record funerary and religious texts. Over time hieroglyphs evolved into a form of cursive handwriting called hieratic, which was used primarily for administrative and literary texts.

Only a small minority of the population were literate in ancient times. Professional scribes were members of an elite class, passing their skills from father to son. Using ink cakes and reed brushes wetted with water, they wrote on papyrus and other surfaces, and

Hieroglyphs, proclaiming the pharaoh's names and titles, run down an obelisk's four sides.

these hieratic writings preserved on ancient papyri have provided priceless data to Egyptologists. By the 5th century BC, hieratic script had been replaced by a simplified script called demotic, which often appeared beside Greek script. With the arrival of Christianity in Egypt came the Coptic language, written using a modified version of the Greek alphabet. Many of the Greek words have remained in common usage, such as pyramid (from the Greek word *pyramis*) and pharaoh (from a Greek word meaning 'great house').

The famous **Rosetta Stone**, found in 1799 by Napoleon's soldiers and now on display in the British Museum, is inscribed in three scripts and two languages: Egyptian hieroglyphs, Egyptian demotic script, and Greek. It was the Greek version of the Egyptian

texts that helped scholars, after 20 years of study, decipher their meaning and begin to understand the far-reaching and complex legacy of ancient Egypt.

Ancient Beliefs

Ancient Egyptians believed the world was shaped like a disk. In the centre lay the flat plains of Egypt, surrounded by a rim of mountainous foreign lands. Below were the deep waters of the underworld and above stretched the sky. Animals were the first to be worshiped in predynastic Egypt and sacred species

Amun, in the form of a ram, protects the pharaoh who stands between the god's paws.

included the cat and the Apis bull. As civilization progressed, the deities were gradually humanized and portrayed in various forms, often half human/half animal.

The major gods were supported by cults, their followers building temples for worshiping a specific deity. The dominant god of the Old Kingdom pantheon was **Ra**, the sun god, whose daily journey across the sky, from birth to death, was a fundamental theme in Egyptian religion. Worship of Ra reached its peak during the Old Kingdom's 4th Dynasty when the Great Pyramids were built.

Osiris, god of the underworld and protector of all, symbolized the imperishability of life and was often depicted in mummy wrappings, wearing the crown of Upper Egypt and holding a crook and flail. **Horus**, god of the sky, was often depicted with a hawk's head for his swift flight across the sky. **Amun**, another important god, rose to prominence during the Middle Kingdom (2055-1650 BC) when the capital of Egypt moved to Thebes, where Amun was worshiped as a local deity. Often depicted with a ram's head, Amun was combined with the sun-god Ra to become the powerful god Amun-Ra.

Ultimately, Egypt's pantheon of gods influenced both the Greeks and Romans, who adopted various Egyptian deities and fused them with their own gods. **Isis** the nature goddess was widely worshiped throughout the Hellenistic world and the Roman empire, and she seriously rivaled both the traditional Roman gods and early Christianity.

The ancient Egyptians believed their pharaohs descended from the gods, and the sun god Ra was considered the direct ancestor of the first pharaoh. The living pharaoh, whose role was to impose order and prevent chaos, was linked with the falcon-god Horus, while the deceased kings were associated with Osiris.

THE PHOENICIANS

The Phoenicians traded with the Egyptians as early as 2800 BC. Large cedars grew in their homeland and this source of wood, which was in short supply in Egypt, was of great value to the ancient Egyptians. Skilled artisans, the Phoenicians also traded with the Greeks and were known for their textiles, especially a purple-coloured cloth they made using dye from shellfish. The Greek word for purple – *phoenicia* – became the name by which their territory (modern-day Lebanon) was known.

The Phoenicians were also accomplished architects, their cities built to withstand attacks, but their greatest contribution to western civilization was their development of a standardized phonetic alphabet, which served as a basis for the Greek alphabet and became a key factor in the development of Greek literature. In the 6th century BC, Phoenicia fell under the influence of the Persian Empire and, with the rise of Greek maritime power, Phoenician cities began to fade in importance. The last traces of Phoenician civilization were eventually absorbed by Hellenistic culture.

ANCIENT GREECE

A recurring theme throughout the history of ancient Greece is the seaborne search for fertile lands. Facing chronic food shortages at home, the people of ancient Greece frequently cast their fate to the wind and set off across the Mediterranean Sea to seek a better life on distant shores. The mountains that isolated mainland Greece's city-states from one another were an abundant source of timber, their slopes covered with forests of oak, pine and fir from which the early shipwrights built sturdy vessels for seagoing trade and migration. Between the 8th and 6th centuries BC, Greek civilization spread eastward to the shores of the Black Sea and west to the coast of southern Spain. The coastlines of France, North

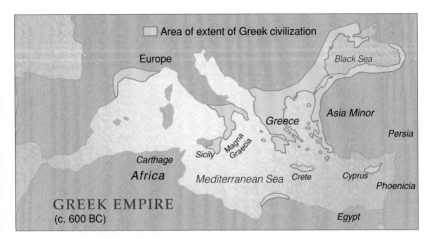

☐ Area of extent of Greek civilization

Europe

Black Sea

Asia Minor

Greece

Persia

Sicily   Magna Graecia

Carthage

Africa   Mediterranean Sea   Crete   Cyprus

Phoenicia

GREEK EMPIRE
(c. 600 BC)

Egypt

Africa, Sicily and southern Italy (Magna Graecia) were all colonized by Greek emigrants, and this period of mass migration marked the greatest geographical extent of Greek civilization.

Long before development of Greek civilization proper, the Aegean Islands were inhabited by a primitive Stone Age people who can be traced as far back as 4000 BC. Over time, they evolved into a Bronze Age civilization which gave rise to three main cultures: the Cycladic on the islands of the same name, the **Minoan** on the island of Crete, and the Mycenaean on the Peloponnese peninsula. The Minoans were skilled sailors who engaged in seagoing commerce. Although influenced by the advanced civilization of Egypt, which was located only 400 miles away, the culture they created was distinct. They built palace cities of multi-storied pavilions set amid gardens and pools, and their wall art was fluid and dynamic, with marine life and other scenes of nature portrayed in a joyful, vibrant style. The bull was a sacred animal, and frescoes often depicted a popular ritual in which young Minoans would vault over the back of a leaping bull.

Minoan culture eventually dominated the Aegean, and from 1600 to 1400 BC, both the Minoan and **Mycenaean** civilizations flourished. There were stark differences in the two cultures, with the Minoans on Crete building no fortifications, in contrast to those erected on the mainland by the warrior Mycenaeans, whose massive hilltop fortresses at Mycenae and Tiryns were regarded by later Greeks as the work of the Cyclopes, those mythical one-eyed giants who were strong enough to move the huge stone blocks into place.

After several devastating earthquakes struck **Crete**, the centre of Aegean civilization shifted to Mycenae on the mainland, where it was eventually absorbed by waves of invasions from the north. About 1400 BC, the first of these northern war-like tribes began invading Greece, sweeping southward onto the **Peloponnese** peninsula. The first to arrive were

ANCIENT GREECE

the Ionians and Aeolians, followed in 1100 BC by the **Dorians**, who pushed their way south to the Peloponnesus where they established their chief cities, **Sparta** and **Corinth**. The **Ionians** fled the Peloponnesus and eventually migrated to the coast of Asia Minor where they established the great city of **Ephesus**.

As Greek civilization spread seaward across the Aegean Sea to the shores of modern Turkey, its mainland harbours and close-lying islands were linked by mariners, resulting in the development of a homogeneous culture. Calling themselves Hellenes (the

A Minoan mural at the Palace of Knossos, Crete.

Ancient Corinth was one of the oldest and most powerful of the Greek city-states.

name of one of the original tribes), the Aeolians, Dorians and Ionians shared a growing racial pride. The Hellenes' mythology became the basis for an intricate religion with a pantheon of immortal gods and legendary heroes. One of the most famous of the Greek heroes was Odysseus, the archetypal Greek sailor whose maritime adventures inspired a great seafaring civilization.

Odysseus was a hero of the **Trojan War**, a 10-year battle between the Greeks and the Trojans, who once inhabited Asia Minor (modern Turkey) at the mouth of the Hellespont Strait (Dardanelles). The Trojan War likely occurred around 1200 BC when invading Greeks may have sought control of trade through the Dardanelles. In mythological terms, the war began after the

Trojan prince Paris abducted Helen, wife of Menelaus of Sparta. Menelaus persuaded his brother Agamemnon to lead an army against Troy, and troop ships were gathered by Achilles, Odysseus and other Greek heroes. After nine years spent ravaging Troy's surrounding cities, the Greeks finally defeated the fortified city of Troy with a cunning plan. They constructed a hollow wooden horse outside Troy's walls, then boarded their ships and pretended to sail for home. One Greek soldier remained, and persuaded the Trojans to bring the horse within the city walls. When night fell, the Greek ships returned and some soldiers who were hiding inside the horse opened the city gates.

The Trojan War is the subject of **Homer**'s epic poem the *Iliad*, and Odysseus's struggle to return home to Ithaca after the fall of Troy is the basis of the *Odyssey*. These poems rank among the finest literature ever written, and were likely repeated by word of mouth in Homer's day. The great poet himself is shrouded in myth. His birthplace is not known for certain but was most likely the island of Chios or Smyrna in Asia Minor. He lived sometime before 700 BC, and he may have been blind. The period of which he wrote is now referred to as the Homeric Age.

While ancient Greece displayed cultural homogeneity, it did not comprise a single political entity; rather, it consisted of small economic and political units called city-states, with each encompassing a city and its surrounding territory. The Greek city-states often quarreled and waged war against one another, but they shared a sense of unity based on their Hellenic culture and religion, which encompassed a vast set of myths and legends. The sanctuary of **Delphi** became a national shrine, and national festivals included the important Olympian games, with the Greeks dating their own historical reckoning from the first Olympiad held in 776 BC.

The Greek hero Hercules (foreground) was famous for his strength and courage. (Piazza della Signoria, Florence)

The Gods of Olympus

The Greek gods dwelt on Mount Olympus, and the Olympian games were held every four years were in honour of **Zeus**, the sky god. Zeus was supreme lord of the heavens and earth, and head of a divine family of gods and goddesses. The deities exercised supernatural powers but these were curbed by fate, which the early Greeks defined as the relentless force of destiny. The gods were immortal and physically larger than their human counterparts but they behaved, in many respects, just like people: they squabbled amongst themselves, betrayed one another and took delight in their mortal loves. Their meddling in human affairs was seen as divine intervention and their ability to see the future was relayed through oracles. Each Greek city-state adopted one or more gods as protective guardians, and these civic deities were honoured with temples, statues and religious festivals.

The 12 Olympian gods, who succeeded the Titans as rulers of the universe, were a collection of deities adopted from various cultures that had influenced Hellenic Greece, including Egypt and Asia. Zeus, a god of the invading

Poseidon, god of the sea, was often violent and vengeful.
(Piazza Navona, Rome)

Aryan tribes, shared his dominion with his two brothers, Hades (lord of the underworld) and Poseidon (lord of the waters). Zeus was married to Hera (an Aegean fertility goddess), but it was a match fraught with tension. The divine children of Zeus, begat by various lovers, were Ares, Hermes, Apollo, Hephaestus, Athena, Aphrodite and Artemis.

Apollo (the sun god) and his twin sister Artemis (goddess of the moon) were born on the Cycladic island of Delos, where their mother Leto had fled to escape the jealous anger of Zeus's wife. Apollo was one of most versatile of the Olympian gods. In addition to being the god of youth, manly beauty, music and song, he was also the god of prophecy with a famous oracle at Delphi.

Athena was the goddess of wisdom, war and the liberal arts, as well as the mythological patroness of shipbuilding. She aided the Argonauts in their voyage to the Black Sea in search of the Golden Fleece, and she favoured the Greeks during the Trojan war, mainly because the Trojan prince Paris awarded the prize for beauty to her rival Aphrodite (goddess of love and beauty), who sprang from the foam of the sea. The 12th Olympian was Zeus's sister Hestia, who resigned her place to Dionysus (god of fertility and wine).

The Greek heroes descended from the gods, and one of the most famous was Hercules (Herakles), who performed great feats and was the only mortal ever to ascend Mount Olympus. The son of Zeus and the princess Alcmene, Hercules was hated by Hera, who sent serpents to his cradle, which he strangled. She later drove him mad, causing him to kill his wife and children in a moment of insanity. Afterwards, as an atonement for his crime, Hercules undertook 12 mighty labours (feats of strength) while at the royal court in Tiryns.

The religious importance of the Olympian gods began to decline in the 6th century BC as Greek philosophers sought a more intellectual approach to humanity's relationship with nature.

The Greek City-State

Between the 8th and 6th centuries, **Athens** and **Sparta** emerged as Greece's two dominant city-states, and each united its weaker neighbours into a confederacy under its control. These two city-states were a study in contrasts. Sparta was a militarized state that led by conquest and kept its subject states under strict control. Athens, on the other hand, united Attica through mutual and peaceful agreement. Athenian reforms, first introduced in 594 BC to grant citizenship to the lower classes, eventually led to the establishment of the first ever government based on democratic principles.

Meanwhile, in 546 BC the great Greek centres in Asia Minor had fallen to the Persians. When Ionia revolted in 499 BC, it was aided by Athens. The Persian king Darius I squashed the revolt, swearing revenge on Greece and demanding tokens of submission. All of the city-states complied except for Athens and Sparta, further enraging Darius who sent to Greece a fleet of ships, commanded by his son-in-law, which was wrecked off Mt. Athos.

Darius prepared a second expedition that set sail in 490 BC. The Persian fleet delivered an army three times the size of Athens' army, but it was defeated at a famous battle on the plain of Marathon near Athens and forced to withdraw. A third expedition, this time overseen by Darius's son Xerxes I, was launched by Persia in 481 BC. One of the largest armies in ancient history, it crossed the Hellespont Strait (Dardanelles) over a bridge of boats and marched southward into Athens where it burned the abandoned city. Meanwhile the Persian fleet pursued the Greek fleet to Salamis, an island near Athens. In the ensuing battle, 400 Greek vessels under Themistocles defeated 1200 Persian vessels. Xerxes, who watched from a golden throne on a hill overlooking the harbour, fled to Asia.

The following year the Persian army was driven out of Attica and Athens' brilliant leadership cata-

Horsemen from the north frieze of the Parthenon. (British Museum, London)

pulted the city-state into a position of Greek domination. This period, the apex of Classical Greece, is known as the **Golden Age of Athens**, for it was a period in world history that has exerted a profound influence over subsequent civilizations. The great statesman **Pericles**, who became head of the Athenian city-state in 460 BC, commissioned the famous sculptor Phidias to design and oversee the completion of the **Parthenon** and other architectural masterpieces. Art and culture thrived, and Greek drama reached its highest development with the tragic plays of Euripides and Sophocles.

The Greek Philosophers

Philosophy – the search for wisdom – originated in ancient Greece, where the pursuit of knowledge for its own sake began with speculation about the underlying nature of the physical world. The first school of philosophy, founded near Ephesus in Asia Minor, took the initial radical step of applying a scientific rather than a mythological explanation to natural phenomena.

The great philosopher **Socrates** was born in Athens around 470 BC. The son of a sculptor and a mid-wife, Socrates received a regular elementary education in literature, music and gymnastics. He initially followed his father's craft but he spent most of his mature life strolling barefooted in the streets of Athens, engaging people in conversation. Socrates believed in provoking people to think for themselves. He founded no school of philosophy and left no written records of his teachings, although these were preserved by his famous pupil **Plato**.

The teachings of Socrates, who was considered the wisest man in Greece, were based on self-control and self-knowledge. He inspired other philosophers with both his words ("How many things there are that I do not need") and his actions (wearing one garment in both summer and winter). His religious views were eventually declared blasphemous and he was charged in 399 BC with various offenses, including corrupting the morals of the young. Plato defended Socrates at his trial by jury, but Socrates was condemned by a small majority. Although his friends planned his escape from prison, Socrates refused to break the law and, after spending his last day with friends, he calmly drank a cup of hemlock according to the customary procedure of execution.

Plato continued extolling his teacher's insights. An ethical and social idealist, Plato believed that the ideal personal state – a sound mind in a sound body – required that the intellect control desires and passions, just as the ideal state of society requires that the wisest men rule the pleasure-seeking masses. One of Plato's students was **Aristotle**, whose father was a physician to the King of Macedonia. The king's grandson, who became Alexander the Great, was placed under the tutorship of Aristotle, who took charge of the young Alexander's education. Aristotle remained the single great authority of science and philosophy throughout the Middle

Philosophers such as Socrates would stroll the shaded colonnades of ancient Athens.

Ages, laying the foundation for modern science with his accumulation of facts and observations. A prolific author, he wrote on many subjects including logic, metaphysics and politics.

The Decline of Athens

While **Athens** thrived both economically and artistically in the 5th century BC, its foreign policy proved its undoing. **Sparta**, ever envious of Athenian prosperity, led the Peloponnesian League in a power struggle with Athens.

Greece's internal strife eventually resulted in its northern neighbour, Macedon, slowly gaining military and political control of the Greek states under the leadership of Philip II. The Macedonian king was preparing for war with Persia when he was assassinated in 336 BC. He was succeeded by his 20-year-old son **Alexander**, who quickly suppressed any Greek rebellion by razing Thebes as a warning to other city-states. As head of an allied Greek army, Alexander (the Great) embarked on the greatest conquest of ancient times, overthrowing the Persian Empire and extending his empire into India. In the process, he spread Hellenistic culture throughout the eastern Mediterranean. While the city-states of Greece stagnated, their culture flourished elsewhere, most notably at **Alexandria** in Egypt. Founded by Alexander the Great in 332 BC, the city became a great centre of Hellenistic culture, its famous university and celebrated libraries perpetuating the art and learning of classical Greece.

THE ROMAN EMPIRE

The rise of Rome, from city-state to empire, is one of history's most gripping epics of war and conquest. Founded around 750 BC, **Rome** grew from a salt port on the River Tiber to a sizeable city governed by a republic. The leaders of the Roman Republic eventually embarked on a campaign of military expansion that marked the beginning of Rome's long march to empire.

Moving southward across Italy to the shores of Sicily, the Romans eventually came face to face with the imperial ambitions of **Carthage**, a city-state that controlled northwest Africa and the islands of the western Mediterranean. The two powers engaged in a titanic struggle called the **Punic Wars**, which unfolded in three distinct conflicts between 264 and 146 BC. During the Second Punic War the Carthaginian general Hannibal led a famous military expedition, transported by elephants, across the Alps into Italy where he was initially victorious against Rome. However, Carthage was ultimately defeated, and the weakened city was finally blockaded and razed by the Romans during the Third Punic War.

Rome's territorial gains continued expanding both eastward and westward. **Julius Caesar**, born into one of oldest patrician families in Rome, left his mark across Western Europe, from the Alps to the Atlantic. From 58 to 49 BC he fought in the Gallic Wars, by the end of which all of Gaul – the seed of modern France – had fallen under Roman control. Caesar also defeated the Britons, and his military campaigns established him as one of the greatest commanders of all time. His willingness to endure hardships and his personal attention to his troops (he was said to know all by name) earned him the devotion of his men. Caesar eventually became leader of the democratic (or popular) party and an adversary of the senate. Against their opposition, Caesar organized a coalition – the First Triumvirate – which consisted of **Pompey** (commander-in-chief of the army), Crassus (the wealthiest man in Rome) and Caesar, whose forceful personality kept the coalition intact despite an ongoing animosity between Pompey and Crassus.

Upon the death of Caesar's daughter Julia, who was married to Pompey, the principal personal

Britannia

Germania

Sarmatia

Gallia

Italia   Illyricum   *Pontus Euxinus*

Hispania   **Roma** ●   Pontus

Mare Nostrum
(Our Sea)   Pharsalus

Carthage   Asia Minor

Mare Internum
(Internal Sea)   Judea

ROMAN EMPIRE

■ Area of extent of Roman conquest
c. 2nd century AD   **Alexandria** ●   Arabia

tie between the two men was broken and Pompey's jealousy of Caesar's military victories came to a head when Crassus died and the First Triumvirate ended. The senate feared Caesar, a military hero and champion of the people, and supported Pompey. In December, 50 BC, the senate demanded that Caesar relinquish his army. He responded that he would do so only if Pompey relinquished his. This enraged the senate which drew up a bill demanding the dismantlement of Caesar's army. **Marc Antony** and Cassius, who remained faithful to Caesar, vetoed the bill and were expelled from the senate. They joined Caesar, who mobilized his army and, upon declaring that "the die is cast," crossed the Rubicon to enter Italy and thus begin a civil war. His triumphant march to Rome caused the senate to flee.

Caesar pursued Pompey to Greece and, with a much smaller army, routed Pompey's fleet near Pharsalus. Pompey then fled to Egypt, again with Caesar in pursuit, and was killed there. At Alexandria, Caesar lived for a while with **Cleopatra**, establishing her firmly on the Egyptian throne. He then headed to Asia Minor, where an easy victory over the ancient country of Pontus prompted his famous words "Veni, vidi, vici" – I came, I saw, I conquered. When a triumphant Caesar returned to Rome in 47 BC, the great leader pardoned all his enemies, then set about improving the living conditions of the people. His dictatorial powers aroused widespread resentment, however, and Caesar was stabbed to death in the senate house on March 15, 44 BC.

Antony, who gave a famous funeral address in Caesar's honour, stirred the mob into anger and drove Caesar's conspirators from Rome. Antony then formed an alliance with **Octavian**, Caesar's grand-nephew and heir, who arranged a Second Triumvirate consisting of himself, Antony and Lepidus, which ruled Rome for five years amid political turmoil and the ongoing threat of civil war. Antony, who had a notorious reputation for riotous living, met Cleopatra in 42 BC and fell hopelessly in love. Five years later, he settled with her in Alexandria to pursue a life of pleasure. Back in Rome, the growing ill will towards him culminated in the famous naval battle off Actium in 31 BC, at which Octavian's fleet, commanded by Agrippa, defeated the less-maneuverable ships of Antony and Cleopatra. The two lovers fled to Egypt where they committed suicide.

Octavian became the first emperor of Rome in 27 BC, receiving from the senate the title **Augustus**. His rule began a long 200-year period of peace, during which an extensive system of roads was built, linking Rome with its most distant provinces. Remarkably durable, these roads were built in four layers, the uppermost layer consisting of a pavement of stones or pebbles set in concrete. The Appian Way was one of the first of these great highways, many of which are, in part, still used today.

Augustus also patronized the arts and letters, which were largely an imitation of Greek culture. Many of the Greek gods had been adopted by the Romans, who also became influenced by Greek mysteries – secret cults based on primitive fertility rites, including the worship of Isis, the nature goddess of ancient Egypt. The mysteries, which fulfilled an individual's desire for personal salvation, created a religious climate conducive to the eventual ascent of Christianity.

Meanwhile a line of notorious emperors left their mark on the Roman Empire. **Tiberius**, stepson of Augustus, was unpopular in Rome and spent his latter years ruling the empire by correspondence from Capri. **Caligula**, a cruel and insane tyrant, was eventually murdered. His successor, **Claudius**, found by soldiers hiding behind a palace curtain when Caligula was murdered, was hauled forth and proclaimed emperor. During his reign, Claudius had one of his wives killed and he himself was eventually poisoned by his wife Agrippina. Her son **Nero**, begat from a previous marriage, became emperor. Cruel and calculating, Nero eventually murdered his step-brother, his mother and his wife Octavia. When a fire destroyed half of Rome in 64 AD, Nero accused the Christians of starting it and thus began a barbarous persecution, with St. Peter and St. Paul among the many Christians killed. Nero rebuilt much of the city on the right bank of the Tiber, with broader streets and impressive buildings, but a series of revolts caused him to commit suicide and his memory was publicly execrated.

The death of Nero marked the end of the Julio-Claudian line. After a brief struggle, Vespasian became emperor, followed by his son **Titus** in 79 AD. A benevolent ruler, Titus completed the Colosseum and built a luxurious

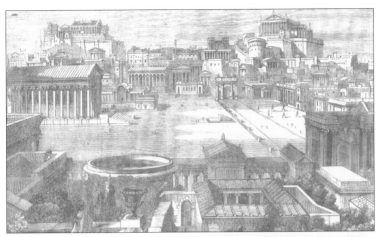

Rome became a city of grandeur as each succeeding emperor after Augustus (shown here) added his own monuments.

bath. He also lent aid to victims of the volcanic eruption of Vesuvius, which buried Pompeii and Herculaneum. Before becoming emperor, his military campaigns had included the capture and destruction of Jerusalem in 70 AD.

Several great emperors ruled during the 1st century AD. **Trajan**, born in Spain and the first non-Italian to head the empire, pushed its eastern borders past Mesopotamia. His successor **Hadrian** pulled Roman rule back to the Euphrates, and in Britain he built Hadrian's Wall to keep out the northern barbarians who were threatening Rome's developing province. **Marcus Aurelius** ruled during the Golden Age of the empire, from 161 to 180 AD. A humanitarian, he improved the living conditions of poor children and tried to curb the brutality at gladiatorial shows. He was also a

man of letters, whose philosophy was based on Stoicism, a Greek school of philosophy which incorporated the Socratic ideals of virtue and self-sufficiency.

Roman law forms the basis of modern civil law, and the greatest figure in its development was the learned jurist Papinian. A close friend of the emperor **Septimius Severus**, who ruled from 193 to 211, Papinian was a stern moralist whose chief works became the foremost authority in legal decisions.

As the 2nd century drew to a close, the decline of the Roman Empire began. A series of emperors ruled in rapid succession during the 3rd century and, with the capture of the emperor **Valerian** by the Persians in 260, the empire fell into anarchy. **Diocletian**, named emperor by the army in 284, divided the empire into four political sections: two eastern and two western. In 330, **Constantine I** moved the empire's capital to Byzantium and renamed it Constantinople. He also granted universal religious tolerance, which allowed Christians to worship without fear of persecution.

The Roman empire became permanently divided into East and West after the death of

Constantine the Great

(Museo dei Conservatori, Rome)

Theodosius I in 395. As the Dark Ages descended on Europe, Rome's western empire soon foundered, and not until the 19th century did Italy recover from the fall of Rome. The eastern (**Byzantine**) empire, however, endured for a thousand years despite constant invasions, religious controversies and internal political strife.

THE MIDDLE AGES

The Middle Ages, between the fall of Rome and the beginning of the Renaissance, were once viewed as a thousand years of darkness. The designation of Dark Ages now refers strictly to the Early Middle Ages (c. 450-750), when the collapse of the West Roman Empire plunged western Europe into turmoil. The year 476, when emperor **Romulus Augustulus** abdicated, is regarded as the end of Rome.

The seeds of Rome's demise were sown by the emperor Constantine. Within 15 years of taking the reins of power, **Constantine** made two decisions, either of which alone would have changed the future of the world. The first was to embrace **Christianity** as the official religion of the Roman Empire and the second was to transfer the capital from Rome to the city of Byzantium, which became known as **Constantinople**.

Constantine's disillusionment with Rome – its republican and pagan traditions matched with its inferior location – was confirmed on his second visit to the city in 326 AD. To him, the old city seemed decadent, tired and vul-

nerable. Constantine's vision was to create a New Rome where its citizens were Christian, its streets and public buildings clean and new, and its grandeur supreme in the world. In a period of just three years, he stripped cities throughout the empire of monuments, columns and artwork for his new capital, and in 330 he formally dedicated Constantinople to the God of the Christians.

Moving the capital east resulted quickly – and unexpectedly – in splitting the realm, and eventually led to a schism between the Roman (Catholic) church and the Eastern (Orthodox) church. While the Eastern (Byzantine) Empire became a military, commercial and cultural power, focused on regaining territories from the Persians, the West Roman Empire suffered waves of Germanic invaders. The emperors of Constantinople tried to hold on to the empire's western province but their attention was soon directed at a new threat to their eastern frontiers – the rise of **Islam**.

Constantine's arch was raised in 312 AD to commemorate a military victory that made him the unchallenged ruler of Rome's west empire.

With lightening speed this new religion, founded by the Arab prophet **Muhammad** in 622, spread outward from his birthplace of Mecca. By 732 the Arabs had swept across northern Africa into Spain, threatening to add southwestern France to their conquests. Called Saracens by the Christians (Moors in Spain), the Arabs closed the Mediterranean to outside commerce, thus isolating western Europe. Amid the political and social upheaval of western Europe, in which the Germanic and Roman cultures were assimilating, Christianity became a unifying force – despite an ongoing dispute between the pope in Rome and the patriarch in Constantinople, both of whom claimed leadership of Christendom.

In 800, **Charlemagne**, the Carolingian king of the Franks, was crowned emperor of the West by the pope in Rome, and this symbolic ceremony introduced a new concept: the interdependence of church and state. Such sharing of power did not exist in the Orthodox East, where the emperors embodied both spiritual and secular authority, regularly installing patriarchs of their choice. Charlemagne's splendid court was located not in Rome but in Aachen (now part of West Germany), and the centre of civilization in western Europe shifted northward. The Mediterranean, once a great highway of commerce and cultural exchange, became a border zone dominated by the Arabs and the Byzantine Empire.

Feudalism, originating in the empire of Charlemagne, spread to neighboring countries and provided protection from attack by plundering Germanic bands. An agricultural-based system of distributing wealth, feudalism was based on a hierarchy of king, nobility and peasantry. The nobles, who held land directly from the king, provided protection to the serfs who worked the land. **Chivalry**, a fusion of Christian and military concepts, grew out of feudalism and inspired the **Crusades** – an attempt by western Europeans to regain the Holy Land from the Muslims. Monastic orders of knights were sworn to uphold the Christian ideal, and tournaments were staged in which knights could prove their chivalric virtues.

The **Holy Roman Empire**, successor state to the empire of Charlemagne, was established in 936, but its emperors, who were initially elected by German princes and crowned by the pope, were constantly struggling to assert their control over a fragmented western Europe. The papacy, surrounded by corruption, was weakened in 1083 when Rome was sacked by the Normans. In 1305, Pope Clement V moved the papal court to **Avignon**, where it came under French control until its return to Rome in 1378.

Meanwhile, the Byzantine Empire had spiralled into a slow decline upon the death of one of its greatest emperors, **Justinian**, in 565 AD. Although the empire stayed more or less intact over the next four centuries, encompassing the area of present-day Turkey and most of Greece, it was riven from within by political and religious intrigues. Yet it remained a bulwark against waves of Arab attacks during a time when most of Europe was vulnerable and in chaos.

Then, during the 11th and 12th centuries, as the Franks and Southern Italians grew in strength and the rift between the Catholic Latins and the Orthodox Byzantines grew, Constantinople found itself fighting on two fronts and becoming progressively weaker. In 1071, the Seljuk Turks finally broke into the Byzantine heartland of Antolia in a decisive battle at Manzikert. Although this led to the fall of most of the empire's Asian possessions, the death blow was administered not by the determined Turks, but by a

90-year-old man from Venice. His name was **Enrico Dandolo** who, as doge of Venice, led a fleet of Crusaders to take the fabled city of Constantinople – the largest and most splendid city of medieval Europe. In 1204, the Crusaders breached the seawalls of the city and Dandolo, who was blind, led his troops into the 'Queen of Cities' and stripped Constantinople of its wealth. It was a blow from which Byzantium never recovered.

In the middle of the 14th century, a tribe broke away from the crumbling Seljuk Turk nation and became, under a series of strong leaders, the rapidly growing **Ottoman Empire**. In 1451, with the accession of **Sultan Mehmet II**, the city of Constantinople (all that remained of the Byzantine Empire) found itself surrounded. In preparation for a siege of the great city, Mehmet built the largest cannon the world had ever known, and in 1453, the Ottoman Turks broke through the great Theodosian land walls and seized Constantinople. The glorious capital of one of the world's longest-lasting empires had fallen.

(Above right) The famous bronze horses displayed at Venice's St. Mark's Cathedral were looted from Constantinople in 1204. (Right) Medieval ports were entered through fortified gates. Shown here is Porta Soprana in Genoa.

By the late Middle Ages, feudalism was firmly entrenched in France and southern Italy, but not in northern Italy, where the rise of the city-state had begun in the 10th century. The two great Italian seaports of **Venice** and **Genoa**, distinct in character and constantly warring with each other, enjoyed a material prosperity based largely on trade with the Middle East. The Christian crusades generated additional wealth for these and other city states, and influential banking firms came to dominate Genoa and the powerful republic of **Florence**, where the prominent Medici family rose from bankers to dukes. Although guilds perpetuated the medieval concept of collective wealth and regulated competition, the growth of cities and the ascent of the merchant class eventually brought about the demise of feudalism, marking the end of the Middle Ages and the dawn of the Renaissance.

THE RENAISSANCE

Called the *rinascita* in Italian and the *renaissance* in French, this 'rebirth' of classical antiquity's arts and sciences not only produced an outpouring of creativity never before seen, it ultimately ushered in modern civilization. The Renaissance, which originated in Italy, did not begin with a single momentous event but began as an artistic and intellectual movement that gradually gained momentum and eventually spread across Western Europe to Great Britain, where humanist thought influenced the works of Ben Jonson and William Shakespeare.

The seeds of the Renaissance's flowering were planted during the late Middle Ages, when a rediscovery of Greek and Roman literature led to the eventual development of the humanist movement. The Italian poet **Petrarch**, who lived from 1304 to 1374, is con-

Paganism & Christianity

During the Middle Ages the pagan rituals of ancient Rome were slowly assimilated into Christian festivals. **Christmas** (Christ's mass) became a widely celebrated feast day in western Europe in the 4th century AD. December 25th was chosen as the date to celebrate the nativity of Jesus Christ, a date coinciding closely with winter solstice, which was traditionally a time of pagan rejoicing. Saint Nicholas was the patron saint of children and sailors in Greece and Sicily, and the December 6th feast day of St. Nicholas eventually became a children's holiday in parts of Europe. Called Sint Nikolaas in Dutch, the saint was adopted by the English in colonial New York and transformed into Santa Claus, and the children's festival was moved to Christmas Day.

sidered the first modern poet and the father of **humanism**. By proclaiming pagan antiquity as the most enlightened stage of history, and the centuries that followed as a time of darkness, he set in motion the pursuit of learning based on a secular rather than a religious framework. This humanistic challenge to scholasticism advocated not a pre-Christian paganism but a reconciliation of classical antiquity's artistic and intellectual achievements with Christian beliefs.

The Renaissance began around 1400 in Florence, where local writers and artists cultivated an interest in the classical teachings of Greek scholars. The mid-15th century was marked by the rise of the **Medici** banking family. Politically powerful and generous patrons of the arts and letters, the Medicis founded a library and filled it with Greek and Roman books. When Constantinople fell to the Turks in 1453, Greek scholars fled to Italy with manuscripts documenting the civilizations of ancient Greece, further fuelling a thirst for knowledge and an active search for classical works. The bronze and marble sculptures excavated in Rome and other ancient sites, which had previously been treated as scrap metal or mortar, were now highly valued by collectors.

As medieval courtliness and codes of conduct gave way to a new era that focussed on expressiveness and emotionalism, the social status of the artist was elevated. Lorenzo de Medici's Florentine court became known as the **Platonic Academy** and

The Vatican, Rome

prominent members of this circle included the artists Botticelli and Michelangelo. Stressing human values and capabilities, humanism's rejection of medieval religious authority climaxed in 1517 when the German cleric **Martin Luther** sparked the Protestant Reformation with his open attack on the doctrines of the wealthy and corrupt Catholic church. Condemning such practices as the sale of indulgences (pardons for sin), Luther believed individuals could communicate directly with God and could seek salvation by reading the Bible, obtaining grace not through the sacraments (reli-

Leonardo da Vinci's Mona Lisa.
(The Louvre, Paris)

gious ceremonies conducted by priests) but through faith.

The growth of literacy, education and middle-class wealth provided a fertile environment for the new Protestant culture, which adopted an austere taste in Christian art, in contrast to the worldly opulence of Rome. New subject matters – landscapes, still lifes and scenes of daily life – formed part of the Renaissance taste in personal artwork, as did portraiture, and artists found new clients in wealthy townspeople. The church, however, continued to be the foremost patron of the arts. In the 16th century, the centre of Italian art shifted from Florence to Rome, where the

Vatican commissioned Michelangelo, Leonardo da Vinci and Raphael for various projects, resulting in some of the greatest masterpieces of Renaissance art. Venetian art also came into its full glory in the 16th century. The Venetian school was known for the superb colouring of its oil paintings, created by such masters as Bellini and Giorgione, and later succeeded by Titian, Veronese and Tintoretto.

The sciences were also advanced during the 16th century, aided by the rediscovery of Galen's anatomical studies and Ptolemy's *Geography*. Scientific thinkers began refining the theories of classical physics, with Copernicus proposing the heliocentric model of the solar system, and **Galileo** inventing an accurate telescope for viewing the heavens.

Leonardo da Vinci, the consummate Renaissance man, studied anatomy and astronomy, his copious notes covering everything from the curved trajectory to metallurgical techniques. In his paintings, accurate depictions of the human form were based on his anatomical observations. Other sciences that were developed during the Renaissance included botany, zoology and astrology.

The scientific and intellectual achievements of the Renaissance, along with seaborne exploration and the discovery of new lands and cultures, fostered further learning in the 17th century. The rationalism of Descartes, the empiricism of Francis Bacon and John Locke and the ground-breaking achievements of Isaac Newton, widely considered the greatest scientist of all time, reflected an intensifying belief in natural law, universal order and human reason. The Renaissance also set the stage for an emerging middle class of merchants and craftsmen which eventually spearheaded the revolutionary upheavals of the 18th century.

THE GRAND TOUR

The 18th century in Europe was called the **Age of Enlightenment** – an era marked by colonial expansion, scientific discoveries and mechanical inventions. The first geographical survey was undertaken in France, as was the first flight in a hot-air balloon. Captain James Cook and other explorers opened up new territories across vast expanses of the Pacific Ocean while Wolfgang Amadeus Mozart entertained the courts of Europe with his musical genius.

Rational and scientific approaches were now applied to all issues – whether social, economic, religious or political. Amid a stimulating atmosphere of skepticism and idealism, Christianity was questioned and classical teachings were scrutinized. The French philosopher Voltaire even dared to declare that Plato "wrote better than he reasoned."

The most cataclysmic event of 18th-century Europe was the **French Revolution**, which began in 1789 and eventually affected the entire world as it tore down the medieval structures of Europe and made way for 19th-century

A British tour group at Giza.

liberalism and nationalism. France, not yet free of feudalism, was ripe for rebellion. The country was still ruled by two privileged classes, the nobility and the clergy, and a simmering resentment among the oppressed bourgeoisie and working classes led to widespread violence and anarchy. A Parisian mob's storming of the Bastille, a prison fortress, symbolized the revolt of the lower classes. In 1793, to the horror of other European monarchs, the king of France was beheaded, along with hundreds of aristocrats.

The army general **Napoleon Bonaparte** rose to dictatorial power in 1799 and had himself crowned emperor in 1804. Although the British navy defeated the French and Spanish fleets at Trafalgar in 1805, Napoleon soon controlled the European continent. The Holy Roman Empire dissolved in 1806, and Napoleon installed his brothers on the thrones of Europe. Napoleon was defeated by the allied forces of Britain, Prussia, Sweden and

Austria in 1814 and exiled to the island of **Elba** off the coast of Italy, but he returned a year later, only to be defeated in the Waterloo Campaign and sent as a prisoner of war to the isolated British island of Saint Helena in the south Atlantic, where he died six years later. The French monarchy was restored, but unrest and rebellion continued, culminating in a bloody insurrection in 1848. The collapse of the French monarchy and the establishment of a new republic caused a chain reaction across Europe, spawning public demonstrations and a general cry for the overthrow of monarchies as an urban bourgeoisie called for constitutional, representative government.

Propelling this massive upheaval was the **Industrial Revolution**. Originating in England in the mid-1700s, it marked Europe's transition from an agricultural-based society to a modern industrialized society. The steam engine was invented in England in 1698 and by the early 1800s the steam locomotive was being used to power early rail travel, followed by the first steamship crossing of the Atlantic in 1819. Europe began rapidly industrializing, building roads and rail lines. A line from Marseille to Cannes was laid in 1863 and extended a year later to Nice, with Tsar Alexander II and his wife among the first to arrive by train in Nice. The railroad line was extended to Monaco a few years later, transforming the tiny principality into a gambling mecca, and by 1870 the rail line reached the Italian border. The railroad revolutionized travel,

for people could now journey across the continent in a fraction of the time it had once taken. Leisure travel, formerly the reserve of the privileged wealthy, would soon become the domain of the masses.

Leisure travel to the Mediterranean originated with the grand tours of the British aristocracy. By the mid-18th century, it was commonplace for the young men of Britain's upper class to embark on an educational tour of Europe to acquaint themselves with the famous classical ruins and Renaissance art of Rome and other Italian cities.

Although politically fragmented and in a state of economic decline, **Italy** was still considered the heart of western culture. Britain had become the wealthiest nation in the world due to its colonial trade, but its privileged classes, who were schooled in Latin and the classics, felt isolated from the cultural riches of Europe. Thus, a Grand Tour was considered necessary for a person to become a fully educated member of elite society.

Italy, and the Mediterranean in general, also held a sensual allure. Escaping damp winters and the prevailing work ethic of the Protestant north, young Englishmen were understandably eager to sojourn in the sunny south of Europe where warm weather and uninhibited attitudes extended to the pleasures of the flesh.

Reaching the Grand Tour's 'must-sees' – namely Rome, Florence, Naples and Venice – entailed a lengthy and at times arduous journey by boat and stage-coach. Early tourists included James Boswell, who achieved fame with his *Account of Corsica* (1768), and Edward Gibbon, who claimed that a walk through the Forum's ruins inspired him to write *The History of the Decline and Fall of the Roman Empire*. Goethe, the German poet and scientist, was smitten with Naples and its bright colours and carefree mood. As there were no guidebooks for the early travellers, works by Vergil and other ancient classics were used as references.

The French Revolution and the Napoleonic Wars interrupted continental touring by the British, but these conflicts didn't stop **Lord Byron** from voyaging to the Mediterranean in 1809. Fresh from Cambridge, he sailed to Lisbon, then entered the Mediterranean Sea, stopping at Gibraltar, Sardinia and Malta before embarking on an overland tour of Greece and Turkey.

The defeat of Napoleon at Waterloo in 1815 brought peace to the continent and one of the first postwar travellers to return was Lord Byron, who lived for three years in Venice before settling in Genoa. Other Romantic poets followed suit, including Keats, who died in Rome, and Shelley, who drowned while sailing in the Bay of Spezia on the Italian Riviera. Byron died of a fever in 1824, while working for the cause of Greek independence.

The Romantic poets' literary works spawned a fresh interest by the British in the antiquities of continental Europe, and the first modern guidebooks appeared around this time, with the Mediterranean homes of Byron joining the lists of local attractions. William Thackery, Charles Dickens and Mark Twain were among the popular writers given free passage on steamships in exchange for writing a book about their travels. By the end of the 19th century, the Americans were second only to the British in

Basin of San Marco, Venice

terms of numbers touring the Mediterranean.

In 1841, an English cabinet maker named **Thomas Cook** organized the first group excursion when he obtained reduced train fares for members of his temperance society, who were travelling to a regional meeting. His organizational skills soon led to a new concept – the guided tour. These packaged holidays appealed to average Britons of modest means who wanted to travel abroad and see the sights previously enjoyed only by the wealthy, who would spend months, even years, completing their grand tours.

As British and American tourists began travelling through Europe in steadily increasing numbers, the wealthy elite sought ever more exclusive and exotic destinations. Egypt became a popular winter destination, with tourists arriving by steamer at Alexandria and spending a few days in Cairo to view the pyramids before heading up the Nile aboard a hired *dahabeeya* (a river sailing craft). Cook's tours expanded into Egypt as well, when regular steamer service was introduced in the early 1870s, and within a decade Cook's Nile fleet had grown to 40 vessels.

A Middle East grand tour wasn't complete without a pilgrimage to the Holy Land, with tourists travelling by horseback across the desert accompanied by an army of servants, including armed guards, who would set up tents for sleeping each night. This was luxury camping, with meals served in dining tents on white linen and fine china, and the sleeping tents outfitted with iron bedsteads and clean sheets.

Luxury travel, in the form of Pullman rail cars, grand hotels and palatial steamships, enabled the wealthy to isolate themselves from the travelling masses. By the end of the industrial revolution, the 'high bourgeoisie', consisting of rich industrialists and bankers, were distinguishing themselves from the 'petty bourgeoisie', which comprised tradespeople and white-collar workers. The bourgeoisie's preoccupation with status and material gain had long been ridiculed, beginning in the 17th century with witty satires by the French playwright Moliere, who was himself the son of a merchant. Some of society's commentators rose to the defense of working men and women, including Karl Marx, who interpreted attacks on the upwardly mobile classes as an effort to subdue the wage-earning proletariat.

Archaeology, which originated in Renaissance Italy with the excavation of ancient Greek sculptures, was advanced in the 18th century by the chance discovery of an ancient Roman resort called Herculaneum, on the Bay of Naples, followed a few decades later by the unearthing of **Pompeii**. Both places had been buried in ash when Mt. Vesuvius erupted in 79 AD, and their discovery triggered a new wave of interest in antiquarian culture, with parties of fashionable ladies and gentlemen, equipped with shovels and picnic baskets, digging for bronze and marble statuary to add to their collections. In

1764 the German archaeologist Johann Winckelmann published a scholarly account of the Bay of Naples discoveries – the first such report in the field of classical antiquities.

Another movement, fostered during the Age of Enlightenment, was the construction of art museums, galleries and academies, including the famous **British Museum**, which was established in 1753 and began occupying its present buildings in 1829. The Athenian monuments of ancient Greece sparked public interest in England when Lord Elgin, the British ambassador to Turkey (which at that time ruled Greece), removed numerous marble sculptures from the Parthenon. Byron was among those critical of Elgin, who defended his actions in a pamphlet he wrote in 1820, claiming he wanted to protect the Greek sculptures from destruction under Turkish rule. In any event, the **Elgin Marbles**, currently in the British Museum, stimulated a strong interest in ancient Greece among the English Romantic poets and became the subject of a poem by John Keats entitled 'On Seeing the Elgin Marbles'.

Egypt also became a source of historical interest when the **Rosetta Stone**, a slab of black basalt engraved with hieroglyphics, was discovered at the mouth of the Nile by scientists accompanying Napoleon on his Egyptian campaign of 1798. Deciphered a quarter of a century later by the French scholar Jean Francois Champollion, the Rosetta Stone's inscriptions provided the first key to understanding the language and lives of the ancient Egyptians. Scientific findings from Napoleon's Egyptian campaign were published in 21 volumes over a 20-year period, thus launching Europe's fascination with ancient Egypt.

Museums began indiscriminately collecting Egyptian antiquities, as dozens of explorers and collectors dug through the desert sands in search of treasures.

A group of 19th-century British tourists at the ruins of Pompeii.

Eventually a more systematic process was enforced following the British occupation of Egypt in 1882, with all excavated objects recorded and catalogued. Meanwhile, the Egyptian government had made diplomatic gifts of several New Kingdom obelisks, presenting France with one from the Luxor temple, which now stands in the Place de la Concorde in Paris, and sending one of Cleopatra's Needles to England where it was re-erected on the Thames Embankment.

Famous archaeological treasures were also discovered in the Aegean region in the latter half of the 19th century, most notably the discovery of the ruins of Troy by German archaeologist Heinrich Schliemann, a wealthy businessman and student of Homer who used the Homeric poems for reference when searching for ancient sites and identifying the unearthed objects. Schliemann also excavated the ruins of Mycenae, Ithaca and Tiryns. As the century drew to a close, the English archaeologist Arthur Evans began devoting his time to the excavation of the Minoan ruins on Crete.

By the end of the 19th century, advancements in science, mathematics and engineering had produced the diesel and turbine engines, the electric motor, the automobile, the light bulb and the camera. The invention of photography introduced a new medium to the visual arts, and helped fuel the growth of tourism, as people were increasingly exposed to photographic images of faraway lands and exotic cultures.

The opening of the **Suez Canal** in 1869, linking the Mediterranean to the Red Sea, transformed the Mediterranean from a vast seawater lake into a direct seaway between the Far East and Europe, making it one of the most strategically important areas in the world. The British built a great naval dockyard at Valletta, Malta, as a base for its British Mediterranean Fleet, and other maritime nations maintained fleets in the Mediterranean to protect their seagoing trade. The canal, which is level and has no locks, is about 100 miles (160 km) long. Its construction took 10 years and was supervised by the French engineer Ferdinand de Lesseps, who later faced bankruptcy and was convicted for misappropriating funds when attempting to build the Panama Canal.

THE MODERN MEDITERRANEAN

The 20th century began with optimism, preceded by a long era of relative peace. However, the decaying Ottoman Empire had left the Balkan territories susceptible to diplomatic intrigue among the European powers of Austria, Britain, Prussia, Russia and France. The imperialistic, territorial and economic rivalries of these countries, along with a rampant spirit of nationalism, all contributed to the outbreak of **World War I**. Called the Great War, it was the largest war the world had yet seen. Fought chiefly in the trenches of Europe, it spread to the Middle East where Britain stopped a Turkish drive on the Suez Canal, then proceeded to destroy the Ottoman Empire. The British soldier **T.E. Lawrence** (Lawrence of Arabia) became a leader in the Arab revolt against Turkish domination, and British field marshal Edmund Allenby invaded Palestine, taking Jerusalem in December 1917.

When the First World War ended on November 11, 1918, without a single decisive battle having been fought, at least 10 million people had been killed and 20 million wounded, with additional deaths from starvation and epidemics in the war's aftermath. The face of Europe had radically changed, and a general revulsion to the destruction and suffering of war was symbolized by the creation of the **League of Nations**. Still, a fervent nationalism soon resurfaced in several countries where the hardships of the Great Depression made the masses vulnerable to the promises of demagogues. In Italy, **Benito Mussolini** and his Fascists rose to power in 1922. Mussolini gradually turned his premiership into a dictatorship, then began his

imperialist designs with the conquest of Ethiopia in 1935. Meanwhile, **Adolf Hitler** had risen to power in Germany in 1933, where he began rebuilding the German army in preparation for a war of conquest. Both he and Mussolini helped the fascist general Francisco Franco win the Spanish Civil War in 1939.

When Germany invaded Poland on September 1, 1939, the democratic governments of Britain and France declared war. Soon all of the Mediterranean region was pulled into World War II, with the Axis powers (Germany, Japan and Italy) occupying North Africa, Greece and Yugoslavia. The German commander Rommel seemed about to take Cairo when British General Montgomery routed the German forces at Alamein in October 1941. Less than a week later, US troops landed in Algeria, helping to clinch an Allied victory in

Florence's Ponte Vecchio was the city's only bridge left standing by retreating Germans in WWII.

North Africa. Italy surrendered in September 1943, following Allied invasions of Sicily and southern Italy, but German resistance continued until Hitler's suicide in April 1945.

An Allied victory in the Pacific brought the war to an end in August 1945, but the devastation it wreaked remains horrifying to contemplate. Modern warfare had brought upon the world a barbarism of such scale that previous wars paled in comparison. The blanket bombing of cities, and Germany's systematic attempt to exterminate entire racial groups, terrorized civilians as well as soldiers and caused millions to die.

In post-war Europe, a widespread aversion to the national rivalries that had provoked such bloodshed and destruction prompted the idea of a united Europe as a way to provide strength and security to the wartorn region and prevent further hostilities. The **European Economic Community** (known informally as the Common Market and today called the European Union) was established in the 1950s as an economic and political confederation of European nations.

A central banking system was provided by the 1992 Maastricht Treaty, and the gradual introduction of a common currency – the euro – was completed in 2002, the national currencies of 300 million Europeans replaced with 10 billion new bills and 50 billion new coins. Not since the 8th century, when Charlemagne circulated his own silver coinage throughout his empire, had

Europe used a common currency.

Joining the European Union has been a hotly debated issue for the citizens of Europe, in both its member and candidate nations. Fierce national rivalries remain, as do economic disparities.

Western Europe's societies have become increasingly diverse in recent decades, with several countries now containing substantial Muslim minorities. The accompanying cultural and religious tensions have resulted in immigration becoming a key election issue in countries such as Italy, where conservatives want to preserve the country's Christian roots.

In France, a fiercely secular nation, the government has banned the wearing of ostentatious religious symbols by workers in the public sector and by students in public schools. The ban includes Jewish skullcaps and large Christian crosses, but it was the refusal of Muslim schoolgirls to remove their head scarves – perceived by many French citizens to be a symbol of militant Islam – that prompted the appointment of a presidential commission to address this controversial issue in a country containing the largest Muslim population of western Europe.

According to scholars, Europe's fear of a Muslim invasion dates to medieval times, when Islam was poised to conquer Europe and three-quarters of Spain was under Moorish (Muslim) rule. For most westerners, the year 1492 marks Christopher Columbus's famous voyage from Spain to the New World, but for fundamentalist Islam this date marks the end of a halcyon age of Muslim culture and the decline of Muslim power when the Moors were driven from Spain by Christian monarchs Ferdinand and Isabella.

As Europe faces new challenges, old scores are still being settled. Efforts to regain the spoils of Holocaust plunder have intensified, including art treasures seized during the war, with governments and individuals pressuring museums to return plundered artwork. The question of rightful ownership is, of course, a contentious issue, and one that existed long before WWII.

The Greek government has pleaded for decades with the British Museum to return the marble sculptures taken from the Parthenon in 1802 by Lord Elgin, British ambassador to Greece when it was under Turkish occupation. Meanwhile, Egypt has sought the return of the Rosetta Stone and a fragment of the Sphinx's beard, both of which are housed in the British Museum.

But these attempts to repatriate cultural property have clashed with the mandate of museums, which is to preserve artifacts that might otherwise have been lost or damaged.

During construction of a new airport and highway outside Athens prior to the 2004 Olympic Games, archaeologists unearthed enough antiquities to fill 4,000 crates. Another 30,000 ancient objects were uncovered in a 10-year dig during construction of the city's new subway system, and some of these artefacts, or their replicas, are now displayed at several subway stations. Construction projects in Rome often face delays because almost any digging there leads to the discovery of antiquities, bringing all work to a halt until study and/or removal can be completed. The past is a constant companion to the peoples of the Mediterranean.

Workers repair a cobblestone street in Rhodes, Greece.

Michelangelo's David
Galleria dell'Accademia,
Florence

ART
ART

&

Western civilization's vast treasury of art and architecture began with the ancient Egyptians, whose megaprojects involved the construction of massive temple complexes. These colossal creations later inspired the Athenians of Classical Greece to transform the Acropolis into a showpiece of artistic and architectural perfection. Two

Bernini's colonnade
St. Peter's Square, Rome

architecture
architectu

cornice

frieze

entablature

architrave

Corinthian capital

thousand years later, when Renaissance artists looked for inspiration, they turned to the classical antiquities of Greece and Rome. In this section, we embark on a visual journey that covers nearly 5,000 years of artistic vision.

The glossary on the next two pages contains terminology used by artists and architects.

TALKING ART & ARCHITECTURE

arcade – a series of arches supported by piers or columns; called a 'blind arcade' when attached to a wall.

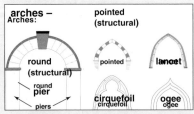

arches –
pointed (structural)
round (structural)
round pier
piers
pointed
lancet
cirquefoil
ogee

art categories – fine art is any painting, drawing or sculpture that is aesthetically beautiful. In free art, the object is purely ornamental. Decorative art adorns a useful object, such as a flower painted on a plate. The applied arts are functional and include the crafts of weaving, furniture-making, glassmaking and ceramics.

balustrade – railing supported by short pillars, called balusters.

basilica – in ancient Rome, a large rectangular building containing the law courts and serving as a public meeting place. Elements of the Roman basilica were later implemented in Christian churches. Differing from the longitudinal, basilica-plan church is the central-plan church (also called Greek-cross church) which has four arms of equal length.

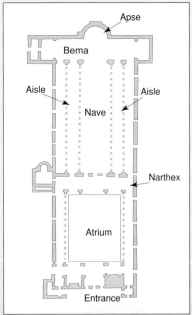

Apse
Bema
Aisle
Aisle
Nave
Narthex
Atrium
Entrance

campanile – bell tower, from the Italian word for bell, *campana*.

caryatid – a sculptured female figure serving as a structural support, used in Egyptian and Greek architecture. A celebrated example is the Porch of the Caryatids atop the Acropolis in Athens.

cathedral – church in which a bishop resides. Important medieval cathedrals include those of Florence, Pisa and Barcelona.

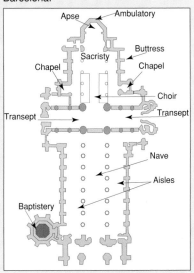

Apse
Ambulatory
Buttress
Sacristy
Chapel
Chapel
Choir
Transept
Transept
Nave
Aisles
Baptistery

clerestory – an upper row of openings or windows that is higher than the rest of the structure. Implemented in certain Egyptian temples, this feature was later used in the great halls of Roman basilicas and became a characteristic element of Gothic churches.

colonnade – a row of columns supporting either an entablature or a series of arches.

fresco – the Italian word for 'fresh'; a technique of painting on wet plaster so that the paint becomes part of the wall.

frieze – a continuous band of painted or sculptured decoration.

gold leaf – gold beaten into very thin 'leaves' and applied to illuminated manuscripts and panel paintings.

hypostyle hall – an outer courtyard bordered with columns

TALKING ART & ARCHITECTURE

icon – small panel painting of a sacred image, usually Christ, the Virgin Mary or a saint.

Iconoclasm – a movement in 8th and 9th century Byzantium to destroy all figurative religious images.

loggia – an open-air, covered arcade, either free-standing or running alongside a building.

lustreware – pottery finished with an overglaze containing copper and silver to create an iridescent effect. Initially used by Islamic potters, the technique was practiced in Moorish Spain and later adopted by Josiah Wedgwood in 18th-century England.

majolica – a technique of decorating and glazing pottery that was highly developed in medieval Italy, beginning in the 11th century, and named for the island of Majorca where the craft was first introduced by Muslim artisans during the Arab conquest of the western Mediterranean.

minaret – a tall slender tower attached to a mosque from which a muezzin calls the faithful to prayer.

mosaic – decorative work in which surfaces are covered with small pieces of coloured materials, such as marble or glass, that are set in plaster or concrete.

orders of architecture – a system devised in Roman times to categorize architectural styles. The three main orders are Doric, Ionic and Corinthian. Tuscan is a simplified version of Doric, with unfluted columns. Composite combines Ionic and Corinthian. Colossal is any order with columns or pillars rising above one storey.

palazzo – stately residence or government building.

pantheon – temple dedicated to all the gods.

pediment – triangular area formed by a gabled roof. A feature of Greek temples, it later became a decorative motif as well, used chiefly over doors and windows.

peristyle hall – an inner court filled with columns

Pieta – representation of the Virgin grieving over the dead Christ lying in her lap.

pillar – general term for upright structural supports, including columns (which are cylindrical), piers (which are square or rectangular) and pilasters (which are piers that project from a wall surface and are generally decorative rather than structural).

plateresque – earliest phase of Spanish Renaissance art, combining Italian influences with Moorish and Gothic elements.

portal – a monumental door or gate.

portico – a columned porch.

relief – figures carved from a flat surface. High relief is deeply carved so that the figures are almost fully detached from their support. Bas-relief consists of low sculptures that barely protrude.

rose window – a large circular window of stained glass and ornamental stonework (tracery), frequently used in Gothic churches.

rustication – a masonry technique that creates a roughly textured surface by projecting blocks of stone beyond the mortar joints.

sarcophagus – large stone coffin, often ornamented.

stele – an upright stone slab bearing a carved illustration or inscription.

stoa – an ancient Greek portico, providing a sheltered promenade.

tempera – form of painting used before the development of oil painting, in which pigments were mixed with egg yolk and water.

terracotta – Italian word for 'baked earth'; a fired, unglazed clay of varying colour (depending on the type of clay), but often a shade of red. One of the oldest known building materials, it is used for pottery and architectural ornament.

treasury – miniature temple for storing votive gifts.

trompe-l'oeil – French for 'deceives the eye'; painting style that utilizes realism and perspective to create the illusion that what is depicted actually exists, i.e. a door or window painted on a wall.

Egyptian Art

In ancient Egypt, where religion dominated all aspects of society, art and architecture served a religious purpose. Stone construction was limited to tombs and temples while people lived in mud-brick dwellings. Even royal palaces were made of mud-brick or wood, with stone used sparingly. A diverse range of stone types were found in the deserts on either side of the Nile valley, and by 2500 BC there were hundreds of quarries scattered across Egypt. Although slave labour was sometimes used to build royal funerary monuments, most work was carried out by free labourers who lived in villages near the building sites.

The basic post-and-lintel system – later adopted by the Greeks – was used exclusively in building temples. Their general design consisted of a massive entrance gate (called a pylon) which opened onto an outer courtyard bordered with columns, which in turn led to an inner court filled with columns. The capitals of Egyptian columns often depicted the closed bud or open flower of the papyrus and lotus flowers, symbols of Lower and Upper Egypt.

The art of ancient Egypt changed little over the centuries, and features of the highly admired Old Kingdom art were imitated by subsequent dynasties. Subjects were portrayed in a formulaic manner so they would be easily recognized and fulfill their symbolic roles. There was an emphasis on symmetry and separate components, with the human torso and an eye viewed frontally and the arms, legs and face shown in profile. Outer temple walls were decorated with shallow reliefs depicting the victorious pharaoh smiting the enemy, and those on inner walls depicted the pharaoh performing religious rituals. The colourful wall paintings inside royal tombs portrayed military, hunting and ceremonial scenes, along with domestic activities to be continued in the afterlife. Male figures were depicted with a darker skin tone than female figures, a practice introduced in 2580 BC and later adopted by, among others, the artists of the Renaissance.

Statues of pharaohs were usually huge, to represent their godlike stature, and often combined the human figure, which represented

Entrance to the temple of Horus at Edfu, Upper Egypt.

intelligence, with an animal, such as a lion or eagle, which represented strength or swiftness. A famous example is the Great Sphinx at Giza, with the head of a man and the body of a lion.

Other colossal monuments included obelisks, often in pairs outside temple entrances. These tapering shafts of red granite, dedicated to the sun god, were covered with deeply incised hieroglyphs and terminated in a pyramidal top that was gilded to reflect the sun's rays. Obelisks became popular with other ancient cultures, and many of those erected in Egypt were later removed to imperial Rome. (Please see the Egypt chapter for information on pyramids.)

Greek Art

Greek art was influenced both by monumental Egyptian art and by the more sensual art of Minoan Crete, which dates from about 2000 BC and brought an Oriental opulence to Greek art. Several periods preceded the great Classical Period, including the Geometric Period (1100 to 700 BC) which produced pottery painted with angular designs. The famous Dipylon vases from this period are named for the cemetery near Athens where they were found.

The Archaic Period (700 to 475 BC) reflected an Oriental influence, evidenced by its painted vases with motifs of fighting animals and winged monsters. Greek sculptors of this period, unlike Egyptian

sculptors, began to free their human forms from the stone by carving spaces in between the legs and between the arms and torso, creating the first free-standing statues.

The culmination of these artistic developments was reached in the Classical Period (475 to 323 BC) when Greek art reached its pinnacle of beauty and perfection. With an emphasis on physical beauty, classical Greek art idealized the human form. The marble decorations of the Parthenon included the east pediment's ensemble of deities watching the birth of Athena from the head of Zeus. Their relaxed and reclining forms reflect a complete ease of movement, both in the masculinity of Dionysus and in the flowing drapery of the three goddesses. These marble sculptures, removed by Lord Elgin between 1801 and 1803, are now on display in the British Museum.

A stunning Minoan mural at Knossos, Crete.

The profound influence Classical Greek art would exert on later civilizations began in about 200 BC, during the Hellenistic age, when statues and paintings were first recognized as works of art to be appreciated for their own sake. During this period, the wealthy began decorating their homes with copies of the great works. Hellenistic sculptures were distinctly different from the Classical works in that they conveyed a more pronounced realism. Famous Hellenistic works include the Rhodian *Nike of Samothrace* (c. 200 BC) which portrays the outspread wings of the goddess lifted by a strong head wind as she stands at the prow of a ship.

Until the *Nike* was discovered, the most admired work of Hellenistic statuary had been *The Laocoön Group*, created in the 1st century BC by three Rhodian sculptors. This work depicts the horrible death of Laocoon and his two sons by a pair of sea serpents sent by Athena to punish the Trojan priest for trying to warn his people of the trick wooden horse. Found in a Roman vineyard in 1506, *The Laocoön Group* was

admired by, among others, Michelangelo, who considered it the finest sculpture ever created.

Although the Minoans of Crete began constructing palace complexes some 4,000 years ago, it was on mainland Greece where the building of temples culminated in the zenith of Classical Greek architecture. Between 480 BC and 323 BC all of the major masterpieces were created, including the famous Parthenon. By then three columnar types had evolved, called Doric, Ionic and Corinthian. The Doric order originated on mainland Greece, while the Ionic order developed on the Aegean Islands and the coast of Asia Minor. The Corinthian capital was invented as an elaborate substitute for the Ionic order and was initially used only for interiors.

The Greek orders of column consisted of a shaft composed of sections, called drums, and a capital. A row of regularly spaced columns formed a colonnade that supported an entablature decorated with carved friezes. A triangular pediment atop the entablature held sculptures. The structure was built entirely of stone blocks that were carefully shaped and fitted together without mortar, although metal dowels were sometimes used. Shallow vertical grooves, called flutes, were carved the length of the column once it was erect.

The Parthenon, built atop the sacred Acropolis of Athens

The Laocoön Group (Vatican Museum). The replica shown here is displayed at the Grand Master's Palace, Rhodes.

Doric Column

capital

shaft

flutes

Ionic Column

Corinthian Column

Pediment of the Academy of Athens

ments were made to the colonnade's columns, and these deviations lend the structure an organic quality. For example, the columns all lean inward and their capitals are distorted to fit the architrave, which is slightly curved, so that the centre of the entablature is a bit higher than the ends. Another feature is that the corner columns are spaced more closely to their neighboring columns than are the middle columns.

The Erechtheum, built on the Acropolis between 421 and 405 BC, is one of the finest examples of the Ionic order. The Monument of Lysicrates in Athens, built a century later, is the earliest known example of exterior Corinthian columns. Greek theatres, before the 4th century, consisted simply of stone benches or wooden bleachers placed on a natural slope. This basic seating arrangement evolved into concentric rows of seats built into the hillside with staircase aisles providing seating access. The front-row seats, made of luxurious marble, were reserved for eminent public figures.

between 447 and 432 BC, was a Doric temple dedicated to the goddess Athena. Designed by the architect Ictinus, this columned structure was built using a white, fine-grained marble and is considered a perfect composition of grace and unity. Subtle adjust-

Marble sculptures from the Parthenon's east pediment. (British Museum, London)

Tomb paintings, Tarquinia

T he Etruscans settled in an area known as Tuscany between Florence and Rome in the 8th century BC, about the same time the Greeks were settling along the southern shores of Italy and Sicily. At their height of power in the 7th and 6th centuries, Etruscan cities rivaled Greece's city-states. The Etruscans ruled Rome for about a century, until the establishment of the Republic in 510 BC. They, like the Egyptians, created elaborate sculptures and wall paintings devoted to the afterlife, but Etruscan art also reflects a Greek influence, similar to that created during the Archaic Period.

Roman Art

T he Romans were great builders and architectural engineers. They admired Greek models but their designs stressed power and boldness, in contrast to the Greek emphasis on harmony and beauty. By perfecting the use of brick and concrete, the Romans were able to use arches and vaults to create complex and spacious interiors with soaring roofs that could accommodate large numbers of people. The most famous example of their outstanding engineering is the Colosseum, with its miles of stairways and vaulted corridors.

The Romans created concrete by combining *pozzolana* (a volca-nic earth) with lime, broken stones, bricks and tuff (a rock formed by the consolidation of volcanic ashes). Easily made and extremely durable, this concrete was used in the vast construction projects undertaken to sustain Rome's growing empire, including the building of roads, aqueducts and bridges. Cities and towns were laid out according to a logical plan with an emphasis on drainage, water supply and zoning. The urban centre's focus was the forum, an open public square surrounded by public buildings which included temples, exchanges and basilicas (law courts). Public baths, derived from Greek gymnasia, were built on an unprecedented scale and the

Vaults

Barrel   Cross   Ribbed

Visitors to Pompeii can walk its ancient roads (above) and view Roman frescoes adorning the interior walls of a villa (right).

Romans engaged in ritual bathing in hot, cold and steam baths. These baths also served as community centres with libraries, shops, shaded walks and open areas for poetry reading. A typical town house consisted of rooms arranged around a central atrium with an opening in the roof. Multistorey apartment buildings were also common in the larger cities, in contrast to the spacious country villas of the wealthy which contained central courtyard gardens.

The Roman amphitheatres, unlike their Greek prototypes, were freestanding and oval-shaped. The exposed concrete of Roman ruins, which makes them today look less appealing than those of Greece, would have been covered during ancient times by a facing of brick, stone, marble or smooth plaster. The Roman impe-rial practice of raising free-standing, commemorative columns may have originated from the Egyptian tradition of raising obelisks, but the triumphal arch was a purely Roman invention. Raised to honour an emperor or commemorate a military triumph, these monumental structures were built throughout the empire and would often span a road.

Roman roads were usually built in a straight line, regardless of obstacles, and consisted of four layers, the uppermost being a pavement of flat stones, concrete or pebbles set in mortar. Such roads still exist near Rome and elsewhere, as do some of the aqueducts. The bridge portion of aqueducts consisted of one to three tiers of arches, depending on the depth of the valley crossed. Nine aqueducts brought water to ancient Rome, three of which still supply the modern city, along with another one that was completed in 1585. Other aqueducts still exist in Italy and in France, where the famous Pont du Gard stands near Nimes.

Roman art was highly imitative and eclectic, reflecting the various cultures encompassed by its far-reaching empire. Pseudo-Egyptian statuary were popular and the low reliefs on Trajan's Column mirror the Egyptian illustrative tradition. However, it was the art and culture of Greece that thoroughly permeated Roman tastes. The Romans held Greek art and culture in such high esteem that original sculptures of every Greek period – Archaic, Classical and Hellenistic – were imported and copied by the thou-sands. Modifications were made to reflect the Roman emphasis on action and strength versus the contemplative nature inherent in Greek culture, and a distinct Roman style of portraiture developed which combined Greek idealism with Roman realism. The Italianate tradition of making death masks also led to the Roman style of portrait bust.

In about 200 AD, just as Roman art was fusing with Greek, the doctrines of Christianity, including denunciation of all pleasures of the flesh, shattered the synthesizing process. Eastern influences that had been introduced during the time of Constantine eventually developed into the stiff iconographic forms of early Christian and Byzantine eras. Early churches, inspired by imperial Rome, were basilican in design (an oblong interior divided into three or five aisles by rows of columns) and decorated with Byzantine-style mosaics.

The famous Portland Vase (1st century BC) was excavated near Rome in the 17th century. Made of dark blue glass overlaid with white cameo relief, the vase was widely copied, most notably in jasper ware by Josiah Wedgwood. It was eventually acquired by the Duke of Portland, who lent it to the British Museum. In 1845 a deranged museum visitor smashed the priceless vase to pieces, but it was skillfully restored and remains on display.

Medieval Art

Christian art initially declined in Europe following the fall of the Western Roman Empire, but continued to thrive in the Eastern Roman Empire where Byzantine art, especially mosaic decoration, flourished. Oriental influences combined with Hellenistic and Roman art forms to produce an ornate style.

In Constantinople, Byzantine architects created a medieval masterpiece when they developed the pendentive to elevate the dome of Hagia Sophia. Built in the 6th century, the vaulted and domed Hagia Sophia was daring in design. With the brilliant use of piers, penditives and semi-domes to create an expansive interior, Hagia Sophia's architects successfully captured the splendour of the heavens.

Medieval cities, facing barbarian invasions and pirate attacks, were designed with security in mind and were protected by thick walls. The only open areas amid the narrow winding streets were municipal or church squares. Fortresses, castles, even monasteries were built for defense. The 9th century's Carolingian style, so named for the Frankish emperor Charlemagne, was followed by the Romanesque style ('in the

(Above) Hagia Sophia in Istanbul is considered the greatest monument of Byzantine art. (Below) A medieval street in Rhodes.

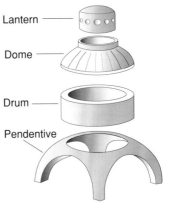

Lantern

Dome

Drum

Pendentive

(Left) Interior view of Hagia Sophia, Istanbul, reveals its revolutionary dome and semi-dome design.
(Below) The Grand Master's Palace in Rhodes is an example of medieval military architecture.

manner of the Roman') and its variants, such as Norman and Gothic. Local styles developed under the generic name Romanesque, but common features included the rounded arch and vault, as well as heavy walls and piers for structural support.

The Gothic style originated in France in about 1150 and flourished until 1450, especially in the cathedrals of northern Europe. Churches became airy and soaring, with pointed arches and vaults, slender piers and counter-balancing flying buttresses. Walls were thin and windows were large to allow a mystical and wondrous light to filter through their panes of stained glass. The sculpting of gargoyles in the form of beasts and grotesque human forms reached its peak in the Gothic period, after which the use of these ornate waterspouts was gradually replaced with lead drainpipes.

In Italy the Gothic style of architecture was tempered by Romanesque proportions, and Spanish Gothic architecture was

influenced by Moorish traditions.

All other visual art forms were dominated by architecture during the Gothic period, with sculpture and stained glass integrated into the churches. The exception was in Italy where medieval painting, long influenced by Byzantine art's use of mosaics and murals, took on a new and revolutionary form in the early 14th century with the works of **Giotto di Bondone**. A Florentine artist, he painted lifelike scenes with a three-dimensional reality and tactile quality, which prompted some to claim that painting had surpassed sculpture as an art form. The newly elevated status of painting was symbolized by Giotto's appointment in 1334 as head of the Florence Cathedral workshop, a position formerly held only by architects or sculptors. The artistic momentum generated by Giotto was, however, temporarily extinguished when an epidemic of the bubonic plague – called the Black Death – swept across Europe between 1347 and 1350, killing about one third of Europe's population.

(Above) Clerestory of Barcelona's Gothic cathedral with 15th century stained glass windows. (Right) Mosaics adorn St. Mark's Basilica in Venice.

Islamic Art

With the Muslim faith discouraging pictorial representation, Islamic art specializes in the decoration of surfaces with patterns that are abstract or geometrical, characterized by interlaced lines and brilliant colors. Calligraphy (Greek for 'beautiful writing') is highly esteemed and used by Muslims to decorate mosques, pottery, metalwork, textiles, as well as books. The Islamic (Moorish) presence in western Europe during the Middle Ages was reflected in such decorative arts as tile work and lustreware.

Early mosques were simple in design, based on the floor plan of the Prophet Muhammad's house. As Islam spread, a variety of existing edifices were taken over and converted into mosques. The Muslim practice of whitewashing the walls of temples and churches when converting them into mosques often resulted in the preservation of the underlying frescoes. Domed mosques were not common until the Byzantine church of Hagia Sofia became a model for mosques following the Turkish conquest of Constantinople in 1453. One famous exception is the Dome of the Rock in Jerusalem, built in 691 AD, which follows an octagonal Byzantine plan and has a wooden dome. Elements of Islamic art were often incorporated in Romanesque, Gothic and Renaissance buildings.

Renaissance Art

The Italian Renaissance, which began shortly after 1400 in Florence, ushered in a new and exciting age. Whereas medieval towns were built with moats, fortresses and city walls for protection from marauding bands, Renaissance cities were built with monumental views provided by wide avenues and long approaches to handsome buildings. New World discoveries contributed to the joy of expansion, but it was a revival of classical antiquity that formed the basis of Renaissance thought and art. The great masters studied the works of Plato and other Greek philosophers, embracing humanism and a belief in man's ability to understand the universe.

In architecture, the classical ideals of order, symmetry and unity were adopted. Rome's structural elements – arches, vaults and domes – were used in original combinations, with the

Self portrait, Leonardo da Vinci

dome symbolizing Renaissance man's pursuit of both learning and clarity. The great Florentine architect **Brunelleschi**, who made several trips to Rome to study classical buildings, incorporated the systematic use of perspective and proportion in his designs, which included the octagonal ribbed dome of the Florence cathedral. The famous sculptor **Donatello** accompanied Brunelleschi on one of his trips to Rome, and the classical influence is evident in such works as his bronze *David*. This statue is one of the earliest free-standing nude figures of the Renaissance, and it marked the end of a medieval interdependence of architecture and sculpture.

In painting, as in the other visual arts, the Renaissance artists sought perfection. Three staggered planes – foreground, middle distance and background – were used to achieve perspective depth, and the painting's figures were harmoniously arranged, their expressive gestures achieving a heightened emotional intensity. The ideal human figure measured seven times the height of the head, and male nudes were painted with golden brown skin in contrast to the pink rose skin of a female nude.

Leonardo da Vinci best personified the ideal 'Renaissance man' with his restless quest for beauty and truth, both in his paintings and in his scientific studies, which relied on a precise observation of the phenomena of nature. Leonardo was one of several supreme artists who generated the great works of the High

Florence Cathedral's dome was designed by Brunelleschi, the first great architect of the Italian Renaissance.

Renaissance between 1495 and 1520. Others included Bramante, Michelangelo, Raphael and Titian. **Bramante**, an architect and painter, designed the original plan for St. Peter's Basilica in Rome, influencing the appearance of many smaller churches. The paintings of **Raphael** (known as 'the Divine') were considered the Renaissance ideal of harmony and balance. And the Venetian painter **Titian**, celebrated for his use of color, was admired by none less than Michelangelo who apparently said, "Only he alone deserves to be called a painter."

Although the Renaissance artist was liberated from medieval con-

the REDISCOVERY of LIGHT

Andrea del Verrocchio and
Leonardo da Vinci
Detail from: The Baptism of
Christ, c. 1470-75
Uffizi Gallery, Florence

Michelangelo
Holy Family, c. 1503-04
Uffizi Gallery, Florence

Titian
Venus of Urbino (1536)
Uffizi Gallery, Florence

Giovanni Bellini
Enthroned Madonna, with
Saints, 1505
San Zaccaria, Venice

Raphael
Madonna with the Goldfinch, c. 1507
Uffizi Gallery, Florence

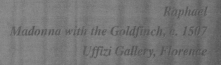

Sandro Botticelli
The Birth of Venus, c. 1485
Uffizi Gallery, Florence

vention, with pagan symbols reappearing alongside symbols of the Christian faith, the challenge of reconciling rational thought with religious belief was personified in the tormented genius of **Michelangelo**. A master of the three major visual arts – sculpture, painting and architecture – he transcended conventions and traditions, and is considered the first truly modern artist. Michelangelo believed that his artistic genius was a divine inspiration, and when sculpting a piece of marble he sought to free its pre-existing figures from the stone.

On the heels of the High Renaissance came mannerism, a style in which scale and spatial relationships between figures were deliberately confused. Mannerism, lasting from about 1520 to 1600, originated in Italy as a reaction to the High Renaissance's equilibrium of form and proportion. While the term 'mannerism' was coined to describe the painting of this period, the characteristics of mannerist architecture included an artificial integration of elements and an emphasis on surface effect, especially through the use of encrusted decoration. Jacopo Sansovino's Library of St. Mark's in Venice is a classic example of this lavish use of sculptural encrustation.

The mannerist schools of painting produced some outstanding artists, including Tintoretto and Veronese, both of the Venetian school. The famous mannerist painter **El Greco**, born on the Greek island of Crete in 1541, was initially trained in the Byzantine tradition of iconography, but he later studied in Venice, then in Rome, absorbing the lessons of the Italian masters, before settling in Spain. In Mannerist nativity scenes, signs of poverty were erased from the manger and the newborn Christ child was transformed into a cherub-like one-year-old perched on the lap of a rosy-cheeked Madonna. This less reverent and more intimate attitude was also reflected in the artists' penchant for painting themselves and fellow artists into scenes – positioning themselves not modestly to one side, as had been the customary position for donors of religious pictures, but squarely in the centre of the canvas. The jubilant and joyous nature of mannerist art was criticized by austere theologians, but the last glorious outburst of Christian art was yet to come in the form of baroque, the dominant art of the 17th century.

Baroque

The baroque style harmoniously united painting, sculpture and architecture. The latter became fluid, like sculpture on a massive scale, with curving forms and undulating facades. Sculptures set within this elaborate architecture seem to spill from their niches or soar heavenward. Famous baroque works include those of the Italian sculptor and architect Bernini, who adorned Rome with his fountains, statues and other monuments, including the elliptical piazza in front of St. Peter's Basilica. Baroque painters used illusionist effects to create a deep sense of space, and its masters included Rembrandt, Rubens and van Dyck. In the late phases of baroque, the centre of the movement shifted from Italy to France, due largely to the patronage of Louis XIV.

As the vitality and force of baroque spilled into the 18th century, its final flowering became known as rococo. Originating in France and lasting from 1700 to 1750, the rococo style, with its light lines and exquisite refinement, was especially popular for interiors and the decorative arts. It was an unfettered style of excessive ornamentation and embellishment, with frescoes travelling across entire walls and ceilings, often multiplied in wall mirrors and reflected in polished parquet floors. In Venice, the painter Tiepolo won international fame with his frescoes in the doge's palace.

Modern Art

The first of a series of overlapping movements and counter-movements began in the mid-18th century. These 'revival' movements were manifested mostly in architecture and began with neoclassicism, which was inspired by the discovery of the ancient Roman ruins of Herculaneum and Pompeii on the Bay of Naples. In tandem with the classical revival was the Gothic revival, which began to dominate after 1800, its largest monument being the Houses of Parliament in London. The final revival phases were the neo-Renaissance and neo-baroque, which dominated from 1850 to 1875 and lingered through the

Rome's Trevi Fountain, completed in 1762, is rococo in style.

turn of the century. Neo-baroque buildings favoured a profusion of ornament, creating an excess of opulence that appealed particularly to the newly rich and powerful of the Industrial Revolution. New materials and building techniques included the use of iron, which was used extensively in the construction of railroad stations, exhibitions halls and public libraries. The Eiffel Tower, erected at the entrance to the Paris World's Fair of 1889, became a famous symbol of 19th-century technology.

Art nouveau, a decorative arts movement lasting from the 1880s to World War I, was originally

The ornate facade of Monte Carlo's opera house.

meant to produce art for the masses. As a reaction to the historical emphasis of mid-19th century art, this new style incorporated dreamlike forms which are best exemplified architecturally in the nature-inspired designs of **Antonio Gaudi**, who lived and worked in Barcelona. Another turn-of-the-century style was associated with the Ecole des Beaux-Arts in Paris and became fashionable both in Europe and North America. Beaux-arts buildings were an eclectic mix of styles, often incorporating Greek, Roman and Egyptian elements.

Romanticism was another artistic movement that arose in the late 18th century. Inspired by ideals of the Enlightenment, the romantics revered nature and the individual's freedom to act naturally. As artists and intellectuals scrutinized classical thought and Christian beliefs, two conflicting views emerged: one supporting scientific and material progress, which was identified with the middle class; the other regarding the bourgeoisie as the enemy of culture. It was the second view that became the battle cry of modern artists, many of whom fervently challenged accepted perceptions of the world with the avant-garde, a term from French warfare meaning 'vanguard'.

After romanticism, most painters rejected traditional subjects taken from the Bible, the classics or the life of the courts, and turned instead to everyday scenes around them. No single movement has dominated modern western art for long periods of time since the 18th century, and there has been a speeding up of successive styles and ideas. The impressionist movement, originating in late-19th century France, rejected the romantics' emphasis on emotion and instead pursued objectivity when painting visual impressions, often directly from nature.

Following the impressionist movement, artists sought new inspiration in fresh landscapes. Fleeing the industrial north, **Vincent van Gogh** headed to the south of France to be 'near Africa', **Paul Cezanne** retreated to his native Provence, and **Gauguin** eventually left Europe for the tropical island paradise of Tahiti. Van Gogh's dark and somber early paintings gave way to swirling brush strokes and intense yellows, greens and blues found in his later works, which represented the archetype of expressionism's emotional spontaneity in painting.

20th Century Art

Artists in the early 20th century, attempting to express an inner vision, intensified their search into the subconscious.

The French painter Henri Matisse, considered one of the foremost artists of the modern period, began using strong primary colours while living in the Mediterranean village of Collioure, and he became a leader of Fauvism, a style emphasizing the use of vivid colour.

Pablo Picasso, who played a leading role in 20th-century art movements, created cubism's most significant work when he painted Les Demoiselles d'Avignon in 1907. Surrealism, a movement founded in Paris in 1924 and influenced by Freudian theories, uses dream-inspired symbols. The paintings of Salvador Dali, born near Barcelona in 1904, combine dream imagery with near-photographic realism.

Umberto Primo Arcade, Naples (above). Chapelle St. Pierre, Villefranche, painted by avant-garde artist Jean Cocteau.

Preserving & Restoring Art

Art museums take extraordinary precautions to preserve their priceless works, using climate control systems that filter dust and chemical pollutants from the air, and sensors that monitor temperature and humidity. Even the wrong kind of carpet, when walked on, can produce dust and lint that settles onto paintings. When Leonardo da Vinci's masterpiece *The Last Supper* was reopened to the public in Milan, visitors were required to pass through three antechambers designed to remove dust, dirt, car exhaust and other particles from their clothes. A bubble of clean air surrounds the restored painting, which covers most of one wall in the refectory of Santa Maria delle Grazie. The original painting was applied to a dry finished wall, rather than on wet plaster, and shortly after its completion it began to deteriorate.

Art restoration is as old as art itself, with early restorers using varnishes made of animal glue to temporarily brighten fresco paintings. When modern restorers cleaned Michelangelo's frescoes in the Sistine Chapel, their painstaking methods involved washing an area with deionized water and an organic solvent, then sponging ammonium carbonate onto the area through layers of absorbent paper, which were left in place for several minutes before being removed. Any loosened dirt was wiped away and the area given a final rinse with water.

Space age technology is also used in art restoration, with a NASA researcher developing a way to use corrosive, atomic oxygen to dissolve sticky soot left on paintings after a fire. Modern laser and microwave techniques were used to clean the marble sculptures that once adorned the Parthenon in Athens, a technique approved by Greece's Central Archaeological Council only after experts spent two years practicing this method on other marbles. In Florence, a thorough cleaning of Michelangelo's statue *David* came to a halt when experts disagreed over the cleaning technique to be used.

When paintings travel to other museums, there is always the risk of damage, despite careful handling by white-gloved workers and the use of custom-designed metal cases fitted with high-density foam. Concerns include potential damage from jet engine vibrations, which can gradually shiver paint from a fragile canvas, and sudden decreases in humidity which can cause a canvas to shrink and possibly crack.

Preserving outdoor monuments is another challenge. Ancient marble monuments are threatened by air pollution, as well as microorganisms such as algae, lichens and fungi, which discolour surfaces and burrow beneath the surface. Ongoing restoration work on the Acropolis is estimated to take several more decades to complete and cost millions of dollars. Scaffolding is a fact of life in Europe, where restoration work by skilled marble masons is time-consuming and extremely costly.

Gardens have been cultivated since antiquity. The ancient Egyptians built walled gardens centred around a pool stocked with ornamental fish and shaded by fig and date trees. Lotus flowers (a kind of water lily) often grew in these garden pools. The revered olive tree, described by Homer as a source of liquid gold, has also been cultivated since ancient times along the Mediterranean coast, and today Italy, Spain and Greece produce 75% of the world's olive oil. Green olives are full-grown but unripened when picked, and ripened olives are purplish black and richer in oil.

Vineyards were introduced to Europe by the Greeks from Asia Minor in about 600 BC. The warm, dry Mediterranean climate was so ideal for the proliferation of viticulture that the Roman Emperor Domitian, fearing grain scarcity, had to restrict the spread of vineyards in Italy during the 1st century AD. During the days of the Roman Empire, landscape gardening was highly developed and formal gardens, designed by architects, were often terraced and adorned with statuary and fountains. The emperors in particular enjoyed retreating to their country villas, replete with formal gardens. According to Edward Gibbon, when Diocletian retired permanently to his estate on the Dalmatian coast in the early 4th century, he dismissed with a smile his former co-emperor's urgings to return by remarking that "if he could show Maximian the cabbages he had planted with his own hands at Salona, (Maximian) would no longer be urged to relinquish the enjoyment of happiness for the pursuit of power."

Early gardens were often simple plots for growing herbs and vegetables. In fact, throughout antiquity and the Middle Ages, herbs were highly valued for their medicinal and curative properties. Saffron, which is featured in Mediterranean cooking, was also a source of yellow dye in the ancient world. Thyme was used by the Greeks as a temple incense and by the Romans who put it in

(Above) Ancient olive trees grow in Jerusalem's Garden of Gethsemene, where Jesus spent his last hours before his arrest. The courtyard garden at House of Vetti in Pompeii (below).

their bath water to energize themselves. Rosemary, a name derived from Latin and meaning 'dew of the sea', grows along coastal cliff tops where it draws moisture from the sea mists. Rosemary's aromatic leaves are used for seasoning and its small blue flowers are the source of an extract used in perfumes and medicines.

Other flowers native to the eastern Mediterranean include the tulip, hyacinth, crocus and hibiscus. Scrubby woodlands dominate the coastline, where prevalent types of trees include the umbrella pine tree, its nuts used for cakes and sauces. Cork oak is also native to the Mediterranean, which is where most of the world's commercial cork is harvested and processed. The bark of these trees is stripped off every 10 years.

During the Middle Ages, various citrus trees were introduced to the Mediterranean area by the Arabs, including tangerines, oranges, lemons and limes. The Crusades also introduced new plants and gardening techniques to Europe, as did the Moors of Spain and Portugal. During the Italian Renaissance the classical garden was revived, and leading artists of the day were commissioned to design elaborate hillside landscapes of fountains, waterfalls and ponds, mingled with statuary and topiary, often in geometrical designs.

(Above) Gardens outside Palma's cathedral, Mallorca. (Right) An Egyptian lotus pond.

Italian-designed gardens lie outside the Grand Master's Palace in Rhodes, Greece.

PART II

—— *The Voyage and the Ports* ——

PORTUGAL

In Portugal, all school children are taught the words to *The Lusiads* by Luis de Camoes. This epic poem is based on the famous voyage of explorer Vasco da Gama, the first European to journey by sea to India. He left Lisbon in 1497, rounded the Cape of Good Hope and sailed across the Indian Ocean to Calicut. The discovery of this sea route gave Portugal access to the riches of the Indies, and marked the beginning of the Portuguese empire.

Camoes, the greatest figure of Portuguese literature, was born of a poor Lisbon family but he pursued a life of romance and adventure, one that provided inspiration for his fiery love poems. Banished from the royal circle after falling in love with a lady of the Lisbon court, he was imprisoned a few years later for wounding a court aide in a street fight. To obtain his release, Camoes served military duty in India. When the ship carrying him from Macao to Goa was wrecked, Camoes managed to save his manuscript of *The Lusiads*.

The Portuguese people's love of poetry and song is an integral part of their culture, best exemplified by the troubadour-style *fado*, which is a melancholy poem or story accompanied by the guitar. *Fado* can be heard throughout the country, from village pubs to the sophisticated clubs (*casas de fado*) in Lisbon. Listening to *fado*, which speaks through its melody, is an excellent way to get to know the Portuguese soul.

Portugal At A Glance

About 10 million people live in Portugal, which includes the Madeira Islands and the Azores in the Atlantic Ocean. The country's last overseas territory, Macao, reverted to Chinese sovereignty in 1999.

Roman Catholicism is Portugal's major religion, and the mother tongue is Portuguese, its vocabulary based on vernacular Latin but also containing words absorbed from Arabic, French and Italian. English and French are the second languages of Portugal.

The country's post-revolution constitution of 1976 established a parliamentary republic with an elected president.

The Tower of Belem stands at the entrance to Lisbon's port.

Travel Tips

Currency – The unit of currency is the euro. Credit cards are widely accepted and ATMs are located throughout Lisbon. Banks are open Monday to Friday, from 8:30 a.m. to 3:00 p.m.

Dining – Sitting at a café sipping a *bica* (espresso) or a glass of port is a popular pastime in Portugal. Portuguese cuisine is noted for its seafood such as Caldeirada (a fish stew), its pastries (including custard tarts) and its fortified wines. Grapes from the Douro district produce the country's famous port wines, which are blended and stored in Oporto. Fortified wine is also produced on Madeira Island, a port of call for westbound sailing ships, which transported this wine to America. The signing of the Declaration of Independence was toasted with Madeira wine.

Opening Hours – Museums and historic attractions are generally open from 10 a.m. to 12:30 p.m. and from 2 p.m. to 5 p.m. Most close on Mondays (some also close on Wednesdays).

Shopping – Shops are open Monday through Saturday from 9 a.m. to 1 p.m., reopening (except on Saturdays) from 3 p.m. to 7 p.m. Shopping malls are open daily, from 10 a.m. to 11 p.m.

Locally made wares include gold filigree jewelry, azulejos (decorative tiles), pottery and embroidered cottons.

Telephoning – Portugal's dialing code is 351. To phone long distance from Portugal, dial 00 followed by your country code, area/city code, and local number.

Portuguese History

Portugal's history began in ancient times. Among its early tribes were a Celtic people called Lusitanians, who came to the area around 1000 BC. The Lusitanians fiercely resisted Roman invasion until their leader, Viratus, was killed in 139 BC. Under Roman domination, the province of Lusitania thrived and Roman ways were adopted, including the Latin language from which Portuguese is derived.

Lusitania was overrun by Visigoths in the 5th century AD, and they in turn were conquered by the Moors, who invaded the area in 711. But it was the Christian reconquest of the Iberian peninsula that created the country of Portugal, and this process began with the arrival in 1095 of Henry of Burgundy, a French nobleman summoned to assist in the fight against the Moors. Henry was granted the title Count of Portugal and the territory eventually became the independent kingdom of Portugal under his son Alfsono.

Alfonso I spent much of his life embroiled in ceaseless fighting, driving the Moors from Lisbon in 1147. The royal court – a tumultuous place – was the scene of family estrangements, shifting alliances, power struggles against the church, and wars with the kings of Castile.

The most glorious period of Portuguese history began with the reign of John I. Rising to power in 1385, he ushered in an era of maritime exploration and colonial expansion never before seen. His son, Henry the Navigator, established an observatory and a school of navigation at Sagres, in southwest Portugal. Trained mariners would set off from the nearby port at Lagos to explore the African coast, pushing further south with each voyage.

This period of prosperity reached its zenith during the reign of Manuel I (1495-1521), when the Portuguese empire extended across the seas to Africa, Asia and America. Lisbon became the centre of the lucrative European spice trade, and Portuguese seafarers would return home with priceless ivory sculptures from Africa and decorated porcelain from China. A distinct style of Portuguese decoration developed, called Manueline, which reflected the country's maritime expansion. Gothic structures were embellished with shells, twisted ropes and strange aquatic shapes, these elements mixed with religious or heraldic symbols to create sumptuous ornamentation.

In 1496, Manuel agreed to expel all Jews and Moors from Portugal as a condition for marrying the eldest daughter of Ferdinand and Isabella of Spain, and this drained the country of communities that had contributed to its learning, science and artisanship. Foreign competition began cutting into Portugal's shipping profits, and the West's centre of trade eventually shifted from Lisbon to Northern Europe.

Portugal's monarchy endured until 1910, when a revolution established a Portuguese republic. A military coup in 1926 was followed by the right-wing dictator-

The Discoveries Monument honours Henry the Navigator.

ship of Antonio de Oliveira Salazar from 1932 to 1968. A bloodless coup in 1974 finally brought democracy to Portugal.

Lisbon

Lisbon (Lisboa) is situated on seven terraced hills that border the banks of the Tagus River where it broadens to enter the Atlantic. Ships entering this ancient trading port are greeted by the sight of the **Tower of Belem 1**, a 16th-century fortress built at the mouth of the Tagus River. It once marked the starting point for Portuguese caravels setting off on voyages of trade and conquest. Nearby is the **Discoveries Monument 2**, erected in 1960 to mark the 500th anniversary of the death of Henry the Navigator.

Getting Around

The cruise ships dock at one of two terminals. **Gare Maritima de Alcantara** is located about two miles (3 km) east of the city centre. The newer terminal, **Santa Apolonia**, is located beside the Alfama neighbourhood. **Taxis** are plentiful at both terminals, and a standard meter fare is charged in the city (outside the city limits, the charge is per kilometre). Some ships provide a shuttle to Commerce Square and to the Belem district.

Lisbon's historic centre of steep, narrow streets that wind up and down the hillsides can be explored on foot. The city's **tram cars** are a pleasant alternative to walking and are popular with tourists. The trams cover five different routes and an interchange station is located near Commerce Square. The fare can be paid to the driver. Tram 28 is a vintage wooden tram that winds through Lisbon's picturesque neighbourhoods, from Sao Jorge Castle to Bairro Alto. Belem can be reached on Tram 15.

The elegant, 18th-century Commerce Square overlooks Lisbon's waterfront.

The Lisboa Card (18.50 euros per adult for one day) provides unlimited use of Lisbon's public transport, including the trains to Sintra and Cascais, and free entry to 26 museums and places of interest. The card can be purchased on the Internet or at tourist information booths in Lisbon, including the main one in Commerce Square and the one at the airport. The Number 91 (Aerobus) is the fastest bus line between the airport and downtown Lisbon.

Shopping & Dining

Rua Augusta, in the Baixa neighbourhood, is the city's main shopping street. This wide pedestrian mall runs through a bustling area of small shops and street cafés. Designer shops are found along **Avenida da Liberdade**, the city's main avenue where banks and grand hotels are also located.

Outdoor cafés, including the art deco Café Nicola, can be enjoyed at **Rossio Square**, which is situated at the south end of Avenida da Liberdade. Nearby is Rua das Portas de Santo Antao – a pedestrian street lined with seafood restaurants. Trendy bars and fado restaurants are concentrated in the bohemian neighbourhood of

Bairro Alto. Wedged between Bairro Alto and Baixa is the upscale **Chiado** area, featuring stylish shops and elegant cafés, including Brasileira – which was a favourite rendezvous for writers in the 1920s. A life-size bronze of Fernando Pessoa, Portugal's most famous 20th-century poet, is seated at one of its outdoor tables.

In Lisbon it's customary for waiters to bring unordered aperitifs and appetizers to your table. You have the choice of declining these items or paying for them if you decide to sample them.

For a delicious Lisbon specialty – Pasteis de Belem (custard tarts) – visit Antiga Confeitaria de Belem at 84 Rua de Belem.

Local Attractions

Castelo de Sao Jorge 3 is a hilltop fort that dominates the city. Possibly built by Romans who occupied the town in 205 BC, the fort stands on the site of an earlier citadel whose inhabitants traded with the Phoenicians and Carthaginians.

At the base of the fort is a maze

of Moorish-built alleys surrounding the 12th-century cathedral, the Se **4**. Built to withstand attacks, the cathedral resembles a fortress, its twin towers supplied with arrow slits for defence. The strength and thickness of its walls saved the cathedral from total destruction during an earthquake that destroyed parts of the city in 1755. Nearby is the Museu de Artes Decorativas (**Museum of Decorative Art) 5**, housed in a handsome four-storey mansion. About a mile to the east is the Museu dos Azulejos (**National Tile Museum) 6**, located in the cloisters of the Madre de Deus Church, where an array of beautiful tile panels are on display.

Shore Excursions

Ship organized tours of **Lisbon** focus on the city's many historic sites. Scenic drives to nearby **Sintra** and **Cascais** are also offered by some cruise lines, as is a tour to **Fatima**. (8 hrs).

The following is a sampling of Lisbon shore excursions. The selection will vary with each cruise line. For more detail, log onto your cruise line's website.
• **Lisbon Highlights**, visit Alfama, Jeronimos Monastery and Maritime Museum with stops at Belem Tower and Monument to the Discoveries (4 hrs, $50+).

• **Lisbon Walking Tour** – explore Alfama and Se Cathedral, Rua Augusta, Rossio Square and Chiado quarter, and ride the funicular up the steep hillside to Bairro Alto (4.5 hrs, about $50+).
• **Baroque Art of Tiles** – This popular excursion visits Basilica da Estrela and the Tile Museum (3.5 hrs, $50+)
• **Panoramic Coach Tour** of Lisbon's highlights; visit Cascais and Sintra for lunch and free time to explore (7.5 hrs, $150+)
• **Lisbon by Private Vehicle** with guide and driver (4 hrs/ 8 hrs, about $600-$1200 per vehicle)

These colourfully painted tiles, called *azulejos*, are seen on buildings throughout Lisbon and are a decorative tradition traced to the Moorish presence in Portugal during the Middle Ages.

Immediately west of Alfama is **Baixa**, Lisbon's most central neighbourhood which was rebuilt by the Marques de Pombal following the 1755 earthquake. A monumental square was built on the former site of the royal palace and called **Praca do Comercio** (Commerce Square) **7**. This lovely square facing the Tagus River contains a massive statue of King Jose I and a triumphal arch that opens onto **Rua Augusta.**

Rua Augusta leads up to **Rossio Square** **8**, Lisbon's liveliest square with atmospheric cafés, baroque fountains and the neo-classical National Theatre. The **Rossio Train Station** **9** features a fanciful facade of Victorian, Moorish and Gothic architectural styles. A few blocks south of Rossio Square, where Rua de Santa Justa intersects with Rua Augusta, is the **Santa Justa Lift** **10**, an open-work iron elevator built by a protégé of Gustave Eiffel.

Just past Rossio Train Station is **Restorers Square**, where the art deco Eden Cinema is now a hotel. Leading off this square is **Avenida da Liberdade**, a stately avenue of statues and leafy trees that's lined with hotels and shops, and ascends to Edward VII Park where the views are more spectacular the higher you climb.

Gloria Elevadore **11**, a funicular on the west side of Avenida da Liberdade, can be taken up to **Bairro Alto**, an old-quarter neighbourhood of cobbled lanes which survived the earthquake and now bustles with night life at its fashionable bars and restaurants. Amid the art galleries and antique shops is the 16th-century **Church of St. Roquem** **12**, its rich interior beautifully decorated with baroque mosaics, precious marbles and gold gilt.

About 1.5 miles (2.5 km) west of the cruise pier is the city's **Belem** section, where some of Lisbon's most famous landmarks

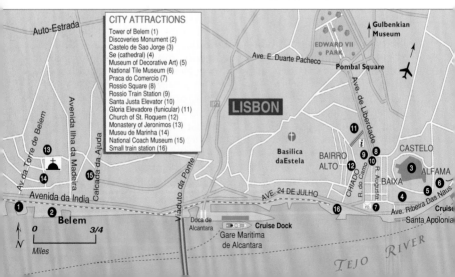

CITY ATTRACTIONS
Tower of Belem (1)
Discoveries Monument (2)
Castelo de Sao Jorge (3)
Se (cathedral) (4)
Museum of Decorative Art (5)
National Tile Museum (6)
Praca do Comercio (7)
Rossio Square (8)
Rossio Train Station (9)
Santa Justa Elevator (10)
Gloria Elevadore (funicular) (11)
Church of St. Roquem (12)
Monastery of Jeronimos (13)
Museu de Marinha (14)
National Coach Museum (15)
Small train station (16)

are located, including the modern **Discoveries Monument** in honour of Henry the Navigator. The 16th-century **Tower of Belem**, an example of Manueline architecture, was built by Manuel I to commemorate the discovery of the route to India by Vasco da Gama. The beautiful cloister of the nearby **Monastery of Jeronimos**  is another excellent example of Manueline ornamentation. Other attractions in this area are the **Museu de Marinha** (Maritime Museum) **14**, one of the finest maritime museums in the world, and the **National Coach Museum 15** where beautiful gilded coaches are displayed.

Out-of-Town Attractions

Trains run regularly between Lisbon and outlying towns, departing **Rossio station** for the 20-minute ride to **Queluz**, where an 18th-century palace with beautiful gardens and rococo rooms once served as a leisure residence for the Portuguese court. Another 20 minutes further by train is the town of **Sintra**, described by Byron as a 'glorious Eden'. The National Palace stands in the centre of town, while a nearby mountaintop is the setting for romantic **Pena Palace**, a fairy-tale castle featuring Arab minarets and medieval battlements.

A half-hour train ride from the small station **6** near **Commerce Square** will take you to the seaside town of **Cascais**, which became a fashionable summer resort in the late 19th century. Further west are the windswept beaches of Guincho and the dramatic cliffs of Cabo da Roca - Europe's most westerly point.

Some 70 miles (110 km) northwest of Lisbon is the hamlet of **Fatima** where the nearby shrine of Our Lady of the Rosary of

(Above) Pena Palace in Sintra.
(Below) The 18th-century Quelez National Palace near Lisbon.

Algarve coastline

Fatima became a centre of pilgrimage after three local children reported apparitions of the Virgin Mary in 1917. Our Lady of Fatima Basilica was built in 1944.

Portimao

Situated in the Algarve region of Portugal, Portimao is a port of call providing access to a rugged coastline of golden sand beaches lying at the base of rocky cliffs. The town itself contains an 18th-century palace and some ruins of its ancient walls. In the nearby town of Alvor you'll find the ruins of a Neolithic village and a 16th-century Moorish church.

Madeira Islands

The verdant, mountainous Madeira Islands were originally known to the Romans as the Purple Islands. Rediscovered by the Portuguese in the early 1400s, settlement took place under order of Prince Henry the Navigator. The British temporarily occupied the islands in the early 19th century but they are now an autono-

Shore Excursions

Madeira shore tours feature a variety of scenic island drives to mountain valleys and secluded villages, such as Camacha (centre of Madeira's wickerwork industry), and along stunning coastlines.
• Scenic Island Drives (4 to 7 hrs)
• Cable Car & Botanical Gardens (4 hrs)
• Funchal tour with wine tasting at Fortress of Sao Tiago (3.5 hrs)

mous region of Portugal. They lie closer to Africa than to Portugal, with the shores of Morocco only 400 miles away.

The archipelago's largest island is Madeira, its steep slopes terraced with green fields and dotted with villages of red-roofed houses. Flowers such as bougainvillea and hibiscus flourish in the balmy climate, and coastal roads cling to mountainsides ribboned with cascading waterfalls. Precipitous viewpoints include the one atop Cabo Girao, the world's second-highest sea cliff.

The ships dock in the port of **Funchal**, a favourite winter retreat of Sir Winston Churchill, who came here on painting holidays. Situated on a beautiful harbour at the base of a mountain, Funchal has a bustling local market where fresh flowers, hand-sewn linens and wickerwork are sold. Fine local wines can be enjoyed at one of the local bodegas, and afternoon tea is served at the classic Reids Hotel. A popular pastime for visitors is to take a cable car to the village of Monte, located uphill from Funchal, and from there embark on a 10-minute ride back down the steep street in a wicker sledge on runners, which is steered by two men dressed in traditional white flannels and straw boaters.

Funchal was founded in 1421 by Joao Goncalves Zarco, whose tomb lies in the local convent church. Other historic attractions are the 15th-century cathedral, the governor's house, and Parque de Santa Catarina, with its harbour views. The main tourist office on Avenida Arriaga hands out a list of scenic island drives and standard taxi fares. For about US$40, a taxi can be hired for the 30-minute drive to Curral das Freiras (Shelter of the Nuns), a spectacular valley where nuns hid in the 16th century whenever pirates pillaged the island.

The Azores

These Atlantic islands lie about 900 miles (1,500 km) west of mainland Portugal. There are nine main islands, two with cruise ports – Ponta Delgado on St. Michael Island, and Horta on Faial Island. First reached by Portuguese sailors in the 15th century, these fertile islands are volcanic in origin. Visitors can view the craters of dormant volcanoes, now filled with lakes, or take a whalewatching excursion to sight sei whales, bottlenose dolphins and sperm whales, among other species attracted to local waters.

(Above) Visitors to Madeira enjoy their ride in a wicker sledge. (Below) The Madeira Islands' rugged coastline.

SPAIN

Sunny Spain – land of fiestas and flamenco – is one of the world's most popular tourist destinations. Traversed by mountains and valleys, Spain occupies most of the Iberian peninsula and is separated from the rest of Europe by the peaks of the Pyrenees. Its fertile coastal plains are cultivated with citrus groves and olive trees, while the country's fishing fleet nets sardines and anchovies. But tourism is the economy's bread and butter. Lined with golden beaches and blessed with a mild Mediterranean climate, Spain is second only to France for the number of foreign visitors it receives annually.

Spain at a Glance

Spain's population, which numbers about 47 million, is predominantly Roman Catholic. Castilian is the standard Spanish language but other languages are spoken in their respective districts, such as Catalan (akin to Provencal), Galacian (akin to Portuguese) and Basque (an independent language). Spain has had a constitutional monarchy since 1975, when King Juan Carlos I became head of state upon the death of the military dictator Francisco Franco.

Spain consists of 17 geographic and historic regions, which generally correspond to the old Christian and Moorish kingdoms.

Administratively, the country – which includes the Balearic Islands and Canary Islands – is divided into 50 provinces. This rich regional diversity has at times fermented separatist tendencies, especially among the Basques of Northern Spain and the Catalans, whose historical capital is Barcelona.

The 1978 Spanish Constitution established autonomous communities and granted them their own regional administrations. Spain's capital is Madrid, and the Spanish enclaves of Ceuta and Melilla in Morocco are remaining remnants of Spain's former empire.

Children file past Valencia's 13th-century cathedral during an annual fiesta.

Travel Tips

Currency – The unit of currency is the euro. Banks are generally open from 8:30 a.m. to 2 p.m., Monday thru Saturday, except in summer when they close Saturdays.

Dining – Spanish cuisine is as varied as the country itself. Catalonia is renowned for its sauces such as *ali-oli* (made with olive oil and garlic) and for the innovative tapas restaurants that thrive in the culinary capital of Barcelona. Valencia, famous for its rice dishes, is where *paella* originated, and Andalusia is the place to order *gazpacho* – a spicy vegetable soup served cold. Mayonnaise was originally created in Mahon, Minorca; other celebrated specialities of the Balearic Isles include *sobrasada* (a sausage-meat spread) and Majorca's *ensaimadas* (exquisitely light pastries). The Canary Islands feature fish, tropical fruits and a hot sauce called *mojo picon* in their dishes. Spain's fine sherry, called Jerez, is a fortified wine from Andalusia.

Restaurant hours are generally 1:00 to 3:30 p.m. for lunch and 8:30 to 11:00 p.m. for dinner, with extended hours in tourist areas. French-bread sandwiches, called *bocadillos*, are a popular fast food served at cafés and tapas bars. Tapas are bite-sized snacks, often served hot, and these are ordered at the counter.

Opening Hours – Museums and historic attractions are generally open from 9:30 a.m. to 2 p.m. and from 4 p.m. to 7 p.m., Tuesday through Sunday. (Some are closed on Sundays.)

Shopping – The traditional 'siesta hours' are still common in much of Spain, with some stores closing between 1:30 and 4:30 p.m. although major shopping malls and department stores stay open without a break from 10 a.m. to 9 p.m. Spain is known for its finely crafted ceramics, coloured tiles, handmade lace, Andalusian leatherwork and colourful handwoven rugs.

Telephoning – Spain's country code is 34. To place a call to Spain, dial your country's exit code (011 in U.S. and Canada; 00 in UK) + 34 + area code + local number. Barcelona's area code is 93; Madrid's is 91. To phone home from Spain, first dial 00 (International), then your country code (1 for U.S. and Canada; 44 for the UK), followed by the area code and local number.

A restaurant in Valldemossa on the island of Majorca.

A History of Spain

Spain has been uniquely influenced by its proximity to Africa. With the coast of Morocco lying only nine miles across the Strait of Gibraltar, it's not surprising that Spain was first inhabited by an ancient people from Africa called Iberians. Next came the Phoenicians, followed by the Carthaginians, who founded Cartagena in the 3rd century BC. Carthage eventually surrendered their Spanish province to the Romans, after which the Iberian population became thoroughly romanized except for the Basques of northern Spain.

Spain endured its first wave of Germanic invaders from the north in 409 AD. These included the Visigoths, who established their capital at Toledo. In 710, a nobleman named Roderick succeeded King Witiza, whose thwarted heirs turned to the Moors of North Africa for military help in overthrowing the Visigothic usurper. A Berber army, led by Tarik Ibn Ziyad, crossed the Strait of Gibraltar into Spain where it defeated Roderick. Tarik, however, did not restore the heirs of Witiza but instead sent for African reinforcements. Within a few years, he had conquered most of the Iberian Peninsula, and Moorish domination endured for nearly eight centuries, bestowing on Spain a rich cultural legacy.

Interior of the Great Mosque of Cordoba in Andalusia.

The Moors, who were Muslims of Berber and Arab stock, built cities of great wealth and splendour. Their ornate palace complexes, decorated with glazed tiles and alabaster, contained open courts adorned with a multitude of low arches and marble columns. Moorish craftsmen were famous throughout Europe for their lacy wooden carvings and fine pottery called lustreware.

Ruled by various Berber dynasties, Spain's flourishing south was a constant temptation to the Christian nobles of the north who had retained a pocket of resistance in Asturias. Over time these nobles slowly regrouped, forging alliances through marriage and retaking, one by one, the Moorish strongholds. By the time the kingdoms of Aragon and Castile were united under Ferdinand V and Isabella I in 1479, most of Andalusia had been conquered.

Riding a wave of religious zeal, the Christian rulers expelled all Jews and those Muslims who

hadn't converted. The infamous Spanish Inquisition – established to punish Christian converts who were deemed insincere – became so zealous in its search for heretics that soon no Spaniard was immune from its harsh censorship.

The 16th century was Spain's Golden Century, when it became the world's first superpower, with fleets on every sea and an empire encompassing the Philippines, Central America and most of South America. Year after year Spanish galleons would return from the New World, their holds brimming with gold and silver. Yet, by the end of the 16th century, Spain's gradual decline had already begun with England's defeat of the Spanish Armada in 1588. While buccaneers preyed on Spain's treasure fleets, centuries of war slowly weakened the Spanish kingdom.

Following the abdication of Queen Isabella II in 1868, Spain embraced various forms of government, including a republic in 1931. But civil war broke out a few years later, with pro-republican forces (Loyalists) pitted against the Insurgents, who won the civil war in 1939 under the leadership of General Francisco Franco. A ruthless dictator, Franco declared Spain a kingdom with himself regent, retaining power until his death in 1975, at which time his chosen successor, Juan Carlos, ushered in a new and enlightened era for Spain.

The first Spanish monarch since his grandfather was deposed in 1931, Juan Carlos surprised the world when, instead of following in Franco's footsteps, he quickly guided Spain down the road to democracy. The country's first free elections since 1936 were held in 1977, marking Spain's dramatic transition from military dictatorship to parliamentary democracy.

Barcelona

Spain's largest port and second largest city with a population of 1.6 million (4.5 million if outlying areas are included), Barcelona is a fascinating mix of modern and medieval architecture. Broad avenues and *modernista* buildings stand in contrast to the city's historic heart – the Gothic Quarter – which is a labyrinth of narrow winding streets.

The Med's busiest cruise port, Barcelona is considered the cultural centre of Spain. Modern art thrives in this city where Picasso began his formal art training and where the visionary architect Antonio Gaudi was a leading figure in the city's Modernismo movement.

Founded by Carthaginians, Barcelona flourished following the Roman conquest, and eventually fell to the Moors in the 8th century only to be taken by Charlemagne in 801. The city became a prosperous centre for banking and maritime trade, rivaling the Mediterranean seaports of Genoa and Venice at its peak in the late Middle Ages.

In the mid-19th century, as Catalonia strove to regain its regional identity separate from Castillian Spain, Barcelona's leading intellectuals and artists championed a movement to transform their city into a showpiece of Modernism while also reflecting the Catalan soul.

The result is best portrayed in the works of Gaudi, who grew up in the Catalan countryside. Inspired by nature, Gaudi designed fanciful buildings with undulating lines and organic shapes sheathed in fragments of tile or glass. His most famous work is La Sagrada Familia, still under construction but uniquely Gaudi with its forest-like design of soaring spires and columns.

Barcelona's newest iconic landmark, Torre Agbar, was designed by the French architect Jean Nouvel and inspired by Gaudi's architectural legacy. Completed in 2005, this geyser-shaped skyscraper is covered in different-coloured louvers of glass that sparkle in the sunlight and are brilliantly illuminated at night.

Christopher Columbus

Born in Genoa in 1451 to a family of wool weavers, Columbus went to sea as a lad. By his mid-twenties he was serving as a ship's master and was married to the daughter of the governor of the Madeira Islands. While living in Funchal, Columbus formulated a plan of reaching the Far East by sailing due west. Finding no support in several other countries, Columbus turned to Spain.

In 1486 he presented his plan to King Ferdinand and Queen Isabella and for five years Columbus (known in Spain as Cristobal Colon) campaigned for financial support. Finally, upon the Christians' defeat of the Moors, Columbus was outfitted with three ships, setting sail from Palos, at the mouth of the Rio Tinto in Andalusia, on August 3, 1492. After stopping at the Canary Islands to make some repairs and take on provisions, the fleet sailed due west on the easterly trade winds, reaching the Bahamas on October 12th.

When Columbus returned to Spain, 33 weeks later, he received a hero's welcome. Ferdinand and Isabella summoned him to the Court at Barcelona, where he was received with honours and granted the titles and privileges he had requested, including support for a second voyage. A brilliant navigator, Columbus proved to be less competent as a colonial administrator and his third voyage to the West Indies ended with his being brought home in chains, charged with misrule of Spain's colony in Hispaniola.

His last voyage to the West Indies ended in shipwreck off the coast of Jamaica, and Columbus returned to Spain in 1504, the year of Queen Isabella's death. Wracked with arthritis and nearing the end of his own life, Columbus was shunned by King Ferdinand. Outraged by the Spanish crown's lack of gratitude, the world's most famous explorer died in neglect, a disappointed man.

Columbus monument in Barcelona

Getting Around

Barcelona's cruise port is located in the heart of the city and is about 10 miles (16 km) from El Prat Airport. Transfer between the airport and city centre can be arranged beforehand with your cruise line, or made independently by taxi, train or bus. The drive by taxi takes about 30 minutes, depending on traffic, and the cost is 25 to 30 euros. A taxi is the most convenient, taking you right to your hotel or cruise terminal.

Trains depart twice an hour from the airport's T2 Terminal and there's a free shuttle bus between terminal T1 and T2, but it's usually more efficient timewise to take the airport buses which run regularly between the airport and Plaça Catalunya (in front of El Corte Inglés department store). If you're heading from downtown to the airport, be sure to board the bus going to your terminal of departure – either T1 or T2. A one-way ticket is about 6 euros and you can pay the driver. The bus ride is about 40 minutes, depending on traffic.

Barcelona's main tourist office is at Plaça Catalunya underneath El Corte Inglés (stairs lead down to the entrance near the fountain), and another tourist information office is on the ground floor of Barcelona City Hall (Plaça de Sant Jaume). A smaller office is located near the Columbus monument (Pl. Portal de la Pau).

When exploring downtown Barcelona, taxis are plentiful and the fare from the cruise port to the Columbus Monument is 6 euros. Cruise port shuttle buses transfer passengers from the terminals to the Columbus monument and back (5 euros for a full-day pass). A cable car runs from La Barceloneta to the Montjuic area, which can also be reached by funicular from the green Metro L3 station on Avda. del Parallel.

A good way to explore the city is by purchasing a one- or two-day Bus Turistic ticket which allows you to ride the sightseeing buses. There are three routes that stop at numerous attractions. You can get on and off at any of the stops, and a Bus Turistic ticket comes with a booklet of discount coupons to the main attractions. Tickets are sold on board the bus and at tourist information offices.

Young dancers perform near Gaudi's famous church.

Shore Excursions

Barcelona This is a sampling of shore excursions offered by most cruise lines. These will vary with each cruise line. Several sightseeing excursions can be combined with an airport transfer.
• Narrated motorcoach drive past the city's landmarks with a stop atop Montjuic (2.5 hrs, $55)
• Scenic motorcoach drive to Montserrat (one hour each way) and visit to the monastery (4 hrs, $70)
• Explore La Boqueria food market and sample tapas at some Catalan restaurants (4 hrs, $100)
• Bicycling tour of city (2.5 hrs, approx $120)
• Flamenco dance demonstration and overview tour of city (4 hrs, $110)
Consult your cruise line's website for details on excursions offered..

The Barcelona Card includes travel on city buses and trains along with discounted admissions to a list of attractions.

Barcelona has a reputation for attracting high numbers of pickpockets to its tourist-frequented sites, so exercise due caution (see 'Security' on page 24).

Where to Stay

Choices in Barcelona range from Euro-chic boutique hotels, such as the Hotel Villa Emilia on Carrer Calabria, to the classic elegance of the Hotel Colon standing opposite the cathedral. Luxury hotels include Le Meridien on Las Ramblas. A hidden 2-star gem is El Jardi, with rooms overlooking a quiet square in the heart of the Gothic Quarter.

Dining & Shopping

Barcelona has become an exciting dining city with its assortment of cafés, restaurants and tapas bars. For a casual outdoor meal of fresh market cuisine, try one of the eat-

Las Ramblas, Barcelona's famous pedestrian street.

MUST SEE:

First-time visitors to Barcelona will want to see Gaudi's famous landmarks – **La Sagrada Familia** (expect long lineups), **Palau Guell**, **Casa Mila** and **Casa Battlo**. Be sure to stroll through the **Gothic Quarter** and along **Las Ramblas**. If time allows, visit Gaudi's **Parc Guell** as well as **Parc Ciutadella** and **Montjuic**.

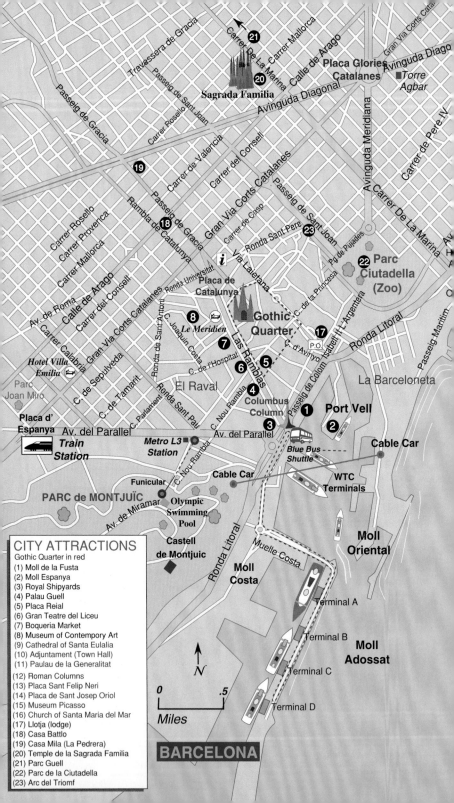

CITY ATTRACTIONS

Gothic Quarter in red

(1) Moll de la Fusta
(2) Moll Espanya
(3) Royal Shipyards
(4) Palau Guell
(5) Placa Reial
(6) Gran Teatre del Liceu
(7) Boqueria Market
(8) Museum of Contempory Art
(9) Cathedral of Santa Eulalia
(10) Adjuntament (Town Hall)
(11) Paulau de la Generalitat

(12) Roman Columns
(13) Placa Sant Felip Neri
(14) Placa de Sant Josep Oriol
(15) Museum Picasso
(16) Church of Santa Maria del Mar
(17) Llotja (lodge)
(18) Casa Battlo
(19) Casa Mila (La Pedrera)
(20) Temple de la Sagrada Familia
(21) Parc Guell
(22) Parc de la Ciutadella
(23) Arc del Triomf

BARCELONA

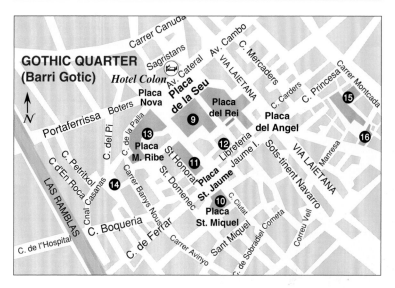

eries in La Boqueria (Barcelona's famous produce market). La Fonda restaurant near Plaça Reial is popular and moderately priced (arrive early if you want to avoid the dinnertime lineups). The city's hottest restaurant for tapas cuisine is Tickets, located on Avda. del Paral and run by the Adria brothers.

Restaurants and souvenir shops are found throughout the Gothic Quarter, amid the narrow winding streets. Carrer Petritxol is where you'll find several commercial art galleries, including Sala Parés (the city's oldest), as well as *granjas* – eateries that serve coffee, hot chocolate and bakery items. More shops and restaurants are found on Carrer del Pi, which leads to Plaça del Pi and adjacent Plaça de Sant Josep Oriol, where arts and crafts fairs are held.

Plaça du Catalunya is the location of El Corte Inglés department store. Leading off this main plaza is Passeig de Gracia with its designer shops. More stores are found along Avda Diagonal, and commercial art galleries are concentrated on Carrer Consell de Cent between Carrer Aribau and Passeig de Gracia.

Local Attractions

The port of Barcelona is serviced by shuttle buses that run between the terminals and the Columbus Monument. A waterside promenade called Moll de la Fusta **1**, lined with bars and restaurants, overlooks the port and is connected by a drawbridge to Moll Espanya **2**, location of the city's aquarium, IMAX theatre and Maremagnum with its restaurants and designer shops.

Across the harbour is **La Barceloneta** – a tongue of land formed by accumulated sand after the port was built in the 17th century. Beaches line the east side of La Barceloneta, and the cable car to Montjuic (Transbordador Aeri del Port) is located here. Adjacent

to La Barceloneta is the **Olympic Port**, a lively spot with a marina, waterfront restaurants and the luxury Hotel Arts, in front of which stands a giant bronze fish sculpture designed by Frank Gehry.

The **Columbus Monument**, which is 200 feet tall, stands near the waterfront in the centre of **Placa del Portal de la Pau**. An elevator can be taken to the top of this monument for a view of the entire city. On the west side of the square is the **Drassanes Reials** (Royal Shipyards) **3**, the largest and most complete shipyard to survive from the Middle Ages. Built in 1378, this fine example of Gothic architecture now houses the Maritime Museum, with reproductions of historical ships.

Barcelona's most famous street, **Las Ramblas**, stretches for three-quarters of a mile, from the Columbus monument to fountain-filled **Plaça de Catalunya**, in the heart of the shopping district. A wide pedestrian promenade flanked by traffic lanes, Las Ramblas is well suited for strolling, with its outdoor cafés, flower stalls and street entertainers. Points of interest just off Las Ramblas include **Placa Reial 4**, a 19th-century arcaded square adorned with Gaudi-designed lamp posts, and **Palau Guell 5**, a colourful medieval-inspired mansion with fairytale flourishes designed by a young Gaudi for his patron Count Eusebi de Guell.

(Above left) Barcelona's famous cathedral. (Left) Its soaring interior is a splendid example of Gothic architecture.

Other attractions along Las Ramblas include the city's opulent opera house, the **Gran Teatre del Liceu** , which was rebuilt following a devastating fire in 1994, and the bustling **Boqueria Market** , filled with delicatessens and stalls selling fruit, vegetables and seafood, and bars serving grilled prawns and other Catalan dishes made from the market's fresh ingredients. The pavement at nearby Pla de la Boqueria was decorated in 1970 with a design by Joan Miro. A few blocks west, at Pl. del Angels, is the **Museum of Contemporary Art** .

Until the mid-19th century, Barcelona's medieval city was surrounded by walls. Today the central part of the medieval city is known as the **Barri Gotic** (Gothic Quarter), the heart of which is **Placa del Rei** – the city's oldest square. It was here that Ferdinand and Isabel received Columbus upon his return in 1493 from his historic voyage to the New World. The buildings facing the square include the Chapel of Santa Agata, the Museu d'Historia de la Ciutat (The City's History Museum) and the Palau Major Reial (Royal Palace). The latter, built from the 11th to the 14th centuries, was the residence of Catalan counts.

Overlooking **Plaça de la Seu**, where Barcelona residents gather on weekends to perform a circular folk dance called the *sardana*, is Barcelona's famous **Cathedral of Santa Eulalia** . Begun in 1291, this Gothic cathedral took 150 years to build. Its west front remained unfinished until the late 19th century, when a local indus-

A trompe-l'oeil façade overlooks a square of the Gothic Quarter.

trialist financed the completion of a neogothic façade based on a 15th-century drawing. Treasure-filled chapels line the cathedral's interior, which features a breathtaking display of medieval masonry with ogival ribbed vaults, slender piers and fine cloisters surrounding a tropical garden. The alabaster tomb of St. Eulalia is an exquisite piece of carving by a disciple of Italian sculptor Giovanni Pisano.

Plaça de Sant Jaume is flanked by the 14th-century **Adjuntament** (Town Hall) and the **Paulau de la Generalitat** , a Gothic palace with a Renaissance façade, which is the seat of the Catalan government. In Roman times, Plaça de Sant Jaume was the site of the town's ancient forum and a 1st century BC temple dedicated to Emperor Augustus was built here. Four remaining columns stand at the end of Carrer Paradis, hidden inside a medieval building's courtyard .

Plaça Sant Felip Neri **13** is a peaceful square located in the old Jewish Quarter (El Call), while nearby **Plaça de Sant Josep Oriol 14** and adjacent **Plaça del Pi** are lively squares featuring outdoor cafés, street musicians, and weekly art and antique markets. The Gothic church of **Santa Maria del Pi** – its bells heard ringing throughout the Gothic Quarter – features a gigantic rose window.

Separated from the Gothic Quarter by Via Laietana, but still medieval in origin, is the **Ribera Quarter**, which became the centre of Barcelona in the 14th century when wealthy merchants built elegant mansions along **Carrer Montcada**. The popular **Museu Picasso 15** is housed here in five adjacent medieval palaces. Picasso, born in Malaga in 1881, was admitted at the age of 15 to the Royal Academy of Art in Barcelona, and some of his early sketches are among the works on display in the museum. Close by, on Barra de Ferro, is the **Museu Europeu d'Art Modern**, which opened in 2011 in the beautifully renovated Palau Gomis.

Also in the vicinity is the 14th-century Church of **Santa Maria del Mar 16**, considered the foremost achievement of Catalan Gothic architecture. A few blocks south of the church is the **Llotja** (Lodge) **17**, a 14th-century structure housing the Barcelona Stock Exchange

Casa Battlo (above left) and La Sagrada Familia (left).

Library and the Academy of Fine Arts. Remodeled in the 18th century, its interesting features include a courtyard and large Gothic hall.

In 1860, Barcelona dismantled the city walls and underwent a major expansion. The city's new section, called **El Eixample** (The Addition), was laid out in a grid pattern of streets with diamond-shaped intersections. Many of the buildings were designed in the art nouveau style, called Modernismo in Spain, and several famous examples are located on **Passeig de Gracia**. A block named **Mancana de la Discordia** (Apple of Discord) features three buildings of contrasting architecture, all of them built during the first decade of the 20th century by Barcelona's three leading architects. Casa Lleo Morera presents a modernist floral façade; Casa Ametller, in the middle, is a neo-Gothic building, its façade decorated with polychrome ceramic; the most famous of the three, **Casa Battlo 18**, stands at the corner of Passeig de Gracia and Carrer d'Arago. Designed by Gaudi, it features a sparkling mosaic façade and a roof shaped like a dragon's tail. The mezzanine is open daily to visitors.

Another famous building by Gaudi is **Casa Mila 19**, also on Passeig de Gracia. Known as La Pedrera (The Stone Quarry), this large apartment house of cut stone appears to have been sculpted from play dough, with chimneys squeezed from a pastry tube. Open daily, visitors can view the attic, rooftop and an apartment.

Gaudi's most famous work, and

(Above and right) Citadel Park

a beloved Barcelona landmark, is **Temple de la Sagrada Familia** (Temple of the Holy Family) **20**, begun in 1882 and still under construction. The intensely pious Gaudi envisaged this work as a Bible made of stone. The church's west facade represents the Passion of Christ, the east facade represents the Nativity, and the Glory is planned for the south. The four towers on each of the three main facades represent the twelve Apostles. You can climb to the top of these towers or use the lift. A complicated structure of

The celebrated monastery in Montserrat. (Below) Arc del Triomf in Barcelona.

inclined columns and parabolic arches, this unique church is the ultimate example of Gaudi's ingenious approach to construction. A museum is located in the basement of the Passion façade.

Parc Guell 21, located about a mile northwest of the La Sagrada Familia, is another showpiece of Gaudi's work. The park, named after Gaudi's main patron, is filled with fantastic and dreamlike forms, such as undulating benches and large, multicoloured lizards. The house where Gaudi spent the last 20 years of his life is now a small museum, and inside one of the park's gatehouses is an interpretive centre with displays providing an understanding of Gaudi's building methods.

The **Parc de la Ciutadella** (Citadel Park) **22** occupies the former site of an 18th-century fortress. The park, built for an 1888 exhibition, offers a tranquil setting with a small lake and monumental waterfall featuring rocks designed by Gaudi as a young student. The nearby **Arc del Triomf 23**, a red-brick arch, was erected as a grand entrance to the exhibition.

When Barcelona hosted the 1929 World's Fair, the venue for this event was the imposing hill of **Montjuic**, overlooking the harbour. Redeveloped for the 1992 Summer Olympic Games, Montjuic can be reached by cable

car from the cruise port or by funicular from the Metro L3 station on Av Parallel. Montjuic's attractions include an artisans' village, botanical gardens, Mies van der Rohe's iconic Barcelona Pavilion and a spectacular fountain where a light and music performance takes place nightly. Several museums are found on Montjuic, including the Joan Miro Foundation and the National Art Museum of Catalunya, situated near Plaça Espanya where the view over the city is spectacular. If you want to travel to the very top of Montjuic, a small 8-passenger cable car can be boarded opposite the Olympic swimming pool for the ride up to Montjuic Castle (now a military museum). Providing panoramic views over the city is the belvedere Mirador de l'Alcalde.

Montserrat – Thirty-five miles northwest of Barcelona, clinging to the terraced cliffside of Monserrat mountain, is one of Spain's greatest religious shrines. Only ruins remain of the original Benedictine monastery, the present structure having been built in the 18th century. A gilded black image of the Virgin held in the 16th-century Renaissance church is believed to have been carved by St. Luke and brought here by St. Peter, then hidden in a nearby cave during Spain's Moorish occupation. A cable car takes visitors up the mountainside to the monastery, church and museum, where cafés and shops are also located. Montserrat monastery can be reached by ship-organized excursion or by train from Placa Espanya station (Line R5 Manresa). When purchasing your ticket, be sure to indicate if you want to ride the cable car or the funicular from the base of Montserrat mountain up to the monastery. The price is the same (18 euros each) but you will get off the train at Montserrat Aeri station if taking the cable car or at Montrisol if taking the funicular.

Tarragona – Situated 50 miles west of Barcelona at the mouth of the Francoli River, this Catalonian port flourished during Roman times. Ruins of the town's ancient walls, amphitheatre and aqueduct can be viewed, as can the 13th-century Romanesque-Gothic cathedral, with one of the finest cloisters in Spain.

Palamos – This small, scenic port is nestled among the coves and beaches of the Costa Brava, where area attractions include several museums dedicated to the life and art of Salvador Dali. His birthplace of **Figueres** is the location of the Dali Theatre-Museum, which holds the largest collection of his works. In nearby Pubol is a medieval castle Dali bought for his wife and is now a museum called Gala Dali Castle. Yet another museum is House Salvador Dali in **Port Lligat**. For detail on these museums, including ticket reservations and opening times, visit salvador-dali.org.

Other places of interest in this area include the seaside resort of **Rosas**, which began as a Greek colony and boasts an 11th-century monastery and 16th-century castle. The medieval walled town of **Girona** features a well-preserved Jewish Quarter. Barcelona is a 2-hour drive from Palamos.

Balearic Islands

Lying off Spain's Mediterranean coast, the idyllic Balearic Islands – with their stone watchtowers and hilltop villas – have provided refuge to pirates and princesses, artists and aristocrats. Luxury yachts call at these islands throughout the summer, a custom that began when Archduke Salvador used his steam yachts to explore the Mediterranean in the mid-1800s and soon discovered Mallorca. A century later Prince Rainier and Princess Grace called at Mallorca on their honeymoon cruise. Prince Charles and Princess Diana vacationed here with their two young sons at the invitation of the Spanish king and queen. And in 2010, Michelle Obama and her daughter Sasha were guests of the Spanish royals.

Mallorca (Majorca)

The largest of the Balearic Islands, Mallorca is a beautiful mountainous island, with pine-covered slopes and meandering donkey trails. The island's north coast is especially scenic, its terraced cliffsides overlooking rocky headlands and hidden coves. This quiet corner of Mallorca is a hideaway for celebrities seeking seclusion and is a stark contrast to the island's bustling capital of **Palma** (pop. 400,000), which stretches along the Bay of Palma, its streets swelling with tourists in summer.

Getting Around – Most cruise ships dock at Estacio Maritima, which is located on the far side of the Bay of Palma, nearly 4 miles (6 km) from the city centre. It's possible to walk into town along the waterfront but most cruise lines provide a shuttle. Also, Palma's hop-on/hop-off bus stops in front of the cruise terminal. Taxis are metered and the one-way fare is 10 euros. Once you're in the centre of Palma, the historic attractions, restaurants and

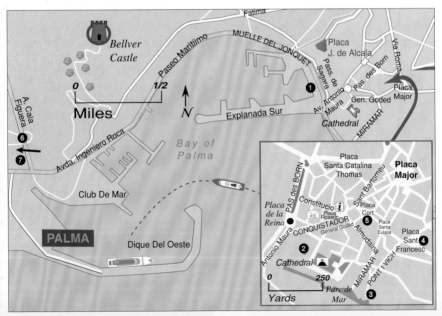

shops are within easy walking distance of one another. Bikes can be rented near the cathedral (PalmaOnBike.com) and a cycle path traces the bay southward past pleasant beaches.

Should you choose to tour the island, car rental agencies are located at the terminal and for about US$60 you can hire a vehicle for the day. Another way to see the island's scenic north coast is to take the vintage train from Palma to Soller, which departs from Pl. Espanya. Local buses also run between Palma (Pl. Espanya) and Soller, following a coastal route with stops at Valldemossa and Deja.

Shopping & Dining – The old town is filled with shops and sidewalk cafés. The narrow streets surrounding **La Lonja** **1**, the 15th-century Maritime Stock Exchange, are lined with restaurants and tapas bars, including one of the same name (La Lonja) where drinks and traditional tapas can be enjoyed on the spacious terrace with views overlooking the harbour. Fashionable boutiques line Avinguda Jaume III and Passeig des Born – a tree-lined boulevard with a pedestrian promenade. Local products include wood carvings, Majorica pearls and leather goods. A crafts market is held several times a week in Plaça Major. Nearby on Plaça Weyler is **Forn des Teatre** (Theatre Bakery), well known both for its delicious pastries; light meals are served in the adjacent café.

Palma's Gothic cathedral

Shore Excursions

Ship-organized excursions on **Mallorca** include sightseeing in Palma (4 hrs) and scenic island drives to Valldemossa and Son Marroig (4 hrs), La Granja (4 hrs), the wine-making village of Santa Maria (4 hrs), and the Caves of Drach (4.5 hrs). Also offered is a train ride (in vintage carriages) from Palma to Soller. The train ascends the mountains through 13 tunnels, providing spectacular vistas along the way, and the return trip is by motorcoach (4 hrs total, about $65). Boat tours take you past the royal summer palace at Cala Major to Palma Nova, the island's first custom-built beach resort catering to British tourists, its seafront promenade lined with pubs. Other excursions include mountain biking, kayaking and a cooking tour that features the preparation of paella.

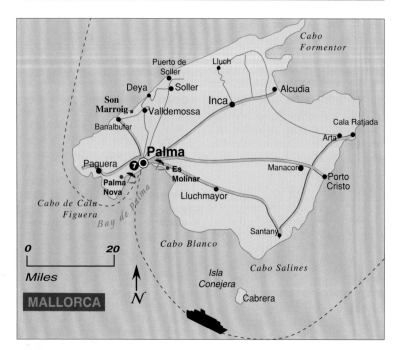

The monastery at Valldemossa where Chopin stayed one winter.

Local Attractions – On a hill overlooking the port is the 14th-century **Bellver Castle**, one of the few circular castles in Europe with a magnificent inner courtyard and sweeping views from its ramparts. Give yourself at least an hour to explore inside and out.

Palma's old town was once encircled by walls, a section of which still stands along the waterfront. Just inside the fortifications is Palma's splendid Gothic cathedral, begun in the year 1230, after James I of Aragon seized Palma from the Moors. Much of the interior was remodeled at the beginning of this century by Antonio Gaudi. The bell tower holds nine bells with the largest, cast in 1389, weighing four tons.

Opposite the cathedral is **Castillo della Almudaina** **2**,

originally a Moorish citadel, then a summer palace for Spanish royalty. Today the palace is the official office of the Spanish king during his annual summer holiday on Majorca. The grounds contain a lovely fountain-filled garden. Other structures of note include 10th-century **Arab baths** **3**, 13th-century **Church of San Francisco** **4**, and 17th-century **Ajuntament** (Town Hall) **5**.

The sea views at Deya (above) and Son Marroig (right) along Mallorca's northwest coast.

The Spanish painter Joan Miro, whose mother and wife were from Mallorca, moved to the island in 1941 in search of spiritual solace. The studio he established in Palma is now a museum, the **Joan Miro Foundation** **6**, containing his paintings, drawings and sculptures. The Spanish royal family's summer residence, **Marivent Palace** **7**, is located nearby on a secluded headland overlooking Plaça Major.

Island Attractions – Mallorca's rugged north coast contains rustic stone villages and secluded country estates. The village of **Valldemossa** is the location of La Cartuja, a Carthusian monastery that was converted into lodgings in 1835. Chopin stayed here in the winter of 1838 with his companion Mme Dudevant (George Sand) who later wrote a book titled *A Winter in Majorca*. The weather during their stay was rainy and the locals did not approve of their love affair. The apartments where Chopin stayed are now a museum furnished in period style with a piano he used while composing his preludes.

The English poet and novelist Robert Graves spent half of his life in the artists' village of **Deya**, not far from Valldemossa. The 1929 success of *Good-bye to All That* allowed Graves to buy land and build a house (now a museum), where he wrote, among other works, *I, Claudius*. In 1936, with the Spanish Civil War looming, he left Mallorca aboard a British destroyer and returned to England. Ten years later Graves and his family returned to Majorca where his house and garden were just as he had left them.

Other famous residents of Mallorca's north coast include Andrew Lloyd Webber, and numerous celebrities have stayed at La Residencia, a luxury boutique hotel near Deya which was once owned by Richard Branson.

Majorca's craggy northwest coast is dotted with spectacular viewpoints, including the one at **Son Marroig**, a residence built by Austrian archduke Luis Salvador, who visited Mallorca in the mid-1800s and decided to stay, buying up estates and olive plantations to save them from development. While much of his property is now owned by the actor Michael Douglas, including S'Estaca (a Moorish-style palace), the Archduke's main residence at Son Marroig has been converted into a museum. The view from the mirador looks down nearly 1,000 feet to a rocky headland from which the waves have carved, over time, a sea arch called Sa Foradada ('perforated').

Other picturesque villages along the northwest coast include **Puerto Soller**, with a natural harbour and fine beaches. Inland, the mountain village of **Lluch** is the location of a monastery set into the side of a cliff.

At the north end of the island is historic **Alcudia**, where a twice-weekly market selling handicrafts is held outside the restored remains of its Moorish city walls. A nearby Roman amphitheatre was excavated in the 1950s. Golden beaches stretch from the cruise port to Playa de Muro.

On the island's east coast, near the fishing port of Porto Cristo, are the **Caves of Drach**, which contain one of the world's largest underground lakes. The pearl factory at nearby **Manacor** is another popular attraction.

Minorca (Menorca)

One of the Mediterranean's most desirable holiday islands, Minorca has been inhabited since Neolithic times. Several monuments of huge undressed stone stand amid the island's gentle terrain of low hills, patchwork fields and narrow hedge-lined lanes. In the 18th century, England, France

Cala Galdana, Minorca

and Spain fought for control of Minorca, but the island was held mostly by the British who gave **Port Mahon** (Mao) its Georgian-style architecture. Mahon's picturesque harbor is overlooked by two fortresses, and the tourist information office is at Plaça de S'Esplanada. Local highlights include the Ajuntament (City Hall) and Church of Santa Maria. The island was awarded to Spain in 1802, but still retains some British flavour.

Ciutadella (Ciudadela), at the island's west end, was Minorca's capital before the arrival of the British and its interesting architecture includes medieval churches and splendid palaces. Beautiful beaches line the island's south coast, such as the protected cove at **Cala Galdana**, and the sandy beach at Cala 'n Porter which is sheltered by cliffs.

Ibiza

A scenic island, with terraced farmland and ancient remains, Ibiza was a popular artists' retreat in the 1960s. The island's first hippy market was located at Patio de Armas, inside the medieval town of **Eivissa** (traditionally called **D'Alt Vila**). Declared a UNESCO World Heritage Site, the town's sights include a Dominican convent (now the Town Hall), a cathedral, episcopal palace and numerous shops, cafés and art galleries. Ship shore excursions feature a walking tour of D'Alt Villa (3 hrs) and a fast ferry ride to the unspoilt island of **Formentera** to spend time at beautiful Illetes Beach (7 hrs).

Valencia

Valenica is Spain's third largest city and the capital of Valencia province – the 'garden of Spain' where the famous Valencia oranges are grown, as is the rice used in making paella, a regional specialty.

A rival of Barcelona during the late Middle Ages, Valencia became a literary and cultural centre with a university founded in 1501 and a famous school of painting. Today the city is quite striking, with narrow streets and blue-tiled church domes in the old quarter and tree-lined avenues in the modern section where an enormous cultural and leisure complex called the City of Arts and Sciences has transformed a former riverbed into a showplace of futuristic architecture. Designed by Valencian architect Santiago Calatrava and Madrid-born Félix Candela, the complex contains an interactive science

One of the many beautiful fountain squares in Valencia.

museum, sculpture park, aquarium and planetarium designed to resemble a giant eye.

Major landmarks in Valencia's historic quarter include a 13th-century cathedral with a Gothic bell tower (called El Miguelete), 14th-century fortified towers (called Torres de Serranos) which were built on Roman foundations, and the 15th-century silk exchange (La Lonja), which is considered one of Spain's finest Gothic buildings.

Valencia's main shopping streets of Colon, Don Juan Austria and Jorge Juan are in the southern part of the historic quarter where you'll find fashion boutiques, shoe stores and shops selling handmade ceramics. Some shops close during the afternoon but many stay open all day, as do department stores such as El Corte Inglés. Unique souvenirs include exquisite handmade fans crafted by the Carbonell family since 1860 and sold at Abanicos Carbonell (Calle Castelon 21).

For refreshment, be sure to try a traditional Valencian snack of *horchata* (made from the chufa root) and *fartons* (a kind of bread for dunking). One of Valencia's most famous *horchaterias* is at Plaza de la Reina, opposite Iglesia y Torre Santa Catalina. A good restaurant for sampling the local paella is La Pepica, next to the America's Cup port.

Valencia hosted the 2007 America's Cup and the facilities built for this international yachting event are now a popular tourist attraction, as are the golden beaches with their waterfront promenades and beachfront bars.

Trams and buses provide local transportation, and a hop-on hop-off tourist bus operates a route in the port area with stops at Las Arenas beach and the City of Arts and Sciences. Consider purchasing the Valencia Card, a tourist card that provides free transport on the metro, buses and trams, free or discounted admission to major attractions, and a discounted ticket on the Tourist Bus.

Alicante

This port on the **Costa Blanca** is dominated by the great Moorish castle of Santa Barbara. Perched upon a rocky peak, the fortress provides breathtaking views of the city's plazas, beaches and palm-lined Explanada de Espana, which runs along the waterfront. A lift, its shaft running deep inside the mountain, transports visitors to the castle. The tourist office is located near the waterfront, in the arcaded Plaza de Ayuntamiento. Behind is Plaza Santisima Faz, an inviting plaza filled with outdoor cafés and restaurants. Nearby is the Museum of 20th Century Art, housing a small collection of works by Dali, Miro and Picasso. Playa Postiguet is the city's main beach, while those north of the city are cleaner and less crowded.

Cartagena

This ancient city has recently reinvented itself as a tourist destination. Founded by Carthaginians in the 3rd century BC, Cartagena thrived under Roman rule before eventually falling to the Moors in the 8th century AD. Recovered by

Spaniards in the 13th century, Cartagena was sacked by Sir Francis Drake in 1585, and was a Loyalist naval base during the Spanish Civil War.

Historic sites include the restored Roman theatre of Carthago Nova, and the city's museum holds excellent pre-Roman and Roman collections. The ruins of the medieval Castillo de la Concepcion, surrounded by fine gardens, command a sweeping view of the city and harbour where waterfront restaurants and a pedestrian seawall can be enjoyed. More restaurants are located in the old town, around Plaza del Ayuntaminento and Plaza Maria Jose Artes. The city's main shopping street is Calle Major, which is also the location of Casa Cervantes and Casa Llagostera, designed by the Modernist architect Victor Beltri.

Ship-organized **shore excursions** in Cartagena include a walking tour, and motorcoach tours to Murcia's 17th-century shrine of Fuensanta, to the hilltop fortress at Caravaca, and to the palm forest in the Moorish town of Elche.

Malaga and Granada

Sunny **Andalusia,** the southernmost part of Spain, is best known for the **Costa del Sol** where a mild climate, lush vegetation and beautiful beaches attract plenty of tourists, and for the famous Alhambra palace located inland at Granada. There are several ports of call providing access to Granada along this stretch of coastline, including Almeria, Motril and **Malaga**.

Malaga, birthplace of Picasso, is a mostly modern city despite its millennia of history. Founded in the 12th century BC by the Phoenicians, the city passed from empire to empire and flourished as a seaport of the Moorish kingdom of Granada before falling to Ferdinand and Isabella in 1487. Its historic buildings include a 16th-century cathedral, the ruins of a Moorish alcazar, and an imposing citadel called the Gibralfaro on a hilltop overlooking the harbour. The Museo Picasso, which opened in 2003, is

Malaga is a popular port on the Costa del Sol.

Shore Excursions

First-time visitors to **Malaga** will want to visit Granada to view the famous Alhambra palace complex (9 hrs). Other ship-organized shore excursions in Malaga include city tours, tapa tasting, and scenic drives along Costa del Sol to Marbella (4.5 hrs), to the stalagmite caves at Nerja (4.5 hrs) and to the Andalusian village of Mijas with its square bullring (4 hrs).

housed in the Buenavista Palace, which is a short walk from the cathedral.

The Malaga cruise terminal is a 30-minute walk to the city centre and a shuttle service is usually available. A hop-on hop-off tourist bus operates in Malaga with stops at the major sites, including the Gibralfaro fortress.

Good shopping is found in the historical quarter along the streets surrounding the cathedral. Malaga's main shopping street is traffic-free Marqués de Larios with its upscale boutiques selling designer fashions. An El Corte Inglés department store is located on Avenida de Andalucia. (In mid-August many of the shops close while the city celebrates a 10-day street fair of festivities.)

Tapas bars are plentiful in Malaga, as are delicatessans selling traditional treats such as turron (a confection of almonds and honey).

Granada, which began as a Moorish fortress, is beautifully

Granada's famous Moorish palace, the Alhambra.

situated at the foot of the Sierra Nevada, where the Darro and Genil rivers flow together. It became a city of great splendor with construction of its famous palace complex, the **Alhambra**. A hilltop group of buildings, the Alhambra (which means 'the red' in Arabic) was built between 1230 and 1354. This luxurious royal palace and citadel are considered the finest examples of Moorish architecture in Spain. The halls and chambers surround a series of open courts, including the Court of Lions, which contains arcades resting on 124 white marble columns. The palace's sumptuous interior of alabaster and glazed tile is adorned with geometric ornamentation of minute detail and intricacy.

When American author and diplomat Washington Irving came to live in the Alhambra in 1829, the palace was crumbling from rot and decay. His book of Spanish sketches, called *Tales of the Alhambra*, helped revive interest in the palace's preservation and, since 1862, an ongoing program of restoration has been in effect.

Sharing the Alhambra's hilltop site are the palace of Emperor Charles V, built in 1526 on the site once occupied by the sultan's private apartments, and the celebrated gardens of the Palacio del Generalife, a summer residence of the Moorish rulers. Granada's 16th-century cathedral was built in the late Gothic and plateresque style. The adjoining royal chapel, a masterpiece of ornate Gothic architecture, contains the marble tombs of Ferdinand and Isabella.

Cadiz and Seville

Cadiz, once one of the world's major ports, is an ancient city rich in naval history. Founded by the Phoenicians in about 1000 BC, Cadiz became the wealthiest port in Europe after the discovery of America, when Spanish treasure ships, returning from the New World, unloaded their cargoes here. In 1587 Francis Drake burned a Spanish fleet in Cadiz's harbor, in an operation known as 'the singeing of the King of Spain's beard', and nine years later another English squadron captured and sank most of the ships in this harbour.

Attacks on Cadiz continued but its wealth, based on trade with Spain's colonies, continued to grow, especially after Seville's port – reached by river from Cadiz – became partially blocked by a sandbar. The port of Cadiz was blockaded by the British in 1797, and bombarded by Sir Horatio Nelson in 1800. Five years later, a Franco-Spanish fleet sailed from Cadiz and met its destruction at the Battle of Trafalgar.

Shore Excursions

Ship-organized shore excursions include walking tours of **Seville** (9 hrs) and Cadiz (3 hrs), as well as sherry tasting at Jerez de la Frontera, visting an Andalusian horse school (5 hrs) and watching a performance of flamenco. A ship shuttle can be taken from Cadiz to Seville (70 miles away) for exploring this fascinating city on your own.

Today cruise ships pull into Cadiz's natural harbour where disembarking passengers can enjoy the palm-lined promenades of this fine old city. Its 13th-century cathedral was rebuilt in the Renaissance style, and a new cathedral was begun in 1722. In 1980 some Phoenician sarcophagi and a Roman theatre were discovered here. A hop-on hop-off tourist bus operates in Cadiz (about 13 euros per adult; 6 euros for children)

Seville, which is connected with the Atlantic by river and canal, has been the chief city of Andalusia since ancient times. The Romans made Seville a judicial centre of Baetica province and built the nearby city of Italica, where the emperors Trajan and Hadrian were born. The city fell to the Moors in 712 AD, and eventually became a flourishing commercial and cultural centre. Two parts of its famous mosque remain, the Court of Oranges and the Giralda tower, which was built between 1163 and 1184.

After a long siege, Seville fell in 1248 to Ferdinand III of Castile, and about 300,000 Moors – the majority of the population – left. Following the discovery of the New World in 1492, Seville again prospered as a chief port of trade. A beautiful **1 Gothic cathedral**, one of the world's largest, was completed in 1519 on the site of the main mosque, its square minaret (the Giralda tower) converted to a bell tower in 1568 with the addition of an ornate Renaissance superstructure. Inside the cathedral are invaluable works of art and the tomb of Christopher Columbus. Adjoining the cathedral is the **Alcazar 2**, built by Moorish

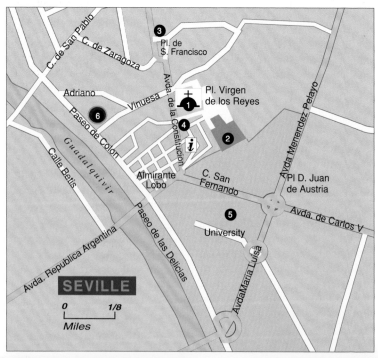

artisans, its splendid halls and exquisite decorations rivaling the Alhambra in Granada.

In addition to Seville's numerous churches and private castles, other notable buildings include the 16th-century **town hall** , the **Ionja** (former exchange) containing archives of Spanish America, and the city's **university buildings** which were formerly a large tobacco factory and a setting featured in Bizet's *Carmen*. Seville is the country's bullfighting capital, and **La Maestranza Bullring** , completed in 1763, is the oldest and most beautiful in Spain.

Cervantes wrote his masterpiece, *Don Quixote*, while living in Seville in the late 16th century, penning parts of this parody about chivalry while in prison.

Galacia

In northwest Spain's Galacia province, the Atlantic ports of **La Coruna** and **Vigo** both provide access to **Santiago de Compostela**, one of the chief shrines of Christendom. In the early 9th century, Alfonso II of Asturias had a sanctuary built on the presumed site of the apostle St. James The Greater's tomb. The city, which grew around the shrine, became an important place of pilgrimage during the Middle Ages, second only to Jerusalem and Rome. The Moors destroyed

BULLFIGHTING

Bullfighting, an important part of Spanish culture, was introduced by the Moors who fought bulls from horses and killed them with javelins. This Moorish practice evolved into the sport of bullfighting, called *corrida de toros* in Spanish. A controversial spectacle, criticized by some as a form of animal torture, the bullfight remains popular in Spain, although it's been banned in Catalonia. Held in a large outdoor arena, the modern bullfight unfolds in three ritualistic parts. First, toreros wave capes at the bull and mounted picadors thrust at it with lances. The next stage involves banderillos who, while on the run, poke short barbed sticks into the bull's withers. Finally the matador, holding a small cape and a sword, makes daring passes at the bull who eventually stops charging and succumbs to the matador's dominance. When the bull strikes a stationary stance, with its four feet square on the ground and its head hung low, this is the moment when, according to ritual and law, the matador must shove his sword into the bull's heart. Fighting bulls are specially bred, and successful matadors are highly paid and admired for their skill and courage.

the sanctuary in the 10th century, and a Romanesque cathedral was built on the site between the 11th and 13th centuries, with baroque and plateresque additions made during later restorations. The Hospital Real was built in the early 1500s by Ferdinand and Isabella to accommodate poor pilgrims. Today millions of Christians annually make the pilgrimage along part or all of the paths that lead to the shrine.

The port of **Bilbao**, in the Basque region of northern Spain, was transformed from medieval town to showcase of contemporary architecture upon completion of the Guggenheim Museum in 1997. Designed by Frank Gehry, this iconic building houses a museum of modern and contemporary art and is the main attraction at this port of call.

Canary Islands

These Atlantic isles, lying off the coast of Africa, are volcanic in origin and immensely appealing to pleasure-seeking visitors because of their subtropical climate, clear waters and expansive beaches. Starkly beautiful, the islands are a study in contrasts. Sea cliffs and craggy coves give

way to massive sand dunes and vast beaches. Mountain villages with whitewashed houses and red-tiled roofs seem far removed from the resort areas' modern hotels and championship golf courses. Millions of visitors arrive annually by air, while those arriving by cruise ship pull into historic ports of cobblestone streets and Spanish colonial architecture – the same ports that greeted famous sea captains in centuries past.

The islands' original inhabitants were a cave-dwelling people called Guanches, who likely migrated from Africa. The islands were visited by Romans as early as 40 BC, and several classical writers referred to them as the Fortunate Islands. The Middle Ages brought the occasional visit by Arabs and Europeans, but no permanent settlement until 1402, when a Norman named Jean de Bethencourt arrived at Lanzarote. In 1479 a treaty between Portugal and Spain gave the latter sovereignty over the Canaries, and the Spanish conquest of the Guanches was complete by 1496.

The islands became an important base for voyages to the Americas, and they were frequently raided by pirates and pri-

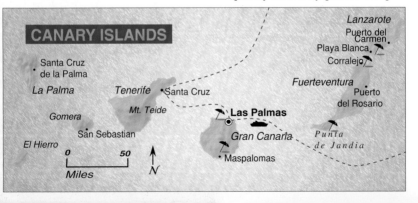

vateers. England's Francis Drake attacked Las Palmas in 1595 but was repulsed; the Dutch were more successful four years later, when they ravaged the port. Two centuries later, in 1797, Horatio Nelson tried to capture a Spanish treasure ship at Santa Cruz but was repulsed, losing an arm in the battle. The Canaries, comprising two provinces, have been an autonomous region of Spain since 1982. Santa Cruz de Tenerife, whose capital is Santa Cruz on the island of Tenerife, encompasses the western islands; Las Palmas, whose capital is Las Palmas on the island of Gran Canaria, encompasses the eastern islands.

Tenerife is the largest of the Canary Islands. Its northern valleys are filled with banana and pineapple plantations, and the entire island is dominated by the snowcovered summit of Mt. Teide – Spain's highest point at 12,162 feet (3,707 meters). The visitor centre at Teide National Park provides guided hikes and bus tours, and a cable car carries visitors close to the top of the volcano, where the final ascent is made on foot to the edge of the crater. Tenerife's port city of **Santa Cruz** has several museums and historic structures, including a Moorish bell tower. The 18th-century cannons that held off an attack by Horatio Nelson are still in place. A hop-on hop-off tourist bus operates in Santa Cruz and the cruise terminal is on its route. The fare is 13 euros for adults and the bus stops at major attractions, including Plaza de Espana in the city's oldest district.

The cliff-edged island of **Gomera** is where Columbus made his last stop, his ships pulling into the port of San Sebastian, before sailing across the Atlantic Ocean in 1492.

La Palma, also called La Isla Bonita ('The Pretty Island'), is a verdant island of volcanic mountains, including Cumbre Vieja, which erupted in 1971 and is slowly sliding toward the sea at a rate of half an inch per year. The island's capital of **Santa Cruz de la Palma** is situated on the edge of a crater. A bustling ship-building centre in the 16th century, the port has retained its colonial appearance. A hop-on hop-off tourist bus (12.50 euros for adults) will take you to the city's museums, the shopping area of Las Arenas or the golden sands of Playa de las Canteras.

Las Palmas, capital of Las Palmas province, is situated on **Gran Canaria**, an island famous for its enormous beaches and sand dunes, such as those found at

A whitewashed village on Gran Canaria island.

Maspalomas. The city of Las Palmas was founded in 1478, and its nearby harbour at Puerto de la Luz is the Canaries' chief port and one of the busiest in Spain. An impressive castle, Castillo de la Luz, protects the harbour, and a Gothic cathedral, dating to the early 1500s, stands in the city's old quarter. It took four centuries to complete the cathedral, hence its 19th-century exterior. The Casa Museo Colon (Columbus Museum) is housed in the palace where Columbus likely stayed in 1492. Not far from Castillo de la Luz, is a fine beach called Las Cantara.

The port of **Arrecife** is on the island of **Lanzarote**, declared a World Biosphere Reserve with its which has an unusual lunar-like landscape of volcanic expanses, black and red beaches, bubbling geysers and grottoes of emerald-coloured water. **Fuerteventura** offers stunning beaches along the island's south coast.

Gibraltar

A British crown colony, Gibraltar is a military fortress perched on a narrow peninsula, called the Rock of Gibraltar, which is connected to the Spanish mainland by a low sandy area of neutral ground.

In ancient times, the Rock was regarded as one of the two mythological Pillars of Hercules – the other being Mt. Acha at Ceuta in Africa. These two promontories flank the east entrance to the Strait of Gibraltar and were said to mark the end of the world by the Ancient Greeks.

The name Gibraltar is Arabic in origin, derived from Jabal-al-Tarik ('mount of Tarik'). In 711, the Moorish leader Tarik captured the Rock of Gibraltar and built its first fortifications, upon which enlargements and improvements have been made over the centuries. The Moors held Gibraltar until 1462, when the Spanish seized control of the fortress. The British gained possession of 'the Rock' in 1704 and have held it ever since, fending off several sieges by the Spanish and French in the 18th century. During the Spanish civil war (1936-39), refugees fled to Gibraltar. Most civilians were evacuated during World War II, when its fortifications were strengthened

Gibraltar is only three miles long and less than a mile wide but, as a strategic naval and air base, it has been an ongoing source of friction between Great Britain and Spain.

Despite Spain's persistent claim to Gibraltar, its residents voted in 1967 to maintain their ties to Britain, and in 1981 Gibraltar's small civilian population, mainly of Spanish, Italian, Portuguese, Maltese and Jewish descent, were granted full British citizenship. In 1985 Spain reopened its border with Gibraltar, after closing it in 1969, and today many of the colony's labourers live in the Spanish border town of La Linea. A proposed plan in which Britain would share sovereignty of the colony with Spain was rejected by Gibraltarians in a 2002 referendum.The Rock of Gibraltar is made of Jurassic limestone, and is honeycombed with caves, arsenals and a tunnel bisecting the rock from east to west. Valuable archaeological finds have been made in **St. Michael's Cave** 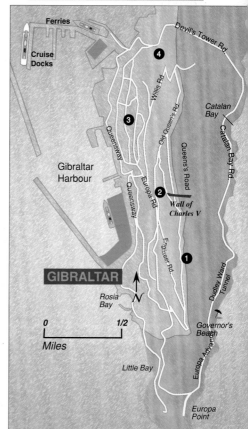 where stalagmites and stalactites create a dramatic setting for the daily sound-and-light shows. Tours are available of the tunnels leading off the cave's main chambers. From St. Michael's Cave, it's about a 20-minute walk to the **Apes' Den** where the famous Barbary Apes – a breed of monkey native to Morocco – are fed twice daily. In between feedings, they pass the time snatching purses and cameras from curious tourists.

The view from the Rock's summit is spectacular, looking across the Strait of Gibraltar to Africa. This lookout, as well as the Apes' Den and St. Michael's Cave, can all be reached by **cable car** from the town , where a tourist office is located in **Cathedral Square**. Local attractions include the Governor's Residence, the Law Courts, the Anglican cathedral and the Catholic cathedral. Main Street is lined with shops, pubs and restaurants. At the north end of town is the **Moorish Castle** , its Tower of Homage dating from 1333. At the south end of town, just past the harbour, is Rosia Bay. Following the Battle of Trafalgar in 1805, Nelson's flagship *Victory* was brought here and the dead on board were transferred to Trafalgar Cemetery at the south edge of town. Nelson's body was shipped back to England, preserved in a barrel of rum.

Shore Excursions

While it's fairly easy to explore **Gibraltar** on your own, taking a ship's shore excursion is an option. An historical tour, which includes a 45-minute guided walk through the siege tunnels (begun by the British in 1782) and a motorcoach ride to the Trafalgar Cemetery and Moorish Castle, takes about four hours. Other ship excursions worth considering include a two-hour boat ride across the Bay of Gibraltar where dolphins are frequently sighted, or a narrated driving tour of the major sights with a visit to the World War II tunnels (3.5 hrs).

FRANCE

French culture has been widely admired since the 13th century, when its language, poetry and manners were adopted as a model by the other courts of Europe. Today it's the food, the wine and the *joie de vivre* of the French that many of us admire. In a nation where dining is an art form, and where the arts are for all to enjoy, the many aspects of gracious living fall into fascinating perspective. Politics are important, but so is lunch. And for the average visitor to France, figuring out the lunch menu could well be easier than understanding the many departments, districts, cantons and communes of French government.

France has had a centralized administration since the Revolution of 1789, yet each region has retained its own distinct character. This diversity harks back to the Middle Ages when provinces were ruled by dukes and counts, and feudal power was held by nobles, guilds and the clergy.

France was first settled by Greek and Phoenician traders who landed on its Mediterranean coast in about 600 BC. Conquered by Julius Caesar in 58 BC, Gaul (as the Romans called it) was under Rome's rule for the next five centuries. Then, in 486 AD, the Franks – a Germanic tribe – routed the last Roman emperor of Gaul and the region soon lay in ruins. The only remnant of Roman civilization was the church, which also faced ruination when Saracens invaded in the 8th century.

The Carolingian dynasty, led by Pepin the Short, rescued the region. His son Charlemagne (Charles the Great) became a legendary figure. Crowned emperor of the West on Christmas Day in the year 800, Charlemagne ushered in an intellectual renaissance. A great leader and administrator, Charlemagne also promoted the rebirth of learning and the arts, and was immortalized in medieval poems as the champion of Christendom.

A thousand years later Napoleon drew on Charlemagne's example when forging his own empire, and his liberal reforms lay the groundwork for modern-day France. The glory days of empire are over for France, but the country's artistic and culinary culture remains the envy of the world.

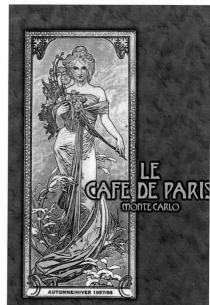

LE CAFE DE PARIS
MONTE-CARLO

AUTOMNE/HIVER 1997/98

France at a Glance

About 66 million people live in France, and Roman Catholicism is the major religion. French, spoken in a variety of regional dialects, is the major language, except in Corsica where an Italian dialect is spoken.

Some basic words to know in French: *bonjour* (hello), *au revoir* (good-bye) and, when asking for assistance, *pardonez mois* (pardon me), *parlez vous Anglais?* (do you speak English?) and *merci* (thank you). When ordering in a restaurant, begin with *s'il vous plait* (if you please).

The capital is Paris and the country is governed by a president (directly elected for a seven-year term) who appoints a premier and cabinet that are responsible to the national assembly. France is divided into 22 planning regions, two of which are covered in this chapter, namely Provence-Alpes-Côte d'Azur and Corsica.

France is an industrial nation and major economic power, yet more than half of its land area is still used for agriculture. Tourism is also a major industry, with France receiving more international tourists than any other country in the world.

The south of France, where cities, towns and fishing villages dot the Mediterranean coastline, is renowned for its scenic beauty and abundant sunshine. Cruise ships dock at the larger ports, such as Marseille, Toulon and Nice, but tendering is the only option at some of the smaller, picturesque ports of call such as Villefranche.

Travel Tips

Currency – The unit of currency is the euro and major credit cards are widely accepted, although some small businesses accept only cash. ATMs are plentiful and banks are generally open Monday through Friday, from 9 a.m. to 5:30 p.m.

Dining – Fresh herbs, grilled fish, olives, garlic and goat cheese are all featured in the local cuisine of southern France. Famous regional dishes include bouillabaisse (a fish stew) and salad niçoise, which features tuna, tomato, hard-boiled egg and anchovies.

The wines produced in the south of France include the famous white wine of Cassis. The grenache grape is used to make the fruity rosé wines for which Provence has a particularly good reputation.

Restaurants usually offer a *plat du jour* (menu of the day) featuring two or three courses at a set price, which is less expensive than ordering a la carte. Most restaurants include a 15% service charge in their prices. Opening times for lunch are usually noon to 2:30 p.m., and dinner is generally served from 7 p.m. to 11 p.m.

Opening Hours – Museums and historic attractions generally open in summer from 10 a.m. to 6 p.m. or later, often closing on Mondays or Tuesdays. Some shops are closed on Sundays and Monday mornings.

Shopping – The south of France is famous for its Provencal style of country decor, which is rustic and romantic, featuring cane beds, rush chairs and tapestry throws. Handcrafted items are created in earthy textures, such as wood, pewter and wrought iron, and local specialties include ceramic pots, hand-painted dishes and colourful table linens. Stores are generally open 9:30 a.m. to 7 p.m. When entering a shop, be sure to greet the proprietor before you start browsing or you'll be considered rude. It's also polite to say good-bye when leaving the premises.

Telephoning – France's country code is 33. To place a call to France, dial your country's exit code (011 in U.S. and Canada; 00 in UK) + 33 + area code (4 in SE France) + local number. To phone home from France, first dial 00 (International), then your country code (1 for U.S. and Canada; 44 for the UK), followed by the area code and local number.

A sidewalk café in
Aix-en-Provence.

The French Riviera

One by one they were drawn to the vivid colours and shimmering sunlight of the Côte D'Azur (Azure Coast). Renoir, Matisse, Picasso – these and other great figures of modern art have lived and worked along the French Riviera, a narrow coastal strip squeezed between the Alps and the Mediterranean Sea. Sheltered from winds and blessed with a mild year-round climate, it was only a matter of time until the entire world discovered the Riviera's natural beauty.

One of the first 'tourists' to the area was Lord Henry Brougham, a British baron who stopped for a night in December 1834 at a hostel in **Cannes**. Enchanted by the village's seaside setting, Lord Brougham decided to have a residence built there and two years later members of London's high society flocked to its opening.

The small fishing port of Cannes quickly became a gathering place for European aristocracy. Villas were built and the barren countryside was transformed when Lord Brougham built a canal to supply water to the town and irrigation for the lawns and gardens at the palatial estates.

A railroad line was built in the 1860s to provide access from Marseille to Cannes, Nice and

Not all visitors were titled. The recently rich and powerful of the Industrial Revolution celebrated their wealth with opulence and excess, as characterized by the Riviera's Belle Epoque hotels, such as the Victoria and Negresco in Nice. The architect of the Carlton, which opened in Cannes in 1911, reportedly modelled the hotel's two domes after the bosom of a famous courtesan.

In the 1920s the American writer F. Scott Fitzgerald began touting the Riviera as a summer resort and the idea quickly caught on. Panoramic highways, busy with summer traffic, now hug this scenic coastline where once only footpaths led to fortified towns set high in the hills.

(Above) Canne's Carlton Hotel. (Left) Flower market in Monaco. (Below) Vieux Port, Antibes

Monaco. High society of Europe and America journeyed to the Riviera each winter, including Tsar Alexander II and his wife, who arrived in Nice a week after the railroad opened in 1864.

Getting Around

The Côte d'Azur's famous resorts lie between **Saint Tropez** and **Monaco** (a distance of about 60 miles/ 96 kilometres), and are connected by roads and regular train or bus service. Cruise passengers arriving at a French Riviera port can visit one or two nearby resorts independently by train, taxi and/or bus. For exam-

ple, the train ride from Villefranche to Nice is only 15 minutes; Villefranche to Monaco is 20 minutes; and Villefranche to Cannes takes about an hour and costs about €8. There's no train station at Eze but the train does stop at Eze-Sur-Mer, from where it's a two-mile bus or taxi ride up to the village. Buses run regularly between Nice and Saint Paul de Vence (one-hour ride each way). Bus fare is usually €2.

Taxis are metered, with a start price of €8. Some approximate sample fares: Villefranche – Nice (6.5 km) = €18; Villefranche – Monaco (11 km) = €27; Villefranche – Cannes (40 km) = €90. Rental cars are also available, especially in Nice, but most are standard shift. The cost is approximately 90 to 120 euros per day, depending on the size of the vehicle. The coastal highway is especially scenic (and busy in summer) along the Corniche du Littoral between Nice and Monaco. There are no border restrictions upon entering Monaco, where the euro is the official currency.

Ports of Call

Saint-Tropez (pronounced *san-tro-pay*) is situated about 30 miles west of Cannes. A picturesque fishing port, it was made famous by film stars in the 1960s. The local Musee del'Annonciade, housed in a 17th-century church, contains works by Matisse, Dufy and others.

Cannes

Home to the illustrious international film festival, Cannes (pronounced *kon*) has long been subject to foreign invasions. Throughout the Middle Ages,

(Above) The Villefranche train station. (Below) A street scene in Monaco's La Condamine.

Shore Excursions

When visiting the **French Riviera**, a leisurely day spent exploring your ship's port of call is of course very appealing.

However, should you wish to visit one of the other Riviera resorts while you're there, this can be done **independently** (see 'Getting Around'). For example, if your ship stops at Villefranche, you could catch a morning train to Monaco/Monte Carlo and return on an afternoon train to stroll around Villefranche before heading back to the ship.

The same applies to the other French Riviera ports: take a train or taxi to a nearby resort in the morning, returning in the afternoon to explore your ship's port of call before reboarding the ship. Lunch can be enjoyed ashore anywhere along the French Riviera, where restaurants are plentiful and most are reasonably priced (menus are posted at the entrance).

Ship-organized shore excursions are another way to see several places along the French Riviera; cruise passengers can choose from a variety of scenic motorcoach drives along the Cote d'Azur with stops at famous beach resorts and medieval hilltop villages. Refer to your cruise line's shore excursions booklet or website for details.

Cannes experienced repeated raids by the Saracens, and by soldiers passing through on their way to battle. In the 5th century, Saint Honoratus founded a monastery on the offshore isle that bears his name. A fort was built on the neighbouring Ile Sainte-Marguerite where, in 1667, a man whose face was hidden behind a velvet mask was imprisoned. Immortalized by Voltaire and Alexandre Dumas, he became a mysterious figure of literature called The Man in the Iron Mask. His identity has long been open to speculation but he may have been a valet to Louis XIV who knew a scandalous secret about the French king.

On March 1st, 1815, Napoleon landed near Cannes when returning from exile on the island of Elba and, with a handful of followers, began his triumphant march northward to Paris. Two decades later, Lord Brougham began transforming Cannes into a holiday resort. The town's seaside path, called the Chemin de la Petite Croix after a small cross that marked the gathering spot for pilgrims to Ile Saint-Honorat, was gradually widened into a road. Today that same path is an upscale esplanade called the **Promenade de la Croisette**, its deluxe hotels and famous blue chairs looking out over a beautiful bay where the fine sand beaches are regularly cleaned by tractor-drawn machines and the water is hydraulically vacuumed.

Cannes held its first film festival in 1939, as an alternative to the Venice Film Festival, which had fallen under the control of the Fascists and Nazis. A 'steamship of stars' arrived that September from America – Gary Cooper, Douglas Fairbanks and Mae West were among its passengers. The festival opened under the presidency of Louis Lumiere, the inventor of cinema, only to be cancelled the next day when Germany invaded Poland. When the war ended, the festival was revived, its principles espoused in the words of writer, visual artist and filmmaker Jean Cocteau, who described the new festival as "a microcosm of what the world would be like if its inhabitants had direct contact with each other and they all spoke the same language."

Roberto Rosellini's *Open City* won the top prize among 44 international films entered in 1946 and the festival quickly became a social event. Financial difficulties, however, forced the Festival's cancellation in 1948 and 1950.

In 1951 the film festival was held in May instead of September so as not to conflict with the one held in Venice. In 1953 Brigitte Bardot appeared on the Croisette in a bikini, and in 1954 a starlet named Simone Silva bared her breasts for attentive photographers who wired the picture to newspapers around the world, dramatically increasing the festival's exposure and turning it into a major media event. The following year American actress Grace Kelly was invited to Cannes to help re-establish the artistic merit of the festival. At a press conference she met Prince Rainier of Monaco and a year later they

(Above) Ste. Maxime Beach, near St. Tropez. (Below) The beach and cruise port at Cannes.

were married at a lavish wedding held during the festival.

The Croisette Palace was eventually replaced with the **Palais des Festivals**, which was inaugurated in 1982 and is a venue for other festivals, as well as concerts, operas, recitals and ballet performances. The auditorium is named after the composer Claude Debussy, who, as a young boy learning to play the piano, would visit the home of his music teacher at the tip of the Croisette.

The most famous grand hotel on the Croisette is the Carlton. Scenes from Alfred Hitchcock's *To Catch a Thief*, starring Cary Grant and Grace Kelly, were shot at the Carlton – on the hotel's beach, in its gala room and outside the door of Suite 623.

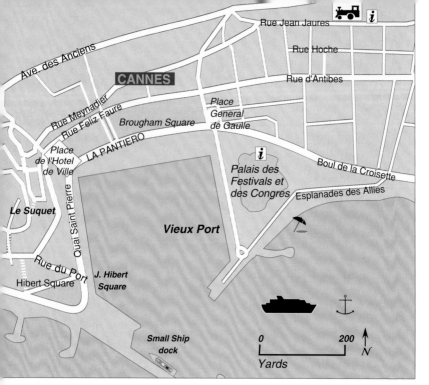

The Majestic, which opened in 1926, is a favourite rendezvous for film festival stars. Excellent **bistros** line the Croisette, and prestigious restaurants include La Cote in the Carlton, La Palme d'Or in the Martinez, and La Scala in the Noga Hilton.

Shopping streets abound, including the popular Rue Meynadier and the Rue d'Antibes. The historic heart of Cannes is **Le Suquet**, a hill mounted by winding alleys with marvellous views from the old watchtower. In addition to its restaurants and shops, attractions include the Sarrazine tower, the 17th-century church of Our Lady of Good Hope, a 12th-century chapel and the Castre museum. Regular boat tours to Ile Sainte-Marguerite are available in summer.

The highway leading north of Cannes to **Grasse** is called the Route Napoleon, for it traces the dirt track Napoleon took after landing near Cannes in 1815. The hilly countryside through which he trekked is now a prime flower-growing region and Grasse is the centre of the French perfume industry. In addition to its numerous perfume factories, Grasse attractions include an early Gothic cathedral, a town hall partially built in the Middle Ages, and a museum containing paintings by Jean-Honore Fragonard who was born in Grasse.

The fortified seaport of **Antibes** (*an-teeb*) is another centre of this famous flower-growing region. The Grimaldi chateau, built in the 14th century, houses a museum containing numerous works of Picasso, who stayed here for a few months in 1946. Fort Carre,

(Right) Cannes viewed from Le Suquet. (Below) The cobblestone lanes of St. Paul de Vence.

built in the 16th century, over-looks Vieux Port. Nearby Cap D'Antibes is a fashionable resort.

The walled town of **St. Paul de Vence**, set in the hills above the Bay of Angels, is protected by 16th-century ramparts, and can be explored on foot along its wind-ing cobblestone lanes. Near the town entrance lies a park and museum, Fondation Maeght, built in 1964 by a Paris art dealer. It houses an array of modern sculp-ture and paintings.

Nice

Nice (pronounced *nees*), with a population of 350,000, is the major city of the French Riviera. Founded as a Greek colony (Nicea in Latin) in the 5th century BC, the city has endured numerous attacks over the centuries – from pillaging by Saracens in the 9th century to occupation by Mussolini during World War II. At the beginning of the French Revolution in 1789, Nice was a haven for Royalists. Annexed to France in 1793, Nice was restored to Sardinia in 1814, then again ceded to France in 1860. Nice became known as the Queen of the Riviera when the British aristocracy began arriving on winter sojourns.

A **Tourist Office** is annexed to the Nice train station, where detailed walking maps are avail-able. The city's trams and buses are a good option should you get tired of walking. **Avenue Jean Medecin**, a busy **shopping** thor-oughfare, leads from the train sta-tion to **Place Massena**, the city's main square, where gardens lie on either side.

Nice is a treasure trove of art museums, including the **Musee Chagall 1** on Boulevard de Cimiez, which houses a collec-

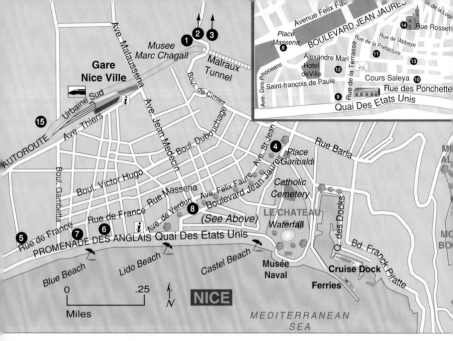

tion of 20th-century religious works by the Russian painter Marc Chagall. **Musee Matisse 2** (at the top of Nice's Boulevard Cimiez) houses the personal collection of Henri Matisse in a 17th-century Genoese villa surrounded by gardens and set amid Roman ruins. Nearby is the **Franciscan Monastery and Museum 3**, with a reconstructed chapel and monk's cell.

The four gray marble towers of the **Musee D'Art Moderne 4**, on the north side of the Old Town, contain an outstanding collection of works by avant-garde artists from the 1960s to present day.

West of the **Old Town**, a few blocks off the Anglais Promenade, is the **Musee Des Beaux-Arts 5**, housed in a late 19th-century mansion built for a Russian princess. Its fine art collection includes paintings by Renoir, Degas and Monet, and ceramics by Picasso. The **Musee D'Art et D'Histoire 6**, with exhibits

focusing on the Napoleonic era and the life of locally born general Andre Massena, is housed in the sumptuous Palais Massena, set on grounds overlooking the **Anglais Promenade**.

The Anglais Promenade traces the curving shoreline of the **Baie des Anges** (Bay of Angels), past Nice's fine pebble beach. Originally a wide path, this broad boulevard of flower beds and palm trees was begun by an Englishman in 1820 and inaugurated in its final form in 1931 by the Duke of Connaught, a son of Queen Victoria. The Queen herself also visited Nice, staying at the luxurious Hotel Victoria. The **Negresco 7**, another palatial hotel of the Belle Epoque, was built in 1912 by an eccentric Romanian named Henry Negresco.

From **Place Massena 8** the waterfront promenade leads past the **Opera House 9**, built in 1885, to the main entrance of Nice's charming Old Town, which

is a maze of narrow pedestrian streets, open-air markets, public squares and outdoor cafés. **Cours Saleya** 10 is the scene of Nice's famous flower market – a daily event except on Mondays when a flea market, complete with antique dealers, takes over this bustling strip. Two streets over, on Rue de la Prefecture, is the former **Royal Palace** 11, built in the early 17th century to accommodate the visiting Princes of Savoy. A fine 16th century house is located at No. 18, Rue de la Prefecture.

(Above and right) The beautiful buildings of Old Nice. (Below) A beach at Nice. (Bottom) Nice's cruise ship harbour,

There are numerous churches to admire in the Old Town, including the 18th-century **Eglise St-Francois-de-Paule** 12, and the 17th-century **Eglise St-Giaume** 13. **La Cathedrale Sainte-Reparate** 14 built in the 17th century to honour the town's patron saint, overlooks **Place Rosetti** – the centre of Old Nice, with outdoor restaurants and ice-cream parlours.

Rue Rosetti leads from the square and winds up the hillside to **Le Chateau** – a hilltop park with an artificial waterfall overlooking Nice. More panoramic views can be enjoyed west of the Old Town, atop **Mont Alban**, with its 16th-century bastions and

Place Rosetti, Old Nice

Villefranche

Villefranche, perfectly situated in between Nice and Monaco, is one of the most picturesque ports in the Mediterranean. It's an authentic fishing village surrounded by the glamour of the French Riviera. The beautiful Bay of Villefranche lies between Cap Nice and Cap Ferrat – this latter point of land being an enclave of opulent villas owned by some of the world's wealthiest. The Rolling Stones' famous *Exile on Main Street* album was recorded at a Belle Epoque villa (Nellcôte) on the east side of the bay in 1971.

watchtowers, and from **Mont Boron** where the hillside homes include Chateau de L'Anglais, a pink-colored Scottish manor. Other unexpected sights in Nice include the onion-shaped cupolas of the **Russian Orthodox Church** **15** located a few blocks west of the train station.

Ships anchor outside the small harbour and tender passengers ashore. A tourist information office is located in the small terminal at the head of the harbour. The train station is a 10-minute walk from the harbour along Quai Courbet and up some stairs.

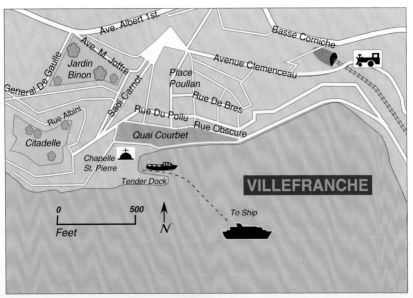

Beside the tourist office is the 14th-century **Chapelle St Pierre** (see photo on page 101) which was restored and redecorated in 1957 by artist and filmmaker Jean Cocteau, a leader of the French avant-garde movement. The nearby **Citadelle** was built by the Duke of Savoy in 1560 and now contains the town hall, museums and gardens.

Monaco

An independent principality and coastal enclave within France, Monaco is less than a square mile in size. It is easily walkable (from both the cruise port and the train station). Public elevators are strategically situated to help people ascend some of the steep streets, including one that takes you up to the Oceanographic Museum where the Azur Express Tourist Train departs every half hour on sightseeing circuits of Monaco-Ville and Place du Casino in Monte Carlo. The local buses, which are clean and efficient, follow five regular routes and an all-day pass can be purchased.

(Above) Villefranche's colourful waterfront and medieval citadel.

A bus boat connects the cruise dock area with Quai Kennedy in Monte Carlo; tickets (€2 per crossing) can be purchased on board and it takes five minutes to cross the harbour. The two main taxi stands are at the railway station and near the Casino.

The tiny kingdom of Monaco has been ruled by the Grimaldi dynasty since the 13th century, when a Genoese family first

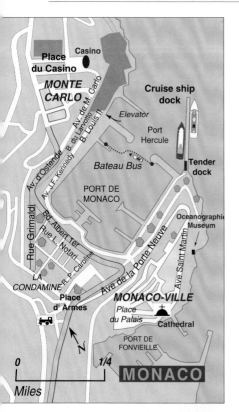

seized control of the fortified medieval town. When the family's male line died out, a French successor by marriage assumed the name Grimaldi. In 1861 the principality was returned to France and until 1911 the prince of Monaco was an absolute ruler. A 1918 treaty stipulated the French government must approve the succession to the throne and, should it become vacant, the principality becomes an autonomous state under French protection.

Monaco consists of several sections. The business district, called **La Condamine**, is where the train station is located. This area is a pleasing mix of open-air markets and residential streets leading to the harbour. La Condamine is flanked on its northeast side by **Monte Carlo**, site of the famous casino, and on its southeast side by **Monaco Ville**, the capital, which is set upon a rocky promontory. Avenue de la Porte Neuve leads off Place D'Armes up to **Place du Palais**, where Monaco's reigning prince resides in a grand Italianate palace. A changing of the guard takes place at the palace entrance every day at five minutes before noon. One wing of the palace, which contains the Musee Napoleon and royal apartments, is open to visitors.

In 1956 Prince Rainier married the American film star Grace Kelly. She arrived for their fairytale wedding on board the *Constitution* and the famous couple were married in Monaco's neo-Romanesque **cathedral**, built

Monaco's neo-Romanesque cathedral.

in 1874 to replace the 13th-century Church of St. Nicholas. The cathedral is also the burial place of Princess Grace (Gratia Patricia on her tombstone) who died in a tragic automobile accident in 1982.

Upon his death in 2005, Rainier III was succeeded by his son Albert who, like his father, governs with the assistance of a minister of state, a cabinet and the National Council, which is elected every five years.

Avenue Saint Martin leads from the cathedral to the **Oceanographic Museum**, which was founded by Rainier's great-grandfather in 1910. The underwater explorer and filmmaker Jacques Cousteau was the former head of this important research institute.

Monte Carlo's famous **casino** opened in 1858, was briefly controlled in 1954 by Aristotle Onassis, and is now overseen by Monaco's Societe de Bains de Mer (SBM). Somerset Maugham once described Monaco as "a sunny place for shady people" and by the 1960s Monaco had become such a tax haven for French citizens that the government of France insisted a new

(Above) Port Hercule, Monaco. (Below) A sentry at Place du Palais, Monaco-Ville (bottom).

Monte Carlo's Place du Casino (Below) Street in Monaco-Ville.

constitution be created for the principality. Less than a quarter of Monaco's 38,000 residents are citizens (Monegasques) and they are not admitted to the gambling casino; neither are visitors wearing shorts or flip flops. The entrance fee is €10, photo ID is required, minimum age is 18 and all hand bags are checked. The casino is open in the morning for tours, but daily admission to the table games and slot machines is from 2 p.m. until the last table closes. The casino complex, a dazzling display of gold-leaf and gilt, includes an opera house and private gaming rooms.

The Casino overlooks the gardens of Place du Casino, as does the palatial Hotel de Paris, where Alain Ducasse's **Louis XV** restaurant enjoys a three-star Michelin rating. On the opposite side of Place du Casino is the historic **Café de Paris**, a good spot to have lunch at affordable prices.

PROVENCE

Inspired by its luminous land-scapes and sun-soaked colours, the Dutch painter **Vincent Van Gogh** called Provence a 'king-dom of light.' This is a land of white limestone cliffs and cobalt blue skies, of yellow sunflowers and ochre earth. The Rhone flows across Provence's western plain, its flat river delta lying in contrast to the rolling hills and mountain ridges which rise in the east and stretch northward from the Mediterranean coast to the French Alps. The countryside is clothed in vineyards and dotted with medieval villages, their winding streets too narrow for cars, their weathered stone houses adorned with painted shutters and window boxes filled with flowers.

The Romans marched through this landscape and made it a prov-ince of Rome in the 2nd century BC. They built roads and bridges, amphitheatres and public baths. By the 4th century AD, the region had become a haven for Christian monasteries.

A courtyard in Aix-en-Provence.

The Middle Ages brought inva-sions by the Visigoths, Franks and Arabs. In 879 the Count of Arles gained control of the region and Provence became part of the Kingdom of Arles. For much of the 14th century, the seat of the Pope was located in **Avignon**, on the banks of the Rhone, where a beautiful papal palace was built and fine wines were produced at the village of Chateauneuf-du-Pape. In 1481 Provence was bequeathed to the French crown.

Flowers, fruits and vegetables all flourish in the fertile Rhone valley, and when Van Gogh arrived at **Arles** from Paris in 1888, he came in search of sensu-al beauty. Both he and **Paul Gauguin** had rejected industrial society and were drawn to the pastoral life of Provence. Yet, the two artists found little peace at Van Gogh's house in Arles where they engaged in heated quarrels.

Gauguin left Provence, but Van Gogh remained in Arles, painting his famous series of sunflowers as well as *The Night Café*. He was eventually confined in the Arles Hospital, and later in the asylum at Saint-Remy where in 1889 he painted *Starry Night*.

Meanwhile, **Paul Cezanne** was living outside **Aix-en-Provence**. Discouraged by ridicule from the critics, he too had fled Paris and the industrial north, returning to his place of birth. Working in seclusion, Cezanne developed his own style while repeatedly painting the craggy peak of Mont Ste-Victoire. Both he and Van Gogh painted numerous scenes of the countryside, yet the nearby Mediterranean Sea was a perva-

sive presence. In Van Gogh's *Wheat Field and Cypress Trees*, the fields resemble a stormy sea and the hills rise like waves into a turbulent sky of swirling clouds.

Marseille

The Ancient Greeks landed on the shores of Provence in 600 BC. Arriving from Asia Minor, they established a colony called Massalia, which the French now call Marseille, and this thriving seaport soon dominated the Mediterranean coast for miles in either direction. It was incorporated into the Kingdom of France in 1481, growing steadily until the start of the French Revolution in 1789.

The Revolution's battle hymn originated in Marseille, where volunteer fighters marched to the army song *La Marseillaise*. Marseille's maritime commerce suffered during the long Napoleonic wars but prosperity returned with the French conquest of Algeria and the opening of the Suez Canal in 1869.

Today Marseille is one of the world's great seaports, its commerce fed by the rich hinterlands of Provence, and is connected with Arles and the Rhone Valley by a canal. Marsaille is the oldest city in France and, at 850,000, the country's second largest with a substantial immigrant popula-

(Left) The Night Café by Van Gogh. (Right) Marseille's city hall.

tion. Marsaille's seamy side was captured in the 1971 crime thriller film *The French Connection.*

Situated on the Gulf of Lions, Marseille overlooks several islands, including a small rocky islet upon which the **Chateau d'If** was built in 1524 and used as a state prison, made famous by Alexandre Dumas's novel, *The Count of Monte Cristo.*

Getting Around

The cruise ships dock north of the city centre. Small ships dock close in at the Joliette piers (J4 Terminal) and large ships dock at the Mole Léon Gourret (Gate 4), which is 2.5 miles (4 km) from Vieux Port. Most ships offer a shuttle service (about €8 each way) to Vieux Port with a drop-off near City Hall. Bus 35 can be taken from Gate 4 to Place de la Joliette but it's a half-mile walk from your ship to Gate 4 (following the green line) if your ship is docked at the far end of the jetty.

Taxis are available for hire at the large-ship pier; sample metered fares: €15 to Gare Saint Charles; €23 to Notre-Dame de la Garde.

Notre-Dame can be reached by bus from the head of Vieux Port or by tourist train (boarded near City Hall) or on foot – it's a quarter-mile hike up the hillside from Abbey St. Victor. One option is to take a taxi from your ship to Notre-Dame, spend some time at the church, then walk back down the hillside to explore Vieux Port.

Shuttle boats run regularly from the head of Vieux Port to Chateau d'If (a 20-minute ride). Note: Admission fee to Chateau d'If (which is closed on Mondays except during school holidays) is not included in the boat ticket. Also departing from the harbour's head are boat tours (3.5 hrs) of the Calanques coastline lying between Marsaille and the seaside village of Cassis where white-limestone sea cliffs rise above narrow inlets.

Trains and buses run regularly from Marseille to other Provencal cities and towns. First-time visi-

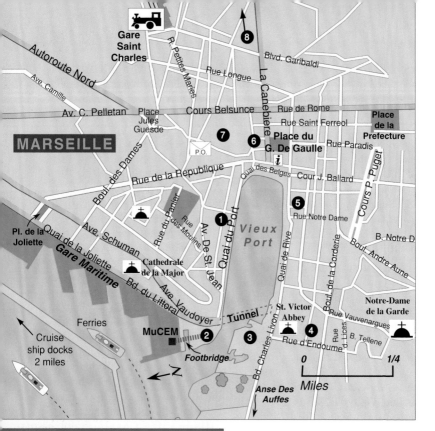

MARSEILLE

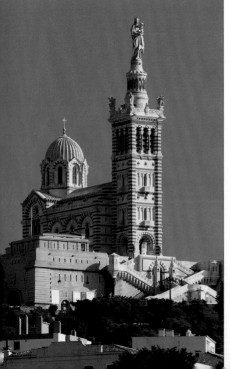

tors should consider taking the bus or train to lovely Aix-en-Provence, where numerous attractions and inviting restaurants are within walking distance of the bus and train stations. The train departs from Marseille's St. Charles station (be sure to buy a ticket for Aix Centre, <u>not</u> Aix TGV). The express bus to Aix, which costs about €4, departs every 10 minutes (more frequently than the train) and the drive takes about 40 minutes, as does the train ride. Whether you arrive at the Gare Routier bus station in Aix, or at the nearby train station on Avenue Maurice Blondel, it's a short walk into the city centre.

Notre Dame de la Garde overlooks Marseille's Old Port.

Marseille Attractions

Busy and brash, Marseille is first and foremost a port city, its historic heart residing in Vieux Port – a harbour filled with fishing boats and sailing yachts. The Tourism Office is located at the head of the harbour and the 17th-century **Hotel de Ville (City Hall)** ▮1 stands on its north side.

The medieval Abbey of St Victor.

Fort Saint-Jean ▮2 and Bas **Fort Saint-Nicolas** ▮3 guard the harbour entrance, which can be traversed by an underwater tunnel. Access is free to the battlements of Fort Sain-Jean, which is connected by a footbridge to the Museum of European and Mediterranean Civilizations (MuCEM), a national museum inaugurated in 2013.

Nearby is the city's Cathédrale de la Major (Nouvelle Major), which stands on a site occupied since the 5th century. A national monument, this 19th-century cathedral was built in the Byzantine and Romanesque architectural styles. Alongside the new cathedral are remains of the old 12-century cathedral (Vieille Major).

On the harbour's south side is the **Abbey of St. Victor** ▮4, founded in the 5th century (as evidenced by ruins in its crypts). The church's door (c.1140) is one of the oldest in France.

The basilica of **Notre-Dame de la Garde** stands on a ridge overlooking the harbour, its bellfry surmounted by a gilded statue of the Madonna and Child. Built on the foundations of an ancient fort and consecrated in 1864, this neo-Byzantine church is the site of an annual pilgrimage on Assumption Day (August 15).

Shore Excursions

Marseille Ship-organized excursions include city tours of Marseille and day trips to other parts of Provence, such as **Les Baux**, a medieval town carved out of white limestone atop a huge plateau, its Citadelle providing panoramic views of the valley below. Another interesting stop is **Arles**, its Roman remains including a theatre and an arena built in the 2nd century AD, that provided seating for 26,000 spectators and is now used for staging bullfights. **Avignon** is also covered by ship shore excursions, as is **Aix-en-Provence** (see pg 171). Some cruise lines offer excursions to **Cassis**, a fishing port and summer resort stunningly situated at the base of Europe's highest cliff – the 1,300-foot **Cap Canaille**. For detail, consult your cruise line's website or shore excursion booklet provided upon boarding.

(Above) Place d'Albertas in Aix-en-Provence. (Below) Flower market at Place de L'Hotel de Ville in Aix.

Also on the harbour's south side is the **Place Thiars** 5 pedestrian zone, an inviting neighbourhood of outdoor cafés. La Samaritaine at the harbour's head is a bar and coffee shop which appeared in *The French Connection*, as did several streets in Quartier du Panier. Another scene from the movie was shot at the seafood restaurant Chez Fonfon, famous for its bouillabaisse, which is located on the waterfront at Anse des Auffes (about 1 km west of St. Victor Abbey).

The city's main avenue, running eastward from the harbour, is Rue Canebiere – named for the old ropewalks that used to operate along its length. On Rue Canebiere's north side, housed in the **Palais de la Bourse** 6, is the city's maritime museum. Behind this large white building is the **Jardin des Vestiges** 7, a public park containing Greek ruins and a small museum housing a 60-foot Roman boat.

Leading south from Rue Canebiere are the fashionable **shopping streets** of Rue Paradis, Rue Saint Ferreol, Rue de Rome and Boulevard Garibaldi. Boulevard d'Athenes, leading off the north side of Rue Cannebiere, is a direct route to the bus station and train station (Gare Saint-Charles). A half-mile east of the train station at the top of Longchamp Boulevard is **Palais de Longchamp** 8 – a 19th-century palace adorned with fountains and gardens, now housing an art gallery and museum.

Cathedral of Saint-Sauveur

Aix en Provence

The capital of Provence since the 12th century, Aix was founded in 123 BC by the Romans near the site of some mineral springs. A popular spa town, its university was founded in 1409, after which Aix became a centre of literature and music, and a sojourn for painters. Students make up nearly a quarter of its population of 160,000, and the town's main attractions are easily explored on foot.

Avenue des Belges leads from the Gare Routiere bus station and Avenue Victor Hugo leads from the train station to Place Gal De Gaulle, where the local tourist office overlooks **La Rotonde**, a huge traffic circle with a fountain in its centre. Leading eastward off La Rotonde is **Cours Mirabeau**, the town's main avenue. On its south side are streets lined with 18th-century baroque mansions; on its north side are narrow medieval streets with shops, cafés and various attractions, such as **Place d'Albertas** **1** where you can admire the sculpted facade of the Hotel d'Albertas (1707), and the nearby Hotel Boyer d'Eguilles (1675), which now houses the Museum d'Histoire Naturelle. City hall and a 16th-century belfry overlook the square at **Place de l'Hotel de Ville** **2** where a bustling flower and produce market is held several mornings each week

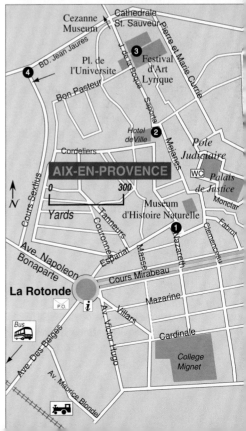

Other places of interest include the 13th-century **Cathedral of Saint-Sauveur** ▮3▮; and the formal French gardens and 17th-century mansion at **Vendome Pavilion** ▮4▮.

While strolling the streets of Aix you will notice bronze studs on the pavement stamped with the letter 'C' – these symbolize the footsteps of **Cezanne** and mark historic places associated with the great artist (a brochure is available at the Tourist Office). His studio, located off avenue Pasteur on avenue Paul-Cezanne, has been preserved as the Musee-Atelier de Paul Cezanne.

Toulon

The most sheltered port in the French Mediterranean and an important naval base, Toulon has two docking areas – the downtown pier and La Seyne pier, which is 10 minutes to Toulon by shuttle boat. Located 30 miles (48 km) east of Marseille, Toulon is a port of access to the attractions of Provence. Marseille is about an hour away by train and an hour and fifteen minutes by motor vehicle. Shore excursions include a scenic drive and walking tour of Aix en Provence (5 hours), and a drive to the medieval hilltop village of Castellet and the port of Sanary Sur Mer (4 hours). The fishing village of Cassis is a 1.5-hour drive from Toulon.

Seté

The scenic fishing port of Seté, with canals crisscrossing its lower town, is situated in the Languedoc region of southern France. The region's name derives from a medieval dialect – langue d'oc – that was spoken throughout the south of France back when the counts of Toulouse ruled this former Roman province, their brilliant court a centre of literature that attracted troubadours.

Seté is a port of access to the nearby medieval cities of Carcassonne and **Montpellier**, the latter's old quarter of winding streets and squares dating to the 8th century. Montpellier's famous university was founded in the 13th century, and outside the city are country chateaux overlooking estate wineries.

Carcassonne is home to an impressive hill-top fortress, considered one of Europe's architectural marvels. The hill was fortified by the Romans in the 1st century BC and the towers (still intact) were built in the 6th century, with fortifications added by the viscounts of Carcassonne in the 12th century. The ramparts had fallen into disrepair when restored in the 1800s.

Corsica

Described by Balzac as a "French island basking in the Italian sun," the mountainous and sparsely populated island of Corsica was known to sailors as the Scented Isle for the fragrance of its wildflowers wafting out to sea. Much of the island is wild, the ground covered with an undergrowth of flowers called Maquis. Corsica is also referred to as 'the mountain in the sea' with snow-covered summits exceeding 6,000 feet and Monte Cintu approaching 9,000 feet.

The Romans first set sail for

Corsica in the 3rd century BC. Their rule ended in the 5th century AD, and throughout the ensuing centuries the island changed hands numerous times. By the mid-15th century the island was under Genoese control and the port city of **Ajaccio** was established in 1492. But public unrest, fueled by the harsh and unpopular Genoese rulers, led to rebellions and often bloodshed.

Genoa finally sold Corsica to France in 1768. The Corsican rebel leader and president, Pasquale Paoli, was soon defeated by the French and fled to England where his friend James Boswell introduced him into the circle of Samuel Johnson. The outbreak of the French Revolution brought Paoli back to Corsica,

A pedestrian street in medieval Bonifacio, Corsica.

(Above) The town of Piana overlooks Corsica's scenic west coast. (Right page bottom) Bonifacio began as a clifftop citadel guarding the harbour.

Shore Excursions

Corsica ship-organized excursions vary, depending on which port your ship pulls into. Generally speaking, these include scenic drives to various sites around the island, such as the Calanches, the megalithic ruins at Filitosa, the ancient Greek village of Cargese and the medieval village of Sartene. One or two places are visited on a 4-hour tour, such as the Prunelli Gorges and the artificial lake of Tolla, which provides hydroelectric power to the island. Longer, 8-hour tours include lunch. Walking tours of Ajaccio and Bonifacio are each about 3 hours, as is a visit to the European Tortoises Protection Center, created in 1985 and home to over 150 species of turtles and tortoises.

where he served as governor until accused of counter-revolutionary activities and summoned to Paris in 1793. Paoli drew on British support to expel the French from Corsica, but within a few years the island was recovered by the French under Napoleon.

World War II brought more invasions, this time by Italian and German troops, who were expelled in 1943. A post-war exodus prompted the French government to stimulate economic development, but the island's separatist sentiment carried on into the 1970s and '80s with occasional bombings and protests.

Attractions in Ajaccio, the capital, include the Maison Bonaparte, where Napoleon was born and raised; the Salon Napoleonien (in the Hotel de Ville), which displays memorabilia of the emperor; and the Musee d'Histoire de la Corse, with exhibits on Corsica's military history. The 16th-century cathedral contains the marble font

THE BONAPARTES

Napoleon's father, Carlo Bonaparte, was a nobleman and lawyer who lived with his wife and large family in Ajaccio and sent his sons to be educated in France. Initially a supporter of the Corsican patriot Pasquale Paoli, Bonaparte changed sides in 1769 and became a leader of the pro-French party in Corsica. When civil war broke out in 1793, Carlo and his family were condemned for opposing Corsican independence and they fled the island. Upon becoming emperor of France, Napoleon named his brothers and sisters as titled heads of Europe and arranged politically advantageous marriages for them. But his siblings resisted many of Napoleon's wishes and resented being left out of the line of succession, their bitterness fostering ongoing scenarios of intrigue, exile and reconciliation.

Napoleon Bonaparte

used for Napoleon's baptism. The Fesch Museum displays works by Botticelli, Veronese and Titiano.

North of Ajaccio, near the coastal towns of **Porto** and **Piana**, is the UNESCO-protected site of the **Calanches**, which takes its name from *calanca* – the Corsican word for inlet. Unusual patterns of erosion here have created fantastic cliffs and pinnacles of red granite rock. Hour-long boat excursions depart daily from Porto to view the Calanches, and cost about 18 euros. North of Piana is the small tendering port of **Calvi**, which is a popular beach resort.

Bonifacio, the oldest town of Corsica, is medieval in character. Founded in 828 on the site of a citadel built by Boniface I, Count of Tuscany, the town is situated atop a limestone cliff overlooking the harbour, and is surrounded by a rampart complete with drawbridge. The 12th-century Pisan-style church dates from Pisa's ownership of Corsica before losing the island to Genoa. The coast of Sardinia lies just seven miles across the Strait of Bonifacio.

NORTHERN ITALY

Italy lies in the heart of the Mediterranean. The north of the country is rooted in Europe while its southern shores stretch, like a bridge, toward the coast of Africa. Many an ancient mariner has landed on Italy's shores, and the eventual rise of Rome turned the Mediterranean into a Roman lake which they called Mare Nostrum (our sea).

When Rome fell, the northern cities of Genoa, Pisa and Venice emerged as great sea powers and rival city-states. Then came the Italian Renaissance, born in Florence in the early 1400s, and beauty became the byword of Italy. Glorious churches, grand palaces and landscaped gardens were built. Marble fountains and statues soon adorned the squares, and a sense of style became an Italian birthright.

The outpouring of artistry that began with the Renaissance spilled over into all areas of Italian life. Opera flourished in the 19th century, followed by film making and high fashion in the 20th century.

The country's creative force, fuelled throughout the centuries by political turmoil and military conflicts, has been described by the art historian Bernard Berenson as "the intensification of life." Visitors come to Italy to see the ancient ruins and famous works of art, and soon find all of their senses awakened. While pausing to enjoy a glass of Chianti wine or a freshly brewed espresso, they find themselves listening to animated conversations spoken in a language that rolls eloquently off the tongue, and they begin to notice the touches of beauty around them – whether it's a flower box beneath a baroque window or the pleasing arrangement of umbrella tables at an outdoor café. This sense of living each moment in a state of beauty, this is the Italian style.

Italy at a Glance

About 60 million people live in Italy, and the faith of the majority is Roman Catholic, the state religion. Italian, spoken in regional dialects, is the major language and English is widely understood. The country, proclaimed a republic in 1946, consists of twenty diverse regions which were unified in 1870. Vatican City and San Marino are independent enclaves.

Bernini fountain in St. Peter's Square

The industrial north has always been more prosperous than the agricultural south which, for centuries, languished under French and Spanish rule. Much of Italy is mountainous or hilly and the country's combination of striking scenery, mild climate, ancient ruins, artistic treasures and a vibrant culture makes it one of the world's most popular tourist destinations.

Travel Tips

Currency – The unit of currency is the euro. American currency is widely accepted but local currency is needed for trains, buses, casual dining, museums and other tourist attractions. Most shops and formal restaurants accept credit cards.

Dining – Delicious, bountiful meals are enjoyed throughout Italy, with some regional variations. Risotto and cream sauces are popular in the north, while the south offers spicier foods. Rome's native rustic cuisine has been influenced by other regions, but classic Roman dishes include spaghetti carbonara and trippa (tripe). Tuscan and Sicilian restaurants are known for their multi-course meals which begin with an antipasto such as bruschetta, which is grilled bread rubbed with garlic and topped with tomato salad or prosciutto (a dry-cured, thinly sliced ham). Granita is a refreshing fruit-flavoured, semi-frozen dessert which originated in Sicily but is now enjoyed throughout Italy, especially in summer.

Italy is famous for its coffee culture, and there are a few rules of etiquette involved in ordering a coffee, which is served black in small cups with sugar provided. If you want milk in your coffee, order a cappuccino – but only in the morning, unless you want to look like a tourist. The Americano is a watered-down espresso that was developed for American soldiers stationed in Italy during WWII and is considered too weak by most Italians' standards. Because Italians drink their coffee in a bar and not while walking the streets, visitors shouldn't expect to order a large cup to go.

Bars are open all day and serve pastries, alcoholic drinks and small sandwiches in addition to coffee. There is a service charge for sitting at a table, which is why patrons often stand at the bar.

Other casual eateries are a *panineria* (sandwich bar), *pizzeria* (specializing in pizza) and *gelateria* (ice-cream parlour). A *trattoria* is an informal restaurant while a *ristorante* offers formal, unhurried dining.

A trattoria in Venice.

Opening Hours – Museums, galleries and historic sites are often closed on Monday, sometimes Tuesday, but this can vary. Daily hours are generally 9 a.m. to 1:30 p.m., although some stay open longer. Most churches are open daily for non-religious visits from 10 a.m. to 5 p.m. except on Sunday, when the public is welcome in the afternoon.

Shopping – Stores are generally open 9 a.m. to 1 p.m. and 4 p.m. to 8 p.m. Many stay open late on Saturday evening, and are closed on Sunday and Monday morning. Stores catering to tourists will usually stay open all day, every day. Bartering is acceptable only at open-air markets, and these are often closed on Sunday.

Taxi fares – Taxi tariffs are set by local authorities and vary from city to city. The average start charge is €4 plus €1 to €2 per kilometre. Rounding up to the nearest euro instead of tipping is common for metered rides. The hourly rate is about €30.

Telephone – Italy's country code is 39. City codes include 06 for Rome, 055 for Florence, 041 for Venice.

Genoa

Italy's chief seaport, Genoa is one of the busiest in the western Mediterranean with its fine natural harbour and modern port facilities. Historic attractions are concentrated in the city centre, and can be **explored independently** on foot. The nearby **Italian Riviera** ports of Camogli, San Fruttuoso and Portofino can be reached by **mini-cruises** from Genoa's harbour.

Shopping & Dining – Via XX Settembre and Via Luccoli are two of Genoa's most exclusive shopping streets. Via Orefici is lined with goldsmiths, and the market in Piazza Banchi is a good place to buy leather, silver and ceramic handicrafts.

Genoa is the place to sample pesto (served with pasta) and freshly baked focaccia, which is sold at walk-in shops like the one on Via Canneto il Curto leading to the Cathedral of San Lorenzo. A good lunch spot is the Garibaldi café, in a tiny alleyway off Via Garibaldi.

Piazza De Ferrari in Genoa's historic city centre.

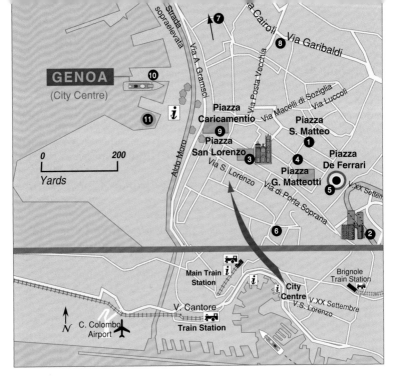

A seaport since ancient times, Genoa built a powerful navy that drove the Arabs from Corsica and Sardinia in the 10th century. The city's wealth and power grew, and it became known as *La Superba* (The Proud). In the early 1500s the naval hero **Andrea Doria** established his family as rulers of Genoa. The family home is located in **Piazza San Matteo** **1** and his tomb is in the church of San Matteo, which dates from the 12th century.

Shore Excursions

Genoa ship excursions include walking tours of the city (3-4 hrs), a tour of the art galleries housed in elegant palazzi along Via Garibaldi, a boat or coach tour to Portofino (4-5 hrs) and a harbour cruise and visit to the Aquarium of Genoa (4 hrs). A motorcoach tour to Milan is about 10 hours.

The other famous mariner associated with Genoa is **Christopher Columbus**. Born Cristoforo Colombo in 1451 to a family of wool weavers, he grew up illiterate and helped his father at the loom before heading to sea as a young lad. He served as a seaman in the Mediterranean but his ambitions would eventually take him far away from his childhood home which stands at the base of **Porta Soprana** **2**. This 12-century gate, built as a defensive rampart, stands at the old entrance to the Roman road that led through Genoa.

Other historic highlights in Genoa's medieval section of steep, narrow alleys (called *caruggi*) are the 12th-century **Cathedral of San Lorenzo** **3**, built of black and white marble, and the nearby **Palazzo Ducale** **4**, built in the 16th century. The Teatro Carlo Felice and Academy of Fine Arts overlook **Piazza De Ferrari** **5**.

Churches of note include **San Donato** [6], a 12th-century Romanesque building, and the 16th-century baroque church of the **Santissima Annunziata** [7].

Via Garibaldi is lined with Renaissance palaces built by Genoese nobility, their frescoed rooms now housing several art galleries, including the collection in **Palazzo Rosso (Red Palace)** [8], which displays works by Titian, Veronese, Rubens and the Flemish painter Van Dyck, who once lived there.

Palazzo San Giorgio [9], overlooking the harbour and now housing the Genoa Port Authority, was built in part with masonry taken from Venice. When 7,000 Venetians were captured at the naval battle of Curzola in 1298, among them was Marco Polo, who dictated his book *Il Milion* while a prisoner in this palace.

A large and modern **aquarium** [10] is located on the harbour, along with the **Bigo elevator** – a lift which takes visitors to the top of a mast-like structure for great views of this seafaring city. These contemporary works were erected to celebrate the 1992 Columbus Quincentennial and were designed by Renzo Piano, who was born and raised in Genoa

Italian Riviera

The Italian Riviera, extending from **La Spezia** to the French border, is an international playground of fashionable resorts, hotels and villas. It was once a secluded coast of craggy coves and tree-clad hillsides where medieval monasteries and tiny fishing ports – their colourful houses built by fishermen and lace makers – led a quiet existence. Today these hidden harbours are among the most picturesque ports of the Riviera.

Best known is **Portofino**, where summer villas, tucked among the umbrella pine and cypress trees, overlook a harbour filled with luxury yachts at the height of the season. The small cruise ships pull right into port, but the larger ships anchor out in the bay and tender their passengers ashore. A haunt of the rich and famous, Portofino is notoriously expensive, but a very pleasant place to stroll and soak up the atmosphere.

Portofino on the Italian Riviera.

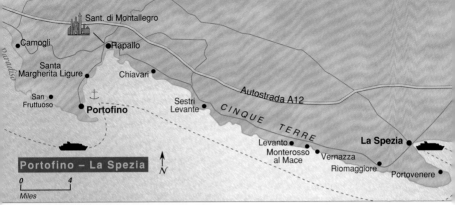

From the main square overlooking the harbour it's an easy hike up to the **Castello di San Giorgio (Fort of St. George)**, built in the mid-1500s, to enjoy excellent views. Just beyond the fort is the church of San Giorgio, said to contain relics of St. George brought back from the Holy Land. Another path leads from the village to the lighthouse at **Punta del Capo**. Portofino's neighbouring seaside villages can be visited by **ship-organized excursions** or by taking the local ferries that connect these small ports. They include the seaside resort of **Camogli,** and the medieval Benedictine monastery of **San Fruttuoso**, situated on a secluded cove around the headland from Portofino.

Portovenere and Vernazza (below)

In the other direction from Portofino is the resort of **Santa Margherita Ligure,** with elegant shops and lively cafés. Nearby **Rapallo** is another beach resort, its historic attractions including a medieval castle, basilica and Renaissance church. Sanctuary of Our Lady of Montallegro, set on a ridge above the bay, can be reached by cable car from Rapallo.

Trains run regularly between Camogli, Santa Margherita Ligure and Rapallo. The rail line bypasses Portofino, which is located two miles from Santa Margherita (about a US$15 taxi ride).

South of Rapallo is **Cinque Terre** National Park, where five villages cling to coastal cliffs and are accessible only by boat, with tours departing regularly from **La Spezia**. A growing cruise port, La Spezia also provides access to Florence, Pisa, Lucca and Genoa. Shore excursions are offered to all of these places, as well as bus and boating tours to Portofino and Santa Margherita, and cooking lessons at a Tuscan farmhouse

A stone farmhouse in the rolling hills of the Tuscan countryside.

TUSCANY

Tuscany is one of Italy's most scenic regions, its gently rolling and verdant hills dotted with stone farmhouses. Vineyards of the Chianti wine region lie between Florence and Siena, and the northwest part of Tuscany is where the famous Carrara marble is quarried. Dante, born in Florence in 1265, established Tuscan as the literary language of Italy with publication of his masterpiece, *Divine Comedy.*

Tuscany, called Etruria in ancient times, was home to the Etruscan civilization before it was conquered by the Romans in the 4th century BC. The northern Lombards controlled the region next, followed by the Franks who, in the 12th century, bequeathed Tuscany to the papacy, which set up a longstanding strife between the pro-papal Guelphs and pro-imperial Ghibellines.

Amid the political turmoil and bloody battles, the towns of Tuscany prospered. **Pisa** initially emerged as the most powerful city of the region, but **Florence** eventually gained control and Tuscany became a grand duchy of Florence's ruling Medici family.

The small city of **Siena**, despite frequent wars with Florence, retained its independence and today draws visitors to its rich array of art and architecture. Gracing the fan-shaped main square are the Gothic Palazzo Pubblico and slender Mangia tower. Adorning the city's Italian Gothic cathedral is a striped marble facade by Giovanni Pisano, and the adjoining library contains famous frescoes by Pinturicchio.

Throughout the Renaissance, Tuscany was a centre of learning and art. Florence overflowed with famous artists such as Michelangelo and Leonardo da Vinci, both born in one of the hill towns surrounding Florence. Other famous Tuscans included Petrarch, Galileo, Machiavelli and Puccini, as well as Carlo Collodi, the 19th-century author of the children's classic *Pinocchio*.

Livorno, the major port for Florence, is one of Italy's most important sea ports and home to the Italian naval academy. The port

Good-quality leather goods are sold at Mercato Nuovo.

evolved from a fortified castle in the Middle Ages into a flourishing city when developed by Florence's powerful Medici family in the 16th century. Livorno was considered the ideal Renaissance town, until it was bombed during World War II. Parts of its 17th-century city wall still remain and the 16th-century cathedral was restored after the war.

Getting Around

Pisa is located about 15 miles north of Livorno, and Florence is a distance of 60 miles – an hour-and-a-half drive through the rolling hills of Tuscany. Trains run regularly to both cities (Pisa is a stop along the Livorno-Florence route). The Livorno train station is about three miles from the cruise ship pier. The pierside shuttle service into Livorno isn't recommended because the drop-off is at Piazza Grande, which is about a mile from the Livorno train station (€15 taxi fare). It's more time efficient to take a taxi directly from the ship to the train station; the taxi fare is about €25. The train ride to Florence takes approximately one and a half hours and the one-way fare is about €12 per person; the train trip to Pisa takes about 15 minutes. Most ships offer a round-trip motorcoach transfer from the ship to Florence (US $100).

Most of Florence's monuments are located within walking distance of one another but be prepared for a wait when visiting some of the popular galleries and museums (unless you reserved tickets online). Their opening hours vary; many are closed by

2:00 pm (especially on Sundays) and remain closed on Mondays.

No tour buses are allowed into the town centre and passengers (including those on ship-organized excursions) are dropped off a few blocks east of the **National Library** 1 in the vicinity of Piazza Piave. The train station is located on the other side of the town centre.

Shopping & Dining – Florentines are renowned for their skilled craftsmanship, especially in ceramics, leather goods, art reproductions and high fashion. Boutiques selling fine leather goods and designer clothing are found on Via de'Tornabuoni and Via della Vigna Nuova. More fine leather shops are found across the river on Via de' Guicciardini between Ponte Vecchio and Pitti Palace. Ponte Vecchio is a good place to shop for jewellery. For antiques, explore the shops along Via Maggio (one block west of Pitti Palace). Shoppers looking for inexpensive souvenirs and leather goods should check out Mercato Nuovo (also known as the Straw Market or Mercato del Porcellino for its bronze statue of a wild boar). More leather goods and gifts can be found at the San Lorenzo Market stalls in the streets around Mercato Centrale, which is a food market containing an upstairs food court of specialty shops, coffee bars and restaurants – a good place to have lunch and sample the local cuisine.

Florence

The Italians call her *Firenze* (the 'flowering city'), thus named by the Romans when this early Etruscan settlement became a town along the Cassian Way. Centuries later, Florence did indeed flower when the Italian

Shore Excursions

Tuscany The following is a sampling of excursions from Livorno. These are usually a combination of motorcoach ride and walking tour, with a mid-day lunch stop.

• Florence & Pisa – guided walking tours of Florence and Pisa's Field of Miracles (11 hrs, $200)

• Tuscan Countryside – visit Lucca and a Tuscan farmhouse for lunch (9 hrs, $195)

•Siena & San Gimignano - visit the medieval city of Siena and walled town of San Gimignano, with lunch at the San Donato Farmhouse (10.5 hrs, $225)

• Scenic drive to Cinque Terre on Italian Riviera (11hrs, $185)

Excursion Suggestion: One of the best ways to see Florence is to take a ship-organized motorcoach ride from Livorno to Florence, where you are dropped off at a central location within walking distance of the city's highlights. After exploring the city on your own, you reboard the coach at a pre-set time and place for the return drive to Livorno. This excursion allows you to maximize your time in Florence, with no concern about getting to or from the city. A tour guide provides informed commentary during the drive into Florence and answers any questions you may have. On the return drive, you can lean back in your seat and relax after a full day of sight-seeing.

MUST SEE:

There are several must-see attractions for first-time visitors to Florence. Here is a good starter list:

Michelangelo's David, either the original housed in the Galleria dell'Accademia, or the replica standing outside Palazzo Vecchio.

The Duomo, Florence's celebrated cathedral.

Church of Santa Croce, containing the tombs of Michelangelo and Galileo.

Church of San Lorenzo's Medici Chapel.

Ponte Vecchio, beautiful, busy, with a 15th-century atmosphere.

Renaissance began here in the early 1400s. Lying at the foot of the Apennines, in the broad valley of the Arno River, Florence is a small city. Her beauty is subtle, her colours muted, and just as that famous Florentine, Mona Lisa, leaves you wondering what's behind her mysterious smile, so too does Florence, with her narrow medieval streets and fortress-like buildings, their austere exteriors offering few clues to the artistic treasures awaiting inside.

After Rome fell, Florence was controlled by various invaders until gaining autonomy in the 12th century. Then, in the 13th century, the pro-papal Guelphs and the pro-imperial Ghibellines fought for control of the city. By the end of the century, the Guelphs had captured the city but they then split into warring factions called the Blacks and the Whites. The poet Dante, a White Guelph and member of the losing side, was banished in 1302.

Florence also warred against other cities, such as Pisa, and gradually grew as it absorbed neighbouring towns and villages. Bankers and merchants made both themselves and the city wealthy by selling Florentine silks, tapestries and jewellery.

The Black Death of 1348 struck a terrible blow to the city, killing more than half the population. But Florence's most glorious days still lay ahead, her golden age ushered in by the rise to power in 1434 of a man named Cosimo de' Medici. A wealthy and powerfully connected merchant banker, Medici and his descendants would determine the destiny of Florence for the next 300 years. Despised by their enemies and denounced as tyrants, the Medicis were initially a tolerant and positive force in Florence. Through their passionate patronage of the arts, literature and learning, the early Medicis financed Florence's growing concentration of architectural monuments and artistic masterpieces, the likes of which had not been seen since the Athens of Pericles.

Cosimo de' Medici, founder of the Medici Library, was a generous supporter of such artists as Brunelleschi and Donatello. His grandson, Lorenzo de' Medici, (il Magnifico) became a towering figure of the Italian Renaissance and was a patron of Michelangelo, Botticelli and others. An astute politician, he held no official title but tactfully wielded power while conducting the affairs of the Florentine state. In 1478 he survived a bloody conspiracy by the rival Pazzi family in which his brother was stabbed to death during Mass at the cathedral. A wounded Lorenzo managed to escape.

The Florentine republicans also tried to drive the Medicis from power. Each attempt was, ultimately, a failure because the early Medicis enjoyed popular support among the Florentines. There were, however, serious challengers. In 1494, Lorenzo's son and successor, Pietro, was expelled from Florence, and Girolamo Savonarola, a zealous religious reformer and enemy of the Medicis, became the spiritual leader of the city, his impassioned sermons inspiring Florentines to toss their offensive secular artwork into a huge bonfire that was lit in the Piazza della Signoria. However, his incessant preaching and rigid moral demands eventually got on people's nerves, and his attacks on the corrupt Borgia

(Right) The Bargello, built in 1255, later became a Renaissance prison. (Below) Ponte Vecchio bridge spans the Arno River in Florence.

pope resulted in his being excommunicated in 1497. Savonarola was hanged a year later for heresy and the Medicis were eventually restored to power.

The Medici dynasty became affiliated with the royal houses of Europe through marriage and produced two queens of France and three popes. However, in the process, the Medicis gained a reputation as arbitrary and ruthless rulers. Alessandro, who governed in the 1530s, was so generally hated that his cousin Ippolito was sent by the people of Florence to complain to the Holy Roman Emperor.

Alas, Ippolito died en route and many believed he was poisoned by order of Alessandro. Another member of the Medici family finally murdered the despised Alessandro but his successor, Cosmo I, was no better liked, although he did expand Florence's territory to include most of Tuscany and he became the first grand duke of Tuscany.

The Medicis were influenced by Niccolo Machiavelli, author of *Il Principe* (The Prince), a famous work describing the amoral, calculating and tyrannical means by which an 'ideal' prince may gain and maintain political power. Machiavelli was born in 1469 to an impoverished branch of a distinguished Florentine family and he rose, in the aftermath of Savonarola's death, from obscure bureaucrat to high-profile republican. His fall came with the return of the Medicis in 1512. Briefly imprisoned and tortured for allegedly plotting against the Medicis, Machiavelli later retired to his country estate to write.

In 1610 Galileo was appointed court philosopher and mathemati-

The cloister of the Church of San Lorenzo.

cian by Cosimo II de' Medici. However, by the late 1600s the Medicis had descended into bigoted and corrupt despotism. The family continued to rule the grand duchy of Tuscany until 1737, when the last male member of the line died. Eventually, Tuscany was annexed by the house of Hapsburg-Lorraine to the kingdom of Sardinia in 1860. When the new kingdom of Italy was formed, Florence was its first capital from 1865 to 1871.

Few of Florence's art treasures were damaged during World War II, but Ponte Vecchio – built in the 14th century – was the only bridge to survive. A major disaster struck in November 1966 when the River Arno flooded its banks. Art experts from around the world came to help repair the buildings and statues damaged by water and mud, and beauty was restored to the city in which the Renaissance first flowered.

Florence Attractions

Located next to the central train station is the **Church of Santa Maria Novella** **2**, built by Dominicans in the late Middle Ages (1278-1350), its patterned marble facade remodeled in the

15th century. The church's Italian Gothic interior contains numerous art treasures, including a famous crucifix carved in 1410 by Filippo Brunelleschi – the first great architect of the Italian Renaissance.

Brunelleschi began his career as a sculptor and goldsmith but, after failing to win a commission to design the bronze doors of the Florence baptistery, he switched to architecture. He went to Rome to study classical buildings and, upon returning to Florence, he launched a new style of architecture based on the systematic use of perspective and a mastery of construction. His elegant designs can be seen all over Florence. Construction of the **Ospedale degli Innocenti** (Foundling Hospital) **3** began in 1419 and its motif – a series of round arches supported by columns – became a prototype of Renaissance architecture. The perfect proportions of the hospital arcade were repeated by Brunelleschi in the **Church of San Lorenzo 4** which he designed in 1421 for the Medicis, who were so impressed with his plans for a burial chapel they were adding to the existing Romanesque church that they asked him to newly design the entire church.

The structure for which Brunelleschi is best known is the soaring dome of the city's Gothic cathedral **Santa Maria del Fiore (the Duomo) 5**. Of revolutionary design, Brunelleschi's dome is one of the most celebrated and original in architectural history. Constructed from 1420 to 1434, this massive dome is the focal point of the city. Its daring structural technique consisted of building the dome in two separate shells, the stronger inner shell supporting the lighter outer shell. An ingenious interlinking of the bricks helped make the counter-balanced dome self-supporting, which allowed Brunelleschi to dispense with the expense and delay of wooden scaffolding and centring. Brunelleschi also designed the lantern atop the dome. The cathedral itself, the fourth largest in the world, was built between 1296 and 1375. The original unfinished facade was torn down in 1587 and not until 1871 was a design by Emilio de Fabris approved for the new

Florence's massive cathedral (the Duomo) is the focal point of the city.

facade. White, green and pink marble – consistent with the rest of the building – was used. The slim campanile (known as 'Giotto's Tower') was designed by the great Florentine artist Giotto di Bondone and begun in 1334. It stands 269 feet (82 m) high.

The octagonal **Baptistery** **6**, originally built in the 4th and 5th centuries when Florence was a Roman town, was considered a classical temple by medieval Florentines. Its current appearance dates from the 11th to 13th centuries, and the panels of its famous bronze doors were designed by two sculptors: Andrea Pisano, whose stories of the Baptist embellish the South Door (1330-1336), and Lorenzo Ghiberti whose submissions won him commissions to design the North Door (1404-1424) and the East Door (1425-1452). The stunningly beautiful East Door became known as the 'The Gates of Paradise' when thus described by Michelangelo.

A copy of the Gates of Paradise now hangs in the east portal, the original restored for exhibition in the **Museo dell'Opera del Duomo** **7** which houses works of art removed from the Duomo, the Campanile and the Baptistery. Works on display include Donatello's *Mary Magdalen* and an unfinished *Pieta* (1550-53) by Michelangelo that was intended for his tomb.

Michelangelo lived with the Medicis from 1490 to 1492, and the family employed him both in Florence and in Rome under the Medici popes Leo X and Clement VII. In between his painting commissions at the Sistine Chapel in Rome, Michelangelo was summoned back to Florence to design a chapel and library, attached to the family's parish **Church of San Lorenzo**.

The **Laurentian Library** was built to house the Medici family's huge collection of books and manuscripts, and its vestibule contains a stairway designed by Michelangelo that has been described as 'nightmarish' for the way it appears to flow downward and outward, defying anyone to mount the steps.

The Church of San Lorenzo's **New Sacristy (Medici Chapel)** **8** was conceived as an architectural-sculptural ensemble and is Michelangelo's only work in which his statues are in the setting specifically designed for them. The plans were changed while work was underway, with Michelangelo completing only two of the four planned tombs, before returning to Rome in 1534. One tomb was for Lorenzo de' Medici, who died at 27, and his statue atop the tomb depicts the young man in a pensive attitude, flanked by the statues *Dawn* and *Dusk*. The opposite tomb of Giuliano de' Medici is watched over by the statues *Night* and *Day*. The meaning of these allegorical figures is described in some notes found on one of the artist's drawings: "Day and Night speak, and say: We with our swift course have brought the Duke Giuliano to death." The statue of Giuliano, set in a niche, bore no resemblance to the deceased but Michelangelo was said to have remarked, "A thousand years from now, nobody will know what he looked like."

Michelangelo's own tomb is in the **Church of Santa Croce** , positioned immediately to the right as you enter. He reportedly chose this spot so that on Judgment Day, when the dead are raised, the first thing he would see through the opened doors of Santa Croce would be Brunelleschi's dome. The tomb of Galileo is situated on the left side of the church, opposite Michelangelo's. Machiavelli's tomb is halfway down the nave on the left, and the composer Rossini's tomb is at the end of the nave. This Gothic church (with a 19th-century facade) also contains the Peruzzi Chapel, immortalized by E.M. Forster in *A Room with a View* when George Emerson shows Lucy Honeychurch the chapel's famous 14th-century frescoes by Giotto. An artist whose works greatly influenced Michelangelo, Giotto departed from the Byzantine style of depicting religious symbols to create, instead, dramatic biblical scenes.

The nave (above) and dome (right) of the Duomo.

The marble facade of Florence's famous Duomo and, in the foreground, the Baptistery.

Also displayed in Santa Croce are works by Donatello, including his *Annunciation* and *Crucifix*. Donatello, an innovative sculptor who freed sculptures of their architectural setting, was interested in ancient monuments and he travelled to Rome in 1430 with Brunelleschi. The **Pazzi Chapel**, annexed to Santa Croce, is a Brunelleschi design and was begun about 1430. He also designed the **Church of S. Spirito 10** begun in 1434, which was about the same time he was designing the **Church of Santa Maria del Carmine 11** – a domed, central-plan church and first of its kind for the Renaissance.

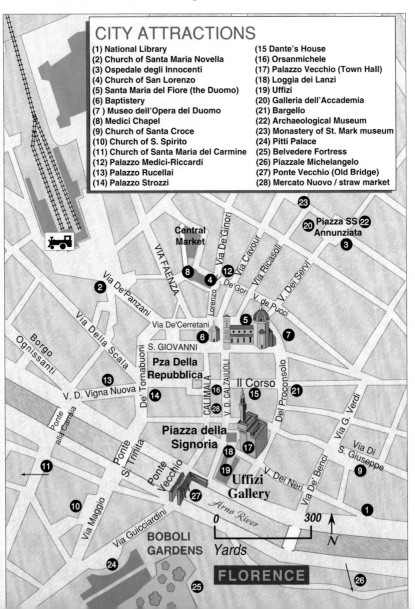

CITY ATTRACTIONS

(1) National Library
(2) Church of Santa Maria Novella
(3) Ospedale degli Innocenti
(4) Church of San Lorenzo
(5) Santa Maria del Fiore (the Duomo)
(6) Baptistery
(7) Museo dell'Opera del Duomo
(8) Medici Chapel
(9) Church of Santa Croce
(10) Church of S. Spirito
(11) Church of Santa Maria del Carmine
(12) Palazzo Medici-Riccardi
(13) Palazzo Rucellai
(14) Palazzo Strozzi

(15 Dante's House
(16) Orsanmichele
(17) Palazzo Vecchio (Town Hall)
(18) Loggia dei Lanzi
(19) Uffizi
(20) Galleria dell'Accademia
(21) Bargello
(22) Archaeological Museum
(23) Monastery of St. Mark museum
(24) Pitti Palace
(25) Belvedere Fortress
(26) Piazzale Michelangelo
(27) Ponte Vecchio (Old Bridge)
(28) Mercato Nuovo / straw market

FLORENCE

The **Palazzo Medici-Riccardi** **12** built from 1444 to 1459, became the model for other private Florentine palaces, such as **Palazzo Rucellai 13** and **Palazzo Strozzi 14**. The Medicis rejected Brunelleschi's model for their new palace, considering it too grandiose, and went instead with a design by Michelozzi, one that did not outwardly flaunt their wealth and power. Its austere Tuscan Gothic exterior of rusticated masonry contrasts sharply with the interior's elaborately decorated salons and the central courtyard's classical arcades, which imitate Brunelleschi's Foundling Hospital. Other buildings of note include **Dante's House 15** and the **Orsanmichele 16**, a granary that was transformed into a church in 1336. The nearby **Piazza della Repubblica**, a 19th-century square dedicated to Vittorio Emanuele II (first king of a united Italy), is situated on the site of the Roman town's ancient forum.

Florence's main square is **Piazza della Signoria**, overlooked by the fortress-like **Palazzo Vecchio (Town Hall) 17** where elected members of the Signoria would temporarily live while serving their term of office. Begun in 1298 and built to withstand armed assault in an era when political turmoil and social tensions often led to bloodshed, the building's tall tower was both

a symbol of civic pride and a watch tower, with the two marble statues flanking the doorway designed for holding chains. Under the arches of the gallery are the coats of arms of the Tuscan communes ruled by Florence. Inside the palace the grand Salone dei Cinquecento (Room of the Five Hundred) is richly decorated with frescoes by Vasari and sculptures by Michelangelo.

(Above right) The Pazzi Chapel is annexed to the Church of Santa Croce (right), which holds the tombs of Michelangelo, Galileo and Rossini.

A replica of Michelangelo's David (detail above) stands outside the Town Hall (below).

The statues standing in front of the Palazzo include a copy of Michelangelo's *David* (1501-1504), one of his greatest sculptural achievements. When commissioned, the statue was supposed to depict a biblical shepherd boy and occupy a pier buttress of the Duomo, but Michelangelo's interpretation of David produced instead a heroic Renaissance man whose masculine nudity made the statue unsuitable for an ecclesiastical site. A committee decided to erect it in front of the Palazzo Vecchio, and it took five days to move the colossal statue (which stands over four metres) to this site. The statue was stoned by citizens offended by its nudity, and David's private parts were covered with gilded leaves until 1545. In 1873 the statue was removed to the Academy and a copy placed on its original site.

The statue to *David*'s left is *Hercules and Cacus* (1525-1534) by Baccio Bandinelli, whose sculptural talents were widely ridiculed by his contemporaries. When the marble block for this statue fell off the transport into the River Arno, the joke was that the stone had thrown itself into the river rather than endure mutilation by Bandinelli. The *Fountain of Neptune* (1560-1575) to *David*'s right was the work of Bartolomeo Ammanati who, soon after its completion, experienced a religious crisis prompted by the counter-Reformation and disowned his works because of their nudity. The Florentines call this sculpture the 'White Giant' because of the enormous size of the white sea god standing in the centre of the fountain. Statues on display in the **Loggia dei Lanzi** **18** include *Perseus* (1533), a masterpiece in bronze by Benvenuto Cellini, and the *Rape of the Sabines* (1581-1583) by Giambologna.

The famous **Uffizi Gallery** **19** is housed in a Renaissance palace that was built to house the administrative offices (*uffizi*) of the Medicis. This U-shaped building was designed by Giorgio Vasari, a favourite portrait artist of the Medici family. When the family installed their art collections here, it became Europe's first modern museum. The gallery, located on the second floor, consists of 45 rooms divided into sections. The famous artists represented in this vast collection of paintings include Leonardo da Vinci, Michelangelo, Raphael and Giotto, with numerous works by Sandro Botticelli.

Other art museums of note are the **Galleria dell'Accademia (Academy)** **20**, which houses the original *David* by Michelangelo,

(Below) The Uffizi Gallery houses a vast collection of Renaissance art. (Bottom) Fountain of Neptune in Piazza della Signoria.

as well as his unfinished *Slaves*. The **Museo Nazionale** in the 13th-century **Bargello** 21, a former Renaissance prison, contains an outstanding collection of Renaissance sculpture with works by Donatello, Michelangelo and Cellini, and the bronze panels submitted by Brunelleschi and Ghiberti in 1402 when they competed for the commission to decorate the north doors of the Baptistery. The **Archaeological Museum** 22 houses Etruscan and Graeco-Roman art, and the **Monastery of St. Mark Museum** 23 contains some of the best works of Fra Angelico, a Dominican monk.

The **Pitti Palace** 24, originally built for the Pitti family in the 15th century, was expanded after it was bought by the rival Medici family. Works by Titian and Raphael are displayed in the Palatine Gallery, which is housed in the Royal Apartments on the right-hand side of the courtyard. Behind the Pitti Palace, which served as the Royal Palace of a united Italy from 1865 to 1870, lie the terraced Boboli Gardens (1550). A back entrance leads to the **Belvedere Fortress** 25, its grounds a popular picnic site for Florentines, with views overlooking the city's medieval maze of churches, squares and red-tiled roofs. The **Piazzale Michelangelo** 26, (farther up the hill) is where the tour buses stop to give their passengers an overview of Florence, the River Arno and its many bridges.

Ponte Vecchio (Old Bridge) 27, was built in 1345 and was the only bridge not blown up by the retreating Germans during World War II. It is lined with jewellers and goldsmith shops, and is topped with a corridor designed by Vasari for Cosimo I de' Medici (1537-1569). Used by successive Medici grand dukes when crossing the bridge, the Vasari Corridor is lined with paintings and, although not open to the general public, the corridor is accessible as part of a city tour called the Prince's Route. The elegant **Ponte Santa Trinita**, the next bridge downriver and the pride of Florence, was designed by Bartolemeo Ammannati in 1567 and was painstakingly rebuilt after the war.

Pisa

Pisa was at the height of its power when the tower for which it's now famous first began to lean. This well-known bell tower was meant to complete the city's splendid ensemble of ecclesiastical architecture, begun in the mid-11th century. Pisa was then a city on the ascent, its growing empire based on naval and economic power. Over the span of two centuries, Pisa's magnificent cathedral, baptistery and campanile ('Leaning Tower') were built at an open-air site north of the city. Called the Field of Miracles, the site proved to be a field of unstable subsoil, for Pisa is situated on the banks of the Arno River, where the ground consists of layers of sandy mud and clay. A former sea port, Pisa now lies six miles inland, its decline as a trading port caused by the silting of the river. Before its decline, Pisa was a powerful maritime republic. When its navy defeated the Arab forces at Palermo in 1062, Pisans built their

Romanesque cathedral from Saracen plunder, the facade's elaborate lace-like ornamentation reflecting Islamic influences.

The Baptistery was modeled on the Holy Sepulchre in Jerusalem, and the entire complex of monuments was an attempt by the Pisans to create their own Holy City. All three buildings are clad in white marble, inlaid with horizontal stripes and ornate patterns in dark-green marble. They contain some of Pisa's greatest art treasures – including bronze panels by Bonnanno Pisano and marble pulpits by Nicola Pisano and his son Giovanni. Soon after construction began on the campanile in 1174, it began to lean. By the time it was closed to the public in 1990, the tower was 16 feet (4.9 meters) out of perpendicular alignment. So close was the 13,050-ton tower to toppling, an earthquake or storm could have demolished it. Upon being closed, the tower was temporarily supported with a steel belt and cables while engineers studied the structure, then began stabilizing it by placing 800 tons of lead weights at the tower's base on the side opposite the tilt. This was fol-

lowed by the removal of tons of subsoil from beneath the tower in an area away from the incline, prompting the tower to bear down and slightly straighten itself. After 11 years of stabilization work, the bell tower was reopened to the public in late 2001, its lean now back to where it was in 1838. Visitors can once again climb to the top of the structure, but only 30 people are allowed inside at a time.

Elba

Lying off the coast of Tuscany, the island of Elba is well known as Napoleon's place of exile from 1814 to 1815. Its principal north coast port of **Portoferraio**, strongly fortified by Florence's Medici family from the 16th to 18th centuries, is today a seaside resort. Napoleon's house, the Villa dei Mulini, where he resided as sovereign of the island, is now a museum. Shore excursions in Elba feature scenic drives to Porto Azzurro (a fashionable resort) and to picturesque fishing ports.

Pisa's medieval cathedral and its leaning campanile.

Venice (Venezia)

Venice, one of world's most beautiful cities, is built on 118 alluvial islets within a lagoon in the Gulf of Venice. It began as a small fishing settlement in the 5th century AD with the first settlers building huts on the mud banks and digging deep ditches to moor their boats. This was the origin of Venice's modern canal system, which now includes more than 100 narrow canals crossed by some 400 footbridges.

Getting Around

Venice, compact and free of motor vehicle traffic, is an intimate city and a delight to explore **on foot**. Narrow lanes (*calles*) lead to hidden squares (*campos*) and the arched footbridges that span the side canals (*rios*). It's easy to become momentarily lost amid the maze of back streets and winding waterways that lead off the Grand Canal, but the bell tower of St. Mark's Square is visible above the surrounding roofs. Most ships dock overnight in

The view of St. Mark's Square as your ship pulls into port.

Venice, so passengers have the opportunity to explore the city at their leisure.

Venice is also a base port, with the Marco Polo Airport located on the adjacent mainland. Road, rail and water bus transportation connect the airport to Venice. The quickest way to get from the airport to your hotel is by water taxi; the fare is about €100 and if you don't have a reservation just head to the water taxi docks. If you're going straight to your ship from the airport, arrange beforehand a transfer with the cruise line.

Once you're in Venice, by water is an ideal way to see the city's sights, and there's nothing more romantic than a **gondola ride** – especially at night when the city's timeless magic is enhanced by the watery reflection of dancing lights and voices echoing down quiet side canals. The daytime rate for a half-hour ride (max. 6 people) is €80; the night rate (after 7 p.m.) is

€100 for 35 minutes. Less expensive is a *traghetto*, a two-man gondola that ferries people across the Grand Canal at various, sign-posted places.

The most popular and reasonably priced mode of transport is to hop on and off the motorized river boats (called *vaporetti*) that are part of the city's water bus service. They run the length of the Grand Canal, making frequent stops along the way. It's a short walk from the cruise terminal to **Piazzale Roma** where a ticket can be purchased at the ACTV booth for a ride along the complete length of the Grand Canal to St. Mark's Square. (A map and water bus schedule is available at the Tourist Information Office located just west of the St. Mark's Piazzetta.)

The cruise lines usually provide their passengers with a reasonably priced boat shuttle that runs regularly between the ship and a drop-off point near St. Mark's Square. Private water taxis can also be hired.

The city's water bus service provides transport to other islands in the lagoon, such as **San Michele** (the city's cemetery), **Murano** (famous for glass making since the 13th century) and **Burano** (a colourful fishing village and lace-making centre).

Shopping & Dining

Venice is the place to shop for leather handbags, fine lace and colourful Murano glassware and jewellery. The city's main shopping area lies between the Rialto Bridge and Piazza San Marco.

Shops featuring finely crafted carnival masks can be found on **Calle dei Fabbri**. A quieter street with shops selling handcrafted items, including leather handbags and beautiful Murano glass jewellery, is **Calle Sant'Agnese** near Accademia Bridge in the Dorsoduro district.

There's a plethora of cafés and sandwich shops in Venice at which to have a light lunch, such as Bar Ae Maravegie on Calle della Toletta in Dorsoduro. **St. Mark's Square** is lined with outdoor cafés, including the famous Caffe Florian, as is the waterfront area beside the **Rialto Bridge**.

Across the Grand Canal in the less touristy **Dorsoduro district,** some recommended restaurants for dinner include **Taverna San Trovaso** on Calle Contarini Corfu, which serves hearty Venetian dishes in a warm rustic setting. For a memorable Venetian meal, reserve a table on the canal-

side terrace at **Ristorante Cantinone Storico** on quiet Rio de S. Vio (shown in photo at left).

Legendary restaurants in Venice include **Harry's Bar** (see map) , which was patronized by Ernest Hemingway, Somerset Maugham and Orson Wells; and the dining terrace of the **Gritti Palace 26**, where former guests include Queen Elizabeth, Winston Churchill and Greta Garbo.

Where to Stay

There is no shortage of luxury hotels in Venice, including **Gritti Palace, Hotel Danieli** and, across the water from St. Mark's Square, the **Hotel Cipriani** on Giudecca Island (George Clooney stays here). If you're looking for more modest accommodation, **La Calcina** is a welcoming, 3-star hotel overlooking Guidecca Canal in the Dorsoduro district, within easy walking distance of the Grand Canal and St. Mark's Square, and a short water-bus ride to the cruise terminal.

A History of Venice

The fishing villages that were built on mud in the Lagoon of Venice eventually organized themselves under a doge (leader) in 697 and began to engage in seaborne trade. The port grew rapidly and by the 9th century Venice's prosperity made it a target of Dalmatian pirates. This prompted the Venetians to build castellated houses for protection and guard the canal entrances

---

MUST SEE: 👁

St. Mark's Square – view it from the ship as you enter Venice, then return by boat for a close look at its famous buildings.

The Grand Canal – board a vaporetto at Piazzale Roma and ride the canal's entire length to St. Mark's Square.

Explore **Venice's back streets** and narrow waterways on foot or by gondola.

Winding canals weave through the enchanting city of Venice.

with chains. But the pirates kept coming, so the Venetians responded by arming their ships. The newly born Venetian Navy defeated the Dalmatian pirates in the year 1000, and this important victory is celebrated with great pomp on Ascension Day.

The Crusades brought great wealth to Venice, her fleet transporting Christian armies to the Holy Land. In 1204 the doge Dandolo led the Fourth Crusade's storming of Constantinople, looting it of treasures. By 1216 the Venetian empire included strategic islands in the Ionian, Aegean and eastern Mediterranean, and the city's native son and world traveller Marco Polo embodied the enterprising spirit of the Venetians. As wealth poured into Venice, its patrician merchants formed an oligarchy and kept a tight hold on power with its secret police and Council of Ten, instituted to punish those who committed crimes against the state.

Intriguing aspects of Venice are found along the back streets and small canals of the city.

Shore Excursions

Venice Ship excursions feature gondola and canal boat rides, as well as visits to various churches and art galleries. Boat tours to the neighbouring islands of Murano and Burano (4-5 hrs) to visit their glass- and lace-making factories are also featured. Tours of the Doge's Palace or St. Mark's Basilica often include special evening excursions featuring a serenaded gondola ride or a boat ride along the Grand Canal to St. Mark's Square for a guided tour of the basilica (which is closed to the public in the evening).

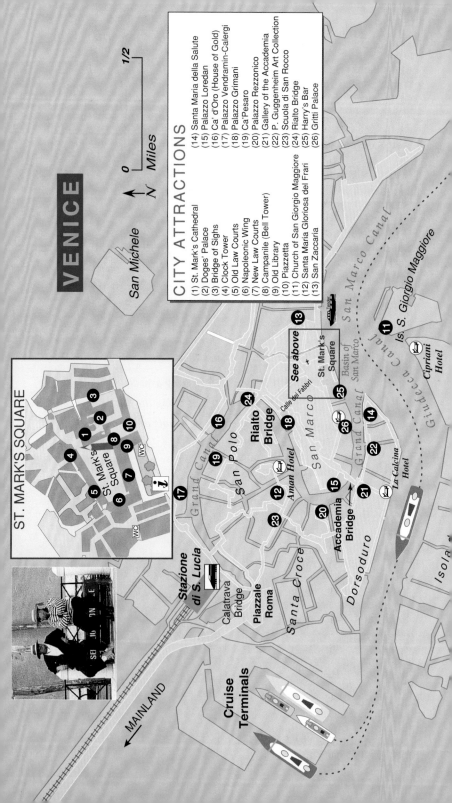

VENICE

CITY ATTRACTIONS

(1) St. Mark's Cathedral
(2) Doges' Palace
(3) Bridge of Sighs
(4) Clock Tower
(5) Old Law Courts
(6) Napoleonic Wing
(7) New Law Courts
(8) Campanile (Bell Tower)
(9) Old Library
(10) Piazzetta
(11) Church of San Giorgio Maggiore
(12) Santa Maria Gloriosa del Frari
(13) San Zaccaria

(14) Santa Maria della Salute
(15) Palazzo Loredan
(16) Ca' d'Oro (House of Gold)
(17) Palazzo Vendramin-Calergi
(18) Palazzo Grimani
(19) Ca'Pesaro
(20) Palazzo Rezzonico
(21) Gallery of the Accademia
(22) P. Guggenheim Art Collection
(23) Scuola di San Rocco
(24) Rialto Bridge
(25) Harry's Bar
(26) Gritti Palace

ST. MARK'S SQUARE

San Michele

MAINLAND

Cruise Terminals

Stazione di S. Lucia

Calatrava Bridge

Piazzale Roma

Santa Croce

San Polo

Grand Canal

Rialto Bridge

Aman Hotel

San Marco

Calle del Fabbri

Dorsoduro

Accademia Bridge

La Calcina Hotel

Isola

Grand Canal

See above
St. Mark's Square

Basin of San Marco

San Marco Canal

Giudecca Canal

Is. S. Giorgio Maggiore

San Giorgio Maggiore

Cipriani Hotel

Venice became the envy of Genoa, a rival republic, and the two maritime powers battled for supremacy. Venice eventually emerged victorious but the city's slow decline began in the mid 15th-century when its lucrative eastern trade was threatened by the fall of Constantinople to the Turks and by the discovery of an all-sea trade route to India and China around the Cape of Good Hope. Much of Venice's seagoing trade went to the Portuguese, Dutch and English, but the city remained a force to be reckoned with, achieving artistic glory during the Renaissance with large-scale construction of churches and palaces designed by renowned architects and embellished by artists such as Titian and Tintoretto.

Venice also shone musically. Monteverdi, the first great figure of opera, was appointed choirmaster of St. Mark's in 1613 and Venice's first public opera house opened in 1637. Antonio Vivaldi, whose father was a violinist at St. Mark's, also lived in Venice in the early 1700s – teaching, playing the violin and writing music.

The 18th century was a period of economic and political decline for Venice, the city's decadence personified in the Venetian adventurer Casanova who supported himself by writing, gambling and seducing women. Venice's upper class indulged in a social life of nightly theatregoing and gambling, their sexual dalliances often taking place in private boxes at the opera or inside parked gondolas.

In 1797, Venice fell without a fight to Napoleon's forces and was transferred by treaty to Austrian rule under which the city chafed for several decades. Meanwhile, opera continued to thrive, with Rossini premiering the first of a string of comic operas in Venice in 1810. Italy's foremost composer of opera, Giuseppe Verdi, also premiered a number of his works in Venice amid an atmosphere of tolerance and freedom of expression, and the German operatic composer Richard Wagner spent his final days in Venice, where he died in 1883. By then Venice had expelled the Austrians and was united with the new kingdom of Italy.

Some Venetians still long for a return to their city's golden era of independence, but secessionist politics are the least of Venetians' concerns. Venice, as everyone knows, is slowly sinking. The city is built on sand, silt and hard clay (which tend to compact over time) and some mainland industries have exacerbated the problem by

Prisoners were led across the Bridge of Sighs to their cells.

St. Mark's Square

The golden facade of St. Mark's Cathedral (above). The Doges Palace reflects the wealth of Venice when it was a great sea power (left).

The Campanile (right) soars above the other buildings of St. Mark's Square.
The Italian Gothic facade of the Doges' Palace (below).

A colourful carnival mask (right).
A young Venetian promotes an upcoming classical concert (below).

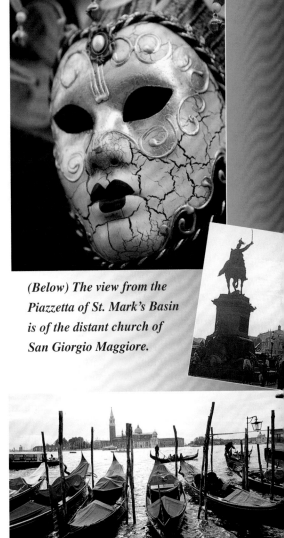

(Below) The view from the Piazzetta of St. Mark's Basin is of the distant church of San Giorgio Maggiore.

PIGEONS

Pigeons have become a problem for the city of Venice. With an estimated population of 100,000, they now outnumber Venetians and anyone (including tourists) caught feeding the pigeons in St. Mark's Square could face a stiff fine. This might seem severe, but the pigeons – many of them diseased – have been put on a strict diet of feed laced with anti-fertility drugs in an attempt to reduce their numbers, as well as the tons of droppings they produce.

lowering the area's underground water table.

In recent years, a shortage of affordable housing has prompted residents to move out of Venice. Thousands of workers commute each day to the city, which is connected to the mainland by a rail-and-road bridge. Many worry that Venice no longer belongs to Venetians, but to tourists and absentee owners who spend little time in their vacation palazzi.

Venice is a busy turnaround port for cruise ships and this has become an issue for some Venetians who resent the increasing size of these ships and the high numbers of passengers they bring to a city already inundated with summertime tourists. Ships entering Venice currently use San Marco Canal, which runs past St. Mark's Square and the entrance to the Grand Canal. There are plans to dredge a new entrance channel to divert the ships but for now the cruise lines have refrained from bringing ships over 96,000 tons into Venice.

Venice Attractions:

St. Mark's Square (Piazza of San Marco) is the central meeting place of Venice and one of Italy's most beautiful squares, dominated by the splendour of **St. Mark's Cathedral** 1. Begun in 1063 and modeled after the Church of the Holy Apostles in Constantinople, this 'Golden Basilica' is an outstanding example of Byzantine architecture. It follows the Greek cross plan, with each arm of the cross emphasized by a dome encased with gilt copper sheet and topped with an ornate lantern, making it visible from a distance

and serving as a landmark for sea-farers. The church's ornate facade consists of clusters of marble pillars and arches containing golden mosaics which glitter in the late afternoon sun. Gold is the dominant decorative element inside the cathedral, its walls completely covered with mosaics from the 12th to 18th centuries.

Entrance to the church is free but there is a fee to enter the Sanctuary (containing the tomb of St. Mark) and the Museum, which houses four gilded bronze horses. These Greek sculptures from the 4th and 3rd centuries BC were brought to Venice from Constantinople in 1204 and were originally displayed on the church's outside gallery, where replicas now stand.

The **Doge's Palace (Palazzo Ducal)** 2, begun in 814, was destroyed four times by fire and each time rebuilt on a grander scale to become a magnificent example of Italian Gothic architecture. The Palace, as residence of the doge and seat of justice, exudes wealth and power in its majestic halls, famous Golden Staircase and elegant rooms with their frescoed walls and ceilings.

The **Bridge of Sighs** (c. 1600) 3 leads from the Doges Palace to the former prisons, a hellish place where prisoners were held either in humid, above-ground cells that were subject to flooding, or in underground cells lined with strips of lead to render them unbearable in the summer heat. Casanova made his famous escape from the latter in 1756.

Other buildings in St. Mark's Square are the **Clock Tower** 4 (built near the end of the 15th century), the **Old Law Courts** (Procuratie Vecchie) which were begun in the 15th century, and the **Napoleonic Wing** (or New Building) , built in 1807, which houses the Correr Museum, its collection of paintings, sculptures and precious objects tracing the history and art of Venice. The **New Law Courts** (Procuratie Nuove) were completed at the beginning of the 18th century. Beneath the portico is the famous **Caffe Florian**, which was frequented by Casanova, Wagner and Proust.

The **Campanile (Bell Tower)** was built in the 10th century and stands 325 feet (99 metres) high. The Loggetta, at its base, was designed by Jacopo Sansovino in the early 16th century and is decorated with bronze statues and marble ornaments. The tower collapsed in 1902 and was rebuilt a few years later as an exact replica of the original. Visitors can reach the balcony near the top by climbing the spiral staircase or by taking the lift.

The **Old Library (Libreria Vecchia)** , its construction started in 1537, was designed by Sansovino as a structural counterpoint to the Doges Palace – the former an educational institute, the latter the political centre of power. The Library became the prototype of Venetian classicism, with its double arcade and lavish use of decorative sculptures. It faces the **Piazzetta** , which leads from the square to the busy waterfront of St. Mark's Basin. The two columns standing here are from the 12th century – one holding a statue of the Lion of St. Mark, the other a statue of St. Theodore. When standing in the Piazzetta and looking across the water of St. Mark's Basin, you will see the church of **San Giorgio Maggiore** , begun in 1566 and designed by Andrea Palladio, who introduced elements from ancient temples to Venetian church architecture.

Venice contains many splendid churches, including **Santa Maria Gloriosa del Frari** with

A ship entering Venice passes St. Mark's Square.

Grand Canal

Motorboats not so swell

When Venice police issue speeding tickets, these go not to motorists but to mariners exceeding the speed limit on the Grand Canal. Supporting local speed limit enforcement are the city's gondoliers, skilled oarsmen who manoeuvre their traditional craft amid the waves caused by passing motorboats. Everyone and everything moves about by boat in Venice, including small barges piled with bags of hotel laundry and crates of fresh fruits and vegetables which are unloaded and wheeled by cart to the local shops. The Grand Canal is reclaimed by rowers when the annual Regata Storica is held on the first Sunday of September. This historic water pageant is followed by rowing races that start in St. Mark's Bay and finish in front of Ca' Foscari where prizes are awarded.

A gondola wedding party (above). Regata Storica is held each September on the Grand Canal (right).

Rialto Bridge (right). Palazzi on the Grand Canal (below and bottom). Gondolas are widely available for hire (below right).

paintings by Titian, **San Zaccaria** ⓭ with the *Enthroned Madonna* by Bellini, and the 17th-century **Church of Santa Maria della Salute** ⓮ which stands on a point of land at the entrance to the Grand Canal.

The Grand Canal

The main thoroughfare of Venice, the Grand Canal is lined with residential palaces (called *palazzi*), their ornate and rippling patterns reflected on the water. The earliest palaces date to the 12th century and their basic features were carried through the centuries. A ground floor portico (for loading and unloading merchandise) led to a large hall where business was conducted; the family's living quarters were upstairs where a large drawing room overlooked the canal.

Each palace was marked by a post, painted with the owner's heraldic colours. Their styles range from early Veneto-Byzantine to Baroque, and Eastern influences are evident in such Oriental touches as delicate lattice work. Because there was little internal strife in Venice, the homes of wealthy Venetian families were built not like fortified castles but as lavish palazzi with fairy-tale facades designed for reflection in the waters of the Grand Canal.

One of the earliest palaces is **Palazzo Loredan** ⓯, now the seat of the City Council, dating from the 13th century and built in the Veneto-Byzantine style. By the early 1500s the Grand Canal was astounding foreigners with its opulent palazzi, such as the late Gothic **Ca' d'Oro (House of Gold)** ⓰. Now housing the Galleria Franchetti, this splendid structure was built by a leading Venetian family in 1420, its lavish stone-carved ornamentation once coloured with red and blue pigments and glistening gilt.

The Renaissance introduced classical elements to the traditional Venetian facade, such as that of the **Palazzo Vendramin-Calergi** ⓱, completed in 1509. This famous palazzo, now a casino, is where the composer Richard Wagner died in 1883 and it became a motif in Thomas Mann's *Death in Venice*.

Ever more and imposing palaces were built along the Grand Canal, including the 16th-century **Palazzo Grimani** ⓲, home of today's Appeal Court, and the baroque **Ca'Pesaro** ⓳, built in 1710 and now housing an art gallery.

The poet Robert Browning lived at the **Palazzo Rezzonico** ⓴, its beautifully decorated and furnished rooms now open to visitors as the Museum of the Venetian 18th Century.

Art galleries of note along the Grand Canal include the **Gallery of the Accademia** ㉑, its 24 rooms containing five centuries of Venetian paintings, with a large number of works by Giovanni Bellini.

The **Peggy Guggenheim Art Collection**, housed in the Palazzo Venier Dei Leoni ㉒, is one of most important collections of contemporary art in the world. The **Scuola di San Rocco** (Great School of San Rocco) ㉓, on Campo San Rocco, houses a series of paintings by Tintoretto.

The Grand Canal is crossed in the centre of the city by the **Rialto Bridge** (Ponte di Rialto) **24**, a single marble arch built between 1588 and 1591. The bridge's arcades are lined with shops and nearby open-air cafés are a good place to watch the constant flow of activity in the Grand Canal.

South of Venice is the port of **Ravenna**, a centre of mosaic art in the 5th and 6th centuries. Shore excursions offered in Ravenna include tours to Florence and to San Marino.

Nestled in the Appenines near the Adriatic Sea, **San Marino** is the world's smallest republic. A Christian stone-cutter from Dalmatia was said to have taken refuge on Mount Titano in the 4th century, and a community soon formed around the mountain's three peaks. Only 24 square miles in size with a population of approximately 25,000 Italian-speaking inhabitants, San Marino's treaty of friendship and economic cooperation was signed with Italy in 1862. The Italian patriot and soldier Garibaldi was granted refuge in San Marino in 1849, and in 1861 Abraham Lincoln accepted an honourary citizenship of the republic.

Italy's Interior

A land tour of Italy is an enticing proposition for passengers beginning or ending their cruise at an Italian port. In the country's north are the majestic Italian Alps, beautiful lakes and Italy's second-largest city, **Milan**. This prosperous city's historic landmarks include the Church of Santa Maria dell Grazie (1465-90), which contains Leonardo da Vinci's famous fresco, *The Last Supper*, and the famous opera house, Teatro alla Scala, which opened in 1778.

The city of **Verona**, a centre of trade since Roman times, reached its apex of power in the late 13th century when ruled by Ghibelline lords. A bloody rivalry between the Ghibellines and the Guelphs, portrayed in Shakespeare's *Romeo and Juliet*, eventually weakened Verona. The 14th-century Casa di Giulietta (House of Juliet) is one of Verona's top tourist spots.

Padua, connected by canal with the Po and other rivers, is home to Italy's second-oldest university (after Bologna's) founded in 1222. Galileo taught here, and Dante and Petrarch were students. Other famous landmarks in Padua include the six-domed basilica of St. Anthony, its high altar adorned with bronzes by Donatello.

Bologna has been a centre of learning ever since the founding in 425 AD of its Roman law school. Bologna's famous university was established in about 1088 and the city's Renaissance architecture includes palazzi, churches and an art gallery featuring works by Bolognese artists.

In **Umbria**, the town of **Orvieto** is famous for its beautiful cathedral, begun in 1290, its black-and-white marble facade decorated with colorful mosaics. **Todi** is another Umbrian town of note, containing Etruscan remains, Roman ruins and Gothic palaces.

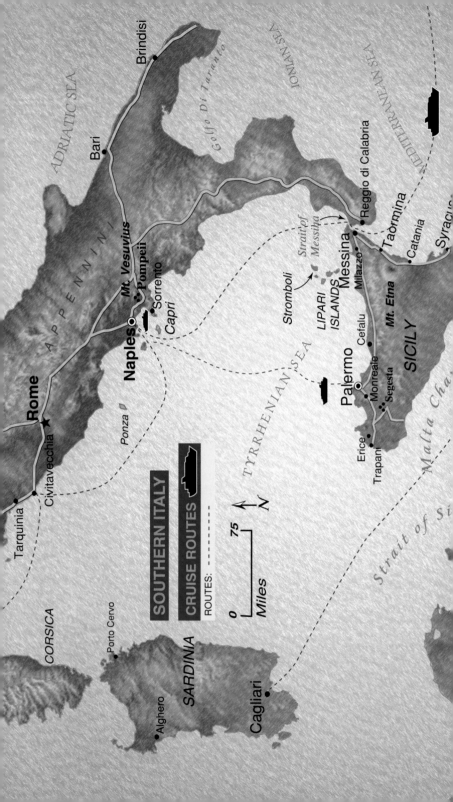

SOUTHERN ITALY

Italy's southern states, rich in natural beauty, have been the poor cousin to the country's industrialized north. Centuries of exploitation by feudal lords and European dynasties had kept the south in a state of backwardness when Italy – which hadn't been a unified political entity since the fall of the Western Roman Empire in the 5th century – began its long struggle toward reunification.

Called Risorgimento (Italian for *resurgence*), this period of cultural nationalism and political activism was inspired by several 18th-century writers. It gained momentum in the early 1800s when the southern states, long dominated by foreign rulers, began to revolt against their repressive regimes. In 1820 there were uprisings in Naples and Sicily, followed by insurrections in Sardinia. Despite severe reprisals, the uprisings continued, led by different factions. One of these revolutionary groups favoured a united Italy under the leadership of Sardinia's King Victor Emmanuel II, and it eventually gained control of the movement. Its cause, supported by the military hero Giuseppe Garibaldi, was ultimately triumphant and in 1861 the kingdom of Italy was proclaimed with Victor Emmanuel as king.

The newly declared kingdom encompassed Italy's northern and southern states, but Rome, situated in central Italy, remained part of the independent Papal States, which were protected by the troops of Napoleon III. The reunification of Italy was finally completed in 1870 when the Papal States were seized by Italian troops. A year later, Rome – the ancient capital of the Roman Empire – was once again the capital of a united Italy.

Victor Emmanuel Monument, Piazza Venezia, Rome

For general information and travel tips on Italy, please see pages 177 and 178.

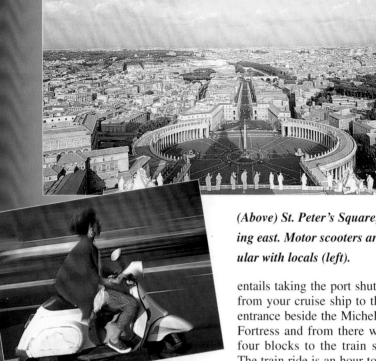

(Above) St. Peter's Square, look-ing east. Motor scooters are pop-ular with locals (left).

Rome (Roma) – The Eternal City

One of the world's most exciting cities, Rome is the intellectual, cultural and religious centre of Italy. Nearly three million people live in Rome, yet no buildings are built higher than the dome of St. Peter's. From hotels' rooftop gardens, sweeping views can be enjoyed of this fascinating city, its famous squares brimming with beautiful churches, fountains and monuments to history.

Getting Around

Civitavecchia, the chief port of Rome, is a 1.5-hour drive from Rome. Independent travellers can hire a taxi or take the **train**. To get to Civitavecchia's train station

entails taking the port shuttle bus from your cruise ship to the port entrance beside the Michelangelo Fortress and from there walking four blocks to the train station. The train ride is an hour to Roma San Pietro station, located 1/4 mile from St. Peter's Basilica.

Another option is to book through your ship's shore excursion office a motorcoach ride into central Rome, where you spend the day sightseeing on your own before catching the motorcoach back to port.

If you're touring Rome on your own, plan your itinerary ahead of time and don't try to see too many attractions – decide beforehand what your priorities will be. Taxis are plentiful, especially at Piazza Venezia and St. Peter's Square. Expect long line-ups to enter St. Peter's Basilica.

If you plan to visit the Colosseum, buy an advance entrance ticket online (www. coopculture.it/en) or purchase a combined ticket at the Roman Forum entrance (where the line-

(Above) The Spanish Steps
(Right) Piazza Della Rotonda

ups are much shorter) which will provide entry to the Colosseum, Forum and Palatine Hill. The Colosseum has free admission on the first Sunday of each month.

Rome's international airport is 16 miles (26 km) from central Rome. The Leonardo Express train connects the airport with Termini station in central Rome, departing every half hour for the 30-minute ride. The cost is €11 if you buy your ticket at the airport counter or at the Termini newsstand (more if bought at the platform). Validate your ticket at the yellow validation machine just before using it (tickets expire 90 minutes after validation).

A taxi from the airport into central Rome is a set fare of €40 (inclusive of luggage) for up to four passengers. Some hotels provide a complimentary airport shuttle that can be booked while making your online reservation through the hotel's website If you're travelling directly from Rome's airport to Civitavecchia cruise port, you're well advised to book a cruise line transfer.

Shopping & Dining

The haute couture world of Fellini's acclaimed film *La Dolce Vita* is found in the area around the Spanish Steps. Famous **shopping streets** leading off Piazza di Spagna include Via del Babuino, Via Condotti and Via Borgognona, all lined with designer boutiques. Less expensive shops are on Via Frattina. In addition to designer goods, Rome has hundreds of specialty shops selling one-of-a-kind hand-made items. Art galleries and antique shops are found on **Via Margutta**, one of Rome's most charming streets and the location of the apartment (#51) featured in *Roman Holiday* as well as the real-life home of Fellini who lived with his wife in apartment #110. Via Margutta leads to **Piazza del Popolo** (a large medieval square with twin churches) where one of Fellini's

The Forum was the centre of republican Rome and the scene of Julius Caesar's assassination.

favourite people-watching spots was **Café Canova**. Another convenient spot to have lunch overlooking a beautiful square is Vacanze Romane in Piazza Navona. However, one of the delights of Rome is to wander its narrow side streets and spontaneously come upon a coffee bar or family-run trattoria.

Where to Stay

Not far from the Spanish Steps are some of Rome's most luxurious hotels, including the famous Hotel Excelsior on **Via Veneto**, where movie stars and deposed royalty held court at sidewalk cafés in the late 1950s, their antics captured in candid photos by paparazzi. Hotel Eden on Via Ludovisi was a favourite haunt of Hemingway, Fellini and Ingrid Bergman.

Recommended 4-star hotels in central Rome include the **Hotel Atlante Star** near Castel Sant 'Angelo (rates from €200 which includes breakfast and airport shuttle). The hotel's rooftop terrace provides panoramic views and is one of the best spots in Rome to have a cocktail while watching the sun set over St. Peter's dome.

Rome's History

Rome, long believed to have originated as a pastoral settlement on seven hills bordering the banks of the River Tiber, likely began as a river port founded by salt merchants. Salt, indispensable for rearing livestock, was brought there from the nearest seaport lying downriver, and a local labour force gathered to unload, warehouse and trade this valuable commodity.

Palatine, a fortified hill of Rome, was taken in the 8th century BC by the Etruscans, one of several tribes in the area. The Etruscans, skilled engineers, built a defensive wall around the seven hills and transformed the existing group of villages into a city, draining the swampy plain of the Forum and building a temple on Capitoline Hill.

In about 500 BC, the Romans overthrew their Etruscan rulers and established a republic that lasted four centuries. As the city grew, so too did its political structure. The ruling patrician class slowly ceded legislative power to the assemblies, and they in turn were eventually controlled by the senate which, as supreme power of the state, led Rome in her quest for empire and world supremacy.

As the empire grew in size, so too did turmoil back in Rome, until Julius Caesar became the new master of Rome. Under the leadership of Caesar, a brilliant orator and patron of the arts, Roman culture thrived and was permeated by Greek thought, literature and language. Caesar's assassination in 44 BC marked the end of the Republic and the beginning of the Empire. Initially there was anarchy, until Octavian, a nephew and protégé of Caesar, emerged as leader and became the first emperor of Rome, receiving from the senate the title Augustus.

Peace reigned for the next two centuries and imperial Rome grew into a city of over two million inhabitants. The city boasted a police force, fire brigades and a postal system. Aqueducts supplied water to public baths, and the wealthy had running water piped right into their villas. Efficient transportation was provided by an extensive system of roads and bridges. Indeed, at the height of Roman imperialism, all roads did lead to Rome for it was the centre of the western world.

MUST SEE:

Rome wasn't built in a day, and it's impossible to see all of Rome in one day. First-time visitors arriving by train from the cruise port should disembark at Roma San Pietro station, which is a short walk to **St. Peter's Square**. From St. Peter's it's a pleasant stroll to **Castel Sant' Angelo**, then across the river to fountain-filled **Piazza Navona** and nearby **Piazza Della Rotonda** (location of the **Pantheon**). It's a short walk from the Pantheon to the **Trevi Fountain.** From here you could head to the **Roman Forum** and **Colosseum**, then catch a taxi in **Piazza Venezia** back to the train station.

If your cruise is beginning or ending in Rome, you should try to stay an extra day or two to view the **Vatican Museums**, **Sistine Chapel** and **Capitoline Hill**, and to soak up the atmosphere around the **Spanish Steps, Piazza del Popolo** and the shopping streets in between.

Rome's decline came quickly as the West sank into anarchy and Italy was ravaged by invaders. Rome was sacked twice and finally fell in 476. However, amid the political disintegration of Rome

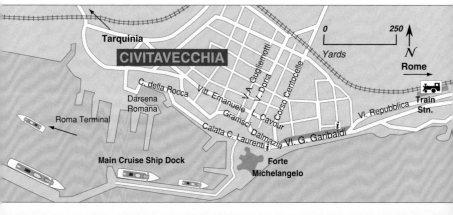

there rose a new power – that of Roman Catholicism. The grandeur of Rome eventually returned with the Italian Renaissance, patronized by a powerful papacy which ruled a swath of central Italy – from Rome to Ravenna – for more than 11 centuries. The Papal States were defeated in 1870 by patriot forces determined to create an Italian nation, but not until the Lateran Treaty of 1929 – which made the pope sovereign within Vatican City – did the papacy recognize the secular state of modern Italy.

Rome Attractions:

The **Colosseum** **1**, completed in 80 AD during the reign of Titus, is a huge concrete amphitheatre containing miles of stairways, and tier upon tier of marble seats which accommodated more than 50,000 spectators. A masterpiece of engineering, the stadium's efficient flow of people in and out of the building was achieved by utilizing 80 ground-floor entrances, each numbered to direct people to the staircases leading to their seats. Entertainment was provided by hundreds of trained gladiators who were slaves or prisoners forced to perform exhibition combats in which they were paired off and would fight to the death – unless the crowd indicated to the victor that he spare the life of the defeated gladiator.

Gladiators were also forced to fight wild beasts, and those who

Shore Excursions

Rome Full-day excursions involve a motorcoach ride from the cruise port to Rome (about a 1.5 hr drive) and an escorted walking tour upon reaching the city centre. Places visited vary (depending on which excursion you book) but usually include three or four famous sites as well as lunch. The following is a sampling of Rome shore excursions. For details, consult your cruise line's website or the shore excursion booklet provided with your cruise documentation.
• Full-day motorcoach and walking tour of St. Peter's Basilica, Vatican Museums and Sistine Chapel (11.5 hrs, $200)
• Highlights of Rome tour to St. Peter's Basilica, Colosseum and Trevi Fountain; includes lunch and free time (10.5 hrs, $200)
• Narrated city drive; major sites viewed from coach; free time for souvenir shopping (6 hrs, $95)
• Tour of Rome's catacombs and the countryside with lunch at a local farmhouse (9 hrs, $180)
Recommended: One of the best ways to see Rome is to take a ship-organized motorcoach ride from Civitavecchia to Rome, where you are dropped off at a central location (usually near St. Peter's Square) within walking distance of the city's highlights. After exploring the city on your own (for about 7 hrs), you reboard the coach at the same spot at a set time for the return drive to Civitavecchia. This excursion allows you to maximize your time in Rome, with no concern about getting to or from the city. A tour guide provides informed commentary during the drive into Rome and answers any questions you may have. On the return drive, you can lean back in your seat and relax after a full day of sightseeing (10 hrs, $95).

revolted against this barbaric treatment were brutally killed by their Roman masters. The famous slave **Spartacus**, who died a century before the Colosseum was built, escaped from a gladiators' school at Capua (near modern Naples) and fled into the mountains, where he organized an army of fugitives who defeated several Roman forces before they were finally crushed.

Southwest of the Colosseum stands the **Arch of Constantine**, a triple-arcaded triumphal arch raised in 312 AD to celebrate Constantine I's victory over Maxentius at the Milvian Bridge near Rome, making him the unchallenged ruler of the West. The road heading south from the Arch led to the Circus Maximus where chariot races were held. The race-track was overlooked by the **Palatine 2**, one of Rome's seven hills and the site of the city's original 8th-century BC settlement. During the city's republican period, notable citizens built homes atop the Palatine, and various emperors built palaces there

(Above) Arch of Constantine. (Below) The Colosseum's interior, missing its arena floor, and an exterior view.

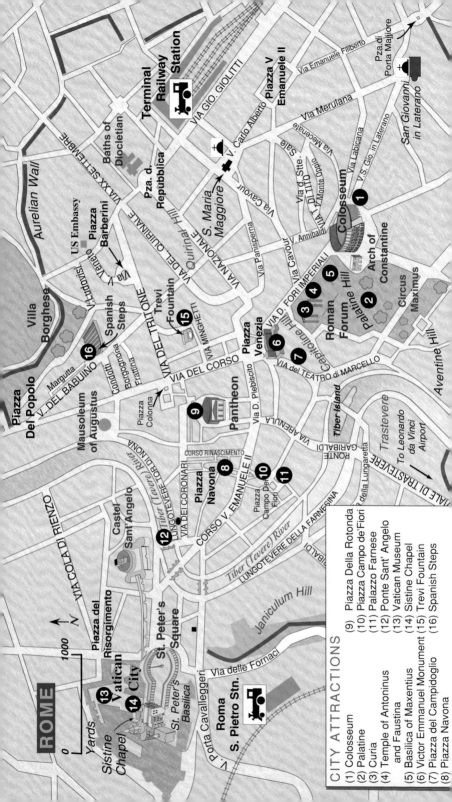

ROME

Yards
0   1000

N

CITY ATTRACTIONS

(1) Colosseum
(2) Palatine
(3) Curia
(4) Temple of Antoninus and Faustina
(5) Basilica of Maxentius
(6) Victor Emmanuel Monument
(7) Piazza del Campidoglio
(8) Piazza Navona
(9) Piazza Della Rotonda
(10) Piazza Campo de'Fiori
(11) Palazzo Farnese
(12) Ponte Sant' Angelo
(13) Vatican Museum
(14) Sistine Chapel
(15) Trevi Fountain
(16) Spanish Steps

during the imperial period.

Lying along the Palatine Hill, in a shallow valley between the Colosseum and Capitoline Hill, is the **Roman Forum** – the centre of republican Rome where the senate met, citizens strolled the basilicas and famous speeches were delivered by such famous orators as Caesar and Cicero. Victorious generals would ride in triumphant procession along the Sacred Way, the most famous street in ancient Rome, which runs the length of the Forum.

The restored **Arch of Titus** (commemorating his conquest of Jerusalem in 70 AD) stands at one end of the Sacred Way, not far from the Colosseum, and the **Arch of Septimius Severus**, raised in 203 AD, stands at the other end. Beside it are the ruins of the rostrum (raised platform) where Mark Antony delivered the funeral address in Caesar's honour. On the other side of the Arch of Septimius Severus is the **Curia 3**, a large brick senate hall dating from the 3rd century AD. Other important monuments in this large complex of ruins include: **The Temple of Antoninus and Faustin, 4**,

(Above) Temple of Antoninus is one of several buildings still standing in Roman Forum (top).

erected in 141 AD to commemorate the emperor and his wife; and the **Basilica of Maxentius 5**, completed by Constantine in 312.

As the empire grew, the Roman Forum could not accommodate additional structures, so certain emperors – following Julius Caesar's example – built along its outskirts. The remains of these imperial forums can still be seen along Via dei Fori Imperiali, a busy main street which leads to

Piazza Navona (above) and the interior of the Pantheon (right).

Piazza Venezia, the hub of central Rome. In the northwest corner of the square is the Palazzo Venezia, an early renaissance palace from which Mussolini, standing in the balcony over the main portal, would deliver speeches to the crowd-filled piazza below. Dominating Piazza Venezia is the **Victor Emmanuel Monument 6**, the huge marble 'wedding cake' commemorating the first king of a united Italy. Begun in 1885, it took forty years to complete. The ceremonial staircase leads to the Altar of the Nation which contains the Tomb of the Unknown Soldier, guarded by two sentinels. Above the shrine stands a statue of Romas flanked on both sides by celebratory reliefs. In the centre of the monument is a colossal equestrian statue of Victor Emmanuel.

Behind the Victor Emmanuel Monument, on **Capitoline Hill**, is the **Church of Santa Maria d'Aracoeli**. One of the oldest Christian churches in Rome, officiated by the Franciscan Friars Minor since 1250, its unadorned brick façade is reached from street level by a long stairway that was built in 1348. Another broad stairway right beside it leads to the **Piazza del Campidoglio 7**, an architectural complex designed by Michelangelo in the 1530s at the request of Pope Paul III and completed long after the artist's death. This complex occupies the most famous of Rome's seven hills – the Capitoline – which was the focal point of Rome's religious life in ancient times. Michelangelo's artistic genius is

(Above) Ponte Sant' Angelo.
(Below) St. Peter's Basilica.

reflected in the harmonious composition of this piazza, its trapezoidal shape created by its three buildings having been placed not at right angles to one other but at an angle of 80 degrees.

Upon ascending the staircase, visitors face the **Palazzo Senatorio** (Senators' Palace), now the Town Hall, which dominates the piazza. To the right is the **Palazzo dei Conservatori** (Conservators' Palace) which displays works of art, including the famous Capitoline Wolf – a 5th century bronze statue of the she-wolf (symbol of Rome) suckling the infant Romolus (founder of Rome) and his brother Remus, figures added by a 15th-century artist. To the left is the Palazzo Nuovo, which houses the **Capitoline Museum**, its works of art including a 2nd-century equestrian statue of the emperor Marcus Aurelius, the only bronze equestrian statue to survive from imperial Rome. It had stood in the centre of the piazza atop a pedestal until it was removed in 1981; an exact replica was mounted in

its place in the spring of 1997.

The main thoroughfare of Corso Vittoria Emanuele II runs through the centre of Old Rome, where narrow, winding streets lead to such famous attractions as the café-lined **Piazza Navona 8**, considered one of Rome's most beautiful squares with its baroque fountains and churches, and the **Piazza Della Rotonda 9** which is dominated by the Pantheon, a domed temple from the early 2nd century AD. The Pantheon is the

(Above) Bernini's baldachino.
(Below) The nave (with its barrel vault) inside St. Peter's Basilica.

best preserved of imperial Rome's surviving structures. It was built as a pagan temple, then converted to a Christian church. Entry is free to the Pantheon.

Piazza Campo de' Fiori (Field of Flowers) **10** is the scene of a colourful outdoor market each weekday morning, and the nearby **Palazzo Farnese 11** is a beautiful Renaissance palace now housing the French Embassy.

The elegant **Ponte Sant' Angelo 12** leads across the River Tiber to Castel Sant'Angelo. Three of the bridge's arches are original – built by Hadrian's successor – and in 1688 the bridge was extended and embellished with ten angels designed by Bernini. **Castel Sant'Angelo**, built in 139 AD as a mausoleum for the emperor Hadrian, was eventually used as a fortress for popes seeking refuge in times of peril. It later served as a prison, and is now a museum containing beautifully decorated papal apartments and prison cells.

Vatican City

A tiny sovereign state in the heart of Rome, Vatican City contains some of the world's most famous buildings and works of art. **St. Peter's Basilica**, the world's largest church, stands on the site of an early shrine to St. Peter. In the 4th century, Emperor Constantine built a church over the grave of St. Peter, and it was in this wood-roofed basilica that Charlemagne and other emperors and popes were crowned. In 1506, Pope Julius II decided a new church should be built to replace the

dilapidated original, and Bramante was commissioned to design it. A succession of architects worked on St. Peter's, including Michelangelo who took over in 1547 and added the gigantic dome. The church was finally completed in 1626 and its sublime interior of creamy marble and glittering gilt is filled with masterpieces. Michelangelo's famous *La Pieta* (sculpted when he was 24) is in one of the side chapels. Bernini's *baldachino* – a bronze canopy – stands above the high altar from which only the pope may read mass. Admission to the basilica is free, but the elevator to the terrace costs €7 (a bit less to climb the dome's stairs to the roof).

(Above) Michelangelo's Creation of Adam, Sistine Chapel, and (below) La Pieta, St. Peter's.

The Vatican Swiss Guards

Since the 15th century, Swiss mercenaries have fought in various European armies. Called Swiss Guards, these mercenaries were put at the disposal of foreign powers in return for money payments. In 1874 the Swiss constitution forbade all recruitment of Swiss soldiers by foreign powers, with the exception of Vatican City. Founded in 1505 as the personal guard of the pope, the Swiss Guard in the Vatican carry on a centuries-old tradition of swearing to serve the pope. Recruited from Switzerland's Catholic cantons, the guardsmen on sentry duty are garbed in colourful costume of Renaissance design and wear ceremonial armour. A 100-member force, its members live in Vatican City and must observe strict rules, including a midnight curfew.

Trevi Fountain

Fountain of the Four Rivers

Fountain Frolicks

Completed in 1762, the **Trevi Fountain** 15 is one of Rome's most popular attractions. Its centrepiece is a statue of the god Oceanus riding in a sea chariot drawn by two Tritons. The fountain was used for a scene in Fellini's famous film *La Dolce Vita*, in which characters played by Marcello Mastroianni and Anita Ekberg go wading in it. Such behaviour is, in real life, frowned upon because of the risk of vandalism, both deliberate and accidental, and the city of Rome imposes a stiff fine on anyone caught bathing in a public fountain.

In addition to Rome's many monumental fountains, the city has hundreds of small drinking fountains, called *nasoni* ('big noses'), from which flows clean, cold water fed by the city's original aquaducts. When walking the streets of Rome you can refill your water bottle at any of these public fountains. Stout and made of cast iron, they're not works of art but on a hot summer's day these fountains are a welcome sight for thirsty pedestrians seeking a drink of cold, refreshing water.

Piazza San Pietro (**St. Peter's Square**) was designed by Bernini in the 1650s at the request of Pope Alexander VII. He called for a grand approach to St. Peter's that wouldn't obstruct the view of the faithful who gather in the square when the pope makes an address from the church's central balcony or from a window of the adjacent Vatican Palace. Bernini met this criteria with a sweeping colonnade that curves along both sides of the square. The Egyptian obelisk in the centre of the square was brought to Rome in imperial times by the Emperor Caligula, and the monumental avenue leading to the piazza was added by Mussolini.

The **Vatican Museums** 13, next door to the Vatican Palace, are a complex of eight museums and five galleries containing one of the world's most extensive art collections, including ancient

Egyptian artifacts, Roman statues and paintings by Raphael. The ceiling and altar wall of the **Sistine Chapel** , where the cardinals meet to elect a new pope, were painted by Michelangelo. Considered works of unsurpassed grandeur, the ceiling frescoes depict biblical scenes and the altar wall was selected for Michelangelo's painting of the *Last Judgment*. A major restoration of these works was undertaken from 1980 to 1992, which entailed cleaning away a layer of dirt to reveal the original vibrant colours of the frescoes. Amid the spectrum of colours used by Michelangelo, the two that stand out are green and violet – the liturgical colours of the Mass.

Tarquinia's museum is housed in a 15th-century castle.

Rome's main shopping area lies between Via del Corso and the **Spanish Steps**  – Rome's most fashionable gathering place. Artists and writers have long been attracted to this area, including the Romantic poet Keats, who lived and died in a house next to the Steps, his residence now a museum. The 18th-century Steps were built by the French to connect the Spanish Quarter at the bottom to the French Quarter at the top. A 16th-century church, built for France's King Louis XII, stands at the top of the Steps, and a boat-shaped fountain designed by Bernini is at the bottom.

Tarquinia

While most passengers arriving in Civitavecchia head straight to Rome for a full day of sightseeing, some choose an excursion to Tarquinia. In 449 BC the Etruscans, whose kings founded and ruled Rome for about a century, established the ancient city of Tarquinni. These people (possibly from Asia Minor) had first settled in the Tuscany area of Italy in the 8th century BC. The Etruscans, their commercial empire rivaling those of Greece and Phoenicia, didn't form a unified nation, but rather a network of city-states, each of which succumbed, one by one, to the Romans in the 5th and 4th centuries BC. Such was the fate of Tarquinni, but its large necropolis of tombs remained intact and today visitors can gaze at their unique murals, inspired perhaps by Egyptian wall art and painted around 500 BC. The **Etruscan National Museum**, housed in a 15th-century castle in the nearby town of Tarquinia, contains an extensive collection of Etruscan artefacts.

Naples (Napoli)

The beautiful Bay of Naples had lured many a visitor to its scenic shores when British admiral **Horatio Nelson** pulled into port during the summer of 1798. Nelson was joining a long list of illustrious guests, including Goethe, who were graciously entertained by Sir William Hamilton, the British ambassador to Naples from 1764 to 1800. Sir Hamilton, after years of scholarly pursuits, had embraced the Neapolitans' carefree attitude to life and thrown himself with gusto into the pursuit of pleasure. His beautiful young wife and former mistress, **Lady Emma Hamilton**, was a confidante of the Queen of Naples – whose court was a centre of scandal and intrigue – and it was through this friendship that the British fleet, under the command of Nelson, was allowed access to the Spanish-controlled ports of Naples and Syracuse to take on provisions when all other Mediterranean ports had been shut off by the French. Nelson went on to destroy the French fleet off the mouth of the Nile River and, upon his return to Naples, he was given a hero's welcome and was

Mount Vesuvius looms above the Bay of Naples.

bestowed with a British peerage. He also fell deeply in love with Lady Hamilton, and so began their notorious love affair.

Such is life in southern Italy, a land of sunshine and song, idyllic islands and fragrant breezes. In ancient times, wealthy Romans built themselves country villas at Herculaneum and Pompeii, situated at the base of **Mount Vesuvius**, and the tiny island paradise of Capri, in the Bay of Naples, became a holiday retreat for the early emperors Augustus and Tiberius. The cataclysmic eruption of Mount Vesuvius in 79 AD brought a thunderous end to the good life when Herculaneum and Pompeii were buried under cinders, ashes and mud, then long forgotten until they were rediscovered in the 18th century.

Mount Vesuvius erupted eight times in the 19th century and three times in the 20th. Its last eruption, which destroyed Thomas Cook's funicular railway leading up to the crater, was in 1944. The ensuing period of inactivity has prompted concerns that the next eruption could be a major one. The volcano's smouldering presence has made Neapolitans somewhat superstitious, and twice a year they gather by the hundreds with their archbishop at the Cathedral of San Gennaro to pray to a 4th-century

A wedding couple crosses a busy street in Piazza Trieste e Trento.

saint and witness a 'miracle' in which his blood, kept in gold vials, liquefies – a sign that disaster will not strike the city.

Getting Around

Naples is not a pedestrian-friendly city. Simply crossing some of the busy streets is challenging, for drivers seem to take no notice of whether a traffic light is red or green. Fortunately, several historic buildings are located a short distance from the **Maritime Station** (Stazione Marittima) **1** where the cruise ships dock. Further afield is the Archaeological Museum, which is a €10 taxi ride away.

The **train station** **2** is on Corso Garibaldi, about one mile from the cruise dock (a €10 taxi ride). Herculaneum, Pompeii and Sorrento can all be reached by train, and tickets are sold in euros. A train runs every 20 to 30 minutes from Naples to **Pompeii**; the ride takes about 30 minutes; disembark at the Pompeii excavation site (Pompeii Scavi). The train

Maritime Station was built during Mussolini's dictatorship.

ride from Naples to **Sorrento** is an hour and 20 minutes.

Catching a ferry from Naples to **Sorrento** is an enjoyable alternative. A terminal is located beside the Maritime Station and the Alilauro Hydrofoil departs from the Moro Beverello pier every two hours; the trip takes about 40 minutes and costs €11 each way. Metro del Mare also provides regular ferry service between Naples and Sorrento.

Several companies operate hydrofoils and ferries between Naples and **Capri**, with numerous departures by hydrofoil to

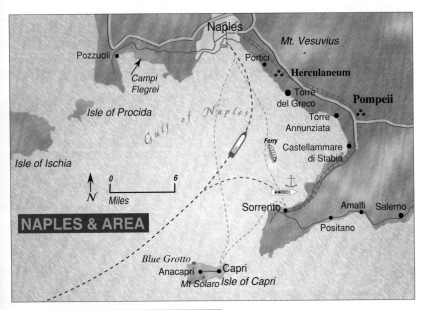

NAPLES & AREA

Shore Excursions

Excursions at the port of **Naples** focus mainly on tours to Pompeii, Capri and the Amalfi coast. Half-day tours of Pompeii and of Herculaneum are offered, along with full-day coach tours that combine a drive to Sorrento with a visit to Pompeii (8 hrs) or a drive along the Amalfi coast with stops at Amalfi and Sorrento (8 hrs). Other excursions include a full-day tour to Capri by hydrofoil or hiking to the upper part of the crater on Mt. Vesuvius (4 hrs).

Capri (approx. €20 and one hour each way). Upon reaching Capri's harbour (Marina Grande), the funicular or bus ride up to Capri town costs about €2.

Boats also run between Sorrento and Capri, and between Naples and Ischia Island, which is where scenes for the movie *The Talented Mr. Ripley* were filmed.

Shopping & Dining

Naples artisans are known for their craftsmanship in cameos, ceramics, wood inlay and embroidered goods. Galleria Umberto I and Via Chiaia both offer upscale shopping.

Naples is where pizza was invented and two of its most popular pizzerias are located off Corso Umberto on the way to the Piazza Garibaldi train station. At **Pizzeria da Michele** (Via Cesare Sersale, 1) customers line up for the Pizza Marinara. More toppings are available at nearby **Pizzeria Trianon** (Via Colletta Pietro, 46), where about 1,000 pizzas a day are baked in its three wood-burning ovens. Another pizzeria, popular with locals who line up outside at lunchtime, is **Di Matteo** on Via dei Tribulani. President Bill Clinton was a customer here while attending the 1994 G7 Summit in Naples.

Naples Attractions

The city's medieval past is evidenced by several Neapolitan castles overlooking the harbour, including the 12th-century **Castel dell'Ovo** **3** which stands on a rocky islet, and **Castel Nuovo** **4**, a symbol of power and the scene of fierce battles between the French and Spanish. Surrounded by a moat, the castle was originally built in 1279 by Charles I of Anjou, then rebuilt by Spanish and Tuscan craftsmen following the bloody wars of the 15th century. Naples became a centre of sculpture under the rule of Alfonso of Aragon, who captured Naples in 1442. His admiration of classical antiquity is reflected in the triumphal arch he had built between the two towers that flank the castle's west entrance. Dozens

West entrance to Castel Nuovo (above), detail of the arch (right).

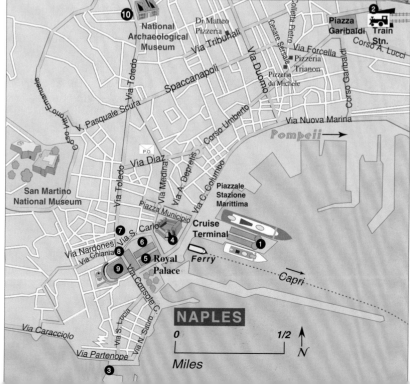

(Above) Galleria Umberto I.
(Below) Gates to Royal Palace.
(Bottom) Piazza Plebiscito.

of Renaissance sculptors worked on its complex design from 1451 until its completion 30 years later.

The Palazzo Reale (**Royal Palace**) **5**, built in the early 1600s, has been damaged, restored and remodeled over the centuries. The past home to various Neapolitan royal families, including the Spanish Bourbons, its sumptuous interior of frescoed walls and grand staircases is filled with baroque furniture, period mirrors and chandeliers, Chinese porcelain vases, gilt bronzes, and paintings by celebrated artists.

Naples is famous for its music,

both classical and popular, some well-known Neapolitan songs being *Funiculi Funicula* and *O Sole Mio*. The great tenor Caruso was a Naples native, and numerous works – including *La Sonnambula* by Bellini – have premiered at the Teatro di S. Carlo (**San Carlo Opera House**) **6**, second in Italy only to La Scala in Milan. It first opened in 1737, then was reconstructed following a fire in 1816. The red and gold interior, which seats 3,000 and provides perfect acoustics, is also a visual feast, with its seven levels of private boxes, each row adorned with gilt balustrades.

Galleria Umberto I **7**, named for King Umberto I, is an iron- and glass-roofed gallery constructed in the late 1800s, which today is filled with elegant shops and cafés. More fine shops are located on Via Chiaia, off **Piazza Trieste e Trento** **8**, a lovely square with a fountain in its centre that connects with **Piazza Plebiscito** **9**, which opens to the sweeping facade of the Chiesa di S. Francesco di Paola (Church of St. Francis). Completed in 1847, the church was modeled on the Pantheon in Rome, while the curving colonnade arcade is reminiscent of the one in St. Peter's Square. A large and majestic square, it is a popular photo shoot for Neapolitan wedding parties.

The highly acclaimed **National Archaeological Museum** **10**, housed in a 16th-century building, contains one of the world's largest collections of classical antiquities, including the historic riches recovered from Herculaneum and Pompeii. Paintings, mosaics, statues, busts, vases and domestic implements are among the discoveries on display.

Pompeii & Herculaneum

Nestled at the foot of Mount Vesuvius, the Roman centres of Pompeii (a prosperous walled city) and Herculaneum (a seaside resort) were both recovering from the earthquake of 63 AD when disaster struck on an August day in 79 AD. It began like any other, the residents of Pompeii going

Classic Cuisine

Pizza is a Neapolitan dish that began as peasant food and is now considered classic Italian cuisine. To meet the certification standards for 'genuine pizza' set by the Italian Standards Institute, a restaurant must dice the tomato a certain size (8 mm), use mozzarella cheese made from buffalo milk, and bake the pizza at 390 to 453 degrees Fahrenheit. Chefs have been baking pizza in wood-burning ovens for more than two centuries in Naples, where the original Pizza Margherita, named for an Italian queen, is made with tomato, mozzarella and basil. Pizza Marinara is a Neopolatin pizza that adds oregano, anchovies and lots of garlic. There are numerous regional varieties of pizza which use different toppings but are always based on the Italian culinary rule of fresh, local ingredients.

The basilica and antiquarium of Pompeii. (Below) Cast of man caught in final moment of life.

about their business as bakers, merchants, artisans, prostitutes and slaves who were in service to the wealthy owners of fine villas. The public baths were busy, as usual, and the city's shops and streets were filled with people, many pausing to read the graffiti written on public walls. Chariots and carts rolled by, following the worn ruts in roads.

Then, suddenly, the ground began to shake and catastrophe struck. A thunderous cloud of ash and lava exploded from the sum-

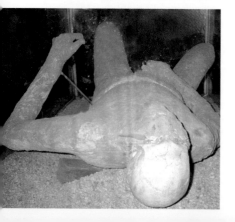

mit of Mount Vesuvius, erupting with such force that it blew away part of the mountain. As people ran for their lives, they were suffocated by gaseous fumes, while those still inside their homes were buried beneath a torrential downpour of cinder and ash. The residents of Herculaneum made a desperate rush for the town exit but there was no escaping the darkness that descended on them. When it was all over, in a space of a few hours, Pompeii lay buried under 20 feet (7 m) of ash and Herculaneum was sealed under a 40- to 100-foot layer of rock that formed when the ash was hardened by falling rain.

Entombed for centuries, the ancient townsite of Herculaneum was first discovered in 1706, when a well was being dug, and systematic excavations began in 1738. The larger site of Pompeii was discovered in 1748, providing the world with a detailed look at everyday Roman life as it existed in 79 AD. Archaeologists discovered hundreds of personal items in the city's private residences, including furniture, ornaments and

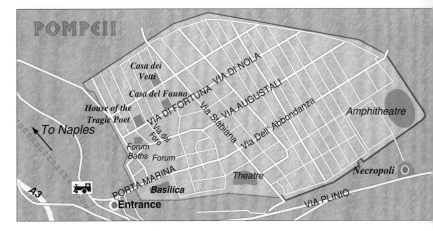

beautifully preserved wall paintings in the villas of the town's patrician class. By pouring liquid plaster into hollows left by disintegrated bodies, they were able to make hauntingly life-like 'impressions', of the people caught in their final moments – embracing, fleeing, retrieving valuable objects from their homes.

Today's visitors to Pompeii enter through the main gate (Porta Marina) near the forum, or through a back gate near the amphitheatre. A restaurant and shop carrying books and maps is located just north of the forum on Via del Foro. Areas of interest include the remains of the civic forum's public buildings and the forum baths.

When the Englishman Thomas Cook brought a group of British tourists to Italy in 1864, the excavated site of ancient Pompeii was perceived as a somewhat shocking, pleasure-seeking city brimming with bars, brothels and priapic statuary. But there was also a refined side to Pompeii, preserved in the luxurious and lavishly decorated villas of the wealthy. A trip to the top of Mount Vesuvius to peer into the volcano's crater was part of a 19th-century Cook's Italian Tour, and the company eventually bought the Italian-built funicular.

Just wandering the streets of Pompeii is a fascinating experience. The raised sidewalks and stepping stones were designed to keep pedestrians' feet dry when rainwater collected in the streets, and cat's eyes – small white marble stones – were set in the streets (and villa floors) to illuminate them at night. At the entrance to the House of the Tragic Poet is a 'Beware of Dog' sign, written in Latin with an accompanying mosaic of a guard dog. The best preserved villa is Casa Dei Vetti, where visitors can admire the home's atrium, frescoed walls and garden courtyard.

Mount Vesuvius, its sides scarred by lava flow, is a Naples landmark. Its fertile lower slopes are cultivated with vineyards that produce the famous Lachryma Christi (Tears of Christ) wine. The base of the mountain is encircled by a railroad and a trail can be hiked to the crater's rim.

(Above) Atop Mt. Solaro on Capri. (Below) Viewing Capri's famous Faraglioni sea stacks from the Hotel Luna's terrace.

Capri

The tiny island paradise of Capri, with its lush vegetation and delightful climate, has been an exclusive retreat ever since the days of the Roman Empire, when Emperor Tiberius owned 12 villas on this craggy island. Twentieth-century residents included Gracie Fields, Rudolph Nureyev and the Swedish physician and writer Axel Munthe, who built Villa San Michele (now a museum) at **Anacapri**, one of two towns on the island which are set atop lime-stone cliffs where herds of *capra* (goats) once roamed.

Capri town overlooks Marina Grande, where the passenger fer-ries dock and a visitor information office is located. A charming town of narrow lanes and tiny squares, Capri is reached by funicular, bus or taxi. Anacapri, which is quieter than Capri, can be reached by bus or taxi from Capri. Monte Solaro's summit, the highest point on the island at 1,900 feet (580 m), can be ascended by chairlift at Anacapri. It's a 12-minute ride up to a dramatic mountaintop belve-

Sorrento overlooks Bay of Naples.

dere dotted with flower-filled urns and café tables. You are literally above the clouds, gazing down at the sea cliffs.

The island's footpaths also provide spectacular sea views as does the Hotel Luna's clifftop terrace (near the Gardens of Augustus in Capri town) which overlooks the iconic Faraglioni sea stacks. Other island attractions include the Blue Grotto (a sea cave bathed in iridescent blue light) which can be toured by boat (€18) from Marina Grande. Shops and restaurants are plentiful in both towns.

Amalfi Coast

The Amalfi coast, from Sorrento to Salerno, is one of the most scenic in the Mediterranean, with its cliff-clinging roads and spectacular views. One seaside resort after another lies along this enchanting stretch of coast, including **Sorrento**, home of the legendary sirens who tried to lure Odysseus onto the rocks. The cruise ships dock within easy access of the town. Ferry boats and hydrofoils run regularly between Sorrento, Amalfi, Capri and Naples.

A tourist shuttle runs between Sorrento and **Positano**, where John Steinbeck, in 1953, lived in one of its multi-coloured houses connected by hillside stairs above a crescent bay. In the hills above Positano is a gem of a restaurant called La Tagliata, with spectacular views and excellent local cuisine. A family-run establishment, it's located at Via Tagliata, 22, Montepertuso (about a $20 taxi ride from Positano).

Amalfi, a small fishing port and picturesque resort overlooking the Gulf of Salerno, was founded by Romans. It became, in the 9th century AD, an Italian maritime republic rivaling Pisa, Venice and Genoa in wealth and power. Its Sicilian-Arab cathedral, built in the 11th century with later additions, reflects the influence of Arab invaders who had seized Sicily in 917 and raided the mainland, until they were driven out by the Normans.

Salerno flourished during the Middle Ages, establishing a medical school in the 9th century and erecting a Sicilian-Norman cathedral in the 11th century. During World War II, allied forces landed on the beaches near Salerno, where fierce fighting forced the Germans to retreat toward Naples.

Sicily (Sicilia)

The largest of the Mediterranean islands with a population of five million, Sicily's mountainous terrain includes **Mt. Etna**, an active volcano and the island's highest point at 10,700 feet. The island, with its fertile soil and long, hot growing season, was a granary of the ancient world. Agriculture remains the major industry – wheat, barley and maize as well as olives, citrus fruits, almonds and grapes are all grown here.

The island's east coast was colonized by the Greeks who founded Syracuse, Catania and Zancle (now Messina), and by 400 BC Sicily was a battleground between the rival empires of Carthaginia and Greece, a situation that would be repeated time and again as foreign powers fought for control of Sicilian soil. During the Punic Wars, Rome and Carthaginia battled for possession of Sicily, and when the Romans eventually seized control of the island, it became the Breadbasket of Rome. After the fall of Rome, the island eventually passed to the Byzantines in 535 AD.

Arabs raided the island for two centuries before it finally fell in the 9th century. Next came the Norman conquest of Sicily in 1060, followed by Spanish rule in 1282. Sicily finally voted to join the kingdom of Sardinia after being conquered in 1860 by Giuseppe Garibaldi, a popular Italian patriot and leading figure in the Risorgimento.

Sicily's most recent invasion came during World War II when, in July 1943, Allied forces staged a large-scale amphibious landing from North African bases and, following a month of heavy fighting, Sicily was once again conquered.

After centuries of exploitation by outsiders, Sicilians today are trying to rid their island of the Mafia – a name that came into use during the 19th century when it was applied to groups of brigands.

Palermo

The capital and largest city of Sicily, Palermo began as an ancient Phoenician seaport. It was during the Arab occupation of 831 to 1072 AD that the city prospered, rivaling Cairo with the Oriental splendour of its palaces, mosques and minarets. An important trading port between East and West, the city continued to flourish under the Normans – most notably during the reign of Roger II, whose court was a centre for the arts, letters and sciences. Today's Palermo, plagued by poverty,

Shore tours are available to Mount Etna, an active volcano.

contains some unique and resplendent works of art which are located within walking distance of one another. Most notable is the Cappella Palatina (**Palatine Chapel**), located inside the **Norman Royal Palace**, which is the seat of the Sicilian parliament. This Arab-Norman chapel, built in 1132 by Roger II, is an artistic treasure containing glittering mosaics and a honeycombed ceiling. The pink-domed San Giovanni degli Eremiti (**Church of St. John of the Hermits**) was built in 1132 on the site of an old mosque, and its lovely cloister is filled with palm and citrus trees. Other historic buildings are the 12th-century cathedral; the 15th-century Palazzo Abbatellis; and the Gothic Palazzo Chiaramonte, built in 1307. Shoppers in search of Sicilian handicrafts should visit the flea market on **Via Papireto**, behind the cathedral.

Shore excursions include a narrated drive through Palmero, a walking tour of a Norman fortified village, exploring the ancient ruins at Segesta and visiting the seaside town of Cefal.

Messina/Taormina

Messina is a busy seaport and gateway to Sicily, with passenger ferries from mainland Italy regularly pulling into port. A modern city, Messina was rebuilt following a devastating earthquake in December 1908 which claimed 80,000 lives and destroyed 90 per cent of the buildings, including fine churches and palaces.

Getting Around

The main attraction for passengers arriving by ship at Messina is the nearby medieval town of

The Messina lighthouse (below).
Mount Etna viewed from
Taormina (bottom).

Messina's Norman-Romanesque cathedral was rebuilt following the 1908 earthquake.

Taormina with its Graeco-Roman theatre. **Taormina** is located 27 miles south of Messina, and can be reached by ship-organized tours, by train, by bus or by taxi. A return taxi ride from Messina to Taormina is negotiable and costs about 150 to 180 euros.

Messina's **train station**  and adjacent bus station are about half a mile from Messina's cruise port. The train ride to Taormina takes from 45 minutes to one hour and 20 minutes; the bus ride takes longer. The Taormina-Gardini train station is situated below Taormina at the base of a hill and from there you can take a taxi up to the town (€12) or take the bus (€2) which departs every half hour for the 10-minute ride up to Via Luigi Pirandello from where you walk the rest of the way up to the town.

If your ship anchors in the Bay of Naxos, there will be a ship's shuttle available at the tender dock (a motor coach transports you to the Lumbi parking lot, which is about half-way up; from there you take a mini-van for the final ascent). Taxis are also available at the tender pier.

Shore excursions from Messina include full-day tours of Taormina and Mount Etna. A unique tour is the one that visits two Sicilian villages - Savoca and Forza d'Agro – where Francis Ford Coppola filmed scenes for The Godfather movies.

Messina Attractions

There are several interesting sights right in Messina, within walking distance of the pier. The main **shopping** area is along Via Garibaldi, Piazza Cairoli and Viale San Martino.

The **Norman-Romanesque cathedral** , was originally built by the Norman king Roger II in 1197. Modified over time and damaged by earthquakes, it has been reconstructed to its original Norman appearance, including most of the mosaics and works of art. The bell tower houses an astronomical clock, one of the largest and most complex of its kind, which was brought from Strasbourg in 1933, and springs into mechanized action at mid-day.

The church of the Annunziata dei Catalani (**The Most Holy Annunciation of the Catalans**) **2** was founded in the 12th century on the ruins of an ancient temple of Neptune. Reflecting both Byzantine and Arab influences, the church today stands several feet below street level because of the city's progressive raising due to earthquakes and reconstructions. Two of the original Quattro

(Top) The Sanctuary of Christo Re. (Above) One of the original Four Fountains on Via Austria.

Fontane (**Four Fountains**) **3** still stand at the former cross-roads of Via Austria and Via Cardines. Baroque in design, two of them are now kept in the **Regional Museum 4** which is about 1.5 miles from the cruise pier along the waterfront and houses a col-

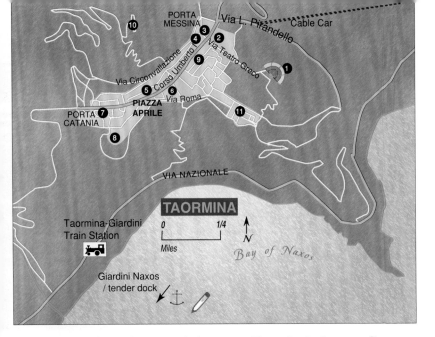

lection of Renaissance paintings, including one by native-born artist Antonello da Messina.

The **Sanctuary of Christo Re** (King Christ) **5** enjoys a prominent position on a hill overlooking the city and harbor. Originally a Norman castle, it may have been constructed by Richard the Lionheart. Serving as a royal residence, then a prison in the 19th century, it was rebuilt after the 1908 earthquake and is now a crypt containing the Messinese who died in World War II.

Taormina Attractions

A medieval town and fashionable resort of undisputed charm, Taormina stands perched above the Ionian Sea, its steep stairways and twisting paths providing views of verdant hillsides covered with palms and pines. On clear days the active volcano of Mt. Etna dominates the southwest horizon, its massive peak rising to nearly 11,000 feet.

Taormina's famous **Graeco-Roman amphitheatre** **1**, built by the Greeks in the 3rd century BC, is beautifully situated to embrace this magnificent coastal setting of sea, sky and snow-capped mountain. Enlarged and rebuilt by the Romans in the 2nd century AD, the theatre today hosts an annual summer arts festival.

Just inside the town's north gate (Porta Messina) is the **Piazza Vittorio Emanuele** **2**, site of the town's ancient Greek agora and later a Roman forum. The **Palazzo Corvala** **3**, now housing a tourist information centre, was restored in 1945 and its features, spanning three historic periods of construction, include an Arab tower. The **Santa Caterina Church** **4** was built in the 17th century on the site of the Roman odeum, the remains of which are visible inside the church. The town's main street of Corso Umberto I, called 'Valeria'

in ancient times, leads to Piazza Aprile – a large square overlooking the sea and site of the 17th-century **Chiesa di San Giuseppe 5** and **Chiesa di Sant-Agostino 6**, built in 1448 and now the town library.

Farther along Corso Umberto I is the town's cathedral – **San Nicola** (Mother Church) **7** – which is similar in plan and from the same period as the Messina cathedral. A slight detour leads to the **Convent of San Domenico 8**, begun in 1374. Other sights include the **Naumachie** (a Roman wall that protected a large cistern) **9**, and the ruins of **Castello Saraceno 10**, which sits on the site of the ancient acropolis and is reached by a long stairway. A stroll through the **public gardens 11** is also recommended. **Shops** selling local handicrafts line the Via Teatro Greco (leading to the amphitheater) and Corso Umberto I.

(Top) Taormina's Graeco-Roman amphitheatre and (above) Piazza Aprile.

South of Taormina are the coastal cities of Catania and Syracuse. **Catania**, like Messina, is a port of access to Taormina. The city was heavily damaged in World War II, and in past centuries has been struck by earthquakes and volcanic eruptions. The 19th-century composer Vincenzo Bellini was born in Catania and his former home is now a museum. The cathedral (originally built in the 11th century) contains Bellini's remains, as well as the chapel of St. Agatha, the city's patron saint.

Syracuse (Siracusa) is best known for its Archaeological Park which contains a 5th century BC amphitheater – one of the most complete Greek theatres to survive from antiquity – as well as the ruins of a Roman amphitheatre. Near the park entrance is Latomia del Paradiso, a garden area where a series of quarries served as ancient prisons.

Sardinia

The large and mostly mountainous island of Sardinia is a favourite holiday destination for Italians living in Rome. Renowned for its beautiful beaches and blue-green sea, this pastoral island was a centre of trade in prehistoric times and became a source of grain and salt for the ancient Romans.

With the fall of Rome, the island was invaded by various forces and was passed back and forth between medieval Genoa and Pisa as they fought for supremacy over the island. Italy's revolutionary hero Giuseppe Garibaldi, born at Nice in 1807, served as a youth in the Sardinian navy. He was a man of action and when revolution swept across Europe in 1848, Garibaldi fought for Sardinia against Austria.

In 1851 he bought part of the small island of **Caprera**, which lies off Sardinia's **Costa Smeralda** (Emerald Coast) of low cliffs and idyllic coves. He had, by then, thrown his support behind Victor Emmanuel II, king of Sardinia, and in 1860 Garibaldi led the victorious conquest of Sicily before crossing to the mainland to conquer Naples. Garibaldi then retired to his island property and shortly thereafter Victor Emmanuel II was proclaimed king of a united Italy.

When the Aga Khan, cruising the Mediterranean by yacht, sought shelter from a storm along the Costa Smeralda in 1965, he was smitten with the scenic beauty that had attracted the seafaring Garibaldi a century earlier. He built the upscale resort village of **Porto Cervo** and thus began the Costa Smeralda's incarnation as a chic enclave for wealthy vacationers, many of whom arrive by luxury yacht. Less-developed (and less expensive) beach resorts lie west of Porto Cervo along the island's northern tip of beach-fringed bays.

Ports of call on Sardinia include **Porto Torres** and **Alghero** – a 14th-century walled town and popular resort with sandy beaches and limestone cliffs where the Grotto of Neptune, a huge cavern, has been carved by the pounding sea. Six miles north of Alghero, on the road to Porto Torres, is a concentration of prehistoric tombs carved into the hillside, their chambers connected by corridors.

Shore Excursions

Sardinia Ship-organized shore excursions from **Alghero** include a walking tour, scenic drives to the dramatic headland at Cape Caccia, a stop at the prehistoric ruins at Palmavera, and a visit to Bosa, where fine lace is made. Shore excursions at **Cagliari** include a walking tour of its medieval Castello district, and a drive to the archaeological site of Nora.

Bronze statuettes depicting people, gods and animals have been retrieved from the tombs and nuraghi of Sardinia's earliest inhabitants. These are on display at the Archaeological Museum in **Cagliari**, the island's capital and a port of call for cruise ships. Cagliari was a Pisan stronghold during the wars with Genoa from the 11th to 14th century, and its Romanesque-Gothic cathedral, extensively rebuilt, reflects this Pisan influence, as does the massive Tower of St. Pancreas, built by Pisans in 1304. The city also has a Roman amphitheatre.

As in the rest of Italy, food in Sardinia is an important matter. If **lunching** in Cagliari, try the Catalan lobster. *Ricci* (sea urchins) are also very popular.

Alghero with the cliffs of Cape Caccia in background.

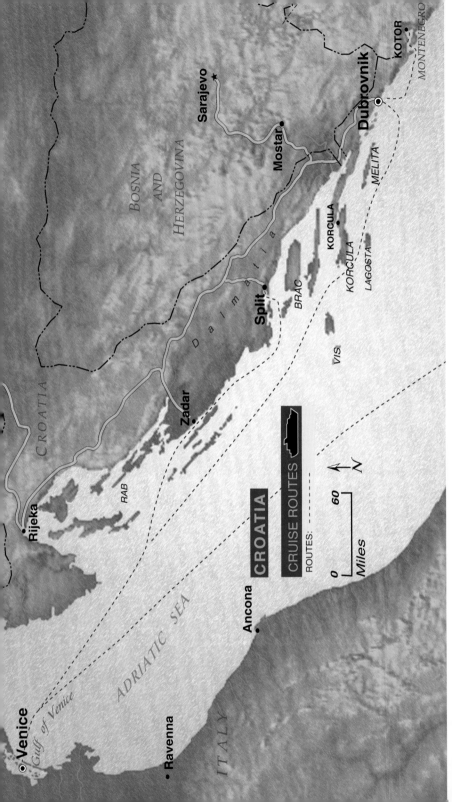

CROATIA
AND MONTENEGRO

The island-dotted Dalmatian coast, famous for its scenic beauty, has been coveted by Roman emperors, Venetian doges, Turkish sultans and Hungarian kings. The mainland is dominated by the Dinaric Alps, their steep slopes forming a dramatic backdrop for the convoluted coastline's harbours and headlands. Immediately offshore lies a string of islands said to number over 1,200, where pine-scented coves and secluded beaches are lapped by the clear blue waters of the Adriatic Sea.

Dalmatia's History

The Ancient Greeks avoided the warlike Illyrian tribes that inhabited the Dalmatian coastline and it was only after the Roman province of Illyria was established in the 3rd century BC that Dalmatia was finally subdued under Augustus (35-33 BC). Two centuries later the future emperor Diocletian was born near the port of Salona (modern Split). He rose from humble beginnings to high military command in the Roman army, which proclaimed him emperor in 284 AD.

After appointing three co-emperors to protect the Roman Empire from invasion, Diocletian retired to his castle at Salona, refusing to return and help restore stability to the empire, despite the urgings of his former co-emperor Maximiam who had abdicated at the same time. Diocletian had discovered gardening and was no longer interested in pursuing power.

The eventual fall of Rome brought chaos to Europe and in the 7th century the city of **Dubrovnik** was founded by Roman refugees fleeing Slav invaders, who in turn settled in Dubrovnik. The medieval city became a link between the Latin and Slavic civilizations, and a powerful merchant republic.

Dubrovnik's medieval walled town is a world heritage treasure.

Over time, massive stone walls and forts were constructed to protect the seaport from enemy attack.

In 1000 AD, Venice sent its newly formed navy to the Dalmatian coast to defeat the pirates who hid out among the many islands and staged repeated raids on Venice. When the Venetian doge Pietro Orsielo II captured the town of Korcula, his victory marked the final defeat of the Dalmatian pirates. Venice soon controlled the Adriatic, with the exception of Dubrovnik, which maintained its autonomy even while under various protectorates, including the Byzantine Empire, Hungary and Turkey. Not until 1808 did Dubrovnik relinquish independence to Napoleon.

Following World War I, Italy regained a foothold in Dalmatia when it received Zadar and several islands under the terms of the Treaty of Rapallo. Croatia, which had been part of the Austro-Hungarian Empire prior to World War I, was incorporated into the new Kingdom of the Serbs, Croats and Slovenes, which became known as Yugoslavia.

The German army invaded Yugoslavia during World War II and Dalmatia was placed under Italian control. Yugoslavia's occupation by Axis Powers was met with organized resistance by guerrilla warriors fighting from mountain strongholds. Leading this resistance was Josip Broz, who had adopted the name **Tito**.

Born in a Croatian village, the son of a blacksmith, Tito began his march to power as a soldier, then as a union organizer and political agitator. By 1945, Tito was the virtual dictator of Yugoslavia. Upon his death in 1980, ethnic tensions amongst the federation's member republics resulted in a violent breakup. Croatia was the second largest Yugoslav republic when it seceded on June 25, 1991. A six-month battle with federal troops (mostly Serbian) ensued and Croatia's independence was recognized by the European Community on January 15, 1992.

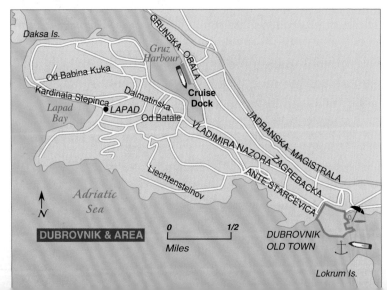

Croatia At A Glance

About 4 million people live in Croatia. The majority (90%) are Croats and a small minority (5%) are Serbs. The country is a parliamentary republic and its capital is Zagreb. Croatian is the official language but most Croats can speak English. Tourism, fishing and farming thrive along the scenic Dalmatian coast, its climate similar to coastal California.

Coastal views are enjoyed on a taxi tour of the Dubrovnik area.

Travel Tips

Currency – The unit of currency is the kuna (HRK), which consists of 100 lipas, but the euro is widely used. The approximate exchange is $1 US = 7 HRK; £1 GBP = 10 HRK. Major credit cards are accepted at most shops and restaurants. ATMs are widespread.

Telephones – Croatia's country code is 385. Dubrovnik's area code is 20 and Split's is 21.

Shopping – Croatian handicrafts include embroidery and fine lace, leather items, woodcarvings, ceramics and filigree jewellery.

Dining – Seafood such as calamari, cuttlefish, shrimp, lobster and oysters are featured in Dalmatian dishes, often cooked in olive oil and seasoned with garlic and local herbs. The Italian influence is enjoyed in a prevalence of pasta, pizza and risotto.

Dubrovnik

An important seaport and tourist resort, Dubrovnik has emerged in recent years as a popular port of call for cruise travellers. Of primary interest is the city's historic section – a medieval fortress built on a promontory which has served as the fictional King's Landing in *Game of Thrones*.

An earthquake and fire in 1667 destroyed much of the city and in 1991-92 Dubrovnik withstood damage while under siege by the Yugoslav army.

Stone walls up to twenty feet thick encircle the old town, which has retained and restored much of its medieval architecture, earning it UNESCO recognition as one of the world's heritage treasures.

Getting Around

The ships either anchor in the bay opposite the Old Town, or dock in Gruz Harbour, about 1.5 miles northwest of the Old Town. A shuttle bus (US$8 each way) runs between the cruise port and a stop just outside Pile Gate, the western entrance into the walled town, which is open to pedestrian traffic only. Public bus No. 8 also goes to the Old Town (the bus station is next to the cruise terminal).

The city walls overlook Onofrio Fountain. (Below) The sea views from atop Dubrovnik's walls.

Taxis (holding 1 to 4 passengers) are available at the pier; €15 to Old Town; €50 for a one-hour tour of the coastal hills with stops at several viewpoints before heading back down to the Old Town with a drop-off at Pile Gate. Similar views can be seen from the cable car (108 HRK return ticket) that runs from outside the Old Town's north entrance to the top of Mount Srdj.

Money exchange offices are located in or near the cruise terminal. Public phones are located at the cruise terminal and these accept personal calling cards. Phone cards can be purchased at the port building's post office.

The Dubrovnik Tourist Board is located near Onofrio Fountain on Cvijete Zuzoric Street in the Old Town. The main shopping streets are Stradun and Od Puca.

Restaurants are numerous in the Old Town. Just outside the Pile Gate entrance is the popular Dubravka Restaurant, offering casual dining on its expansive terrace overlooking the water.

Local Attractions

Pile Gate 1, which dates from 1537, marks the starting point of a walking tour through the Old Town's cobbled streets and marble-paved squares. Set in a niche over the gate's Renaissance arch is a statue of Saint Blaise, the city's patron saint.

After passing through Pile Gate, visitors come upon **Onofrio Fountain 2**, one of Dubrovnik's best-known landmarks and a popular gathering place for locals. Built in 1438 as a water supply system, the fountain was damaged in the 1667 earthquake but 16 of the original sculptures still adorn it.

Opposite Onofrio Fountain is the entrance (tickets cost 100 kuna per person) to the **fortifications** encircling the Old Town, which were built between the 8th and 16th centuries. These massive stone walls and forts provide panoramic views of the city and surrounding sea.

Not far from the Onofrio Fountain is the 14th-century **Franciscan Monastery 3** which houses one of Europe's oldest pharmacies, founded in 1317 and still functioning.

Placa (also called the Stradun) is the Old Town's main street and is lined with **shops** and **restaurants**. Numerous narrow lanes lead off Placa and are interesting to explore. Europe's second-oldest **synagogue 4** is located in the block between Boskoviceva and Zudioska.

At the eastern end of the Placa, overlooking the harbour, is the Old Town's main square, dominated by the **Clock Tower 5**, first built in 1444 and most recently restored in 1929, its two bronze figures regularly ringing out the hours.

Shore Excursions

Dubrovnik Dubrovnik's outlying areas can be visited by ship-organized shore excursions. These include the seaside resort of Cavtat (where Edward VIII and Wallace Simpson honeymooned). Some sample shore excursions:
• Walking tour of Old Town and cable car ride to Mount Srdj (4 hrs, $95)
• Sea kayaking to Betina Cave Beach for swimming and snorkeling (3.5 hrs, $100)
• Biking in the pastoral Konavle valley (4.5 hrs, $130)
Consult your cruise line's website for more detail.

Several historic buildings are located around the square, including **St. Blaise's Church** , constructed in the baroque style in the early 1700s. It occupies the site of a 14th-century church from which were recovered two stone statues and a gilded silver statue of Saint Blaise, now displayed in the existing church's main altar.

The 15th-century **Rector's Palace** , reflecting late Gothic and early Renaissance styles, was built to house the offices and private chambers of Dubrovnik's governing rector. The building, today used for concerts during the Summer Festival, is now a museum with furnished rooms depicting how the aristocracy once lived. The 16th-century **Sponza Palace**  originally served as the town's mint and customs house, and now houses the State Archives, which includes a priceless collection of manuscripts.

The **Dominican Monastery**  was built between the 14th and 16th centuries and contains a collection of Renaissance paintings.

Split

The Roman emperor Diocletian put the seaport of Split on the map when he built his magnificent palace here for his retirement in 305 AD. Situated on the outskirts of Salona, an ancient city founded by the Romans, the palace was transformed into the city of Spalato (now Split) when the people of Salona fled here in the 7th century.

Split eventually became a flourishing port of medieval Dalmatia and is now a major commercial centre, where shipbuilding and other industries thrive. Yet, its scenic location and historic monuments have made this seaside resort an important tourist destination and an increasingly popular port of call. The Riva (waterfront promenade) is pleasant for strolling and sampling the city's stylish seafood restaurants.

Kayakers paddle past the Old Town fortifications.

The cruise ships either dock at St. Duje's pier (a 10-minute walk to the city centre) or anchor in the bay and tender passengers to the jetty opposite Diocletian's Palace. The ancient walls of this palace complex contain most of the city's historic attractions, including the Cathedral of St. Duje (a Roman temple converted during Venetian rule). Entry from the Riva is through the Bronze gate; an open-air market lies outside the Palace's east gate.

The Mestrovic Gallery is a 20-minute walk west of the old town or can be reached by catching the No. 12 bus in front of the Church of St. Francis. The sculpture gallery is housed in the palatial summer home and studio built in the 1930s by the Croatian sculptor Ivan Mestrovic.

Shore excursions include a Split walking tour plus scenic drive to the ruins of the Roman city of **Salonae** or to the medieval

The waterfront area of Split.

town of **Trogir**, which occupies an island (connected by bridge to the mainland) and contains a splendid 13th-century cathedral and several Renaissance palaces. A half-day trip to **Krka National Park** and its famous Krka River waterfalls is offered by some cruise lines, as is kayaking, canoeing and cavern snorkeling .

Rab – The pastoral island of Rab (Ital. Arbe) was under Venetian rule from the 10th century until 1797. Today a popular

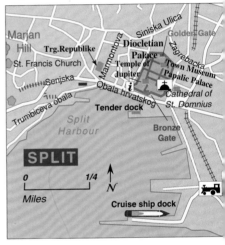

Korcula's inner harbour

seaside resort, the island, 40 square miles in size, has retained its ancient walls and ruins of the palace of the Venetian governors. Also of interest are the 12th-century cathedral and medieval palace where the archbishop resided.

Korcula – The beautiful island of Korcula, lying off the Pelijesac Peninsula, is covered in pine forests, pastures and vineyards. Colonized by Greeks in the 4th century BC, Korcula became a medieval stronghold for pirates conducting raids on Venice. According to some sources, the famous Venetian traveller Marco Polo was born on Korcula. The island's chief town, also called Korcula, has retained its medieval cathedral and fortifications.

Kotor, Montenegro

Forty miles south of Dubrovnik, along the scenic Dalmatian coast, lies the splendid Gulf of Kotor, its fjord-like reaches bordered by limestone cliffs. Hidden at the head of its innermost inlet is the medieval port of Kotor, its well-preserved walls and buildings a World Heritage Site.

Large ships anchor and tender their passengers ashore to the cruise pier, which is just outside the old town's walls and used by the smaller ships. It's a short stroll to one of the medieval gates and into the old town with its pedestrian-only maze of narrow streets

Shore Excursions

Kotor In addition to a walking tour of the walled town (2 hrs) other escorted shore excursions in Kotor include a motorcoach ride to **Perast**, its baroque manors built by merchant sea captains. At Perast Harbour, board a motor launch for a 10-minute cruise across Boka Bay to an islet occupied by the baroque church Gospa od Skrpjela (Our Lady of the Rocks) (3.5 hrs).

Another escorted excursion combines a walking tour of Kotor with a motorcoach ride up a steep, winding road to the village of **Njegusi** and to Montenegro's former capital of **Cetinje**, founded in 1482, where the National Museum is housed in the former royal palace and features the state apartments. (5.5 hrs)

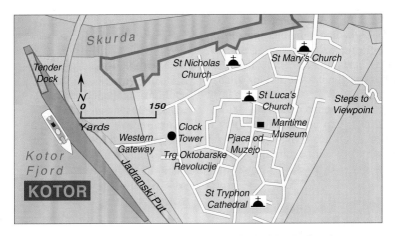

and squares. Historic buildings of note include St. Tryphon Cathedral and the 17-century Grgurina Palace, which houses the Maritime Museum – a tribute to Kotor's seafaring past when it was one of the Adriatic's major naval powers.

Ruled by the Republic of Venice from 1420 to 1797, Kotor's architecture reflects this Venetian influence. Kotor was first colonized by Greeks in the 3rd century BC and is the oldest town in Montenegro. Formerly part of Yugoslavia, the republic of Montenegro declared its independence in 2006. The local currency is the euro and taxis cost about 60 euros per hour.

A steep and rocky path winds up the mountain behind Kotor to the Fortress of St. John. This ancient stone pathway traces the Venetian-built ramparts and consists of 1,500 steps, providing spectacular views as it winds its way up the mountainside. There's a €3 charge to access the trail.

The path leading to St. John Fortress provides spectacular views of Kotor.

MAINLAND GREECE
0
75
Miles
N
CRUISE ROUTES
ROUTES: --------
ITALY
ALBANIA
MACEDONIA
BULGARIA
TURKEY
Istanbul
Thessaloniki
Mt. Athos
LIMNOS
Dardanelles
CORFU
Igoumenitsa
Meteora
Larisa
Volos
AEGEAN SEA
LESBOS
Mitilini
TURKEY
IONIAN SEA
Delphi
Itea
Thebes
Attica
Izmir
CHIOS
ITHACA
CEPHALONIA
Patra
Athens
Corinth
Ephesus
Olympia
Tripolis
Piraeus
SAMOS
Mycenae
Tiryns
Katakolon
Peloponnesus
Epidaurus
Navplion
PATMOS
Cyclades
MYKONOS
Mistras
Sparta
Githio
Monemvasia
(Malvasia)
Dodecanese
KOS
Rhodes
SANTORINI
RHODES

MAINLAND GREECE

Greece is a mystical land of impassable mountain ridges and fertile plains filled with olive trees and orange groves. Monasteries dot pine-forested slopes and isolated valleys run down to the sea. Strabo, a Greek geographer from the 1st century BC, wrote that "the sea presses in upon the country with a thousand arms" for no point in Greece is further than 65 miles from the coast.

With limited natural resources, the Greeks have always looked to the sea for their livelihoods, through fishing, shipping and trade. Today the country's merchant marine is one of the largest per capita in the world, and an extensive ferry system connects Greece's mainland ports and widely scattered islands.

Many of our modern institutions, such as democracy, are based on concepts that originated in classical Greece. Theatre began with the Greek dramatists and the foundations of 20th-century architecture, law and philosophy can be traced to Greece.

The Greek gods and heroes are part of our everyday vocabulary, their names associated with everything from Apollo spacecraft to Nike jogging shoes. And when satellites beam us televised coverage of the Olympic Games, the torch-bearing runner who lights the eternal flame is reenacting yet another time-honoured ritual rooted in ancient Greece.

Porch of the Caryatids

When Athens hosted the summer games in 2004, the Olympics returned to their country of origin for the first time since the modern games began in 1896. The men's marathon was raced on its ancient course, retracing the route run by Pheidippides in 490 BC when bringing news of victory over the Persians. The route starts in Marathon and ends in Athens, at the Panathinaiko Stadium, its horseshoe-shaped marble-clad seating built for the 1896 Olympiad as a replica of the ancient stadium that once stood on this site. Few could witness such an event without recalling the glory that was Greece.

Greece at a Glance

The term Greek derives from *Groeci*, the Latin name for a small Hellenic tribe of ancient Greece, and the Greeks refer to their country as Hellas.

About 11 million people live in Greece and the faith of the majority is Eastern Orthodox. Greek, with a variety of local dialects, is the dominant language, and the well educated speak a more classical version of the language. English is widely spoken. The Greek alphabet has fewer letters than the English alphabet, and when a Greek word is translated into English there are often several variations in the spelling.

In 1974, following the collapse of a military dictatorship, Greece became a parliamentary republic and joined the European Union in 1981. Since 2010 there have been concerns about the prospect of Greece defaulting on its euro denominated debt.

Travel Tips

Currency – The unit of currency is the euro. Most banks are open from 8:00 a.m to 1:00 p.m., Monday through Friday. The currency exchange dispenser at the National Bank of Greece on Syntagma Square in Athens is open 24 hours a day.

Dining – The Greeks usually have lunch at 2:00 p.m. and dinner after 8:30 p.m., but restaurants often open earlier in tourist-oriented centres.

A typical Greek meal begins with a plate of *mezedes* (hors d'oeuvres) such as salami, fish, *dolmades* (stuffed vine leaves) and *tiropites* (cheese pies). Main dishes include *kalamaraki* (squid fried in olive oil) and *moussaka* (a baked casserole of mincemeat, eggplant, onions and other ingredients).

Olive oil is used extensively in Greek cooking and salads, along with fresh herbs and cheeses such as feta. For dessert, try a *baklava* – layered pastry with nuts, which is often served warm. Ouzo, a colourless liqueur and Greece's national aperitif, is served either neat or watered down, which turns it milky.

A restaurant in Navplion

Opening Hours – Most museums in Greece are open Tuesday through Sunday and are closed or open late (1:30 p.m.) on Mondays. They also close on public holidays – Independence Day (March 25), Good Friday, Easter Sunday and May 1st.

Shopping – Stores generally are open Monday thru Saturday, 9:30 a.m. to 8 p.m., some closing for a few hours in mid-afternoon. Bartering is acceptable in Greece. The country's excellent handicrafts include ceramics, wood carvings, handwoven carpets and embroidered tablecloths. Wool sweaters, leather goods and gold or silver jewellery are often good buys. Fishermen's caps and natural sponges are popular souvenirs.

Telephoning – Greece's country code is 30 and the area code for Athens is 21. To call Greece from the U.S. or Canada, dial 011 then 30+area code+local phone number. From the UK, dial 00, then 30, etc. When calling home from Greece, dial 00 followed by your own country code (1 for U.S. and Canada; 44 for the UK), followed by the area code and local number.

Athens

Athens, the capital and largest city of Greece (pop. 3 million), is situated on a plain dotted with low hills, the most famous of which is the **Acropolis** – 'high point of the city.' This is where the **Parthenon**, a masterpiece of classical Greek architecture, has stood for more than 2,000 years. Constructed of white marble in the 5th century BC, when Athens was at its height as a military power and a centre of intellectual life, the Parthenon has survived centuries of wars, sieges, sackings and pilferings. Dedicated to the virgin goddess Athena, this ancient temple rises above the congested streets of downtown Athens as testament to the city's glorious past.

At the foot of the Acropolis lies the ancient marketplace, the **Agora**, where democracy originated and the seeds of Western culture were sown during the Golden Age of Athens under the leadership of **Pericles**, whose reforms included payment for jury duty, enabling even the poorest citizens to serve. A patron of the arts, Pericles commissioned the city's best architects and sculptors to design and oversee the completion of the Parthenon and other monuments, including a theatre for staging the plays of Euripides and Sophocles.

Years later, as the 5th century BC drew to a close, Athens faced ruination at the hands of its rival city-state Sparta. After succumb-

---

MUST SEE:

• The Acropolis, where the Parthenon and other ancient monuments are located, with original artefacts on display in the new Acropolis Museum.
• Ancient Agora, beside the Acropolis.
• Plaka neighbourhood – pleasant for strolling and souvenir shopping
If you're spending more than a day in Athens, also visit Lycavittas Hill (for sweeping views of the city) and the National Archaeological Museum.

The venerable Parthenon stands atop the Acropolis.

ing to Sparta in the Peloponnesian War, Athens attempted to regain its past glory, rebuilding both its navy and the fortified walls that protected the city and connected it to the port of **Piraeus**. But the city-state had lost its imperial status and Athens declined into a provincial city. Its great contributions to civilization endured, however, as Hellenistic culture spread Athenian achievements throughout the world.

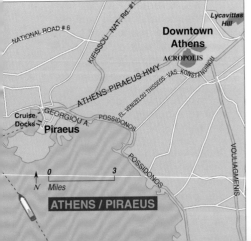

Getting Around

Athens is a sprawling metropolis of over three million people and is one of Europe's most affordable cities. Its major historic sites are situated right in the downtown core, within walking distance or a short taxi ride of one another. The heart of Athens is pedestrian-friendly, with traffic restricted inside the commercial centre.

Transportation improvements were made in and around Athens in preparation for the 2004 Olympics. The new international airport is located at Spata, about 18 miles east of the city centre, and is connected by a six-lane highway and a rapid transit rail line, the latter providing 20-minute connections.

Taxi fares are relatively cheap compared to the rest of Europe, but not all drivers can speak English. Have the name and address of your destination written on a piece of paper and confirm the fare beforehand. If you're setting off from an

Athens hotel, ask the concierge to arrange a taxi for you. Expect a luggage surcharge.

If you are making same-day connections between a flight into Athens and a cruise, you are well advised to arrange for a transfer with the cruise line.

Connections between downtown Athens and the port of **Piraeus** (a distance of six miles) can be made by taxi (about €11, depending on traffic and amount of luggage) or on the subway system. The green subway line (No. 1) connects the port with Monastiraki Square in downtown Athens. If you plan to return to the port by taxi after a day of sightseeing in Athens, be sure to allow at least an hour in case the traffic is crawling.

One of the best ways to visit Athens for the day while your ship is docked in Piraeus, is to book your cruise line's 'On Your Own' shore excursion (if available). This excursion includes a brief city tour by motorcoach before you are dropped off at Syntagma Square. From there, you can explore Athens for about six hours, then reboard the motorcoach at the same spot for the return drive to Piraeus. (4 to 7.5 hrs; $50-$100)

Hop-on hop-off sightseeing buses operate in Athens (€18 adult fare), departing every 30 minutes from Syntagma Square. They also operate in Piraeus (€22 per person), making serveral local stops (including the cruise terminal's gates) before heading into Athens where you can hop off at the Acropolis.

Where to Stay – The legendary Hotel Grande Bretagne, which opened for business in 1874, is a 5-star hotel on Constitution Square in the heart of Athens. The Metropolitan Athens is a luxury hotel on the outskirts of the city, near Piraeus, with views of both the Acropolis and the Aegean Sea.

Dining in Athens – For lunch, try one of the cafés lining Theorias Street just below the Acropolis in Plaka. The second-floor restaurant in the Acropolis Museum provides splendid views of the Acropolis from its terrace. If you're staying a night or two in Athens, try the rooftop garden restaurant of the Titania Hotel at 52 Panepistimiou Avenue. For a truly memorable meal, Orizontes Lykavittou – atop Lykavittos Hill – is widely considered one of the finest restaurants in Athens. At the base of Lykavittos Hill is a square where local families gather at outdoor cafés. Kolonaki Square is where you will find trendy coffee shops and restaurants.

Shopping– Some of the best streets for souvenir hunting are in the vicinity of Monastiraki Square in the Plaka neighborhood. The

market on Pandrossou Street sells a selection of handicrafts, and the pedestrian mall that runs along the north side of the Agora is lined with stalls selling leather goods, silver jewelry and an array of ceramics, including Grecian urns, busts and statuettes. Fashionable stores are found on Ermou Street, while the city's most chic fashion boutiques are on Tsakalof Street off Kolonaki Square.

Shopping in Plaka (above). The changing of the guard in Syntagma Square (below).

Athens Attractions

The main travel information bureau is located on **Syntagma (Constitution) Square** 🔳, a centre of activity with hotels, banks, coffee shops, bars and night clubs surrounding the square. Overlooking the Square's east side is the **House of Parliament**, originally constructed (1836-1842) as a palace for King Otto, Greece's first monarch, and Queen Amalia. The Tomb of the Unknown Soldier (1929) stands in front where it is guarded day and night by two soldiers. A changing of the guard takes place every hour.

Just south of the Parliament Building is the **National Garden** 🔳, designed for the Royal Palace and first planted between 1838 and 1860. Further south along Amalias Avenue is the **Arch of Hadrian** 🔳, built of Pentelic marble. (Penteli is one of the mountains surrounding the basin of Athens.) On the northwest corner of the site is the **Temple of Olympian Zeus** 🔳, completed in 131 AD by the Roman emperor Hadrian.

To the west of Amalias Avenue lies the lovely neighbourhood of **Plaka**, where narrow stone-paved streets wind past neoclassical homes and sidewalk cafés. On foot is the best way to approach

Shore Excursions

Athens The Acropolis is, not surprisingly, featured in many of the shore excursions available at Athens. These usually involve a motorcoach ride from the port to downtown Athens where a walking tour of the Acropolis is combined with shopping in the Plaka district and lunch (6 to 9 hrs, $100-$180)

Some tours combine a visit to the Acropolis with a drive to ancient Corinth or to the ruins of Mycenae on the Peloponnese peninsula. Half-day tours are available to the Acropolis (4 hrs, $100).

Most cruise lines provide a motorcoach shuttle from the port into Athens (see Getting Around).

Consult your cruise line's website for specific shore excursions.

Please note: Excursions to the Acropolis required walking at this ancient site. In summer, be prepared for intense heat and large crowds at the Acropolis.

Temple of Olympian Zeus (right).
A quiet street in Plaka (bottom).

the Acropolis, and a morning ascent along the quiet roads of Plaka will reward you with enchanting, ever-changing vistas. On the upper slopes is **Anafiotika 5**, a village of small white houses erected in the 1830s by master builders from the Aegean island of Anafi, who were hired by the first King of Greece to build his palace. To stave off homesickness while living in Athens, they recreated their island village along the edge of the Acropolis. One of Plaka's most famous structures is the **Monument of Lysicrates 6**, a round structure built in about 334 BC. Its engaged columns are the oldest known example of exterior Corinthian capitals. Along the northern edge of the Plaka area is **Cathedral Square 7** where the city's Great Metropole Cathedral, built in the mid-1800s, overshadows the smaller Little Metropole, built in the 12th and 13th centuries.

The **Acropolis** was regained by Greece in 1833 when the Turkish

The café-lined streets of Plaka lead up to the Acropolis.

guard departed. The sacred rock, which had been used as a fortress for 1,500 years, was declared a national monument and archaeological work began almost immediately to excavate and restore the site. What we see today is the result of extensive reconstruction. A mosque built inside the Parthenon during Turkish occupation was torn down, as were ramparts, walls and a Frankish tower.

Restoration work has taken place within the Parthenon since 1983. Priceless artefacts are displayed in the **Acropolis Museum** at the base of the Acropolis. This modern multi-level structure of concrete and glass opened in 2009 and contains, among its many exhibits, the famous Caryatids of the Erechtheum and original blocks of the Parthenon's frieze. Visitors can view archaeological excava-

tions through glass floors and exhibits are bathed in natural light coming through the glass walls.

Entrance to the Acropolis is made along a processional way that passes through the colonnaded buildings of the **Propylaea** **8**, its interconnected stone structures including the Temple of Athena Nike. This imposing entrance prepares you for the sight of the **Parthenon** **9**, the great temple of Athena. Designed by the architect Ictinus and built using white, fine-grained marble, the columned Parthenon is a masterpiece of refinement and restraint. Originally it housed a colossal statue of the goddess Athena, which was created by the famous sculptor Phidias, her skin made of ivory and her draperies of beaten gold. Other temples on the Acropolis include the **Erechtheum** **10**, the roof of its south porch supported by the figures of six maidens, called the Caryatids. These famous figures are all copies of the originals, four of which are housed inside the Acropolis Museum. The fifth

Monuments atop the Acropolis (above) include the Caryatids of the Erechtheum (right).

is being restored, and the sixth was removed by Lord Elgin in 1806 and is on display in the British Museum.

Situated on the southern slope of the Acropolis are the **Ancient Theatre of Dionysos** 11, originally built of wood then reconstructed with marble during the 4th century BC, and the **Odeion of Herodes Atticus** (the Herodeion) 12, which was built in 161 AD by a wealthy Athenian and is still used

Ancient Theatre of Dionysos (right). Odeion of Herodes Atticus (below).

today for summer concerts. West of the Acropolis is the **Areopagus (Hill of Ares)** 13 on which the city's supreme court of law once stood. This outcrop of slippery stone is also the spot from which St. Paul delivered his first sermon to the Athenians in 51 AD.

The road below the Areopagus connects the Acropolis with the **Agora**, the 'gathering place' of ancient Athens. Political meetings, religious festivals, dramatic contests and athletic competitions took place in this civic and commercial centre, where temples and altars stood alongside law courts and libraries. Philosophers such as Socrates strolled the open squares and shaded colonnades, while chariots wheeled along a

Temple of Hephaistos (top). Tower of the Winds (middle left). Stoa of Attalos (bottom left).

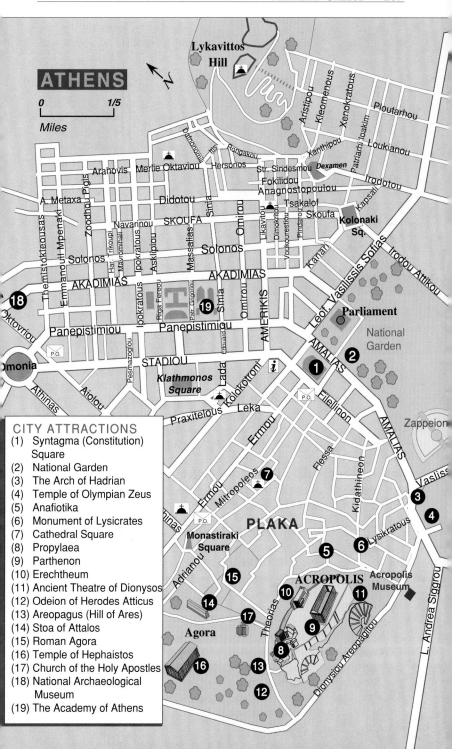

ATHENS

0 — 1/5
Miles

CITY ATTRACTIONS
(1) Syntagma (Constitution) Square
(2) National Garden
(3) The Arch of Hadrian
(4) Temple of Olympian Zeus
(5) Anafiotika
(6) Monument of Lysicrates
(7) Cathedral Square
(8) Propylaea
(9) Parthenon
(10) Erechtheum
(11) Ancient Theatre of Dionysos
(12) Odeion of Herodes Atticus
(13) Areopagus (Hill of Ares)
(14) Stoa of Attalos
(15) Roman Agora
(16) Temple of Hephaistos
(17) Church of the Holy Apostles
(18) National Archaeological Museum
(19) The Academy of Athens

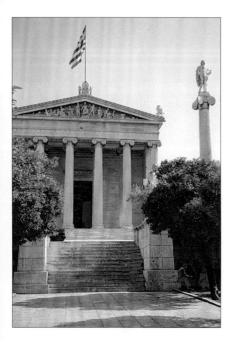

Academy of Athens

broad street called the Panathenaic Way, which was the annual scene of a grand procession that ascended the Acropolis during the festival of the goddess Athena. The town's craftsmen and merchants lived on the southern edge of the Agora, in modest homes with inner courtyards. On the nearby hill of Pnyx, in full view of the Acropolis, Athenians would gather to hear famous orators – such as Pericles – deliver their speeches.

The **Stoa of Attalos 14**, rebuilt in the 1950s according to its original design, is a classic example of Greek civic architecture. Originally a shopping arcade with 21 shops on each of its two floors, the Stoa now houses the **Agora Museum** and contains excavated items of everyday use in the ancient Agora, including bronze ballots from the law courts and terracotta animals from a child's grave. Behind the Stoa of Attalos is the **Roman Agora 15**, a marketplace completed in 10 BC, its marble-paved pedestrian mall once lined with colonnades, shops and shrines built with financial assistance from Julius Caesar and the Emperor Augustus. Still standing is the **Tower of the Winds**, an octagonal structure which served as a water-clock, compass and weather-vane.

The **Temple of Hephaistos 16** was dedicated to the goddesses Hephaistos and Athena, both patron divinities of the arts and crafts. Built in 449 BC, the Temple housed statues of the two goddesses and is today one of the best preserved Greek temples of ancient times. A fountain house, its water supplied by an underground terracotta pipeline, once stood beside the site now occupied by the **Byzantine Church of the Holy Apostles 17**, built in 1000 AD and restored in the 1950s.

The **National Archaeological Museum 18** houses an impressive collection of antiquities extending from Neolithic to Roman times. The **Academy of Athens 19**, completed in 1887 and flanked by columns topped with statues of Athena and Apollo, is a fine example of neo-classical architecture. The summit of **Lycavittos Hill** can be reached by funicular, footpath or road, and provides panoramic views of the city and surrounding area – a spectacular sight when the sun is setting.

Peloponnesus

First inhabited as early as 4000 BC, the Peloponnese peninsula was gradually colonized by Greek-speaking Mycenaeans, whose advanced civilization eventually became the centre of Greek culture. This era is now called the Heroic Age, thus named for the incredible feats of Hercules and the events described in Homer's *Iliad* and *Odyssey*, including the Trojan War (c. 1200 BC).

When a new wave of invaders called Dorians arrived in about 1100 BC, their arrival marked a cultural decline. The conquering Dorians built huge stone buildings, and Argos, Corinth and Sparta became powerful city-states. Corinth, strategically situated on the Isthmus of Corinth, became a wealthy maritime power and rival of Athens. Sparta was Corinth's traditional ally and, by the 6th century BC, was Greece's strongest city.

Located in a mountain-walled valley, Sparta became an armed camp, its culture dominated by war. Sickly boy babies were abandoned in the mountains, while those fit for military service were taken from their mothers at the age of seven to begin training. State business was conducted in secrecy while serfs, closely monitored for fear of insurrection, farmed the land.

All of Greece's city-states participated in the Olympic games, held in summer every four years at Olympia. The warring city-states were as proud of a victory at the Olympic games as they were of winning a battle, and this nationalistic spirit fuelled a keen competitiveness among the participants. Home-coming champions were hailed as heroes and showered with gifts and privileges. The Games began in 776 BC, possibly earlier, and running was initially the only event. Over time, new events were added, including the pentathlon, chariot racing and a foot race with armor. Greek women held their own games called Heraea.

The Olympic games were eventually discontinued in the 4th century AD by the Romans, who had conquered the Peloponnesus in 146 BC. Over time, the once-powerful Peloponnesian League of city-states, weakened by wars with Athens and each other, which weakened the cities, became susceptible to foreign invasions – a situation that would prevail until an 1821 rebellion in the Peloponnesus launched the Greek War of Independence.

Navplion (Nafplio)

Not only is Navplion a fascinating port of call, it provides access to the famous sites of **Mycenae, Epidaurus** and ancient **Corinth**. Ships anchor off Navplion and tender their passengers ashore, where the town's sights are within walking distance, although it's a strenuous hike up to the Palamidi fortress.

Navplion's name derives from Nauplius who, according to Greek mythology, was the son of Poseidon and father of Palamedes, a hero of the Trojan War. The old quarter, situated on a peninsula, is medieval in character. It was originally built by the Venetians when

Venice was a dominant sea power in the Mediterranean.

Navplion Attractions

The **Bourtzi** , an island fortress at the harbour entrance, was built by the Venetians in 1473. Looming high above the red-roofed buildings is another Venetian fortress, the **Palamidi**. It was successfully stormed by the Ottoman Turks in 1715 when they captured the town. The view from the Palamidi is breathtaking and can be gained either by ascending the stone steps that lead to its 700-foot summit (a climb best made in the coolness of early morning) or by taking a taxi or ship-organized excursion.

At the foot of the Palamidi, beside the Cultural Centre of Navplion, is the Tourist Information Office. A few blocks away is **Three Admiral Square**, named for the English, French and Russian admirals who defeated an Egyptian fleet that was bringing reinforcements to the Turks during the Greek War of Independence. Elegant neoclassical townhouses overlook this

Cruise ship anchors off Navplion on the Peloponnese peninsula.

square on V. Konstantinou Street, which leads west to **Syntagma (Constitution) Square** where, on its west side, the Archaeological Museum is situated, housing a collection of Mycenaean artifacts.

Greek insurgents took Navplion from the Turks in 1822 and the town was, from 1830 to 1834, the first capital of an independent Greece, its first National Assembly convening next to the museum in a Turkish mosque on Staikopoulou Street.

Konstantinou and Staikopoulou are picturesque pedestrian streets lined with restaurants and shops. Side streets with stone steps lead off Staikopoulou, up the hillside toward **Akronafplia**, a barren hilltop fortified over the centuries by various occupants and now the site of two hotels which can be reached by a lift or by a road that runs past **Arvanitia**, a fully-serviced beach. The town's **promenade** is pleasant for strolling with its waterfront cafes and views across the harbour.

Ship-organized **shore excursions** from Navplion generally include a half-day coach trip through the scenic countryside to Mycenae, Epidaurus or Corinth, often with a stop at the top of

Palamidi on the way back to the ship. One option for passengers interested in viewing a Mycenaean ruin is to visit nearby **Tiryns**, 3 miles away (US$25 return fare by taxi). Although not as extensive as Mycenae, this ancient citadel was the mythological birthplace of Hercules. Its impressive entrance ramp evokes a sense of past power, when the palace was protected by two massive walls with an outer and inner gate designed to trap attackers between the walls.

Mycenae, 13 miles north of Navplion, is one of Greece's most famous archaeological sites. These ancient ruins, which were the center of the Mycenaean civilization, are shrouded in a dark history of murder and betrayal. Agamemnon, the great king of Mycenae, is a tragic figure of Greek mythology. He belonged to the deadliest of dysfunctional families, a curse having been brought upon it by his grandfather Pelops. Agamemnon's father

The Bourtzi fortress (above).
An elegant square on V.
Konstantinou Street (below).

didn't help matters by murdering his brother's children and serving them for dinner. When Agamemnon left for the Trojan war, he sacrificed his eldest child to guarantee good winds for his sailing ships. This deed incurred the hatred of his wife Clytemnestra, who murdered Agamemnon upon his return. To avenge their father's death, Orestes and Electra murdered their mother.

Several hundred years later, the poet Homer wrote about Mycenae and his writings were eventually used by the 19th-century archaeologist Heinrich Schliemann to provide clues as to where to dig at this ancient site. Spurred by Homer's references to gold, Schliemann's dramatic discoveries included royal tombs filled with gold treasures. The site's

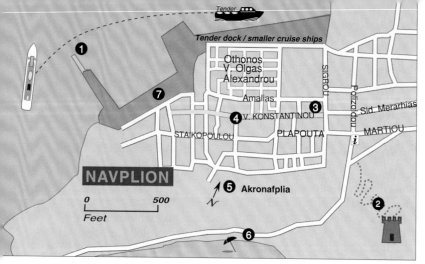

NAVPLION

```
0          500
Feet
```

Tender dock / smaller cruise ships

Othonos
V. Olgas
Alexandrou
Amalias
V. KONSTANTINOU
STAIKOPOULOU
PLAPOUTA
SIGROU
Polizoidou
Sid. Merarhias
MARTIOU

1
7
3
4
5 Akronafplia
2
6

heavy fortifications and massive masonry include the **Lion Gate**, Europe's oldest monumental sculpture, which in ancient times was closed by a double wooden door sheathed in bronze and secured with a wooden bar. The largest of the beehive tombs, located outside the walls of the city, is the Treasury of Atreus (also called Agamemnon's Tomb).

Epidaurus, situated 15 miles east of Navplion (US$60 return taxi fare), is an ancient sanctuary and the site of Greece's best-preserved amphitheatre. Greek drama lives on at the 14,000-seat theatre of Epidaurus, which was considered beautiful and harmonious when built in the 4th century BC and is still acclaimed for its excellent acoustics. Since the theatre's restoration in the 1950s, theatrical events have been staged here each summer, including the late Maria Callas performing the title role of Bellini's opera, *Norma*. In September 1997, to commemorate the 20th anniversary of the famous diva's death, friends from the world of opera gathered for a seaboard ceremony off Epidaurus. As a recording of her voice resounded across the water, olive wreaths were tossed into the Aegean Sea, where her ashes had been scattered two decades earlier.

Old Corinth, 40 miles from Navplion, has been occupied by Romans, Goths, Crusaders, Ottoman Turks and Venetians. Corinth was finally returned to Greece when captured by Greek insurgents in 1822, only to be

Palamidi fortress in Navplion.

destroyed by an earthquake in the 1850s. A new city was founded nearby, and the ancient ruins remaining at Old Corinth include a Temple of Apollo, a Roman amphitheatre and hilltop fortress. A short distance away is the four-mile-long Canal of Corinth, built between 1881 and 1893, which cuts across the Isthmus of Corinth. Its sheer rock walls rise 285 feet above the water on both sides, accentuating the narrowness of the canal, which can be transited only by small ships. Until this canal was built, a narrow neck of land connected the Peloponnese peninsula with central Greece. In ancient times this isthmus served as a land bridge for tribes migrating into the area from the north but it eventually posed a barrier to trading ships travelling between the Adriatic and Aegean seas. The citizens of Corinth, with harbours on both sides of the isthmus, solved the problem and grew wealthy in the process by building a connecting road across which they hauled ships on rollers.

Katakolon

Olympia, located about 15 miles from the port of **Katakolon**, was an important centre of worship and the venue for the Panhellenic Olympic Games. Situated in the beautiful valley of Alpheios, the site contains ruins of the great temple of Zeus which housed a statue by Phidias, the famous sculptor whose works adorned the Parthenon. Counted among the Seven Wonders of the World, this colossal ivory and gold statue of Zeus sitting on an ornamented throne was later removed to Constantinople where it was destroyed by fire in 475 AD. Other sculptures from the Temple of Zeus are on display in the nearby **Archaeological Museum**, along with the outstanding statue of *Hermes with the Young Dionysos* by Praxiteles. Ruins associated with the Olympic games include the remains of the Gymnasium and the Stadium. The sacred flame of the modern Olympic games begins its journey here with a torch-lighting ceremony held in front of the Temple of Hera, the oldest Doric temple in Greece.

Shore excursions from Katakolon focus on Olympia, with motorcoach drives to the nearby site, a walking tour and a visit to the Archaeological Museum (4 to 7 hrs; $80-$120). A

Small cruise ship is towed through the Corinth Canal.

modern train travels the 25 miles from Katakolon to Olympia and takes about 45 minutes; the cost is 1 euro each way. To hire a taxi carrying 1 to 4 people for a half day tour of Olympia, the cost is 80 to 120 euros.

Githio

The hill-top town of **Mistra (Mystras)**, about 30 miles from the port of **Githio**, is the most representative example in existence of a Byzantine city from the 14th and 15th centuries. The medieval castle overlooking the town was built in 1249 by Frankish crusader Guillaume de Villehardouin. He and his knights were defeated 10 years later by the Byzantines, who built a palace for the emperor as well as numerous churches and monasteries decorated with beautiful frescoes.

The town, its wealth generated by a lucrative silk industry, grew down the hillside, with the upper and lower sections connected by two gates. The lower town contains most of the monasteries and churches, while the upper town contains the Palace of the Despot (a rare example of civic Byzantine architecture), an adjacent church and the Frankish castle, which is reached after a 30-minute ascent. The magnificent view from the castle includes a bird's eye look at the gullies of Mt. Taygettus – where the Spartans are said to have tossed sickly babies.

Nearby modern Sparta bears little resemblance to the ancient city-state that once dominated the central Peloponnese peninsula.

Relying on their military power for protection, the Spartans didn't bother building walls, so only a few temple ruins remain.

Malvasia

The fortified island village of Malvasia, a unique and intact medieval town, is joined by a causeway to the Peloponnese mainland where a modern beach resort lies in contrast to the Byzantine churches and Venetian mansions contained within the walls of Malvasia. A fortress in the Middle Ages, Malvasia was also a commercial port which exported malmsey wine.

Itea

On the northern shores of the Gulf of Corinth, the port of Itea accesses the ancient site of **Delphi**, where the great temple to Apollo was first built in the 6th century BC. Apollo, one of the most important Olympian gods, was associated with prophecy, and Delphi was the seat of ancient Greece's most famous and powerful oracle. Pilgrims seeking help brought gifts which lined the Sacred Way leading to the temple, where a priestess sat on a tripod inhaling divine vapours and uttering oracular messages. It has long been speculated that the 'divine vapours' Pythia inhaled were volcanic gases, and geologists now surmise that a major fault zone below the temple provided pathways for seeping gases, including ethylene and methane – known to have narcotic effects. Delphi played a unique role amid the warring city-states for its splendid setting on the lower slopes of Mt. Parnassus was a meeting place for the Amphictyonic League, as well as the site of the Pythian Games, held every four years.

Volos

Meteora, about 75 miles from the port of Volos, is a surrealistic sight of barren rock formations rising from a flat, fertile plain. Their geological origins still a mystery, these pinnacles of rock became a place of refuge for monks during the Middle Ages. What began as small cells evolved into great monasteries holding rich murals and religious treasures, and they form a surreal sight perched atop columns and crags of black rock. Ropes and pulleys are still used for transporting provisions, but visitors can now walk up steps cut into the precipitous slopes. These who make the strenuous climb are rewarded with sweeping views of the plain of Thessaly – ringed by mountains, including Mount Olympus, which separate Thessaly from the plains of Macedonia.

An escorted **shore excursion** entails a two-hour motorcoach ride to Meteora where the road terminates at the base of the rock pinnacles. You are then taken on a guided climb up the stone steps to view the monastic buildings at the top and take in the sweeping views. (8.5 hrs, $100)

Thessaloniki (Salonika)

Macedonia's port of Thessaloniki is Greece's second-largest city

Monastery of Saint Nicholas Anapafsas, Meteora.

and was named the 1997 Cultural Capital of Europe. Its world-renowned museum houses treasures of Philip of Macedon, father of Alexander the Great, and in 1997 it hosted a special exhibit of priceless icons, manuscripts and other objects never before seen outside the monasteries of **Mount Athos**. Consisting of 20 monasteries of the Eastern Orthodox Church, this theocratic community is perched high above the water on the southernmost tip of the Khalkidhik peninsula. Since the first monastery was founded around 953 AD, this community of monks has been allowed to govern itself by committee and its strictly enforced rules include the banning of all females and dogs. When US ambassador Thomas Niles visited Mount Athos in 1994, he chose to sleep outside one of the monasteries on a cot (as did the rest of his large retinue) rather than be separated from his beloved dog, Mr. Wheat.

THE GREEK ISLES

The only way to see the Greek isles is slowly, by boat. At least that's what Cary Grant told Doris Day in the 1962 comedy, *That Touch of Mink*, when he likened these islands to fine paintings. "You mustn't rush up to them," he said. Anyone who has stood at a ship's rail and watched the sun rise above a Greek isle will know exactly what he meant. A sea-borne arrival, as the morning sun warms the terraced hill-sides and whitewashed houses of a sleepy fishing port, is a travel experience of unsur-passed romance.

Greece has more than 2,000 islands, comprising about one-fifth of the country's total land area, yet only some 200 are inhabited. When the Greek gov-ernment announced a plan in 1995 to resettle some of its unin-habited islands, the response – both domestic and foreign – was overwhelming. Thousands of people from all walks of life sought to move to one of the many islands left abandoned after World War II when their inhabi-tants emigrated in droves to the cities. Whether or not Greece's repopulation plan is successful, it's obvious the allure of the Greek isles is as strong as ever.

For general information and travel tips on Greece, please see pages 258 and 259.

THE CYCLADES

The Cyclades, comprising about 220 islands in total, lie spread across 1,000 square miles of the Aegean Sea. They are quintessential Greek islands, with their charming fishing harbours and seaside villages. Box-shaped houses climb the hillsides and dome-roofed chapels cling to cliffsides, their dazzling whiteness appearing in stark contrast against the deep blues of the sky above and the sea below.

Most popular of the Cyclades are the tourist-oriented islands of Santorini and Mykonos, the latter lying close to uninhabited Delos – a centre of Cycladic (Greek for *circular)* culture in ancient times, with the other islands forming a rough circle around it.

Mykonos (Mikonos)

This arid island, 35 square miles in size, is the most cosmopolitan of the Cyclades. Although extremely popular with tourists,

Mykonos has retained a Cycladic charm with its whitewashed houses and hilltop windmills. Shops, cafés and tavernas line the town's waterfront area while serious shoppers will delight in wandering the town's winding backstreets. Originally designed to disorient marauding pirates, these twisting alleyways are now lined with boutiques frequented by the rich and famous. Jacqueline Onassis and Elizabeth Taylor are among the famous women who have shopped at Galatis on the town's **main square (Platia Manto)** **1**, also referred to as Taxi Square.

Little Venice **2**, a neighborhood south of the main harbour, is where you'll find local artwork and handicrafts. The waterfront buildings in this section are a reminder of the island's Venetian period, as is the **Roman Catholic Cathedral** **3**, its entrance hall bearing the coat of arms of the Ghisi family who took over Mykonos in 1207. Next door is the **Greek Orthodox Cathedral** **4** and nearby, on a promontory

Mykonos is a popular port of call in the Greek Islands.

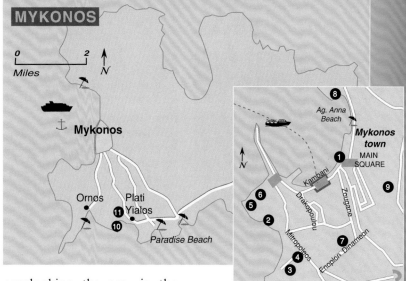

0   2
Miles   **N**

⚓ **Mykonos**

Ornos   Plati Yialos

11

10

Paradise Beach

Mykonos town

Ag. Anna Beach

8

1   MAIN SQUARE

9

Kambani

Drakopoulou

Zouganс

6

5

2

Mitropoleos

7

Enoplon Dinameon

4

3

overlooking the sea, is the **Church of Paraportiani** **5**, its cluster of whitewashed chapels a much-photographed sight. A short distance away is the **Folklore Museum** **6**, housed in the 300-year-old house of a former sea captain. Other local museums are the **Aegean Maritime Museum** **7**, the **Archaeological Museum** **8** and a **working windmill** **9** on the east side of town. More windmills stand on a headland south of Mykonos town.

The island's south coast boasts a string of beautiful beaches, which are a short taxi or bus ride from the town. **Psarou** **10**, one of the finest (and busiest) of these beaches, features restaurants and a variety of watersports. **Plati Yialos** **11** also has restaurants and is popular with families. The beaches lying to the east – Paranga, Paradise, Super Paradise and Elia – are designated nude beaches, and can be reached by boat from Plati Yialos or by road from Mykonos town.

Delos – The smallest of the Cyclades, this tiny island was of great importance in ancient times,

The whitewashed, sunbaked buildings of Mykonos.

A ship at anchor off Mykonos

when its temple of Apollo held the treasury of the Delian League – a confederation of maritime states led by Athens. Today the island group's administrative centre is on Syros, but its historical heart remains on Delos – the mythical birthplace of Apollo.

According to Greek legend, Zeus's lover Leto was cursed by his jealous wife. A pregnant Leto wandered the earth until the god

The ancient ruins on Delos

Poseidon took pity on her and gave her a place to rest by anchoring the island of Delos with four diamond columns. There Leto gave birth to Zeus's children – a girl named Artemis and a boy named Apollo, who became important Greek gods.

Council members of the Delian League, formed to finance a war against Persia, would meet on the politically neutral island of Delos and contribute funds, troops and ships to the league. Its treasury was moved from Delos to the Athenian Acropolis in 454 BC but the island continued to prosper, becoming the site of a thriving slave market in the 2nd century BC. Sacked by Mithridates VI of Pontus (modern Turkey) in 88 BC, Delos never recovered and was abandoned near the end of the 1st century BC.

Excavation of the site began in the 1870s and today the uninhabited island is visited by day trippers arriving solely to see its ancient ruins, which include the small sanctuary of Dionysus (dating to 300 BC), a restored temple to the goddess Isis, and the famous Terrace of the Lions, carved from marble in the 7th century BC.

Naxos

The largest of the Cyclades, Naxos is ringed with beautiful beaches and traversed with fertile valleys where olive trees and grape vines thrive in the fertile soil. An island steeped in Greek mythology, Naxos was once a centre of worship of Dionysus and a member of the Delian League. The town of Naxos (Hora) runs from the harbour up a hillside, its narrow winding lanes lined with stone houses and leading to a Venetian castle. White marble and granite have been quarried on Naxos since antiquity, and monuments from various periods can be found throughout the town, including fine Byzantine churches and the castle with its tower and battlements. The local archaeological museum in Naxos also contains some notable exhibits.

Cruise ships anchor below the spectacular cliff-top town of Fira on Santorini Island.

Santorini (Thira)

Myth and modern science meet on the island of Santorini, believed by many to be the lost kingdom of Atlantis, which was destroyed by a volcanic explosion in about 1500 BC. Crescent-shaped Santorini's stunning setting seems to support this myth. Set on the exposed rim of a submerged volcano, Santorini's harbour is a flooded crater.

Cruise ships anchor in this watery caldera and tender passengers ashore to the base of an idyllic clifftop town where a switchback staircase ascends the crater wall. The town of **Fira** can be reached on foot, by donkey, by cablecar or by motorcoaches used for shore excursions. It takes about 45 minutes to reach the top on foot. Whatever your chosen mode of ascent, the view from above is spectacular.

Across the bay from Fira lies the quiet island of Thirasia, a fragment of the caldera's rim that was once joined to the main

Shore Excursions

Shore excursions in **Santorini** include various motorcoach tours of the island. These usually include a stop at Fira and the village of Oia combined with other attractions, including a local winery (4 hrs, $100-$150) or a visit to a taverna for a dinner of Greek cuisine, music and dancing. Also offered by some cruise lines is a 15-minute boat ride to Nea Kameni volcanic crater for a hike to the summit (2.5 hrs, $100).

island until an eruption in 236 BC. Dotting the bay are the smaller Burnt Islands, which rose from the caldera in subsequent eruptions. Palia Kameni emerged in 196 BC, and Nea Kameni last erupted in 1925. In the past, a reliable warning of an imminent eruption occurred when the surrounding sea turned a milky colour due to an increase in underwater sulphur emissions.

Fira town is perched high above the harbour on Santorini.

Fira is a fashionable resort, its terraced streets of whitewashed buildings lined with chic shops and restaurants, its numerous domed churches still prominent amid the tourist attractions.

The village of Oia at the north end of the island (which can be reached by local bus) is a haven for artists, their original works sold in the array of galleries lining streets that are wide enough for pedestrians but not cars.

Before the catastrophic eruption of c. 1500 BC, Santorini was colonized by Minoans from Crete. Archaeological digs indicate these people heeded the warning earthquakes and abandoned the island before the massive explosion. The island was next settled by Phoenicians, followed by Laconians from the Peloponnese peninsula who estalbished a new centre on the island's east coast under their leader Thira.

From the Middle Ages onwards, the island was called Santorini after St. Irene, protector

of the island. The Greek god of fertility and wine, Dionysus, is also associated with Santorini where wine grapes thrive in the volcanic soil.

Fira Attractions

Near the **cable car ticket office** 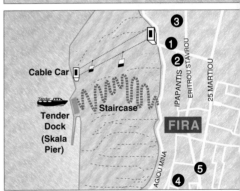 **1** is the **Archaeological Museum 2** which displays artefacts from ancient Thira. A private museum is housed in a restored mansion near the **Roman Catholic Cathedral 3**. More churches, including the **Greek Orthodox Cathedral 4**, are situated a few blocks south of here. **Platia Theotokopoulou 5** is the town's main square, where tourist services are located.

At the south end of the island, near Akrotiri, is the ancient **Minoan site**. Still under excavation, it was discovered in the late 1960s by Professor Spyros Marinatos, who discovered an extensive ancient city preserved for 35 centuries beneath tons of volcanic ash. Streets of multi-storeyed warehouses and homes, their walls decorated with vivid wall paintings, were revealed as the ash was cleared away, but the absence of skeletons indicated there had been a mass evacuation prior to the explosion. Geological evidence indicates the island was racked beforehand by earthquakes, ample warning for the island's residents.

Most of the beaches on Santorini are black, due to the fallen volcanic ash but there is also a well-known red beach near Akrotiri.

Crete

A mountainous island of deep gorges and farm-filled valleys, Crete's long history is one of invasion and resistance. In ancient times, one of the world's earliest civilizations thrived on the island of Crete. Called **Minoan** for the legendary King Minos, its great palaces were adorned with colourful murals and enormous clay pottery.

Minoan habitation of Crete began in about 3000 BC. The

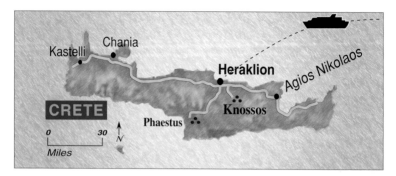

island's forests supplied wood for boat building, and the residents of Crete engaged in seagoing trade. Their island lay only 400 miles from the northern shores of Egypt, where an advanced civilization influenced the cultural development of Crete. Neolithic village life evolved into an urban society centred around great palaces. Minoan art flourished, portraying animals with a joyful fluidity of movement.

When Dorian Greeks settled on the island several centuries after the collapse of the Minoan civilization, they established dozens of city-states, with **Knossos** emerging as one of the most powerful. A centre of trade, the island became a pirate haven until conquered by the Romans in 68 BC. The Byzantines were next to rule Crete, followed briefly by Arabs before the island was reconquered by the Byzantines in 961.

Next to rule the island were the Venetians, who built a wall around **Heraklion** (then called Candia) to defend this important trading port from pirates. When the Ottoman Turks over-ran the island in 1648, the garrison at Heraklion fought off the invaders for 21 years before surrendering.

The statesman Eleutherios Venizelos, born in Crete and educated in Athens, returned in 1896 to play a prominent role in the island's insurrection against Turkish rule. Turkey, at the intervention of European powers, was eventually forced to evacuate,

A quiet square near Agio Titos (above). Minoan vase dating from 1700 BC in Archaeological Museum (left).

and in 1908 Crete proclaimed its union with Greece.

Crete came under invasion once again, during World War II, when British and Greek forces on the island were overwhelmed by a German airborne invasion. The German troops occupying the island eventually surrendered to the British navy in late 1944.

Famous Cretans include the 16th-century painter El Greco, and Nikos Kazantzakis, author of *Zorba the Greek.* The singer Nana Mouskouri was born in Chania, on Crete's north coast, shortly before the Second World War, and her childhood recollections include the excitement of the olive harvest when she dipped her mother's freshly baked bread into extra virgin olive oil, made from the first pressing and flavoured with fresh herbs grown in the mountains.

Getting Around

Crete's main cruise ports – Heraklion (Iraklion) and Souda Port-Chania – are located on the island's north coast. **Heraklion** is the capital and main city of Crete and is conveniently located three miles from the famous Minoan palace at Knossos, which is the main attraction for passengers arriving at this port. In addition to ship's excursions, Knossos can be reached from Heraklion by taxi (15-20 minute drive; €17 each way) or by catching the Knossos bus at the station near the harbour (see map). A taxi from Heraklian's cruise port into the town centre costs about €6, but it's a fairly pleasant and easy walk from the

(Above) Iraklion's Old Harbour.
(Below) Agios Titos Church.

cruise dock into town.

Ship **shore excursions** from Heraklion include half-day tours to Knossos (3 to 4 hrs, $60-$80) often combined with a sightseeing tour of Heraklion or a nearby village. Other excursions include a half-day tour to the Minoan ruins at **Phaestos**. These ruins, set on a plateau, are not as extensive as those at Knossos, but the drive across the island offers an opportunity to see more of Crete's splendid scenery.

The port of **Souda** is located a few miles east of **Chania** and a city shuttle bus provides regular service (the fare is €1.5). Taxis are also available. From Chania it's a 2.5 hour drive to Knossos, so a ship's shore excursion is probably the best way to visit this site (8 hrs, $95). Other shore excursions in Chania include beach transfers ($25) and sightseeing tours (5 hrs, $60-$70). Chania's old town is centred around its Venetian-built harbour and is a pleasant place to have lunch on the waterfront.

Heraklion Attractions

If you're setting off on foot from the cruise dock, follow the waterfront to the **Old Harbour** **1** for a look at its Venetian fortifications. The largest of the six bastions is Martinengo Bastion, where a stone slab marks the buri-

al place of the writer Kazantzakis, who died in 1957.

From the harbour, proceed up Avgoustou (August), a pedestrian street that leads to the town's central platia (square), named for the great statesman Eleftherio Venizelou. Along the way you'll pass some beautiful neoclassical buildings and the Byzantine church **Agios Titos** **2**, named for Crete's patron saint, who converted the people of Crete to Christianity.

At **Platia Venizelou** **3** you'll find outdoor cafes and standing in the centre of the square is a marble Renaissance fountain called The Lions. Across the street is the **Agios Markos** (St. Mark) **4**, built by the Venetians in the 13th century and now housing an exhibition centre. **Market Street** leads south from Platia Venizelou and is a good place to shop for local handicrafts including silver jewellery. The maze of back streets lying east of the square

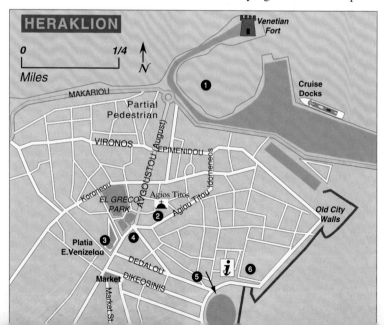

contain outdoor cafés and a selection of shops, including the boutiques on **Daedolou Street**, which leads to **Platia Eleftherias 5**. Here, on the square's north side, is the **Visitor Information Office** and the **Archaeological Museum 6**. Built between 1937 and 1940 in a converted power station, the museum grounds contain gardens, benches and a coffee shop. Inside the museum is an extensive collection of Minoan artifacts, including the Phaestos disc and original wall paintings from the palace at Knossos.

About three miles from Herraklion is the site of the famous Minoan palace at **Knossos**. Built on a hillside, the original palace was destroyed by an earthquake around 1700 BC, then rebuilt on an even grander scale and serviced by a complex drainage and water-supply system. Although it was damaged by another earthquake around 1450 BC, excavations of the 'new' palace have revealed a labyrinth of rooms and passages, porticoes and staircases, richly decorated with lyrical wall paintings.

The palace was built around a central courtyard and boasts excellent masonry construction. The columns were originally made of wood – those we see today are reproductions. English archaeologist Sir Arthur Evans spent decades (1898 and 1935) and his personal fortune uncovering the ruins and reconstructing the buildings. Some archaeolo-

gists have criticized these reconstructions, but they do offer the lay person a good idea of what the palace looked like in Minoan times. Highlights of the site include the Queen's Megaron, approached by the Grand Staircase, which is decorated with the Dolphin Fresco. Adjacent is the Queen's Bath, containing a terracotta bathtub.

Many legends are associated with this great palace, including the myth of the Minotaur – a monster with the head of a bull and the body of a man – who was confined within a labyrinth beneath the palace, where he devoured sacrificial youth sent as tribute from Athens.

Minoan wall art (above right) and palace ruins at Knossos (right).

The Dodecanese

Pronounced *doh dek en ees* and meaning Twelve Islands, this island group in the eastern Aegean Sea lies much closer to the shores of Turkey than those of Greece. Yet Greek culture has endured on these islands, despite centuries of foreign occupation, since antiquity. Initially influenced by the Minoan civilization of Crete, the Dodecanese were eventually settled by the Dorians, who had established the Greek city-states of Sparta and Corinth before migrating across the Aegean Sea. Those who landed on Rhodes discovered a fertile island blessed with a subtropical climate.

Rhodes

When the Greek cartographer Eratosthenes compiled a map of the known world in the 3rd century BC, the central point on his chart was the island of Rhodes.

Situated only 12 miles from the shores of Asia Minor (modern Turkey), the busy port of Rhodes was a trade link between East and West. Built in 408 BC as a planned 'modern' city with a grid system of streets, it was protected by a fortified wall.

These were prosperous times for Rhodes and, after withstanding a siege in 305 BC, the city commissioned three local sculptors to create a colossal bronze statue of Helios, the sun god, which was erected at the harbour entrance but later destroyed by an earthquake. Rhodes was one of the most beautiful and organized cities of the Hellenistic world. The arts and sciences flourished, and Rhodes became a centre of learning, its 800-seat theatre used for teaching philosophy and oration, with Julius Caesar among those who studied there.

Rhodes eventually declined economically, descending into a period of obscurity that lasted until the Knights of St. John landed on its shores in 1306. A religious-military order founded in Jerusalem in the middle of the 11th century, the Knights of St. John had been driven from the Middle East by Arab forces and were stationed on Cyprus when their Grand Master negotiated a deal to purchase Rhodes from the Genoese, who were then administering the Dodecanese Islands.

The Knights of Rhodes, as they called themselves during their 213-year rule of the island, were supported financially by the feudal lords of Europe, for they were

The Colossus of Rhodes

spearheads of Western expansionism and defenders of Christianity. The order was a hierarchical organization of knights (noblemen), chaplains and sergeants (sons of freemen), who hailed from seven European nations – Provence, Auvernge, France, Italy, Aragon, England and Germany. Each national group was called a 'tongue', had its own 'inn' or meeting place within the fortified city, and was responsible for defending a specific section ('curtain') of the wall.

Prosperity returned to Rhodes under the Knights. Their imposing Palace of the Grand Master stood on the town's highest ground, while the winding streets below teemed with merchants, both local and foreign, as well as bankers, artists and tradesmen. Goods arrived and departed by ship and hostilities between the Knights and the Turks were set aside in favour of trade. The sounds of feasting and carousing spilled into the streets while the wealthy nobility strolled the town's beautiful gardens in their elegant clothes.

In 1840 Turkish forces laid siege to mighty Rhodes. With a fleet of 170 ships carrying 100,000 soldiers, the Turks mounted attack after attack, finally taking the Tower of Italy and penetrating the city walls. Knights raced from other parts of the city to fight the invaders, who finally retreated after a bloody battle and sailed away. An earthquake struck Rhodes the following year, completing the devastation wreaked by the Turkish siege, but the Knights rebuilt the town.

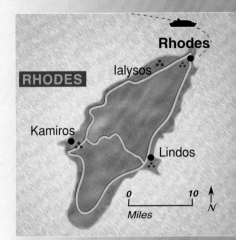

(Above) Back street of Old Rhodes.
(Below) Street of the Knights.

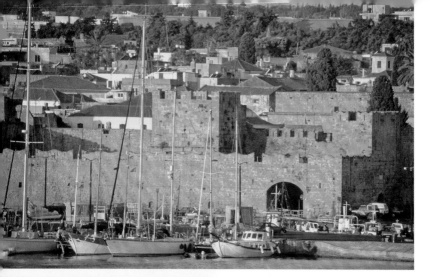

(Above) The walled fortress town of the old city. Sea Gate is one of several fortified entrances (left).

More than 40 years passed before the Turks attacked again, relentlessly bombarding the town's landward fortifications while a huge fleet blockaded the harbour. The townspeople, running out of food and the will to resist, convinced the Knights to surrender. On January 1, 1523, the Knights and about 5,000 Rhodians boarded ships and set sail for Crete, leaving Rhodes to the Ottoman Turks. The Turks held the Dodecanese for the next 400 years, until they were occupied by Italian forces in 1912. Captured by the Allies during World War II, the islands were returned to Greece in 1947.

Getting Around

The cruise ships dock in the city's commercial harbour, opposite the medieval fortress of Old Rhodes. It's a short distance to the walled town where you could easily spend an entire day wandering the cobblestone streets of this medieval fortress. Or, spend half the day exploring Old Rhodes and the other half of the day on an escorted tour to Lindos (see box).

A motorized trolley travels from the harbour to the ancient acropolis (also called Monte Smith, for a British admiral), which overlooks the walled town.

Buses run regularly between Rhodes and Lindos (€5 each way); the Rhodes **bus station** is located north of the Old Town's north wall. Taxis to Lindos from Rhodes is about €55 one way.

Rhodes Attractions

A World Heritage Site, the town of Rhodes was badly damaged by earthquakes in the mid-1800s. Many of its buildings were repaired during the Italian occupation, but further damage was caused by incendiary bombs during World War II. The Greek Archaeological Service is now in charge of its restoration and conservation.

The **Gate of the Virgin 1** and the much-photographed **Sea Gate 2** both provide access into the walled town from the harbour front. Not far from the Sea Gate is busy **Platia Ippokratous 3**, its outdoor cafés, shops and fountains overlooked by the

D'Amboise Gate was named for a French Grand Master.

Kastellania (Courthouse) of the Knights. Nearby, off Mousio (Museum) Square, is the **Archaeological Museum 4**, housed in the New Hospital of the Knights, which is one of the most handsome and best preserved buildings from the time of the Knights. Here the sick were cared for by physicians under the supervision of eight 'brothers' – one

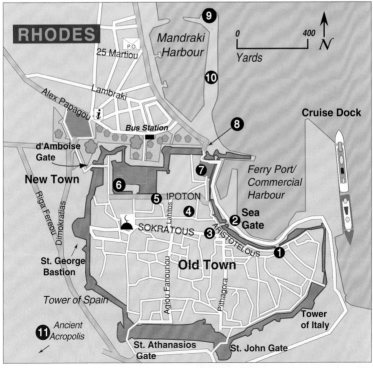

from each 'tongue' (nationality) of the Order.

The Hospital's north side runs along **Ippoton (Street of the Knights) 5**, which was the most important thoroughfare in the medieval town. It ran through the middle of the Collachium, a section of town once separated from the rest by an inner wall. The knights lived inside the

Courtyard (above) and outer gardens (below) at Grand Master's Palace in Rhodes.

Collachium, spending their days engaged in military exercises and prayer. Each 'tongue' had an 'inn' along the Street of Knights at which its members could gather to dine and discuss matters. At the top of the Street of the Knights stands the **Grand Master's Palace 6**. Built on the site of a Byzantine citadel, the Palace became the town's administrative centre and was the last refuge for its citizens during times of attack.

Left to crumble by the Turks and damaged by earthquakes, the final blow to the Palace occurred in 1856 when some gunpowder stored in the vaults of the nearby Church of St. John blew up, leaving only the palace's ground floor standing. The Italians restored and modified the palace between the two world wars, when it became a residence and headquarters for Fascist Minister C.M. de Vecchi. Interior highlights of the Palace include a grand staircase, made of marble, which leads to the upper storey. There a series of vaulted halls contain carved furniture, Chinese vases and marble sculptures from the Hellenistic period, including a copy of *Laocoön* that was created in the 1st century BC by three Rhodian sculptors. The expansive floors of these chambers are covered with Hellenistic and Roman tile mosaics brought by the Italians from buildings on the island of Kos.

North of the Street of the Knights is **Platia Argirokastrou 7** where the ancient ruins of the Temple of Venus (Aphrodite) are situated opposite the **Freedom Gate 8**. Beyond this gate is

Shore Excursions

Rhodes • Walking tour of Old Rhodes and motorcoach ride to Lindos with visit to ancient acropolis; lunch included (8 hrs, $150+)
• Scenic motorcoach ride to Lindos and walking tour of ancient acropolis (4.5 hrs, $50-$100)

Mandraki Harbour, the ancient port that was guarded by the Colossus of Rhodes. Today a bronze deer stands on either side of the harbour entrance. During the reign of the Knights, the **Fort of St. Nicholas 9**, which stands at the end of the stone pier, was an important fortress protecting the harbour from Turkish assaults; the tower now houses a lighthouse. The three windmills still standing on the **Mole of St. Nicholas 10** were used by the Knights for grinding wheat. West of the medieval town is the **ancient acropolis 11** where the walled ruins include the Temple of Apollo, the Odeum and the Stadium.

Lindos – Before the town of Rhodes was established in 408 BC, Lindos was a major naval and trading centre on the island's southeast coast. The town's acropolis – a promontory rock overlooking the sea – was both a fortress and sanctuary housing a temple of Athena. In the year 51 AD, the Apostle St. Paul landed by small boat in the bay and introduced Christianity to the island. The ancient acropolis was further fortified during the Byzantine period, then by the Knights.

Modern-day Rhodians favour scooters for getting around the Old Town (above). Bronze deer at the harbour entrance (below).

A hike up the stairway leading to the fortress rewards visitors with a panoramic view of two crescent-shaped beaches and the hillside village of Lindos, its narrow streets and whitewashed mansions dating from the 17th century. The Byzantine church of the Panayia was built in the 15th century, and later decorated with wall paintings.

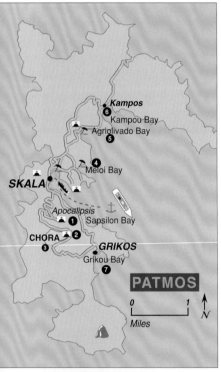

Patmos

The serene and scenic island of Patmos has been a place of pilgrimage ever since St. John the Evangelist landed on its shores in 95 AD. One of three apostles closest to Jesus and author of the fourth Gospel, an elderly John was banished by the Roman Emperor Domitian to the tiny island of Patmos, where he sought shelter in a cave.

Now called the **Holy Grotto of the Apocalypse 1**, it was in this cave that God revealed to John a magnificent yet terrifying vision, described in the Book of Revelation, which John spent the next 18 months dictating to his disciple Prochorus.

Ten centuries later the Byzantine monk Hosios Christodoulos, who had built a monastery on the island of Kos, travelled to Constantinople to request permission to found the **Monastery of Saint John the Divine 2** on Patmos. His request was granted, in exchange for his holdings on Kos, and construction of the monastery commenced in 1088, its thick walls and battle-

A ship's tender heads ashore at the Greek island of Patmos.

Skala's waterfront (above). A shaded street in Skala (right).

ments built to protect the main church, several chapels and a treasury of icons and gold-embroidered vestments. Its forecourt is decorated with frescoes illustrating the life of St. John, and its library contains priceless books and manuscripts, including one from the 6th century containing portions of St. Mark's gospel.

The fortress-like monastery stands on a hill above the charming village of **Chora (Hora)** 3, which is a labyrinth of winding lanes, whitewashed houses and bell-topped chapels.

On Your Own

Patmos is an ideal island to tour independently because it's small and the roads are fairly quiet. The large cruise ships anchor outside the small port of **Skala** and tender their passengers ashore. A taxi stand with a dispatcher is located near the cruise ship quay and tender dock. The taxi fare from Skala to the Monastery of St. John is 5 euros. Buses also run between Skala and Chora, departing every half hour. It takes about half an hour to walk the path up to the cave, then on to the monastery.

Cars, motor scooters and bicycles can be rented in Skala (see www.patmos-island.com).

Beaches on the island can be reached by hired boat or by road. Just north of Skala and within walking distance (about 20 minutes) is the sand and gravel beach at **Melloi** 4. Further along is the sandy beach at **Agriolivado** 5. One of the island's best beaches is **Kambos** 6, a ten-minute taxi ride or 20-minute boat ride north of Skala. **Grikou Bay** 7, below Chora, has a sandy beach.

Shore excursions include a motorcoach ride to the grotto and monastery of St. John (2.5 hrs,

(Above) A tiny square in Chora.
(Left) Fresco in Monastery of St.
John the Divine. (Bottom)
Natural sponges, harvested in
local waters, are sold on Patmos.

$50+), and a scenic drive to the grotto of St. John, the white-washed village of Chora and coastal Grikou (2.5 hrs).

Kos

An ancient cultural centre, the island of Kos is where Hippocrates founded a school of medicine in the 5th century BC. In the following century, the Sanctuary of Asklepios became famous as a healing centre, its ter-raced buildings encompassing the Temple of Asklepios and the Stoa, which housed the medical school. The island also prospered during Hellenistic times as a naval base for the Ptolemaic dynasty of Egypt. The Graeco-Roman town of Kos contains an odeum built in imperial times, as well as a castle built by the Knights of St. John.

Its Roman-era villas were decorated with fabulous floor mosaics, many of which were removed by the Italians in the 1930s to the Grand Master's Palace in Rhodes.

Northeast Aegean Islands

Lying off the coast of Turkey, these remote and widespread islands include rugged **Limnos (Lemnos)**, volcanic in origin, its fertile soil used for growing wheat and fruit trees. Sacred to the Olympian god Hephaestus (originally an Asian fire god), Limnos was a colony of Athens in c. 500 BC and excavations at Hephaestia have revealed a theatre of the Hellenistic period. With the decline of the Byzantine Empire, Limnos was eventually seized in 1479 by the Ottoman Turks. A fortress overlooks the fishing harbour at Myrina, the island's capital and primary port.

Lesbos (Lesvos) became a cultural center of Greece in the 7th century BC. The female poet Sappho, who wrote love lyrics to other women, was born here in the early 6th century BC and the term 'lesbian' is derived from the name of her island home. Aristotle and Epicurus are among those who taught at the island's Philosophical Academy. Lesbos was captured by Ottoman Turks in 1462 and, along with Limnos, was returned in 1913 to Greece. Olive groves and citrus fruits flourish on the island's fertile hillsides. Mitilini is the chief town, its harbour overlooked by Gattelusi Castle, constructed by the Byzantine emperor Justinian.

The ancient ruins on Kos

The Theatre of Mytilene, built in Hellenistic times on the slope of a hill, is where Pompey reportedly sat on a luxurious throne and watched performances lauding his military successes.

Ionian Islands

This chain of lush, mountainous islands lying off the west coast of Greece is shrouded in myth – both ancient and modern. The island of Ithaca was, according to Homer's legends, the home of **Odysseus** who, in the course of his 10-year odyssey, struggled with angry gods and insistent sea nymphs before returning home to his waiting wife and son.

A modern Greek tale unfolded on another Ionian island – the tiny isle of **Skorpios** – when its owner, the shipping tycoon **Aristotle Onassis**, married one of the world's most famous women, Jacqueline Kennedy, in October

The lovely Ionian Islands are known for their dramatic cliffs and sugary white beaches.

1968. Turkish-born Onassis had formed, with his former father-in-law and brother-in-law, the most powerful shipping clan in the world when he set his sights on the widow of President Kennedy.

Shipping has always been big business in the Ionian islands. Over the centuries they have been ruled by various maritime powers, including the Byzantines and medieval Venice. In the early 1800s they were occupied by the British navy and remained under Britain's protection until they were at last ceded to Greece in 1864.

Cephalonia (Kefalonia)

The largest of the Ionian Islands, Cephalonia is known for its beautiful beaches hidden between rocky headlands. Argostoli is the island's largest town and a busy seaport. The cruise ships dock at a new pier right alongside the town of Argostoli, from which several shore excursions can be taken around the island.

Attractions on Cephalonia include the fishing port of Sami, where the 2001 movie *Captain Corelli's Mandolin* was filmed. Fiskardo is another picturesque port. A popular beach on Cephalonia is Makrys Giaios (nicknamed Long Beach) where watersports can be enjoyed along with sunbathing and swimming.

Several caves also dot the island, including Drogarati Cave, which was discovered some 300 years ago when an earthquake exposed its entrance to a dramatic cavern filled with stalagmites and stalactites.

Corfu (Kerkira)

Corfu has long been considered one of Greece's loveliest islands. Homer wrote glowingly about Phaeacia – a luxurious and joyful island whose seafaring people welcomed sailors – and it's quite likely Corfu was this island, upon which Odysseus was shipwrecked. Other poets and writers since Homer have been smitten with the beauty of Corfu, including Goethe, Oscar Wilde and Lawrence Durrell. Shakespeare, in *The Tempest*, may have modeled Prospero's island on Corfu.

The Turks also coveted Corfu, but the island's inhabitants resisted Turkish invasion, including two famous sieges in 1537 and 1716. Corfu is a fertile island, and its major industries are farming, fishing and tourism.

Getting Around

Corfu town, one of Greece's largest medieval towns, is well preserved, its cobblestone alleyways filled with shops and tavernas. The ships dock west of the town and provide a motorcoach shuttle into the town centre (US$16 roundtrip). A taxi ride into town is €10; a 4-hr island tour by taxi is €200; a 1-hr beach visit by taxi to the island's west side is €100. Rental cars cost about €60 + tax.

The sights south of the town centre can be reached by buses that travel regularly between the Esplanade and Kanoni. Buses also run regularly between Corfu town and Palaeokastritsa on the island's west coast.

On the west side of Corfu town stands the Venetian-built **New Fortress** **1**, originally constructed in 1577, its maze of tunnels and moats later modified by the French and British. On the opposite side of town, on a promontory converted to an island by a Venetian-dug moat, are the remains of the **Old Fortress** **2** built by the Venetians in 1546 with modifications and additions under the English Protectorate (1815-1864). This expansive site (€4 entry) is a fascinating place to spend an hour or two exploring

The Old Fortress overlooks Garitsa Bay.

the fortifications, enjoying the sea views and relaxing over lunch at the terrace café.

The town's main square – the **Esplanade 3** – contains a crick-

Shore Excursions

Corfu Shore excursions in Corfu include a walking tour of the Old Town and a motorcoach ride to various island attractions (4 hrs, $70). Mountain biking (4 hrs, $95) and four-wheel drive adventures (5 hrs, $190) are also offered. Check your cruise line's website for details.

et pitch and Victorian bandstand, and is bordered on its west side by Georgian and Venetian townhouses, their overhanging balconies decorated with wrought-iron railings. The Liston – an arcaded sidewalk of cafés and restaurants – was built by the French under Napoleon. This beguiling blend of architecture is repeated throughout the historic quarter – the 16th-century red-domed **Church of St. Spyridon 4**, the 17th-century Venetian lodge now housing the **Town Hall 5**, and the 19th-century colonnaded **Palace of St. Michael and St.**

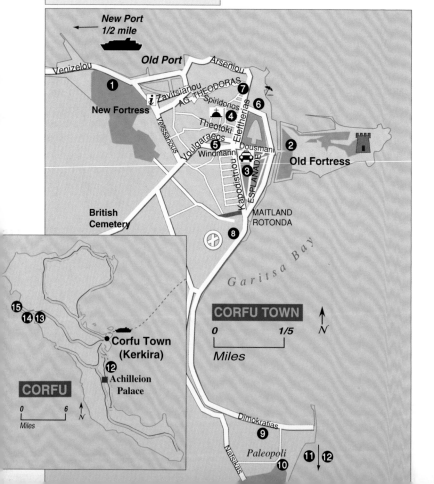

George , built as a residence for the British Lord High Commissioner. Another beautiful building houses the **Corfu Literary Society** , the oldest in Greece.

It's a pleasant walk along Garitsa Bay to the **Archaeological Museum** , with its fine collection of excavated artifacts. At the south end of the bay is the **Church of Saints Jason and Sosipater** , a Byzantine church decorated with beautiful icons. Just south of the bay, near the public beach, is the **Palace of Mon Repos** . Set amid gardens, this mansion (built in 1831) was a summer residence for Britain's Lord High Commissioner. It became a royal residence and is the birthplace of Prince Philip, Duke of Edinburgh, whose Danish grandfather reigned as Greece's King George I from 1863-1913. Greece abolished its monarchy in 1974 and in 1990 the Palace was expropriated by the Greek government.

About a mile past the Palace of Mon Repos is **Kanoni** , with its captivating view across a mountain-bounded inlet dotted with two idyllic islets joined to shore by a narrow causeway and containing the monastery of Vlacherna. South of Kanoni is the gaudily grand **Achilleion Palace** , which was used as a springtime retreat by Germany's Kaiser Wilhelm II in the early 1900s but is perhaps better known as the casino set used in the James Bond movie *For Your Eyes Only.*

The cliff-edged coves of **Palaeokastritsa (Old Castle)** on the island's west coast contain beautiful beaches and turquoise waters. The sea caves here can be explored by peddle boat. For panoramic views of the beach-lined coves, follow the road west of Lacone to the **Paleokastritsa Monastery** , perched atop a cliff, or carry on further to **Bella Vista** – a natural terrace overlooking the sea, which is situated near the ruins of Angelokastro (Castle of the Angel), a Byzantine fortress.

A local swimming beach lies at the base of Corfu's Old Town.

TURKEY,
THE BLACK SEA & CYPRUS

Part European, part Asian, Turkey is a unique Mediterranean destination – exotic, mysterious and steeped in history. Arching gold beaches and lush stands of palm and cypress trees are juxtaposed with ruins dating back to before the Bronze Age.

If ever there was a Garden of Eden, it may well have been situated in a narrow valley of southeastern Turkey where researchers have found DNA traces of the founder crop of einkorn wheat. This region, on the edge of the ancient Fertile Crescent of Iraq, is where agriculture and the origins of collective society began 10,000 years ago.

Yet, despite its ancient past, Turkey is very much a modern nation. A parliamentary republic, Turkey has embraced westernization while retaining its eastern culture.

Turkey at a Glance

Turkey's population, about 79 million, is almost exclusively Sunni Muslim. The official language is Turkish – not Arabic – and Kurdish is spoken by 18% of the population. English, French and German are widely understood. Turkey (770,000 sq km) is slightly larger than Texas. European Turkey is largely rolling agricultural land while the

Asian side of the country is bordered by the Black Sea Mountains to the north and the Taurus Mountains to the south. This part of Turkey is dominated by the vast semi-arid plateau of Anatolia, although parts of the lower interior are lush and fertile, with numerous rivers and lakes.

Travel Tips

Currency – The unit of currency is the Turkish lira (TRY). Introduced as the New Turkish lira in 2005, it eliminated six zeros from the existing lira. The approximate exchange rate is 1USD = 3 TRY; 1GBP = 4.25 TRY. US currency is widely accepted and ATM machines issuing Turkish lira at competitive exchange rates are located at most ports.

A cruise ship departs Istanbul.
Hagia Sophia in foreground,
with Topkapi Palace behind.

The excellent Metro transit system can be boarded near the Eminönü docks with stops throughout "Old Stamboul."

Tourist Visa – Cruise passengers visiting a Turkish port within a single day do not need a tourist visa (this applies to multiple stops). However, if Istanbul is a base port where you plan to stay overnight or longer, a tourist visa is required and can be purchased online at a slight discount (www. evisa.gov.tr). If arriving by air, a tourist visa can be obtained at a kiosk in the airport. The fee for US citizens is $30; for Canadians the fee is US$70; British citizens pay £20.

Health Concerns – Inoculations for cruise passengers planning to stay a few days in Istanbul or along the Aegean coast are not necessary. However, if you intend to travel further inland before or after your cruise, you should consult your physician.

Getting Around – The cruise ships dock in central **Istanbul** at the Karakoy or adjacent Salip Pazari cruise berths. The taxi fare from Ataturk Internaional Airport to downtown Istanbul is about 40 Turkish lira (US$15). Official yellow taxis are a good way to get about in Istanbul and are reasonably priced (see www.taksiyle.

com/en for estimated taxi fares). All taxis have meters and the meter starts at 3.20 Turkish lira and charges 2 lira per km. Pay the fare in liras or you will be charged an unfair exchange.

Another efficient way to get around is by the ubiquitous *dolmus* (meaning 'stuffed' – which they often are at rush hour). These small buses are usually tan coloured, with their destinations displayed on the windscreen. Payment, in local currency, is made as you get off. Istanbul's Metro, a sort of art-deco street car, is also good – and cheap.

Dining – Turkish cuisine is renowned for its excellence and variety. Popular dishes include *kebap* which is grilled or roasted meat, and fish. Restaurant dinner hour normally begins at about 7:00 p.m. A popular alcoholic beverage is *raki* – the grandfather of absinthe-type drinks – which goes well with hors d'oeuvres and is traditionally enjoyed prior to the main meal of the day. Turkey produces some good wines from the Thrace, Anatolia and Aegean regions. *Buzbag*, a popular red from Anatolia, is often touted as

Turkey is a fascinating study between its Muslim traditions and its adaptation to the modern world. (Below) Entrance and interior to Grand Bazaar.

Turkey's most original wine.

Although Turkish coffee is very good, tea is more popular with the Turks. The favourite tea (cay) is deep red and known as 'rabbit's blood.' Served piping hot with sugar in small, tulip-shaped glasses, it's often offered as a traditional expression of hospitality.

Opening Hours – Most stores open by 10:00 a.m. and many businesses hum along well after 6:00 p.m. The covered bazaar in Istanbul is open from 8:00 a.m. to 7:00 p.m. but is closed on Sunday. Bank hours seem to vary but generally the doors open at 8:30 a.m., closing at noon for lunch and re-opening from 1:30 until 5:00 p.m. Museums are open between 10:00 a.m. and 4:00 p.m. every day except Mondays. An exception is Topkapi Palace, which closes on Tuesdays.

Shopping – Turkey is renowned for its carpets and kilims (fine carpets for walls), tiles and porcelain, and silks. Turkey is also an excellent place to buy jewellery, Meerschaum pipes, brass work and leather products. Handmade ceramic tiles, bowls, plates and other pot-

View from the Bosphorus of Istanbul with Blue Mosque at left, Hagia Sophia in the middle, and Topkapi Palace to the right.

tery are also widely available, their colourful designs often replicated from 17th and 18th century works.

Turkish merchants enjoy presale banter and haggling is part of the process. It's very common for a merchant to offer you tea and ask you to sit down while he tells you about his wares. If you are seriously looking to buy something, this is an aspect of Turkish culture to be enjoyed. The art of bargaining starts with a figure about half the asking price and settles at between 60 and 80 per cent of the initial price.

Turkey's History

The world's first settlement dates back over 8,000 years to a Neolithic centre at Çatalhöyük, about 120 miles northeast of the coastal resort city of Antalya. The entire Anatolian plateau harboured numerous tribes, but it wasn't until the Hittites moved west into the Capadocian area around 1800 BC that Turkey's history began. With their capital at Bogazkoy (70 miles east of Ankara), the Hittites became the chief power and cultural force in western Asia but by 1000 BC, the Hittite empire had been subdued by invaders. It was around this time that Ionians, fleeing Dorian invaders on mainland Greece, began settling along the coastline of Aegean Turkey. The region's fertile land and excellent harbours provided prosperity for these Greek pioneers and various cities thrived, particularly **Ephesus**.

Well before the Romans arrived in Turkey, one of the world's greatest cities was being settled by the Greeks on a small promontory on the Sea of Marmara. Legend has it that a Greek soldier named Byzas, upon receiving direction from the Delphic oracle, established a colony where he stood on a hill (the future site of Istanbul's Topkapi Palace) overlooking the Bosphorus and Golden Horn.

Ancient Byzantium was ideally situated to control shipping to and from the Black Sea and, straddling Europe and Asia, it was a critical trade portal between the Orient and Europe. Surrounded on three sides by water and with substantial land walls, it was virtually impregnable to attack.

Eventually, Byzantium, like most other cities of the Mediterranean, fell under Rome's rule, becoming an important port and garrison for the Empire. So things remained until the 4th century, when an event unparalleled in the history of the Roman Empire occurred – the voluntary retirement of Emperor Diocletian. This caused an eruption in the Empire as armies aligned with three competing caesars, one of whom – the victor – became known as **Constantine the Great**.

Some historians point to Constantine as the single most influential ruler in western civilization. Constantine moved the Roman capital to Byzantium and on May 11, 330 AD, he formally dedicated the city, which he called Constantinople, to the God of the Christians. Today, the most visible remains of Constantine's building effort is his column near the entrance to the Covered Bazaar.

The Byzantine Empire reached its apex during the reign of Justinian I, from 527 to 565 AD, when its borders stretched from Spain to Iraq. Many edifices and magnificent churches were built across the Empire during this time, the most magnificent being the Hagia Sophia, built near the acropolis of the city.

Although the Byzantine Empire remained relatively intact for another 400 years, its decline was apparent by the 11th century with the permanent loss of Asia Minor to the Turks.

During a power struggle for the throne in early in the 13th century, the usurper Alexius IV enlisted the Venetians to attack the city under the guise of the Fourth Crusade and for the first time in almost a thousand years the city fell. Pillaging of the city stripped it of most of its wealth and many of these treasures were taken to Venice. This sacking of the Greek Orthodox capital by Latin Roman Catholics made permanent the schism between the two great Christian religions.

The Latins were finally pushed out of Constantinople in 1261 but Byzantium had few allies against the ever-encroaching Ottoman Turks. Finally, in 1453, the Turks surrounded the Queen of Cities and using a specially made cannon (the largest the world had known) they blasted a hole in the Theodosian Walls and took the city. Their leader, Mehmet II, was 21 when he made his triumphal entry into the city.

Mehmet, called Fatih (the Conqueror), made Constantinople his capital and restored the city's greatness with a massive rebuilding program. The Ottoman Empire enjoyed another hundred

Mosiac of Justinian I in Basilica S. Vitale, Ravenna, Italy.

The Byzantine Empire

☐ Extent of Byzantine Empire (6th century)
----- Extent of Ottoman Empire (17th century)

Imperial Byzantine emblem

years of expansion which culminated with **Süleyman the Magnificent's** capture of Belgrade and Budapest. However, the reign of his son Selim II, known as The Sot, marked the slow decline of Ottoman influence. Corrupted from within by palace intrigues and by the violent resistance of the Janissaries – an elite corp of the Ottoman army – to any reforms, the Empire's steady decline followed.

In the early 19th century the sultan Mahmut II ushered in an era of reform but suffered political and military setbacks, such as the loss of Greece in 1830. Mahmut eliminated the Janissary Corps, created a new, more modern army and supported the improvement of education, thus laying the foundation for secularization throughout Ottoman society. He also banned turbans, which were replaced with the Moroccan fez.

Throughout the 19th century, succeeding sultans continued to

spend extravagantly, building huge palaces along the Bosphorus such as the **Dolmabahçe Palace**. Serious conflicts, such as the Crimean War, drained the Empire's finances, and by 1881 the Empire was on the brink of bankruptcy.

The unravelling Ottoman Empire collapsed when Turkey blundered into the First World War on the side of Germany. Despite winning the tactical battle of Gallipoli, Turkey's fate was tied to that of Germany.

With Germany's surrender in 1918, plans were made to alter Turkey's borders, with Greece the main benefactor. European allies landed Greek troops at Izmir in May of 1919, but the Turks rallied around the hero of the Battle of Gallipoli, Mustafa Kemal (known later as Ataturk – "father of the Turks"), who hastily organized an army and routed the Greek invaders in a counterattack that began in late August 1922. Within a few weeks, the Turkish mainland was completely liberated, an armistice signed and the Ottoman dynasty abolished.

In July 1923, the Turkish government signed the Lausanne

Treaty with European powers. Ankara became the capital of a new Turkish state, with Mustafa Kemal its first president. The new nation's ideology was, and remains, Atatürkism. Its basic principles stress the republican form of government, representing the power of the electorate.

The country's democracy is underpinned by a military determined to keep Turkey secular, but public support for the military weakened under the 11-year leadership of former Prime Minster Erdogan, who has been accused of polarising the country. The European Commission, upon reviewing Turkey's case to join the European Union in 2012, criticized the country's record on fair trials and freedom of speech.

(Top) Gentile Bellini's portrait of Fatih (the Conqueror) (Below) Dolmabahçe Palace, Bosphorus

Istanbul

The Queen of Cities, as Istanbul has been called over the centuries, is one of the most fascinating ports in the world. If Istanbul is the home port for your cruise, you should try to add at least two days for touring the city. Although no longer the capital of Turkey, an aura of power remains in Istanbul, for it's still the country's financial and business centre, and home to most of its head offices. Called Constantinople for over 1,500 years, its name was formally changed to Istanbul (meaning 'to the city' in Turkish) in 1930.

Where to Stay

The 4-star Pera Marmara is located a five-minute walk from the famous shopping street of Istiklal Caddesi and this chic hotel's higher-floor rooms provide excel-

lent views. The luxurious Ritz-Carlton Istanbul, not far from Dolmabahçe Palace and the cruise port, offers views of the Bosphorus in spacious rooms that feature Turkish-inspired decor, including huge marble bathrooms decorated with Iznik tiles.

Shopping & Dining

The Grand Bazaar is on everyone's list of places to shop for handcrafted Turkish souvenirs and other items sold at the hundreds of vendors stalls. For ceramics that are beautifully handpainted with classic patterns, visit Iznik Classics.

Should you get hungry while shopping, try one of the food stalls that serve dürüm – a warm, flatbread sandwich filled with grilled lamb and chopped tomatoes. One of the best kabob shacks in the bazaar is Aynen Dürüm (Sok N. 33, Muhafazacilar) where the wraps are delicious.

Istanbul's most famous shopping street is Istiklal Caddesi (Independence Avenue). This elegant pedestrian street in the historic Beyoglu (Pera) district is lined with boutiques, art galleries, cafés, pubs and night clubs.

Another trendy shopping area has sprung up around the Galata Tower where a designer jewellery boutique called Aida Pekin (44A Serdar Ekrem Sk) sells pendants inspired by local landmarks.

The Spice Bazaar (beside the New Mosque) is the best place to buy local spices, dried fruit and nuts, and Turkish Delight – a classic sweet that's called *lokum* in Turkey.

Recommended upscale restaurants in the Sultanahmet neighbourhood include Matbah near Hagia Sophia, which serves authentic Ottoman cuisine on a sunny terrace looking toward Topkapi Palace.

Near the Blue Mosque, a long-standing favourite with locals and tourists is the elegant Albura Kathisma Café & Restaurant; its premises (which include an outdoor patio and panoramic rooftop terrace) occupy an Ottoman-era house that was built on the site of Byzantine ruins.

Fishermen gather near the cruise ship dock at Karaköy.

Istanbul Attractions

Istanbul is a pedestrian friendly city and its main attractions are quite accessible by foot from the cruise docks. The best place to start touring this magnificent city is the **Galata Bridge**, near the cruise port at **Karaköy**. The view is expansive and beautiful, taking in the Bosphorus, the Golden Horn, the Sea of Marmara and the old city. A thousand years of architecture, from the Theodosian walls (completed in 447 AD) to the Topkapi Palace (built in 1465), can be seen at a glance, while below, on the river, ferries jockey for position at the docks.

Galata Bridge joins Karaköy with the Eminönü dock area. Near the bridge is one of the city's important mosques, the **Yeni Cami** , meaning the New Mosque, for it was the last of the great classical Ottoman mosques built (in 1663).

About halfway along the **Eminönü** dock area will be your first opportunity to hitch a ride on

View from Galata Bridge to Kariköy where cruise ships dock.

MUST SEE:

Istanbul has many must-see sites and first time visitors can't go wrong focusing on the old city of Istanbul.

Hagia Sophia, touted by art lovers and architects around the world as the greatest monument of the Byzantine Empire.

Topkapi Palace, a rare glimpse into the mystery and splendour of the Ottoman era.

Blue Mosque one of the most beautiful mosques in the world, renowned for its tiles.

Kapali Çarsi, also known as the Grand Bazaar; whether or not you're in the market for a carpet, you have to visit this fascinating labyrinth of shops.

Istanbul's excellent **Metro**, which winds through the city. You can also catch the Metro just outside of the **Sirkeci Train Station** a few hundred paces further along. However, there is still much to see on foot, as you walk up old Constantinople's first hill, beginning with the Sirkeci Train Station – termination of the famous **Orient Express** which made its first run to Istanbul in 1888. Further along, are the palace walls and **Alay Köskü** (Sultan's Gazebo) **2** where the sultan observed the comings and goings of his Grand Vizier across the street. The entrance to the Vizier's palace and offices was known as the **Sublime Porte**, the diplomatic reference to Turkey for hundreds of years. Nearby is the first entrance to the grounds of **Topkapi Sarayi**, the Great Palace of the Ottomans.

Topkapi Palace 3 – Built by Mehmet the Conqueror in 1467, Topkapi Palace was, for 400 years, the residence of sultans and the centre of imperial administration. The palace is the most extensive structure of Ottoman architecture, covering an area almost half the size of Monaco. It took its name from the Cannon Gate of the Byzantine sea-walls, which translated into Topkapi in Turkish. It was not until the reign of Süleyman the Magnificent (1520-1566), at the urgings of his Russian wife Roxelana, that accommodations for wives and concubines were included at the palace.

Now a museum complex, the Topkapi Palace contains unrivaled collections of porcelains,

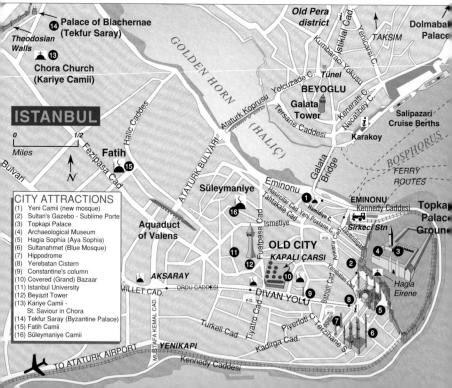

CITY ATTRACTIONS
(1) Yeni Camii (new mosque)
(2) Sultan's Gazebo - Sublime Porte
(3) Topkapi Palace
(4) Archaeological Museum
(5) Hagia Sophia (Aya Sophia)
(6) Sultanahmet (Blue Mosque)
(7) Hippodrome
(8) Yerebatan Cistern
(9) Constantine's column
(10) Covered (Grand) Bazaar
(11) Istanbul University
(12) Beyazit Tower
(13) Kariye Camii -
       St. Saviour in Chora
(14) Tekfur Saray (Byzantine Palace)
(15) Fatih Camii
(16) Süleymaniye Camii

armour, jewels and other objects of art once belonging to the sultans. Visitors can wander freely throughout the grounds' public areas. There are two entrances into the first court, with the northern one (near the Alay köskü) taking you to the **Archaeological Museum** ■4, the Museum of the Ancient Orient and the famous Tiled Pavilion. The southern gate, known as the Bab-i Hümayun or Imperial Gate, is the main entrance. This gate also takes you by the old Byzantine church of **Hagia Eirene**, built during Justinian's reign at about the same time as Hagia Sophia.

The **Archaeological Museum** was the first systematic attempt by the Ottoman Empire to preserve the nation's antiquities and it contains the superb Alexander Sarcophagus, discovered at Sidon (modern Sayda in Lebanon) in 1887. (This sarcophagus derives its name from carved sculptures depicting Alexander the Great

Topkapi Palace

hunting.) The **Museum of the Ancient Orient**'s collection isn't large but is of great importance with its pre-Islamic Arab artifacts, as well as Babylonian and Assyrian exhibits.

Leaving the grounds of the first court, you pass through the

Shore Excursions

Istanbul With ships docking very close to a city crammed with attractions, the cruise lines offer numerous tours.

• **Byzantine Treasures** tour takes you to the Chora Church and Hagia Sophia (4.5 hrs, $50-$100) .

• **Bosphorus Cruise** – affords a rare view of the grand Ottoman palaces along this famous strait. (2.5 hrs, $50-$100).

• **Whirling Dervish Show** is an evening presentation of authentic Turkish traditions (2 hrs, $50-$100).

• **Architectural Wonders Of Istanbul** – Some cruise lines offer tours showcasing the architectural works of Sinan, who designed the Suleymaniye Mosque. Includes two or three mosques and a visit to the Grand Bazaar.

• **Topkapi Palace** tour (5 hrs, about $100). This tour focuses on the famous palace used by Ottoman sultans for 400 years. Visit includes treasury and harem.

Recommended: Most cruise lines offer a Best of Istanbul tour (8 hrs, $150-200) which is a history walk and scenic drive, focusing on the major sites in the old city. Usually includes shopping in the Grand Bazaar. Good value.

impressive Bab-üs Selam (Gate of Salutation). Built into the wall to the right of the gate is the **Executioner's Fountain**, where he would wash his hands and sword after performing a decapitation outside the gate. The inner palace grounds contain many important exhibits and attractions. For Muslims, the most significant is the **Pavilion of the Holy Mantle**, displaying the sacred relics of the Prophet Muhammad, including his sword and robe (the Holy Mantle).

The **Treasury of the Topkapi Palace** is considered one of the richest in the world. Among its priceless artifacts, which were made for the sultans, is the famous **Topkapi Dagger**. The centrepiece of the 1960s film *Topkapi*, the dagger's sheath is pierced with diamonds and its gold hand is set with huge emeralds.

(Top) Magnificent entrance to Topkapi Palace. (Left) Priceless Topkapi Dagger. (Bottom) Court area.

Hagia Sophia (Church of the Divine Wisdom) **5** – On first entering this venerable building, one senses the volume of history it has withstood. First a church, then a mosque, and now a museum, Hagia Sophia has been in existence for nearly 1,500 years. Considered one of the most beautiful buildings ever constructed, it was the largest church in Christendom until the construction of St. Peter's Basilica in Rome.

Standing just outside the Imperial Gate of the Topkapi Palace, the Hagia Sophia is the third edifice of the same name to rest on the site. The first church, dedicated in 360 AD, was destroyed by fire during a mob riot, as was the second church during the Nika Revolt in early 532, during the early years of

THE SULTAN'S HAREM

For the sultans, home was the harem. These private apartments housed the sultan's four main wives (the maximum number under Islamic law), his concubines and numerous relatives (including confined princes), eunuchs, guards and servants. At the height of its use, the Topkapi Palace population numbered over 3,000. Numerous staircases, corridors and courtyards are linked by narrow passageways, exuding the claustrophobic world of palace intrigue where, for generations, the women behind the sultan — often his mother — controlled the reins of power.

On half a dozen levels, hundreds of girls and women lived their existence almost exclusively within the walls of the harem. They usually came from non-Muslim parts of the empire (Islamic law forbidding enslavement of Muslim women) and were almost always captured in war or bought on the slave market. Because life for these women was so privileged, some parents would voluntarily send their daughters to Istanbul, even after slave trading was banned in the 19th century. Girls came to the harem as young as five years of age. After training for domestic duties, they became a cariye (a concubine of the lowest rank) and began to assume greater importance, for each was the potential mother of a sultan. The sultan normally had about a dozen favorite concubines and if one became pregnant she was called *kadin efendi*. If she successfully brought a child into the world, she acquired the title *haseki sultan* and given her own apartment.

If the child was male and the mother a favourite of the sultan, she could become one of his official wives. She then would do her utmost to maneuver her son as heir to the throne. Roxelana, a wife of Süleyman, went so far as to convince the sultan to kill his first son so that her alcoholic son, Selim II, could assume the throne.

(Above) The gardens by Hagia Sophia. (Below) A 19th-century painting of Hagia Sophia.

Emperor Justinian's reign. Successfully putting down the riot with the help of his general Basilierus and the considerable backbone of his wife Theodora, Justinian resolved to build the grandest church ever, regardless of expense.

The architects, given carte blanche and 10,000 workers, began the project just five weeks after the riots. Provincial governors were ordered to send to the capital any surviving classical remains that might be incorporated into the new edifice. In response, eight porphyry columns of the pagan Sun Temple of Rome were sent, as were eight green marble columns from Ephesus.

The church was completed in 537 and according to Procopius, the historian of the day, it greatly impressed the Christian world. With a huge dome over 100 feet in diameter, 160 feet high and pierced with 40 windows, it appeared "suspended from heaven by a golden chain." To most observers, the church seemed nothing less than a miracle. When Justinian first walked into the church, he stood silent for a long time before uttering, "Solomon, I have surpassed thee."

What makes Hagia Sophia such an architectural marvel is not the height and breadth of the dome, but the two semi-domes at either end. In addition to lengthening the nave, the semi-domes give the observer, on first entering the church, an unobstructed view to the top of the church. Decorative aspects of note include the beautiful marble casings throughout the interior, such as the butterfly marble over the main entrance. The unique capitals of the columns, with their surface decoration of acanthus (symbolizing heaven) and deeply undercut palm foliage, produce an effect of lightness and strength. Monograms on the capitals are those of Justinian and Theodora.

The mosaics of Hagia Sophia are one of the most fascinating aspects of this church. Although various figures adorned the church in the 6th through 8th centuries, these were removed during the iconoclastic years which ended in 846 with a burst of new work. Important mosaics include those at the east end of the south gallery, next to the apse, depicting the Empress Zoe and her third husband, Constantine IX, on either side of Christ. Just to the right of this mosaic is an imperial portrait showing John II Comnenus and Empress Eirene with the Mother of Jesus holding an infant Christ. A side panel shows the heir, Prince Alexius, who ascended to the throne at 17 but died shortly thereafter.

The most significant of the Byzantine mosaics in Hagia

(Top) South aisle of Hagia Sophia. (Above) Empress Zoe and Constantine IX with Christ. (Below) The Deesis.

Sophia is the sad and beautiful Deesis, located in the east wall of the buttress in the south gallery. Likely produced in the early 14th century, this work is an example of Constantinople's cultural renaissance after the restoration of the city from the dark years of Latin control. Although most of the mosaic is lost, the facial features of its three subjects remain intact and show Christ, with an expression of grief, flanked by the young Virgin on one side and a pleading St. John the Baptist on the other.

Sultan Ahmet Camii (The Blue Mosque) 6 – Built by the young Sultan Ahmet I between 1609 to 1616, the Blue Mosque is widely considered the city's most splendid. The domes and semi-domes cascade gracefully from the summit within a stand of six slender minarets which represented that Ahmet was the sixth Sultan. Ahmet was an enthusiast about his mosque and often pitched in to speed up construc-

View across Hippodrome and Blue Mosque to Marmara Sea.

tion. He didn't have long to enjoy it for he died of typhus, at the age of 28, within a year of its completion. His tomb is at the northwest side of the mosque.

When walking the short distance from Hagia Sophia to the Blue Mosque, visitors enter a square that was the heart of ancient Byzantium. Law courts, a large public library and a book market all stood where gardens now flourish. The main entrance to the Blue Mosque is at the eastern side of the courtyard and, as with all mosques (*camii* in Turkish) you must remove your shoes before entering.

The Blue Mosque's reputation as a must-see attraction is deserved, for the interior is stunning. Four fluted piers, pushing towards the centre, resemble trunks of huge trees as they disappear into the arching canopy of the dome and four semi-domes. Sunlight, filtered and diffused by coloured glass, pours in from 260 windows. Along the lower part of the walls, especially in the galleries, is a profusion of beautiful blue and green Iznik tiles, for which the edifice is named.

Just to the west of the Blue Mosque is the ancient **Hippodrome 7** where chariot races and other events entertained the citizens of Constantinople. An immense structure, it could seat 100,000 spectators. The central line of the race course is still visible today and was marked by obelisks and columns, three of which remain.

The **Egyptian Obelisk**, from the 15th century BC (erected in the 4th century) is about 65 feet in height and is actually the top third of the original obelisk. The sculpted reliefs around the base depict Emperor Theodosius sitting in his box at the Hippodrome, holding a head wreath to honor a winner.

The middle column, called the **Serpent Column**, is the oldest Greek monument in the city. Erected in 479 BC in the Temple of Apollo at Delphi, it was brought to the city by Constantine the Great. The **third column**, erected by Emperor Constantine VII Porphyrogenitus in 940, is over 100 feet high and was once plated in bronze gilt, which was removed during the Latin conquest. A favourite pastime in early

(Above) Interior of Blue Mosque.

(Below) Egyptian Obelisk.

Ottoman years was to climb this column as a daring feat.

It's about a 25-minute walk from Sultanahmet to the Covered Bazaar and you may want to take this opportunity to board the Metro at the station just west of the Hippodrome on the Divan Yolu. Just a few steps from this station is the fabled **underground cistern 8** known as the **Yerebatan Saratu** (underground

palace). This giant reservoir, built in the 6th century, was supplied with water from the Belgrade Forest 12 miles west. Supported by 336 columns, the cistern was the main water source for the city and was specifically built to survive periods of siege.

The **Divan Yolu** has been the main road of this city for over 2,000 years. The Milion (first mile) started at an archway just beyond Hagia Sophia and from this point all distances in the Byzantine Empire were measured. The first Metro stop along Diva Yolu is called Çemberlitas which refers to the nearby **Column of Constantine** 🔟,, sometimes referred to as the Burnt or Hooped Column. This column was erected in 330 to mark the city's dedication and a number of relics, including bits of the True Cross, are reportedly sealed beneath its foundation.

Turning north from the Hooped Column, you soon encounter the walls of the Nuruosmaniye Mosque and the entrance, through a shaded courtyard, to the Bazaar. Beggars and peddlers often line the walkways leading to the Bazaar and occasionally a musician can be heard.

Kapali Çarsi (Covered Bazaar) 🔟 – Also known as the Grand Bazaar, this is a huge labyrinth of shops, banks, cafes, restaurants, mosques and a post office crammed into a grid of narrow streets and protected from the elements by a multitude of domed and vaulted roofs. Come prepared to spend. It is the world's largest covered bazaar and, with hundreds of shops, the place to buy Turkish souvenirs. Whether you're interested or not in purchasing a carpet, you'll be approached by numerous young men wanting to show you their selection. If you are interested in a carpet or kilim, this is a good place to shop – the selection is excellent and the competition for business is intense.

Located northwest of the Grand Bazaar is the **Istanbul University** 🔟 and the **Beyazit Tower** 🔟 – built as a fire lookout in 1828. The University dates from just after the Conquest in 1453.

West of the Bazaar along Millet Caddesi, are the beautiful **Theodosian Walls**, first built in the fifth century by Theodosias and fortified many times right up to last Byzantine emperor, Constantine XI. The Topkapi Gate is where the Turks first blasted through on May 29th, 1453. These walls inspired Lord Byron to write they were the most impressive of all ancient ruins he had seen. Although crumbling, the walls testify to the survival of this great city for over 1,000 years.

Interior of Grand Bazaar

Extending more than four miles from the Sea of Marmara to the Golden Horn, the walls were actually a system of three defences with an outer moat (where the highway now is), an outer wall and the main inner wall studded with 96 towers. Although the first phase of the walls was completed in 413 under Theodosius II, a violent earthquake in 447 destroyed much of what had been built. Reconstruction began immediately and within two months the walls were rebuilt and were far stronger – successfully repelling Attila the Hun shortly after.

From the Edirnekapi gate, it's a short walk to the beautiful **Church of St. Saviour in Chora (Kariye Camii) 13** and the haunting ruins of **Tekfur Saray 14**, an annex to the nearby Byzantine Palace of Blachernae. The palace facade is decorated with geometrical designs in red brick and white marble, typifying latter Byzantine architecture of the 13th and 14th century.

For many visitors to Istanbul, seeing the Chora church is a priority. The phrase 'in Chora' means 'in the country' and the original church (of which nothing now

THE LOWDOWN ON CARPETS

The creation and use of carpets in Turkey dates back to at least 2500 BC, with depictions on rock tombs showing men with implements used for rug weaving. The cool, mountainous region from Turkey to Persia, where sheep fleece and camel and goat hair grow long and fine, is where the art of carpet-weaving reached its peak in the 16th century. Lying east and southeast of Ankarra, this famous region of carpet production is among the few places in the world where carpets are still hand-made. Marco Polo claimed the most beautiful carpets in the world came from Konya in this area of Turkey.

The most common material used in Turkish carpets and kilims is sheep's wool, and weavers still use the time-honored double knot, or Gordes knot. A well-made woollen carpet can take one or two weavers up to a month to make, and prices range from US$80 for small throw rugs to several hundred dollars for larger carpets. Silk carpets can be priced in the thousands of dollars.

The quality of a carpet depends on the quality and type of wool, and the number of knots per square inch of surface which can vary from 40 to 1,000 knots. Traditional woollen Turkish carpets are more vibrant and brighter than Persian carpets and often contain patterns dating back many centuries. Kilims, flat woven rugs without any pile, are very popular because of traditional Turkish design and deep colors.

Patterns found in Turkish carpets not only indicate the vintage of the design, but also the region where the carpet was most likely produced. Motifs from nature include birds, camels and flowers. Other patterns utilize symbols, such as arrows for courage, and colors, such as blue to represent the infinite. Prayer mats are distinguished by the pointed shape of their central panel.

remains) stood outside the walls built by Constantine. The present building dates from the late 11th century, with elaborate remodelling carried out in the 12th and 14th centuries. The mosaics and frescoes of this church are regarded as the most important series of Byzantine artwork in the world, exquisite in detail and anticipating the great Renaissance which soon took hold in Europe.

A visit to the mosques of **Fatih** **15** and **Süleymaniye** **16** as well as **Valens Aqueduct**, which spans the valley between the two mosques, is well worth the effort. The Fatih Mosque, largest mosque in Istanbul, named after **Mehmet the Conqueror**, is more sombre in appearance than the Blue Mosque, but is nonetheless impressive, if only for its sheer size. It is said that when Mehmet the Conqueror found his mosque was not quite as high as Hagia Sophia he ordered the architect's hands cut off. Both the architect and Mehmet are buried behind the mosque, and visitors can view the tomb of the great conqueror.

The **Süleymaniye Mosque**, the second largest in the city, is one of Turkey's finest imperial Ottoman mosques and is representative of the 'Golden Age' of the Empire. Designed by the great architect Sinan, the Mosque was completed in 1557 and stands just below Istanbul's third hill, on a slope down to the Golden Horn. A structural masterpiece, it assured Sinan's place as a genius of architecture. At the entrance is a grand porticoed courtyard with columns of rich marble and granite. At the corners of the courtyard rise four minarets, representing Süleyman as being the fourth sultan to reign in Istanbul. Cleverly disguising buttresses and eschewing aisles and numerous columns, Sinan created a vast interior enlivened by light filtered through beautiful stained glass windows. Süleyman's majestic tomb is located behind the mosque and his catafalque is capped by the huge white turban he once wore.

The **Valens Aqueduct** was built about 375 AD to bring water from the Belgrade Forest into the centre of the city. Although damaged by earthquakes, it was kept in good repair by the Byzantine emperors and the Ottoman sultans, and was used until the late 19th century when it was replaced by a modern water distribution system.

Dolmabahçe Palace – Many Turks in the late 19th century saw in this palace all that was wrong with the Ottoman Empire. Excessive, expensive and out of touch with the rest of the country, the Dolmabahçe Palace's construction helped bring the empire to the point of bankruptcy. An inlet was filled in to form the palace site

The ruins of the last Byzantine palace – Tekfur Saray.

(Dolmabahçe means 'filled-in garden') and a royal park was created with a series of kiosks and pavilions built close to the Bosphorus. The sultan Abdul Mecit decided to build a much larger and more luxurious palace, designed in a neo-baroque style and completed in 1854. The opulent furnishings of the palace included the largest chandelier in the world, weighing four-and-a-half tons and hanging in the State Room.

The palace was home to the last sultan, Mehmet VI, whose ignominious departure entailed being smuggled aboard a British frigate. The palace was also the principal residence of Mustafa Ataturk, who died here in November 1938.

Karaköy and Beyoglu

The districts of Karaköy and Beyoglu, on the north side of the Golden Horn, are almost as old as the main city and were for centuries home to foreign merchants and dignitaries. Karaköy is the Turkish name for the old **Galata** area, which was once the Genoese stronghold. A walled mini-city, Galata had a reputation for debauchery.

Beyoglu is the Turkish name for the old **Pera** district, and was actually an upper-middle class suburb of Galata. During the 18th and 19th centuries, along a road which became known as the Grand Rue de Pera, palatial mansions and embassies were built. You can take the 19th-century

tram part way along Grand Rue de Pera – now called **Istiklâl Caddesi** – or explore on foot. Just off Galatasaray Square, halfway along Istiklâl Caddesi, is an avenue which leads to **Tepebasi** and the site of some renowned grand hotels. The best known of these is Pera Palas, which was built in 1876 as the terminal hotel for the Orient Express.

At the south end of Istiklâl Caddesi, where the avenue forks to the right, is the entrance to the

(Top) Fascinating old Pera District. (Right) Galata Tower affords good views of old city.

underground funicular railway known as the Tünel, built in 1875 and dubbed 'The Mouse's Hole' by locals. It takes just over a minute to descend to the bottom of the hill near the Galata Bridge. Another route is to turn left down the steep street of Galip Dede Caddesi to see the famous **Galata Tower**. Built in 1348 as the apex of Genoese fortifications, it has been restored and houses a restaurant on its upper levels with magnificent views.

The Turkish Coast

The **Dardanelles**, known in ancient times as the Hellespont, is a famous strait and the site of many legendary events. Leander swam across this strait nightly, from Asia to Europe, to meet his beloved Hero, a Greek priestess. This romantic gesture was repeated by the poet Lord Byron, to prove it could be done. Armies have crossed this strait, including that of Alexander the Great.

One the most tragic battles of the first world war, resulting in the death or injury of over 500,000 soldiers, also took place at the Dardanelles, and is known as the **Battle of Gallipoli** after the nearby town. The plan was set in motion by a young Winston Churchill, then First Lord of the Admiralty, who saw a chance to seize Constantinople and secure a route to Russia, England's ally. However, Churchill prematurely sent a British fleet into easy gun range of the hills overlooking the strait and, after a number of ships went down, the navy retreated to wait for land troops. By the time the Allied army was ready, two months later, the Turks had fortified their position. The landing of allied forces at Suvla on the west coast of the peninsula resulted in severe casualties of British, Australian and New Zealand troops, as well as for the Turks. The man most directly responsible for the Turkish victory was the future president of Turkey, **Mustafa Kemal Ataturk.** Ataturk remains greatly venerated and his picture is often seen in stores throughout Turkey.

About 20 miles (32 km) south of **Çanakkale** lies the ancient Hellenic city of **Troy**, site of the legendary Trojan war described by the Greek poet Homer in his work the *Iliad*. Long dismissed as fiction, the city was only discovered in the latter part of the 19th century by the German archaeologist Heinrich Schliemann. Uncovering the ruins in a series of mounds, Schliemann proved, by Homer's description, that there was indeed a great city just west of the Dardanelles.

Although the ruins of Troy are

Mustafa Kemal Ataturk (1881-1938), first president of Turkey.

not impressive, the fortifications are well preserved and conveys the scene to those familiar with the famous story of Paris, Helen, Achilles and Odysseus. At the entrance to the site stands a replica of the famous wooden horse.

Shore excursions from **Çanakkale** include visits to both Troy and its nearby museum or to the Battlefield of Gallipoli (about 6 hours) which includes crossing the Dardanelles by ferry. Although there is a fair bit of hiking involved, this is a highly recommended tour for war buffs.

Kusadasi

This popular port of access to Ephesus has become a frenetic resort town serving the ruins-bound traveller. Although there are some decent beaches to the south of the town, they are usually busy. However a walk across an extended causeway links the town to pretty **Pigeon Island**, with a 13th-century Byzantine castle surrounded by gardens and restaurants. The town bazaar is a good place to shop.

Ephesus

This is one of the most important archaeological sites in the Mediterranean. not only for the fine examples of classical architecture but for a rare view into the life and architecture of classical Rome. Of great importance for over a thousand years, Ephesus at one time rivalled Rome for opulence and beauty. The ruins are extensive and parts are well preserved. One can easily visualize this bustling port city that was once home to over 300,000 citizens.

Shore Excursions

Kusadasi. Kusadasi, drop port for visits to Ephesus and area, offers travelers various tour combinations, many of which focus on the ruins. A basic tour of Ephesus, $50-$100, takes three or four hours and is good value.

• Ephesus, St. John's Basilica & Virgin Mary Shrine. Great way to see the three most important Ephesus-area sites in a day.

• Turkish village visit (Sirince) and tour of Ephesus Museum with its impressive collection of Hellenistic and Roman artifacts ($100-$150, 6 hours).

Located near the mouth of the river Cayster (now Kuçuk Menderes), Ephesus (Efes in Turkish) was first settled by Ionian Greeks around 1100 BC. The site was a place of worship for a native nature goddess associated with the Greek goddess Artemis, and around 550 BC a large temple was built in her honor. Over the next few centuries the city changed hands many times and continued to thrive as a Greek seaport until 133 BC, when

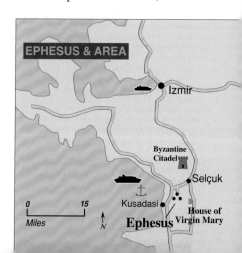

EPHESUS & AREA

Izmir

Byzantine Citadel

Selçuk

Kusadasi

House of Virgin Mary

Ephesus

0 — 15
Miles

N

it was taken by the Romans and used as the leading city of their Asian province. Its great Temple of Artemis, renamed the Temple of Diana by the Romans, was considered one of the Seven Wonders of the Ancient World, although little remains today.

As the terminus of the famous Silk Route and the world capital of the slave trade, Ephesus was wealthy and secure for over 500 years, even surviving a sacking by Goths in 262 AD. In the 5th and 6th century, it remained the second-most important city, after Constantinople, in the Byzantine Empire.

Soon, however, Ephesus began to decline with the sacking of the city by Arabs in 716 AD. The Byzantine government also could not afford the annual expense of dredging and soon the harbor completely filled with silt. The city lost its value as a port and by the end of the 8th century Ephesus was reduced to little more than a village. With the advent of the Ottoman Empire, it was completely abandoned. The site was re-discovered by a British archaeologist in 1869, after six years of searching. Most of the ruins visible today date from the Roman period of the 1st century BC to the 2nd century AD.

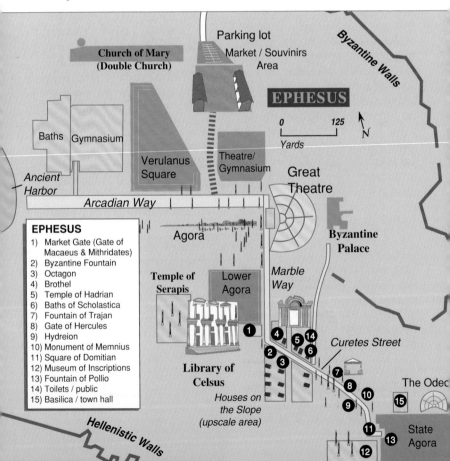

EPHESUS

1) Market Gate (Gate of Macaeus & Mithridates)
2) Byzantine Fountain
3) Octagon
4) Brothel
5) Temple of Hadrian
6) Baths of Scholastica
7) Fountain of Trajan
8) Gate of Hercules
9) Hydreion
10) Monument of Memnius
11) Square of Domitian
12) Museum of Inscriptions
13) Fountain of Pollio
14) Toilets / public
15) Basilica / town hall

Exploring Ephesus

Ephesus actually begins near the parking lot where the original harbourfront existed a few hundred yards to the west. Also near the car park is where the **Church of Virgin Mary** (also know as Double Church), is located. This church got its name after the Church of Councils was held in 431 when it was decided that Mary would be known as the "bearer of God". Pope Paul VI led prayers at this spot when he visited Ephesus in 1967.

From the site entrance at the souvenir market you can walk east along the wide **Arcadian Way**. This avenue was first built in the Hellenistic period but was restored in the fifth century and, as it links the city with the sea, it is also referred to as Harbor Street. Arcadian Way leads east for over five hundred yards to the Great Theatre.

Built during the reign of Claudius in about 60 AD, the **Great Theatre** could seat over 25,000 spectators and was the scene for gladiator fights in the 4th and 5th centuries. If you

(Top) Library of Celsus, (below) Ruins of Prytaneion, (bottom) the Apostle Paul spent two years in Ephesus, mainly in jail.

House of the Virgin Mary was declared a shrine by the Vatican.

climb up to just the first tier of rows, you can enjoy an excellent view over the city's old colonnaded main street, once lined with statues and lit by oil lamps at night. The walk along Marble Way takes you past the Lower Agora (marketplace).

One of the most beautiful pieces of architecture remaining in Ephesus is the **Library of Celsus**, built in the early 2nd century by a Roman consul as a memorial to his father. The library once contained over 10,000 scrolls and books. Statues of the four virtues adorn the niches between the columns.

Along **Curates Street** are many interesting ruins including the Temple of Hadrian and ruins of various houses and public buildings. Under the marble-paved street runs the largest sewer system of the city. At the east end of the ruins is the **State or Upper Agora** where large transactions of government took place. The **Odeon**, a building with a capacity of 1400, was built in the 2nd century AD for concerts and drama.

The **Apostle Paul's** connection with Ephesus (described in Acts 17-19) occurred during his second and third missionary journeys into Anatolia between 53 and 57 AD. For three years, with Ephesus as his base, Paul wrote letters and preached to the locals, urging them to put aside their idols of Artemis. "Gods made by human hands are not gods at all," he wrote. This outraged the local silversmiths, who enjoyed a lively trade making Artemis statues, and they provoked a riot that resulted in Paul's incarceration. Forced to leave Ephesus upon his release, Paul journeyed to Jerusalem where he was arrested, sent to Rome and executed during the persecutions of Emperor Nero.

House of the Virgin Mary: According to legend (which began with a German nun in the 19th century) St. John the Apostle brought Mary to Ephesus around 38 AD. She retired to a cottage at Meryemana near Selçuk and there died a few years later. The stone cottage was declared a shrine by the Vatican in 1896 and several popes have visited the site, including Pope Benedict XVI in 2006.

Selçuk

When the port of Ephesus began to fill in with silt, residents moved a few miles to the northeast and settled near the ancient **Temple of Artemis**. The town was below the prominent Ayasuluk Hill upon which the **Byzantine Citadel** was built in the 7th and 8th century. When the Turks overran Ephesus in the 12th century, the fortress (known as Ayasuluk Castle) was rebuilt and much of what remains

is from the Ottoman era. The town of Selçuk (pop. 30,000), the modern name for Ephesus, benefits greatly from tourism.

St. John's Basilica: Built in the 6th century by the industrious emperor Justinian, the church is regarded as the most magnificent of the buildings from the Byzantine Period. It is located at the southern foot of Ayasuluk Castle and is said to be built over the grave of John. While in Ephesus he wrote the *Book of John* as well as his three letters.

Izmir

Turkey's third largest city and second largest port, **Izmir** is also an important military base and a NATO command centre of southeast Europe. Of the original Hellenistic city-states situated along the Turkish Aegean coast, only Izmir (known until this century as Smryna) survived. It was possibly the birthplace of Homer, and was the largest and most prosperous city of Asia Minor. Unfortunately, it bears little evidence of its ancient past, yet it's an interesting city to stroll with several sites situated close to the downtown. These include the **Roman Agora**, just a few blocks from the main centre of town, the **main bazaar**, the **Clock Tower** and the 16th-century **Hisar Mosque**.

(Top) The Byzantine Citadel with ruins of Temple of Artemis in foreground. (Middle) The important naval port of Izmir also has one of the best bazaars in Turkey. (Below) The Clock Tower and the miniature Hisar Mosque are two landmarks of Izmir.

South of Izmir and Kusadasi is the resort town of **Bodrum** which occupies the site of ancient Halicarnassus. Bodrum offers many attractions, including a fascinating Museum of Underwater Archaeology which features Byzantine ships housed in the magnificent crusader castle overlooking the harbour.

The Castle of St. Peter was built in the 15th century by the Knights of St. John using stone quarried from the ruins of the Mausoleum of Halicarnassus (one of the Seven Wonders of the Ancient World). In the castle's English Tower, the banquet hall has been restored and visitors can enjoy a glass of wine while reading graffiti that was carved into window niches by homesick knights. A dolmus can be taken to the pretty fishing villages of Turgutreis and Gümüslük.

Hadrian's Gate in Antalya, built in the 2nd century, is one of the best perserved gates of ancient Roman architecture.

Antalya

This beautiful city is situated far enough south to receive good weather during the shoulder seasons and is often referred to as the Turkish Riviera, with miles of golden sand stretching south to Kemer. The old port is situated on a small cove surrounded by ancient fortifications. The steep hillside was first settled in the 2nd century BC and fell under Roman control soon thereafter. Emperor Hadrian visited the city in 130 AD, an event commemorated by a triumphal gate, still in excellent condition. During the Middle Ages, Antalya was a Byzantine stronghold and an important staging point for shipping troops and supplies to the Holy Land during the Crusades. Captured by Seljuk Turks in the 12th century, it became the most important port on the Mediterranean coast and fell under Ottoman rule in the 15th century.

Mermerli Beach is situated about one and a half miles from the Kaleiçi District. In between,

Ataturk Park provides cool shade and good views of the Mediterranean Sea and Taurus Mountains.

Perge (10 miles /16 km from Antalya) was settled by the Hittites as early as 1500 BC. St. Paul stopped here on one of his journeys, when Perge was an important city of the area.

The Black Sea

When the Latin poet Ovid, famous throughout the Roman Empire during the time of Augustus, was inexplicably exiled to a Black Sea outpost in 8 AD, he poured his despair into a five-volume work called *Tristia* (Sorrows). By the late 19th century, the Black Sea region was no longer regarded as a place of exile but rather as a fashionable retreat for members of the Russian nobility who came to enjoy the sub-tropical climate. Count Leo Tolstoy spent his last summers at a cottage overlooking the Black Sea, and Anton Chekhov wrote *The Three Sisters* while staying at a Crimean resort.

The Bolshevik Revolution of 1917 replaced the privileged classes of czarist Russia with Communist party leaders and Kremlin military brass, yet they too followed the aristocratic tradition of retreating to a Black Sea *dacha* (country cottage) each summer and Crimea became known as the Soviet Riviera. Former Soviet president Mikhail Gorbachev was vacationing at his Crimean villa in August 1991 when placed under house arrest during an unsuccessful coup d'état in Moscow.

The lands bordering the Black Sea have changed hands many times over the centuries. Navigated since prehistoric times, the Black Sea contains mud that is rich in hydrogen sulphide, which causes the water to look black. Sheltered from the north by mountains, the Black Sea's waters remain warm year-round and its coastline was colonized as long ago as the 8th century BC by the ancient Greeks. Eventually the Greek colonies fell under Roman rule, and the founding of

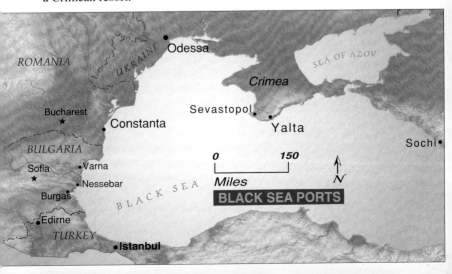

Constantinople increased the strategic importance of the Black Sea. Its southern shores remained mostly under Byzantine control following the decline of the Roman Empire, but its northern shoreline was invaded by Tatars and the area became part of the Mongol empire. In the 13th century, the Genoese ventured into the Black Sea where they established prosperous coastal commercial settlements. The Turks followed in the 15th century, and their expanding Ottoman Empire soon controlled all of the Black Sea coast.

In the 18th century, Russia under Catherine the Great annexed the Crimean peninsula to gain access to the Black Sea's warm-water ports. These imperial ambitions were thwarted by the Crimean War of 1853 to 1856, in which the allied powers of Turkey, England, France and Sardinia defeated Russia when,

after a long and bloody siege, its naval base of Sevastopol in Crimea fell.

Military alliances had changed dramatically by the time a World War II meeting took place at nearby Yalta in 1945, attended by British Prime Minister Churchill, American President F.D. Roosevelt and Soviet Premier Stalin. Cloaked in secrecy, the agreements reached by the 'Big Three' included territorial concessions to the Soviet Union, with Roosevelt later accused of delivering Eastern Europe to Communist domination. The Soviet Union has since collapsed but the Black Sea's growing appeal as a cruise destination was diminished in 2014 when Russia annexed Crimea, followed by military conflicts in Ukraine.

Ports of Call

Yalta is the largest resort in the Crimean peninsula. Many of its hotels, sanatariums and guest houses were built as villas by the Russian nobility, and the nearby town of Livadiya became a summer residence of the Russian czars in 1861. The Livadiya palace, built in 1910, was the meeting place of the Yalta Conference in 1945 and is now a sanatarium.

The Ukrainian port of **Odessa** was the leading Soviet Black Sea port before the dissolution of the Soviet Union, and its cosmopolitan population consists of Ukrainians, Russians, Jews and Greeks. Originally an ancient Greek colony called Odessos, the

(Top) Yalta Conference in 1945 took place at Livadiya Palace.

port became a Tatar fortress and trade centre in the 14th century. Odessa's cultural attractions date mainly from the 19th century and include a university, historical museum, astronomical observatory, ballet theatre, opera house and picture gallery.

The French statesman Armand Emmanuel du Plessis duc de Richelieu served Russia as governor of both Odessa in 1803 and the Crimea in 1805, and a monument to Richelieu stands at the top of a magnificent flight of granite steps leading to the harbour. These steps were the scene of a famous workers' riot in 1905 when the mutinous crew of the *Potemkin*, a Russian battleship of the Black Sea Fleet, arrived in port.

Constanta, Romania's main seaport and a popular seaside resort, began as a Greek colony called Tomi, and became Ovid's place of exile in the 1st century AD. Ovid, whose erotic and mythological poems later became a primary source of inspiration for the artists of the Renaissance, wrote his final works at Tomi. In the 4th century, Constantine the Great changed the city's name to Constantiana. Captured by the Turks in 1413, the port city became part of Romania in 1878. Local sights include an Orthodox cathedral, several museums and extensive Roman and Byzantine remains.

An excursion into **Bucharest**, Romania's largest city, takes visitors into the heart of Walachia. The 'bread basket' of Romania, the principality of Walachia was founded in the late 13th century when

the Mongol wave receded and local inhabitants descended from their mountain refuges. Vlad IV, who ruled Walachia in the mid-15th century, maintained order by sentencing 20,000 people to death in the space of six years. His practise of impaling Turkish prisoners earned him the name Prince Vlad the Impaler and, as the son of Prince Vlad Dracul (Vlad the Devil), he also became known as Dracula or son of the Devil. Bucharest was the residence of the Walachian princes and became the capital of Romania in 1861. Much of the Old City was demolished by President Nicolae Ceaucescu during the 1980s to make room for a model socialist-planned city. Historic landmarks include several churches from the 17th and 18th centuries; the Museum of Romanian History was built during Ceaucescu's dictatorship.

Like many Black Sea ports, **Varna** began as a Greek colony, then passed to the Roman Empire in the 1st century AD. Under subsequent Byzantine rule, the city's

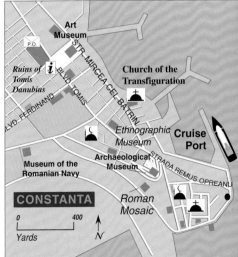

5th-century basilica and 6th-century fortress were built.

In 679, the Byzantine emperor Constantine IV was defeated by the Bulgarians (a Turkic-speaking people called Bulgars who had merged with earlier Slavic settlers and adopted their language) and the first Bulgarian empire was established in 681. It was eventually subjugated by the Byzantines in 1018. The second Bulgarian empire rose in 1186 but was absorbed by the Ottoman Empire. Varna was captured by the Turks in 1391 and the 1444 Battle of Varna was the last major attempt by Europe's Christian Crusader forces to stem the Ottoman tide. Not until 1878 was Varna and the rest of Bulgaria liberated from Turkish rule.

Sofia, the capital of Bulgaria, has undergone several name changes. The city flourished under the Roman emperor Trajan as Sardica. Following its destruction by the Huns in 447, the city was rebuilt by the Byzantine emperor Justinian I and renamed Triaditsa. The Bulgars renamed the city Sofia (Sophya) in 1376. Soon after, Sofia passed to the Ottomans and became the residence of Turkish governors overseeing the Ottoman Empire's Balkan possessions.

Situated on a high plain surrounded by the Balkan Mountains, Sofia is filled with historic churches, mosques and synagogues. City landmarks include the parliament building, the state opera house, the former royal palace, the 4th-century Church of St. George and the 6th-century Church of St. Sofia.

Cyprus

In pagan times, the mountainous island of Cyprus was a centre of the cult worshipping Aphrodite, the Greek goddess of love and beauty who sprang from the foam of the sea. Ruled by a succession of ancient empires, including the Phoenicians, Egyptians, Persians and Romans, the island at one point was given to Cleopatra by Marc Anthony. Saint Paul brought Christianity to the beach-lined shores of Cyprus in the 1st century AD, and in 395 AD the island became part of the Byzantine Empire, its monks retreating into the Troodos Mountains to build secluded monasteries filled with icons and manuscripts.

In 1191 AD, Richard Lion Heart rescued and married his betrothed after her ship, en route to Jerusalem, was caught in a storm and forced ashore at Limassol. Today the island republic of Cyprus, with its liberal marriage laws, attracts Israeli couples who wish to be legally wed without undergoing the stringent rituals of Orthodox Judaism. Wedding packages often include the beach town of **Larnaca**, which is the mythical birthplace of Aphrodite.

Dubbed the Island of Love, Cyprus has also been an island of war. Taken by the Turks in 1571 following seven centuries of Byzantine rule, this bastion of Greek Orthodox Christianity became part of the Ottoman Empire, with colonists arriving in large numbers from Turkey.

When Britain gained administrative control of the island in 1878, the animosity between the

Greek Cypriot population and the Turkish Cypriots was firmly entrenched. Granted independence in 1960, the new country of Cyprus was soon embroiled in ethnic violence, forcing the UN to intervene and eventually partition the island into Greek and Turkish territories, which are separated by a UN-occupied buffer zone.

The northern third of the island is recognized only by Turkey as the Turkish Republic of Northern Cyprus, while the southern two-thirds of the island is internationally recognized as the Greek-occupied Republic of Cyprus. Nicosia is the capital, and **Limassol**, on the south coast, is the chief cruise port and commercial centre of Cyprus.

Limassol's attractions include sandy beaches, an historic town centre and the Limassol Castle, where Richard Lion Heart married Berengaria of Navarre and crowned her Queen of England. About nine miles (14 km) west of Limassol is **Kolossi Castle**, and another three miles (five km) further along is the ancient site of **Curium** (Kourion), where a Graeco-Roman theatre overlooks the blue sea. A few miles west of Curium is the Temple of Apollo, and further to the west is **Paphos**, with its historic harbour. Attractions there include the Paphos Mosaics, which are well-preserved mosaic floors from 3rd-century Roman villas.

Shore Excursions

Limassol From Limassol, there are several shore tours of interest.

• A 4X4 scenic drive through the Phassouri Citrus Groves en route to the Crusader Kolossi Castle; includes a visit to wine-producing region. (7 hrs, $100+)

• Kourion Beach – 20-minute drive to beach (2.5 hrs $50+)

• Kourion, Temple of Apollo and Omodos Village (4 hrs, $50+)

• Nicosia and Lefkara Village includes visit to 17th-century St. John's Cathedral (8 hrs, $100+)

• Trekking in forested Troodos mountain range (4 hrs, $50+)

• Paphos & Kourion Ancient Theatre, with shopping in Old Harbour area (7 hrs, $100+)

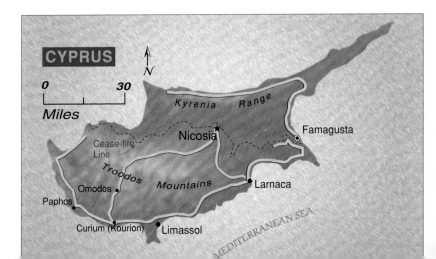

CYPRUS

N

0   30

Miles

Kyrenia   Range

Nicosia   Famagusta

Cease-fire Line

Troodos   Mountains

Omodos   Larnaca

Paphos

Curium (Kourion)   Limassol

MEDITERRANEAN SEA

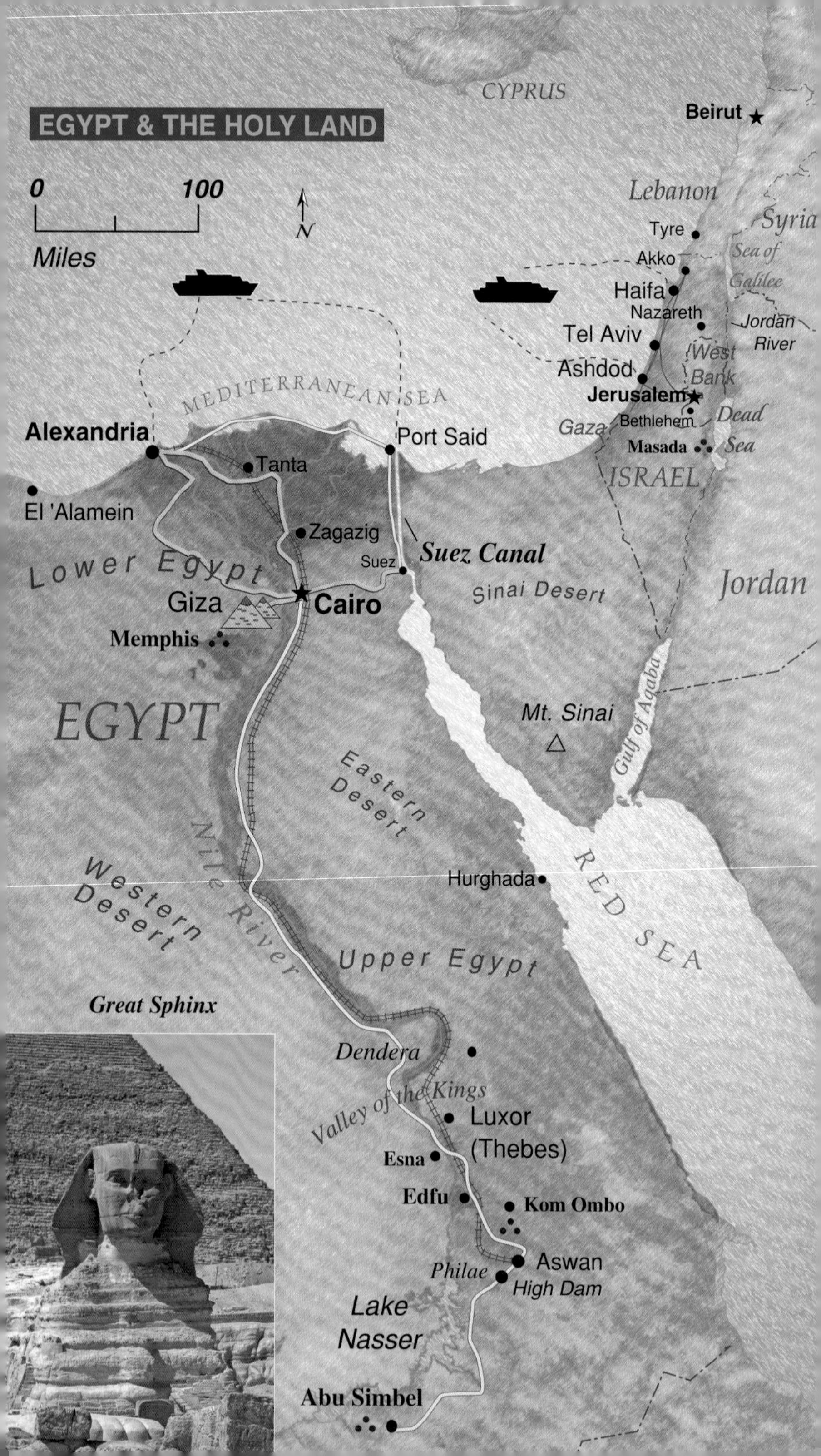

EGYPT & THE HOLY LAND

CYPRUS

Beirut ★

Lebanon

Tyre

Akko

Haifa
Nazareth

Tel Aviv

Ashdod

Jerusalem ★

Bethlehem

Gaza

Masada

Syria

Sea of Galilee

Jordan River

West Bank

Dead Sea

ISRAEL

0   100
Miles

N

MEDITERRANEAN SEA

Alexandria

El 'Alamein

Tanta

Port Said

Lower Egypt

Zagazig

Suez

Suez Canal

Sinai Desert

Jordan

Giza

Cairo

Memphis

EGYPT

Eastern Desert

Mt. Sinai △

Gulf of Aqaba

Western Desert

Nile River

Hurghada

RED SEA

Upper Egypt

Great Sphinx

Dendera

Valley of the Kings

Luxor (Thebes)

Esna

Edfu

Kom Ombo

Philae

Aswan
High Dam

Lake Nasser

Abu Simbel

EGYPT

& THE HOLY LAND

Egypt is a country of epic proportions, both historical and geographical. Its ancient civilization is measured not in centuries but in millennia, and its vast desert, covering 95% of the country's nearly 400,000 square miles, is bisected by the longest river on earth – the Nile.

The story of Egypt is the story of the Nile. Indeed, Egypt owes its existence to this river which flows its length. The river's fertile valley and fan-shaped delta cover only 4% of the country's total area but provide almost all of its arable and habitable land.

The Nile has been the country's lifeblood for some 7,000 years, beginning with hunters who roamed the river valley in pre-dynastic times. Eventually they learned to control the river's annual inundation by digging irri-gation canals, and farming of the fertile floodplain began.

Supported by an agricultural society, a long line of pharaohs became almighty rulers of Egypt. They were divine kings, descended from the gods, and they oversaw the construction of colossal stone structures along the banks of the Nile. Built to preserve life beyond death, these awe-inspiring temples and tombs still stand, their imperious facades exerting a sense of power and mystery on mere mortals gazing up at them. Huge temple gates, massive columns, giant statues and of course pyramids – all were built to last for eternity and many of them have, preserved for thousands of years by an arid climate and a dry soil of sand and silt.

The famous pyramids of Giza

Egypt at a Glance

Egypt, the Arab world's most populous country, has been in political turmoil since President Hosni Mubarak, the regime's autocratic ruler, was deposed in 2011 after losing the military's backing in the face of mass demonstrations. Subsequent elections were won by the Muslim Brotherhood, but the country's educated middle class continues to protest against the government and its lack of reform.

Most Egyptians are of complex racial origin, having descended from ancient Egyptians, Berbers, black Africans, Arabs, Greeks and Turks. About 90% of Egypt's 80 million people are Sunni Muslims, while close to 10% are Coptic Christians. Arabic is the official language; English and French are also spoken by the well educated.

Nearly one third of Egypt's workers are engaged in agriculture and the principal crop is cotton, which is one of the country's main exports along with petroleum and metals. The Suez Canal and tourism – which has suffered from protracted demonstrations in the streets of Cairo – are important sources of foreign exchange.

Travel Tips

Currency - The unit of currency is the Egyptian pound. The approximate exchange is 1USD = 8 EGP; 1GBP = 11 EGP. American and British currencies are widely accepted.

Documentation - In addition to a valid passport, visitors to Egypt need a visa, which must be purchased ahead of time if you are arriving by ship.

Shopping - Always barter – it's expected – except in department stores. Gold cartouches are unique and popular Egyptian souvenirs, but be careful when buying gold jewellery. If you're interested in a piece, ask to see its stamp indicating the number of karats. Egyptian cotton is among the finest in the world and attractive cotton clothes, including the traditional *galibeya*, are widely sold. Handcrafted items in brass, copper and Egyptian alabaster are also popular.

Egypt's History

Ancient Egypt – its fields, towns, temples and tombs lining both banks of the Nile – was buffered from invasion by the river's natural borders. Desert plains lay to

Shore Excursions

Egypt Visitors arriving by cruise ship at Alexandria or Port Said are strongly advised to take a ship-organized excursion into Cairo due to the distances involved and the heavy traffic in Cairo. The drive each way is about three hours and lunch is provided at a hotel in Cairo. Ships docking in Alexandria also offer half-day tours of Alexandria. Some cruise lines offer a special two-day tour that covers all the sights in and around Cairo and includes overnight accommodation at a leading hotel. The following are a sampling of excursions:
• Pyramids of Giza & Egyptian Museum (11.5 hrs)
• Pyramids of Giza & Step Pyramid (11.5 hrs)
• Pyramids of Giza & Nile lunch cruise (11 hrs)

the east and west, the Mediterranean Sea to the north, and a series of cataracts south of Aswan in Upper Egypt. The shepherds then living in the Nile valley were descendants of the Hamitic branch of the Caucasian race, and their villages evolved over time into towns which collectively became the kingdoms of Lower and Upper Egypt. In about 3100 BC, the two kingdoms were unified by Menes, who was believed by ancient Egyptians to be a descendant of the sun god Ra. During his long reign, the city of **Memphis** was founded in Lower Egypt on the Nile delta, 14 miles south of modern Cairo.

Egypt's famous **Old Kingdom** (2682-2181 BC) emerged during the rule of Djoser (Zoser). Memphis had become the seat of the royal government and, under Djoser's reign, Egypt's territory expanded into the Sinai Peninsula. Amid a flourishing era of arts and sciences, the pharaoh's vizier Imhotep designed the **Step Pyramid** – the first great stone structure ever built. Located at the necropolis of **Saqqara**, it consisted of six massive tiers climbing to a height of 200 feet, its pyramid shape clearly visible from Memphis.

Stone construction continued to evolve and, during the reign of Sneferu, the first smooth-sided pyramid was constructed at Saqqara. This is known as the 'bent pyramid' for its sudden change of angle part-way up. Sneferu ordered another one built nearby, which was an architectural success called the 'red pyramid' because of the iron oxide in its stone. However, it was during

Visitors emerge from the Great Pyramid's burial chamber.

the reign of Khufu, Sneferu's son, that the largest surviving pyramid was built at **Giza**, a plateau situated on the southwestern outskirts of modern **Cairo**.

Rising 481 feet above the ground, the **Great Pyramid of Khufu (Cheops)** was built using an estimated 3.2 million blocks of limestone, each weighing an average of 2.5 tons. Khufu's son Khafra built a somewhat smaller pyramid at Giza, although it appears larger than Khufu's because it stands on a slight rise. The **Great Sphinx**, a representation of Khafra carved from a knoll of rock, is located next to the causeway leading from the pharaoh's granite-lined temple to his pyramid. A third pyramid, covering less than a quarter of the area of the Great Pyramid, was built by Menkaura, a son of Khafra.

It took about 20 years to build the Great Pyramid and hundreds of thousands of workers were employed each flood season to labour on this project. After the building site was carefully leveled, the cardinal points were determined through astronomical observations, providing for a precise alignment of the pyramid's sides. The entrance is north-facing, allowing the pharaoh's mummified body to face the north star from within the burial chamber, which is located deep within the pyramid's core and reached by cramped passages. Two air shafts, straight narrow tunnels, lead from the chamber to the outside and are aligned with various stars. The apex was crowned with gold sheet, symbolizing the pyramid's association with the sun god Ra.

Much of the building stone was quarried nearby, and granite, for lining the burial chambers, was transported from Aswan. Work was carried out during the Nile's inundation, when floodwaters would have allowed boats carrying massive granite columns and

heavy blocks of limestone to navigate close to the pyramids. The inundation season, when farmers were idle, was an ideal time for the pharaoh to employ them as labourers, helping to raise the blocks – each weighing about 2 1/2 tons – into place. The method used is still open to speculation. They likely used cranes, levers and rockers, along with ramps built along the terraced sides of the pyramid. It's believed that as the outer casing of limestone was applied from top to bottom, the ramps were removed.

Egypt's second great era was the **Middle Kingdom** (2055-1650 BC). This period lasted nearly 400 years, during which the centre of political power shifted from Memphis in Lower Egypt to Thebes (modern Luxor) in Upper Egypt. Then, in 1550 BC, the Theban ruler Ahmose I ushered in a new era of greatness for the pharaohs of ancient Egypt. Called the **New Kingdom** (1550-1069 BC), these were glory days for the ancient city of Thebes, where columned temples and avenues of sphinxes were built on a massive scale.

Across the river from Thebes, where the sun sets on the west bank of the Nile, lies the traditional burial ground of the New Kingdom pharaohs and their families. Cut into barren cliffsides, the tunnel entrances of these treasure-filled tombs were concealed with rocks and sand in an attempt to foil grave robbers. The Valley of the Kings would eventually contain more than 60 royal tombs, including that of the boy-king **Tutankhamun**, which was discovered intact by Howard Carter in 1922. Priceless treasures found in Tutankhamun's tomb, including the solid gold sarcophagus that held his mummified remains, are on display in the **Egyptian Museum**, which overlooks Tahrir Square in Cairo.

Cairo is the capital and chief city of Egypt, with a population exceeding 11 million. Although a modern city with wide, traffic-clogged streets, its older sections contain famed mosques, palaces and city gates built between the 7th and 15th centuries. The **Citadel of Salah El Din** was built by Saladin in 1179 to protect Cairo from attacks by Crusaders. Cairo's famous bazaar, **Khan el-Khalili**, is across the street from the mosque of Al Azhar, built in 970.

Cairo's famous suburb of **Giza**, on the city's southwestern outskirts, is where the **Great Pyramids** and the mysterious **Sphinx** loom above the desert horizon. The ancient city of **Memphis** once stood a short distance south of modern Giza and its surviving necropolis (the nucleus of which was **Saqqara**) contains the **Step Pyramid**, the first pyramid ever built.

Alexandria

Situated on a narrow peninsula, Egypt's leading port of more than 4 million people is built over the ruins of an ancient city once famous as a centre of learning and culture. The names associated with Alexandria are legendary, starting with Alexander the Great, who founded the city in 332 BC. The city then was considered

Tutankhamun's gold mask (opposite) is displayed in Cairo's Egyptian Museum (above).

more Greek than Egyptian, with its gridded street plan and large population of Hellenistic Greeks. Its famous library and museum, no longer standing, attracted scholars such as the mathematician Euclid and the anatomist Herophilus.

But it is **Cleopatra**, co-regent of Ptolemaic Egypt from 51 to 30 BC, who is most often associated with ancient Alexandria. Famous for her intelligence and political astuteness (her beauty was more myth than reality), Cleopatra conducted her famous love affair with Marc Antony in a palace overlooking the East Harbour. Later submerged when earthquakes altered the city's coastline, the ruins of Cleopatra's ancient court remained hidden beneath the sea until they were discovered in 1996 by a team of French marine archaeologists.

Another famous landmark was the **lighthouse** on the island of

Pharos, joined to the mainland by a causeway. This celebrated lighthouse, one of the Seven Wonders of the World, was built during the city's Roman occupation in about 280 BC. It was destroyed by an earthquake in the 14th century and the fortress of Qait Bey now stands on its site. The greatest of Rome's provincial capitals, Alexandria received antiquities from all over Egypt to decorate its new temples. Under Augustus, Cleopatra's Needle (now standing on the Thames embankment in London) and New York's Central Park obelisk, were brought as a pair to Alexandria from a temple at Heliopolis near modern Cairo.

Although much of ancient Alexandria lies underwater or is covered by modern buildings, there are some accessible monuments, such as **Pompey's Pillar** (a granite column erected in c. 297 AD near the temple of Serapeum) and the **Konel-Shugafa catacombs** – a labyrinth of rock-cut tombs constructed in the first two centuries AD. Excavations near the Mosque of Nebi Daniel have uncovered remains of the central city during its **Roman** period, including an **amphitheatre**, baths and a gymnasium complex.

Port Said

Located at the entrance to the **Suez Canal**, this port was founded in 1859 by the canal's builders and is named for Said Pasha, then leader of Egypt. Port Said is a fueling point for ships using the canal and is also a cruise ship port, providing access by modern highway to Cairo. The canal connects the Mediterranean Sea with the Red Sea, and is level throughout with no locks.

The Holy Land

The Holy Land is a place of pilgrimage for the world's three great monotheistic religions – Judaism, Christianity and Islam. Jews believe it was promised to them by God, Christians believe it was the scene of Jesus's life, and Muslims believe it was the site of Muhammad's ascent to heaven. Lying roughly between the Mediterranean Sea and the Jordan River, this region has long been called Palestine, a name derived from a word meaning Land of the Philistines. The Philistines came to the region from the Aegean in the 12th century BC and were rivals of the Hebrew people of Israel, whose name for Palestine is Eretz Israel, meaning Land of Israel.

The Jews, who had left Palestine to settle in Egypt, returned around 1290. They were led by **Moses**, who delivered to them the Ten Commandments while crossing the Sinai desert. When the shepherd boy **David** killed the Philistine giant Goliath using a slingshot, his divine election was revealed. Crowned king of ancient Israel, David conquered Jerusalem, walled the city and made it his capital. His son **Solomon** built the first Temple in Jerusalem. Following his reign, the kingdom eventually fell under foreign domination, with the Jews exiled and their temple destroyed.

In 63 BC, Palestine became a Roman province ruled by puppet kings of the Herod dynasty. In about 8 BC, when word of the birth of **Jesus** reached Herod the Great, he ordered the massacre of all male babies, prompting the Holy Family to flee into Egypt.

Following a Jewish revolt in the 2nd century AD, Hadrian rebuilt Jerusalem as a pagan shrine. However, when the Roman emperor **Constantine** converted to Christianity in 312 AD, the city became a centre of Christian pilgrimage, especially after Constantine's mother, Saint Helena, found what was believed to be a relic of the True Cross in Jerusalem and the location of the Holy Sepulchre (Christ's Tomb).

The rise of **Islam** and its belief that the Prophet Muhammad had ascended to heaven from Jerusalem, prompted the Muslims to build, in 691, the Dome of the Rock on the site where the Temple of Solomon once stood. When Muslims destroyed the Church of the Holy Sepulchre in 1001, this triggered a call to arms for the Christians of western Europe, and the first of several **crusades** was launched. For the next two centuries, the Christian cause in the Holy Land was carried out by armies of Latin princes and by the great military orders of the Knights Hospitalers and the Knights Templars. The First Crusade was a success, but the Second Crusade ended in dismal failure. The Third Crusade, led by England's King Richard I (Richard Lion Heart) and Philip II of France, failed to recapture Jerusalem. The last Christian stronghold of Akko fell in 1291 to the Egyptian Mamluks, who in turn were defeated by the

Tenth Station of the Cross, Church of the Holy Sepulchre

Ottoman Turks in 1516.

In 1831, following three centuries of Ottoman rule, Palestine began opening up to European influence and Jewish settlement. With approval from the League of Nations, the British began to establish a Jewish homeland within Palestine in 1920. This caused clashes between the Arabs and the steadily growing population of Jews. In November 1947, the United Nations divided Palestine into Jewish and Arab states, with Jerusalem and its environs, including Bethlehem, to be an internationally administered enclave. Six months later the British withdrew and on May 14, 1948, the state of Israel was proclaimed. However, Israel's neighbouring Arab states rejected both the partition of Palestine and the existence of a Jewish state, and fighting broke out in Jerusalem before the partition even went into effect. To this day, ongoing peace negotiations have failed to resolve the situation.

Travel Tips

Getting Around – Israel's two main cruise ports are Haifa and Ashdod. Taxis are available at the port gate in Haifa. A train station is located near the Haifa pier, and it's a half-hour ride from Haifa to Akko. From the Akko train station it's a 20-minute walk to the Crusader fortress. Nearby is a taxi dispatch office where you can arrange for a taxi ride back to Haifa.

Taxis are available on the pier in Ashdod. Tel Aviv is a 30-minute drive from Ashdod, and Jerusalem is an hour drive. Drivers will often accept US currency, but it's best to use Israeli shekels and negotiate a price.

Currency – Israel's currency is the shekel (ILS). Approximate exchange rates: 1USD = 4 ILS; 1GBP = 5.5 ILS.

Language – Hebrew is the official language, although English and Yiddish are spoken.

Shopping – Handcrafted items include leather articles and embroidered, hand-woven clothing. Best buys include olive-wood figurines, gold and silver jewellery and brass candelabras. Be wary of street hawkers in Jerusalem – while one distracts you by unfurling a poster for your perusal, another could be picking your pocket.

Haifa

Haifa, the chief city of northern Israel, is situated at the foot of Mount Carmel. High on the slopes overlooking the port is the **Bahai Temple**, surrounded by Persian gardens. The domed shrine contains the tomb of Baha Allah, the 19th-century Persian founder of the Bahai faith.

Situated at the top of the Bay of Haifa is the ancient port of **Akko (Acre)**, birthplace of the Virgin Mary and the site of a medieval citadel, walled fortifications and several churches dating from the Crusades. Numerous battles have taken place along its walls, outside of which is the al-Jazzar mosque, built in 1781. Next door, housed in the mosque's former Turkish bath, is Akko's museum.

A popular shore excursion from Haifa is a day-long journey to **Galilee**, in northern Israel, where Jesus grew up and spent the first years of his ministry. Places of pilgrimage include **Nazareth**, home of Jesus and site of the Basilica of the Annunciation,

Shore Excursions

Israel Shore excursions from Haifa include a day-long motorcoach tour of Nazareth and Galilee. Excursions from Ashdod include a motorcoach ride to Jerusalem for a guided walking tour of the Old City, lunch in a Jerusalem hotel and a visit to Bethlehem's Church of the Nativity. Other Ashdod excursions include a full-day trip to Masada and the Dead Sea, and a half-day tour to Tel Aviv and Jaffa.

Some cruise lines (on certain voyages) offer a two-day overland tour (between Haifa and Ashdod) to Nazareth, Galilee and Jerusalem. Meals and hotel accommodations are included; advance booking required.

Mary's Well and the Mosque of Peace. Jesus performed his first miracle of turning water into wine at nearby **Cana**, and he began his first ministry at **Capernaum**, home to several of his disciples and the site of a 3rd-century synagogue which has been excavated and partially restored.

Along the shores of the **Sea of Galilee**, also called Lake Tiberias, stand several pilgrim sites, including the famous Place of Baptism at Yardenit, associated with the baptism of Jesus, where the **River Jordan** flows from the lake. The resort town of **Tiberias**, one of the four holy cities of Judaism, was founded by Herod Antipas in 20 AD. Ruins of the Roman baths remain, as do some Crusader fortifications. At nearby **Tabgha**, the Church of the Multiplication commemorates the act of Jesus feeding the multitude with fish and bread, and the **Mount of Beatitudes** is where Jesus delivered the Sermon on the Mount.

Ashdod

Ashdod, a Hebrew name for 'stronghold,' is the modern port for Tel Aviv. Settled as early as the Bronze Age, Ashdod's first modern Israeli settlement was made in 1955 and its deepwater port was completed ten years later, bringing about the closure of Jaffa's ancient seaport. **Jaffa**, situated in a quiet section of Tel Aviv, was founded by the Phoenicians and named a provincial capital of ancient Egypt in the 15th century BC. Conquered numerous times throughout the ages – by Alexander the Great,

Saladin, Richard I and Napoleon, among others – Jaffa today is known for its narrow streets and a thriving artists' quarter.

Tel Aviv, the commercial and cultural centre of Israel, was founded in 1909 by Jews from Jaffa. Its population grew rapidly in the years preceding and following World War II. In 1950, Tel Aviv was merged with Jaffa, and was briefly named the capital of the state of Israel, before the capital was moved to Jerusalem.

The **Holy City of Jerusalem** is the highlight of a visit to the Holy Land. Within the stone walls of Old Jerusalem, amid the maze of narrow alleys and crowded bazaars, stand the holiest sites of Judaism and Christianity, and the third holiest site of Islam.

Standing atop Mount Moriah (Temple Mount), is the **Dome of the Rock** – a magnificent mosque built on the site of the First and Second Temples. It is centered upon the rock from which Muhammad, according to tradition, ascended to heaven on his winged steed. This same rock is where the Jews believe Abraham was poised to sacrifice his son Isaac to prove his faith in God. Dome of the Rock mosque is encased in marble slabs and Persian tiles inscribed with passages from the Koran. The nearby Mosque of El-Aksa was used for a time by the Crusaders as a residence for the knights in charge of the Temple area, who became known as the Knights Templars.

The **Western Wall** of the **Temple Mount** is what remains from the Second Temple. Also called the Wailing Wall, this is

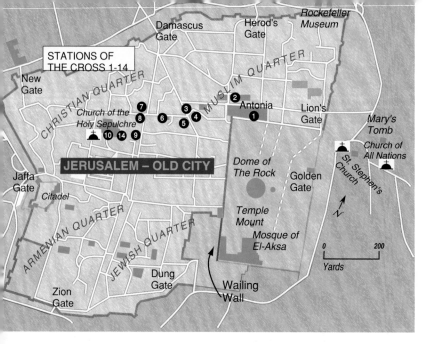

Damascus
Gate

Herod's
Gate

Rockefeller
Museum

New
Gate

CHRISTIAN QUARTER

MUSLIM QUARTER

Church of the
Holy Sepulchre

Antonia

Lion's
Gate

Mary's
Tomb

Church of
All Nations

St. Stephen's Church

JERUSALEM – OLD CITY

Dome of
The Rock

Golden
Gate

Jaffa
Gate

Citadel

ARMENIAN QUARTER

JEWISH QUARTER

Temple
Mount

Mosque of
El-Aksa

N

0   200

Yards

Dung
Gate

Wailing
Wall

Zion
Gate

Judaism's most holy site and it is here that Jews come to pray and bewail the destruction of their Temple.

Christendom's most sacred site is the **Church of the Holy Sepulchre**, which contains the Tomb of Christ. Situated in the Christian quarter of the city, the Church of the Holy Sepulchre houses the last five of the **Fourteen Stations of Cross**. Each station marks an event of sacred memory along the traditional route taken by Jesus, bearing his cross, to his crucifixion. Called the **Via Dolorosa**, this **Way of Sorrow** is Christendom's most hallowed road and it begins at the Antonia Tower, which marks the site of the Roman fortress where Jesus was condemned to death.

The next eight stations are marked by chapels, convents and monasteries built along the Via Dolorosa as it twists and turns its way to the Church of the Holy Sepulchre. The original basilica was built in 325 by order of Emperor Constantine, after the location of Christ's tomb was revealed in a dream to his mother Saint Helena while she was visiting Jerusalem. The first church was destroyed by the Persians in 614, then rebuilt and destroyed once more. The existing structure was built by the Crusaders in 1149 AD. Inside is a Latin shrine marking the place where Jesus was nailed to the Cross (the Eleventh Station), a Greek altar standing over the **Rock of Calvary** where the cross of Jesus was erected (the Twelfth Station), and the Stone of the Anointment where the dead body of Jesus was placed when taken down from the cross (the Thirteenth Station). The Fourteenth Station is the **Chapel of the Angel** – the site of Christ's burial and resurrection.

Opposite the Old City's eastern wall, overlooking the Dome of the Rock, is the **Mount of Olives**.

At its base stands the **Church of All Nations**, also called the Basilica of the Agony. The adjacent **Garden of Gethsemene** is where Jesus and his disciples spent the last hours before his arrest. The present church was built in the Byzantine style in the early 1920s with contributions from 12 nations. It stands on the ruins of Byzantine and Crusader churches, and houses **the Rock of Agony** upon which Jesus prayed the night before his arrest. On Palm Sunday, Jesus entered Jerusalem with his disciples through the Eastern Gate – which is where the **Golden Gate** (a 7th-century Byzantine structure) now stands and has been walled up since the 9th century. On the opposite of the Old City is the **Jaffa Gate,** which adjoins the **Citadel** – originally built by Herod to guard his palace. This famous landmark now houses the Museum of the City of Jerusalem. South of the Old City, in a park-like setting, is the **Keneset** (Israel's seat of government), the Israel Museum and the Shrine of the Book, which houses the Dead Sea Scrolls.

The town of **Bethlehem** – birthplace of Jesus – is about six miles south of Jerusalem, in the West Bank. The first **Church of the Nativity** on Manger Square was completed in 333 by Constantine, then rebuilt and enlarged by Justinian I in the 6th century. The low entrance door, through which visitors must stoop, was built to prevent Muslims on horseback from entering the church. Now shared by monks of Greek, Latin and Armenian orders, the Church of the Nativity is built over a grotto which is believed to be the manger where Jesus was born.

Israel's private and collective farms (*kibbutzim*) have transformed dry desert into arid farmland, irrigated by the **Jordan River**. Deep and turbulent during the winter's rainy season, it becomes a sluggish stream during the summer drought. The **Dead Sea**, fed by the Jordan River, is shrinking due to a combination of the river's reduced inflow and natural evaporation, which is caused by the lake's extremely dry and hot location. One of the saltiest water bodies in the world, the Dead Sea contains no marine life but its waters are extremely buoyant and are a source of mineral salt. The ancient cities of Sodom and Gomorrah once stood on the southwestern shore, and today beaches, spas and tourist hotels line the Dead Sea coast. **Masada**, a nearby mountaintop fortress once occupied by Herod the Great, was seized by Jewish Zealots in 66 AD, who later committed mass suicide when faced with capture by Roman soldiers. Masada was excavated in the 1960s, and today a cable car transports visitors up to the site.

In 1947, the **Dead Sea Scrolls** were found by Bedouin shepherds at Qumran. These ancient leather and papyrus scrolls contain the oldest known books of the Old Testament, and were written or copied between the 1st century BC and the 1st century AD by members of a Jewish sect whose library was secreted in cliffside caves overlooking the Dead Sea.

MALTA,
TUNISIA & MOROCCO

Malta has no rivers or lakes, no natural resources and few trees, but its strategic location in the centre of the Mediterranean has made it the jewel in many a crown. Sir Winston Churchill called this former British colony a "tiny rock of history and romance." For centuries its natural harbour – one of the finest in the world and situated at the crossroads of Mediterranean shipping – brought war and conquest to its doorstep. Following a siege by the Turks in 1565, the Knights Hospitalers fortified the port of **Valletta** so extensively it became one of the greatest strongholds in the Mediterranean.

Malta At A Glance

Malta (pop. 400,000) has been a republic since 1974, when the first Maltese president took office. The country's three inhabited islands are Malta (the largest), Gozo and Comino. The two official languages are English and Maltese (similar to Arabic but with an alphabet and grammatical structure derived from Latin). Italian is also widely spoken, with Malta lying just 58 miles south of Sicily. British colonial influences include driving on the left and an enthusiasm for marching brass bands, which are an integral part of the local festivals. Malta remains a bastion of Roman Catholicism and has retained strong economic ties to Europe.

Shopping - Malta is famous for its handmade lace, silk cloth and filigree ornaments in gold and silver. Other items to look for include pottery and blown glass, especially those made by master artisans on Gozo.

The main shopping area in Valletta is Republic Street. Other shopping venues are the harbourfront promenade in Sliema, and the Ta' Qali Crafts Village near Mdina.

Shops are generally open from 9 a.m. to 1 p.m., and from 4 p.m. to 7 p.m. (or later) except on Sundays and holidays.

Currency - The euro as the country's unit of currency. Banks are open Monday to Saturday, closing in the early afternoon (mid-day on Saturday). ATMs are plentiful, and most larger shops and restaurants accept major credit cards.

Getting Around

The cruise ships dock at Pinto Wharves, within walking distance of Valletta's fortifications (about a 15-minute walk). The quickest way to get from the Valletta waterfront up to the fortified city, is the new panoramic lift that whisks passengers from Grand Harbour to the upper Barrakka Gardens. A Tourist Information Office is located in Freedom Square, just inside City Gate.

Island attractions can be reached by taking the local transit buses, painted orange and yellow,

Shore Excursions

Malta Excursions in **Valletta** include a city walking tour (4 hrs, $50+) as well as scenic drives around the island to **Mdina** (4 hrs, $50+), prehistoric sites (3.5 hrs, $50+) and the **Blue Grotto** for a boat tour (3 hrs, $50+). One excursion includes a walking tour of both Valletta and Mdina (4hr, $50+). Malta can also be explored on half-day 4x4 adventures ($100+), as can the neighbouring island of **Gozo**, which is reached by boat. Consult your cruise line's website for specific excursions offered.

which can be boarded at the main terminus just outside the Valletta city gates. Buses 38 and 138 go to Hagar Qim and Mnajdra; Bus 65 goes to Mdina and Rabat. These towns can be toured on the local

Valletta's natural harbour is one of the finest in the world.

sightseeing train (which is actually on wheels); the train departs every hour from a terminal near the bus interchange in Mdina and the tour lasts approximately 30 minutes (4.5 euros per adult). Hop-on hop-off sightseeing buses also operate in Malta on various routes (15 euros per adult).

Malta's History

Malta contains some of the world's oldest stone monuments, pre-dating those at Stonehenge in England. The island had already been inhabited for some four thousand years when the Phoenicians arrived in about 1000 BC. The Greeks followed, occupying the island in 736 BC and

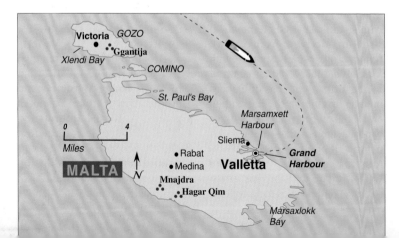

naming their colony Melita – 'island of honey' – for the golden-coloured limestone found here. Malta later passed to the Carthagians, then to the Romans. Saint Paul brought Christianity to Malta when he was shipwrecked on the north coast in 60 AD.

When the Roman Empire was divided in 395 AD, Malta and its smaller neighbouring islands of Gozo and Comino became part of the Eastern Roman (Byzantine) Empire. An Arab conquest in 870 was followed by a Norman invasion in 1090. Malta was a feudal fief of the kingdom of Sicily when Emperor Charles V of the Holy Roman Empire granted the island in 1530 to the Knights of St. John of Jerusalem, who had been driven out of Rhodes by the Ottoman Turks.

The Knights ruled Malta until 1798, when Napoleon invaded and occupied the islands during his Egyptian campaign. The Maltese appealed to Great Britain and in 1799 Lord Horatio Nelson besieged Valletta, compelling the French to withdraw.

For the next century and a half, Valletta was the headquarters of the British Mediterranean Fleet, its harbour further fortified and an extensive naval dockyard built in Grand Harbour. During World War II, Malta withstood almost daily German and Italian air raids, and in 1942 King George VI awarded the British colony the George Cross for heroism.

Malta became independent in 1964 and a few years later Britain handed over the naval dockyards. A haven for NATO warships until 1979, Malta's former naval base has since been devoted to shipbuilding and dry dock repairs.

Upon joining the European Union in 2004, Malta became the smallest member nation. Its small but diversified economy includes financial services, manufacturing and tourism.

Nearly everything in Malta is built of golden limestone, and fresh water is produced at its seawater reverse osmosis plant, one of the world's largest, with the rest provided by wells.

Valletta

Built on a rocky promontory between two deep harbours, Valletta is named for the French Grandmaster Jean de La Vallette, who oversaw construction of the town's fortifications. Described by Sir Walter Scott as "the most superb place I have ever visited,",Valletta is today the capital of Malta, its parliament housed in the Palace of the Grandmasters in the very core of the fortified town. Lining the cobbled streets, which are laid in a grid-work pat-

Malta's golden limestone prompted ancient Greeks to name the island Melita – Island of Honey

tern, are the churches and inns (auberges) built by each nationality (langue) of the Knights.

Valletta Attractions

Republic Street, now a pedestrian **shopping mall**, leads from Freedom Square to three adjoining squares in the town centre where several landmark buildings are located. **St. John's Co-Cathedral** 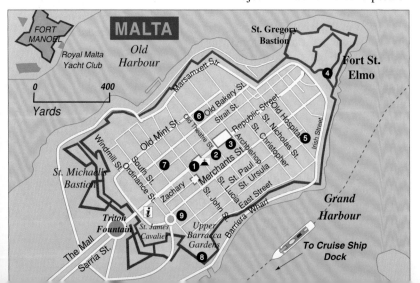 ('co' because there's another cathedral in Mdina, the former capital) was built by the Knights between 1573 and 1577, and contains the crypt of Jean de La Vallette. The magnificent interior of gold and marble contains a succession of chapels, each representing one of the Order's nationalities.

Overlooking Republic Square is the **National Library**, and in adjacent Palace Square stands the **Palace of the Grandmasters**, a masterpiece of military architecture completed in 1574. Its marble halls are graced with priceless paintings and its ground floor armory features weapons and armour from different periods.

The **National War Museum** in Fort St. Elmo commemorates Malta's heroic role in WWII when the island refused to capitulate to relentless bombing by the Italians and Germans.

Mediterranean Conference Centre is housed in the original hospital (Sacra Infermeria) of the Order of St. John, built in 1574. Restored and converted to a conference centre in 1976, the hospital's Great Ward became the Exhibition Hall, one of the longest in Europe. Hospital artifacts, including silver plates upon which patients were served their food, are on display in the Fine Arts Museum, along with paintings by Tintoretto and other Renaissance artists.

Regular performances are held in the **Manoel Theatre**, built in 1731 and featuring an opulent interior.

The **National Museum of Archaeology** is housed in the Auberge de Provence. On display are pottery, sculptures and other objects found at various prehis-

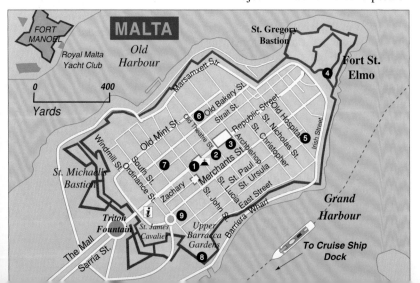

toric sites on the islands. These megalithic stone structures – built between 3800 and 2000 BC, and dedicated to a fertility goddess – are among the world's earliest freestanding structures.

Lovely views of Grand Harbour can be enjoyed from **Upper Barrakka Gardens** **8**, originally the private gardens of the Italian Knights. Nearby is **Auberge de Castille** **9**, one of the Knights' grandest inns.

Across Grand Harbour, south of Valletta, lie the three historic towns of **Vittoriosa, Cospicua** and **Senglea** – referred to as Cottonera (**The Three Cities**). Local attractions include the Folklore Museum (housed in the Inquisitor's Palace) and Maritime Museum, housed in the former bakery of the Royal Navy.

Sites of interest outside Valletta include the ancient stone temples at **Hagar Qim** and Mnajdra, and the nearby **Blue Grotto**, a stunning sea cave. Also worth visiting is the medieval walled town of **Mdina**, its labyrinth of narrow winding streets containing palaces and churches, including the cathedral dedicated to Saint Peter and Saint Paul. Close by, in the town of **Rabat**, are early Christian catacombs (underground cemeteries) and the Museum of Roman Antiquities with fine mosaics on display.

Gozo

Malta's sister island of Gozo is visited by small ships, which anchor or use the mooring buoy that's been installed in the deep waters of Xlendi Bay. Passengers are tendered ashore to enjoy firsthand the unspoilt natural beauty of this sparsely populated island.

Attractions include Calypso Cave and the Ggantija neolithic temples. Historic sites include the ancient citadel in Victoria, its fortifications representing centuries of occupation, including the Romans who turned it into their acropolis and the Knights of St. John who raised the southern flank overlooking Victoria, the island's capital.

Tunisia & Morocco

The coastal lands of North Africa were once called the **Barbary States**. Initially inhabited by Berber tribes who farmed the coastal plains and lived in mountain villages, the region was colonized by Phoenicians in the 9th century BC. They founded **Carthage**, on the Bay of Tunis, which became a powerful city-state.

As the Carthaginian empire grew, its expansion ultimately led to a series of wars with the rising Roman Empire and the Berber States eventually came under Roman rule. Invasions by various barbarian peoples followed the decline of the Roman Empire, and the Barbary States were conquered by Arab Muslims in the 7th century. The Berbers were converted to Islam and formed the backbone of the Arab armies that conquered Spain in the 8th century.

In the 13th century, the Christians of Spain and Portugal began driving the Moors from the Iberian Peninsula, back across the Strait of Gibraltar into North

Africa. Meanwhile, the Ottoman Turks were sweeping westward across North Africa, led by the corsair Barbarossa, who prevented the region from falling to Spain. For the next three centuries the Barbary States were a base for Muslim pirates who staged attacks on Mediterranean shipping. European naval powers often bombarded and blockaded the pirate strongholds, but not until 1830 was piracy eradicated.

Tunisian attacks on Algeria, a French possession, prompted France to invade Tunisia and make it a French protectorate in 1881.

Major battles of World War II were fought on Tunisian soil after British General Montgomery defeated German forces in Egypt and forced them to retreat to Tunisia, where they became trapped by American and British troops occupying territories to the west, including **Casablanca**, which was the scene of a major Allied landing in November 1942. A year later, American president Franklin D. Roosevelt and British prime minister Winston Churchill met in Casablanca, where they issued a joint declaration pledging the war would end only with the unconditional surrender of the Axis powers.

Following the war, nationalist movements intensified in Morocco and Tunisia, with both nations gaining independence from France in 1956. The Moroccan sultan became King Muhammad V, and he was succeeded by his son Hassan II in 1961, who ruled for 38 years until his death at age 70 in 1999. King Hassan was a staunch supporter of the West who worked secretly for Middle East peace.

Tunisia and Morocco are moderate Arab states, and the Arab Spring began in Tunisia, where Islam is the state religion and Arabic is the official language, with French widely spoken.

In Morocco, water for irrigation is drawn from artesian wells, while Tunisia is more dependent on rainfall. Desert oases, found in both countries, form in places where the water table reaches the surface, often as springs. They range in size, from a pond surrounded by date palms to cities surrounded by cultivated fields. In Morocco's oasis city of Marrakesh, an 11th century sultan built a network of underground canals, still in use today, for irrigating the imperial city's extensive gardens and providing water for its citizens.

NORTH AFRICA'S MOVIE ROLES

Numerous films have been shot in the mountains, deserts and walled towns (medinas) of North Africa. Scenes from *Raiders of the Lost Ark* and *The English Patient* were shot in Tunisia, as was footage for the original *Star Wars* movie and *The Phantom Menace*, in which scenes set on the planet of Tatooine were shot near the southern city of Tatouine. Morocco has served as a movie backdrop for decades. Alfred Hitchcock filmed scenes for his 1956 thriller *The Man Who Knew Too Much* at the Hotel La Mamounia in Marrakesh, and David Lean shot *Lawrence of Arabia* at locales in and around Ouarzazate, in the heart of the Atlas Mountains. A permanent film studio was founded at Ouarzazate in 1984, when *The Jewel of the Nile* was filmed there. Ridley Scott shot *Black Hawk Down* and parts of *Gladiator* in Morocco, and Oliver Stone's epic about Alexander the Great utilized the Moroccan army as extras, who slept on the battlefields and provided security for the film crews.

Travel Tips:

Currencies - Tunisia's unit of currency is the dinar (TD) which is divided into 1000 millimes. Morocco's unit of currency is the dirham (DH), which is divided into 100 centimes.

Shopping - Shops in the medinas (old walled towns with narrow winding lanes) are generally open for business from 8 a.m. to 9 p.m. daily, with a Friday break for prayers. Bartering is done at the souks (markets) where rows of stalls sell a variety of handcrafted items in copper, brass and wrought-iron. Silk caftans, painted ceramics, inlaid wooden boxes and Berber carpets are all popular items, as of course are the country's leather goods. They are made of a special goatskin leather, called 'morocco,' that is dyed on the grain side and boarded or embossed to show the characteristic grain. Often crushed and glazed, morocco is hard but pliable, and valued for bookbindings and purses.

Tunisia

Tunis, located on a lake connected by canal to the sea, is the capital of Tunisia, its metropolitan area approaching two million in population. The cruise ships dock at **La Goulette**, a port suburb lying east of the city center. The winding streets of the **medina** (the historic heart of the city) contain colorful souks, the **Great Mosque** and a Turkish palace housing the **Dar Ben Abdallah Museum**. West of the *medina* is Ville Nouvelle, built by the French during the city's colonial era and traversed by the grand

Avenue Bourguiba. The Hotel Majestic, on Avenue de Paris, is an impressive example of French colonial architecture. The famous **Bardo** museum, housing one of world's finest collections of Roman mosaics, is about four miles northwest of the city centre.

The site of the ancient Phoenician city of **Carthage** lies 10 miles northeast of the city core. Its seaside ruins are mostly of Roman origin and include baths, villas and a museum. About two miles past Carthage, along the coast, is the whitewashed, cliff-top village of **Sidi Bou Said**, which is popular with tourists who enjoy strolling the cobble streets of this quiet residential area. Further afield, about 100 miles south of Tunis, past the port of Sousse, is the ancient Roman amphitheatre at **El Djem**. This is the world's second-largest amphitheatre after the Colosseum in Rome, and its thick walls are of staggering proportions.

Shore excursions in Tunis include a walking tour of the medina and the Bardo Museum combined with a drive to Carthage and Sidi Bou Said, with a stop for lunch (8 hrs, $100+). Shorter half-day tours can be taken to the medina and Bardo museum (4 hrs, $50+), and to Carthage and Sidi Bou Said (4 hrs, $50+).

Morocco

Casablanca is called Dar-al-Baida in Arabic, but the city's Spanish name is embedded in the minds of many as the exotic setting for the 1940s film classic starring Humphrey Bogart and Ingrid Bergman. The real city bears little resemblance to the movie, which was filmed in a Hollywood back lot, but it does have a Rick's Café – thanks to the efforts of former U.S. diplomat Kathy Kriger, who formed a company called The Usual Suspects and raised enough capital to open a Casablanca restaurant and piano bar that is reminiscent of Rick's Café, complete with arabesque arches and a pianist playing tunes from the movie. Rick's Café, which opened in March 2004, is set in a courtyard-style mansion and is a 10-minute walk along the harbourfront from the cruise port gate (turn right when leaving the port; most ships provide shuttle transportation to the port entrance.) A red taxi (maximum 3 passengers) costs about 25 dirhams ($3) from the port entrance to Rick's. Credit cards and cash (dirhams, dollars or euros) are accepted at Rick's.

Casablanca, with a population approaching three million, is Morocco's largest city and principal port. Dominating the modern

The village of Sidi Bou Said

city's skyline is the **Hassan II Mosque**, the world's third largest. Completed in 1993 and located near the cruise port (a 20-minute walk from the port entrance; a 10 minute-walk from Rick's). The mosque features marble pillars, ceramic mosaics and carved Moroccan cedar. Its minaret is the world's tallest at 660 feet and the roof over the main prayer hall is retractable.

The former imperial city of **Marrakesh**, founded in 1062, is stunningly situated at the base of the snowcapped Atlas Mountains. The city's ruling sultans and grand viziers built rambling palaces and walled gardens, where reflecting pools and palm trees stand amid a fragrant profusion of jasmine and bougainvillaea. Rising high above the winding streets of the medina is the **Koutoubia minaret**, built by the Almohad dynasty of Berber rulers in the late 12th century. It is the oldest of their three famous minarets – the other two being the Tour Hassan in Rabat and the Giralda in Seville, Spain. Other historical sites include the ornately refurbished Ali ben Youssef Medersa, a religious school founded in the 14th century.

The focal point of Marrakesh's medina is the **Djemaa el-Fna**, a huge square of non-stop activity where snake charmers and fortune tellers jostle for space with acrobats and magicians. Leading off the square is a maze of alleys filled with souks selling spices and slippers, kaftans and carpets. In contrast to the cacophony of customers bartering for wares in the crowded souks, is the nearby

Shore Excursions

Casablanca   Shore excursions in Casablanca include a city walking tour (4.5 hrs, $50+) which includes shopping and refreshments, and a driving/walking tour of Casablanca (5 hrs, $50+). Out-of-town excursions are offered to Rabat (Morocco's capital) for a city walking tour (6 hrs, $50+) and to Marrakesh (12 hrs, $150+), which is a four-hour drive from Casablanca.

tranquillity of the luxurious **Hotel La Mamounia**, set in an enclosed park which was originally a sultan's wedding gift to his son.

This legendary hotel, with its pillared lobby and red-carpeted corridors, opened in 1922. Former guests include the Aga Khan, Richard Nixon, Orson Welles, General de Gaulle and Jimi Hendrix. Winston Churchill was a frequent guest in the 1940s and '50s, and the Churchill Suite is decorated with photos of the former British prime minister and his last unfinished painting of the gardens.

Casablanca's Hassan II Mosque

Azamara Journey (2007)
866 passengers, 30,000 tons

AZAMARA CLUB CRUISES: This upscale brand (founded by Celebrity Cruises in 2007) operates mid-sized boutique ships with a country club atmosphere and all-inclusive cruise fares. Turnaround ports for Mediterranean cruises include Barcelona, Nice, Rome, Venice, Athens and Southampton. Azamara's itineraries appeal to seasoned cruisers seeking out-of-the-ordinary destinations and frequent overnight stays at ports of call. Customized excursions often include night-time shore events. *(azamaraclubcruises.com)*

Carnival Dream (2002)
1,950 passengers, 90,000 tons

CARNIVAL CRUISE LINE: This contemporary cruise line, based in Miami, can take credit for changing the public's perception of cruising back in the 1970s – from being stuffy and formal to being casual and fun. Carnival's large Fun Ships attract a high number of first-time cruisers and families, with extensive facilities and activities for children and teens, and spacious staterooms. Carnival offers cruises from Barcelona, Venice and Athens. *(www.carnival.com)*

Constellation (2002)
1,950 passengers, 90,000 tons

CELEBRITY CRUISES: Founded in 1990 by the Greek cruise line Chandris, Celebrity Cruises is now owned by Royal Caribbean Cruises Ltd. A premium cruise line, Celebrity is noted for its sophisticated service, gourmet cuisine and stylish new ships appointed with modern art. Family staterooms are available on most ships, as are extensive youth facilities. Celebrity features a range of cruises of the Western and Eastern Med from the base ports of Barcelona, Rome and Venice. Cruisetours cover Spain (Barcelona, Madrid) and Italy (Venice, Florence, Rome and the Italian Lakes). Officers are Greek; service staff are international. *(celebritycruises.com)*

COSTA CRUISES: Founded by a Genoa shipping family, Costa introduced its first passenger ship in 1948 and is today Europe's most popular cruise line, offering an international ambiance and authentic Italian cuisine. North Americans comprise 10% to 25% of passengers on Med sailings. Costa's turnaround ports are Savona, Rome, Venice, Trieste, Athens, Marsaille and Barcelona. Officers and service staff are international. *(costacruises.com)*

Costa Mediterranea (2003)
2,114 passengers, 86,000 tons

CRYSTAL CRUISES: This all-inclusive luxury line operates two mid-sized ships which are spacious and beautifully appointed, and offer an easygoing elegance. In addition, the company's 62-passenger luxury yacht, *Crystal Esprit*, takes passengers to secluded coves and islands in exclusive style. Crystal is well known for its fine cuisine and signature shore excursions. Med cruises depart from a variety of base ports, including Athens, Rome, Dubrovnik and Lisbon. Officers are Scandinavian; service staff are international. *(crystalcruises.com)*

Crystal Serenity (2003)
1,080 passengers, 68,000 tons

CUNARD: This prestigious British line began operations in 1840 when Sir Samuel Cunard formed a fleet of ships to deliver mail between Liverpool, Halifax and Boston. Cunard is now owned by Carnival Corporation and currently operates a modern fleet of three classic liners – *Queen Mary 2, Queen Victoria* and, the newest, *Queen Elizabeth* – all featuring traditional elegance and a British ambiance. Cunard's home port is Southampton, from which a variety of round-trip itineraries are offered. A few sailings are one-way between Southampton and Rome. Officers are British and Norwegian; service staff are international. *(cunard.com)*

Queen Mary 2 (2004)
2,620 passengers, 150,000 tons

Disney Magic (1998)
1,750 passengers, 83,500 tons

Westerdam (2006)
1,848 passengers, 85,000 tons

MSC Musica (2006)
2,550 passengers, 89,000 tons

DISNEY CRUISE LINE: This family-friendly cruise line, which has sailed the Med on and off since 2007, offers 7- to 12-night cruises from Barcelona. Disney's premium ships combine traditional ocean liner opulence with elements of fun associated with their storybook characters. Shore excursions are customized by Disney to appeal to children and adults, such as a treasure hunt for hidden artefacts at Ephesus while the parents join an on-site archaeologist. Officers are European. *(disneycruise.com)*

HOLLAND AMERICA LINE: This Seattle-based premium cruise line commands a loyal following, its classic blue-hulled ships featuring wrap-around teak decks, with fine art and fresh flowers displayed throughout the spacious public areas. HAL's mid-sized ships offer amenities and activities for all age groups, including children, and are popular with multi-generational family groups. HAL's Med itineraries are diverse, covering both the major and minor ports. Itineraries include a wide variety of 7- to 36-day cruises between various base ports, including Barcelona, Rome, Venice and Athens, with frequent overnight stays in Venice, Barcelona and Istanbul. Pre-cruise land tours are also available. In business since 1873, HAL operated transatlantic service between Rotterdam and New York before turning to cruises in the late 1960s. Officers are Dutch; service staff are Indonesian and Filipino. *(hollandamerica.com)*

MSC ITALIAN CRUISES: This Italian line is owned by Mediterranean Shipping Company (one of the world's largest freight container companies) and offers cruises out of Genoa and Venice. The company's mid-sized ships, which include the *Lirica* (christened by Sophia Loren in 2003), appeal to experienced travellers who prefer traditional cruise liners. The MSC Yacht Club is an exclusive suite enclave within the ship. The mix of passengers is international. Officers and service staff are Italian. *(msccruises.com)*

NORWEGIAN CRUISE LINE: One of the first lines to invent modern cruising in the mid-1960s, Miami-based NCL remains innovative with its unstructured dining, casual atmosphere, private luxury suite enclaves and single staterooms on some ships. NCL has excellent youth facilities as well as some of the best live entertainment at sea. Med itineraries include roundtrip and one-way cruises from the base ports of Barcelona, Rome and Venice. Officers are Norwegian; service staff is international. *(ncl.com)*

Norwegian Jewel (2005)
2,400 passengers, 92,000 tons

OCEANIA CRUISES: This upscale line's mid-sized ships offer gourmet cuisine, open-seating restaurants and attentive service in a country-club casual atmosphere. The ships' itineraries are a mix of popular and off-the-beaten-track destinations. Base ports include Lisbon, Valletta, Barcelona, Rome, Venice and Athens. Officers and service staff are international. *(oceaniacruises.com)*

Regatta (1998)
684 passengers, 30,000 tons

PRINCESS CRUISES: This premium cruise line, based in Los Angeles, offers a variety of itineraries from base ports of Barcelona, Rome, Venice and Athens. Land tours of Italy are also available. Princess also offers roundtrip cruises of the Western Med from Southampton and cruises from the English port of Dover to Venice. Princess ships appeal to a broad range of passengers with their tasteful, Italian-influenced decor (including an inviting piazza-like atrium), excellent entertainment, extensive children's facilities and flexible dining options. Officers are British and Italian and service staff are international. *(princess.com)*

Star Princess (2002)
2,600 passengers, 109,000 tons

Seven Seas Navigator (1999)
490 passengers, 30,000 tons

Brilliance of the Seas (2002)
2,112 passengers, 90,000 tons

Seabourn Spirit (1989)
208 passengers, 10,000 tons

REGENT SEVEN SEAS: This luxury line (formerly Radisson Seven Seas) offers a variety of itineraries between such base ports as Lisbon, Valletta, Barcelona, Monte Carlo, Rome and Venice. Offering small-ship intimacy, Regent's ships feature all outside suites and all-inclusive fares that include unlimited shore excursions. Officers are Scandinavian; service staff are European. (*rssc.com*)

ROYAL CARIBBEAN INT'L: Miami-based RCI offers a variety of roundtrip and one-way cruises from base ports that include Barcelona, Rome and Venice. RCI cruises departing from Italian base ports attract a high number of Italian passengers, especially in July and August. RCI also offers roundtrip Med cruises from Southampton and one-way cruises to Barcelona. Pre-cruise land tours of Italy, Spain and Paris/London are available. RCI's megaships are known for their stunning atriums, glass-wrapped observation lounges, sports facilities and excellent youth programs, with family staterooms and a nursery for babies and tots on some ships. Each ship's funnel features the company's trademark rock-climbing wall. Officers are Scandinavian; service staff are international. (*royalcaribbean.com*)

SEABOURN CRUISE LINE: This luxury line offers gourmet cuisine, complimentary wines and spirits, and spacious all-suite accommodations on its 200- and 450-passenger mega-yachts. Base ports are Lisbon, Barcelona, Monte Carlo, Rome, Venice, Athens and Istanbul. Itineraries feature less-visited ports and customized shore excursions. Officers are Norwegian and service staff are international. (*seabourn.com*)

SEA DREAM YACHT CLUB: Founded in 2001 by Norwegian industrialist Atle Brynestad (founder of Seabourn) this innovative company's twin yachts each carry 55 couples in relaxed and casual elegance, providing the private-yacht experience on 7- to 14-day voyages. Turnaround ports are Malaga, Barcelona, Cannes, Monte Carlo, Nice, Rome, Venice and Dubrovnik. Officers and service staff are international. (*seadreamyachtclub.com*)

SeaDream II (1985)
110 passengers, 4,250 tons

SILVERSEA: Consistently rated the Number One Small Ship Cruise Line by Condé Nast Traveler, this all-inclusive luxury line offers interesting Med itineraries ranging from 7 to 12 days. Base ports include Lisbon, Barcelona, Monte Carlo, Rome, Venice, Athens and Istanbul. Officers are Italian; service staff is European. (*silversea.com*)

Silver Whisper (2001)
382 passengers, 28,250 tons

WINDSTAR: A premium line of high-tech sailing ships which appeal to passengers seeking both relaxed luxury and the romance of sail, Seattle-based Windstar has also acquired three small luxury ships formerly operated by Seabourn Cruises. Windstar itineraries include small ports along the French Riviera, Italian coast and Greek Isles. Base ports are Lisbon, Barcelona, Rome, Venice and Athens. Officers are British and service staff are international. (*windstarcruises.com*

Wind Spirit (1988)
140 passengers, 6,000 tons

P&O's Ventura (2008)
3,090 passengers, 116,000 tons

Europe-Based Cruise Lines

P&O Cruises, based in Southampton and geared to the British holidaymaker, has been operating passenger ships since the early 1800s when it was a division of the Peninsular & Oriental Steam Navigation Company. Today's modern P&O fleet consists of family friendly ships and those that are exclusively for adults. P&O ships offer a variety of round-trip Med itineraries from Southampton. (*pocruises.com*)

Other British-based lines include **Thomson Cruises** (a budget cruise line), **Fred.Olsen Cruise Lines** (offering Med cruises from Dover, Southampton and Liverpool) and **Swan Hellenic**, which operates *Minerva*, a 350-passenger ship featuring distinguished guest speakers and cruise fares that are inclusive of shore excursions.

Voyages to Antiquity, headquartered in Oxford, England, and founded by Lord Gerry Herrod, offers boutique-style, small-ship cruising on the premium-class *Aegean Odyssey*, which carries 350 guests. The ship's itineraries were crafted by historian John Julius Norwich and are enhanced by an onboard lecture program.

Ponant, a French company headquartered in Marseille, offers small-ship luxury cruises of the French Riviera, Dalmatian coast and Greek Isles.

Cyprus-based **Celestyal Cruises** (formerly Louis Cruises) offers budget cruises of the Greek Isles.

Viking Cruises, well known for its river cruises, has entered ocean cruising with the launch of several new 960-passenger ships which offer Med cruises from Barcelona, Rome, Venice and Istanbul.